Retailing of Financial Services

Retailing of Financial Services

Peter J. McGoldrick and Steven J. Greenland

Peter J. McGoldrick is Littlewoods Professor of Retailing in the Manchester School of Management and Manchester Business School

Steven J. Greenland is a Lecturer in Retailing at the Manchester School of Management, UMIST

McGRAW-HILL BOOK COMPANY

London · New York · St Louis · San Francisco · Auckland
Bogatá · Caracas · Lisbon · Madrid · Mexico
Milan · Montreal · New Delhi · Panama · Paris · San Juan
São Paulo · Singapore · Sydney · Tokyo · Toronto

Published by
McGRAW-HILL Book Company Europe
Shoppenhangers Road, Maidenhead, Berkshire, SL6 2QL, England
Telephone 0628 23432
Fax 0628 770224

British Library Cataloguing in Publication Data

McGoldrick, Peter J.
  Retailing of Financial Services
  I. Title   II. Greenland, Steven
  658.8

  ISBN 0–07–707613–3

Library of Congress Cataloging-in-Publication Data

McGoldrick, Peter J.
  Retailing of financial services / Peter J. McGoldrick, Steven Greenland.
    p.   cm.
  Includes bibliographical references and index.
  ISBN 0-07-707613-3
  1. Financial services industry—Management.
  2. Financial services industry—Customer services.
  I. Greenland, Steven. II. Title.
  HG173.M396 1994
  332.1′068′8—dc20
                                 94-7269
                                 CIP

12345 BP 97654

Typeset by Computape (Pickering) Ltd, North Yorkshire
Printed and bound in Great Britain by the Bath Press, Avon

CONTENTS

PREFACE

Over the last 15 years, many financial institutions have migrated from complacency, to anxiety, to euphoria, to disillusionment, to reflection. Before the 1980s, things changed very slowly in most sectors of financial services. The 1980s was a decade of rapid change, spurred by legislation which stimulated far more inter-type competition within the industry. After initial reluctance, many banks, building societies and insurance companies became infatuated with their newly defined roles as competitive high street retailers. The concepts and tactics of retail marketing were applied with vigour, and usually with cost. After all, who could put a foot wrong during the 1980s' boom years?

Recent history and recessionary conditions have unfortunately shown many of the moves to be wrong-footed. We have seen some very expensive retreats from cherished strategies, withdrawals from the high street, and the takeover of some major players. Were the financial services providers wrong to pursue the retailing analogy, or was it sometimes pursued in the wrong way? Certainly, a strategy that is ideal for one supermarket may be entirely wrong for another supermarket; so why then should it be appropriate for a bank, building society or insurance company? Having said this, much has been gained from this period of rapid change, at least in terms of the choice, flexibility and quality of financial services retailing.

As financial services retailers reflect upon their strategies for the remainder of this millennium, it is timely to take a detailed and analytical look at the relevant concepts, strategies and tactics. This book represents a natural convergence of two streams of interest within this university. Retailing has been researched and taught within the Manchester Business School and the Manchester School of Management at UMIST for over 20 years. This interest culminated recently in the formation of the International Centre for Retail Studies, spanning the two Schools. In 1987, as a result of a generous covenant from the TSB group, the Financial Services Research Centre was founded at UMIST. Some of the chapters of this book draw upon original research conducted within the Centre.

Following an introduction to some of the core concepts, the book is presented in three main parts. Part One examines the processes involved in the effective formulation of retailing strategy. In Chapter 1, a detailed analysis is presented of the financial environment, including the most salient economic, social, political, legislative and structural changes. Strategies formed without a very clear understanding of the consumer are most likely to founder; Chapter 2 takes us through those elements of buyer behaviour that are most relevant to the retail strategist; Chapter 3 illustrates how some of the key frameworks for strategic planning can be applied to the retailing of financial services. Part Two looks at the design of the retail branch network, starting in Chapter 4 with those long term and major decisions on branch location and network strategy. Chapter 5 provides a special look at retail branch security; while rarely cited as an element of the retail or marketing mix, retail security is an issue of major concern and expenditure. A third element of 'place' is treated in Chapter 6, which examines the elements and processes of retail branch design. Part Three considers four other key elements of the retailing mix, starting with product development and product range management decisions in Chapter 7. Pricing is the focus of Chapter 8, which examines the special issues involved in the pricing of each type of financial service. Advertising decisions are the core theme of Chapter 9, consideration also being given to sponsorship and other forms of promotion. Chapter 10 examines the vital topics of customer service and quality, including ways of measuring service quality and the key role of retail personnel.

Peter J. McGoldrick

ACKNOWLEDGEMENTS

We would like to acknowledge with gratitude the work of those colleagues and industry experts who have contributed some of the chapters. Their expertise and deep knowledge of the industry has contributed both strength and diversity to this project. We would like to thank Dr John Hughes, formerly with CACI and now with Bradford and Bingley; Malcolm Hughes, of Watermill Consultants; Roy Palmer and Monica Lucas, of Pragma Consulting; Yvette Kirk of Millward Brown. We would also like to thank our colleagues within the Manchester School of Management; Dr Barbara Lewis and Erica Betts. Names and contact addresses of contributors are listed in the following pages.

We are grateful to the many publishers who gave their permission, usually freely, for the use of data and exhibits. These are acknowledged and attributed at the relevant points within the text. For their many helpful comments and suggestions, we are also grateful to the anonymous reviewers who read the various versions of the book plan and manuscripts.

It is not possible to acknowledge individually all the managers, researchers and organizations who have helped in the writing of this text. We are, however, specially grateful for the assistance provided by the market research department of TSB and for the help and access provided by the Building Societies Association library in Saville Row, London.

Bringing a book from the early drafts to the final manuscript is a task of major proportions, for which I am once again most grateful to my secretary, Mary O'Mahony. Thanks are also due to our resourceful computer officer, Peter Lythgoe, for converting all the disks and for keeping us 'on-line' through no less than three recent office moves! Finally, but by no means least, we are grateful for the help and encouragement of the editorial staff at McGraw-Hill. In particular, we thank Tessa Hanford, Production Editor and Brendan Lambon, Business and Economics Editor at McGraw-Hill, for their patience and professionalism throughout this project.

Peter McGoldrick and Steven Greenland

CONTRIBUTORS

Ms Erica Betts
Manchester School of Management
UMIST
PO Box 88
Manchester
M60 1QD

Mr Steven Greenland
Lecturer in Retailing
Manchester School of Management
UMIST
PO Box 88
Manchester
M60 1QD

Dr John Hughes
Corporate Planner
Bradford and Bingley Building Society
PO Box 88
Crossflatts
W. Yorkshire
BD16 2UA

Mr Malcolm Hughes
Managing Consultant
Watermill Consultants
24 Watermill Lane
Hertford
SG14 3LB

Ms Yvette Kirk
Associate Director
Millward Brown Market Research Ltd
Olympus Ave
Tachbrook Park
Warwick
CV34 6RJ

Dr Barbara R. Lewis
Senior Lecturer
Manchester School of Management
UMIST
PO Box 88
Manchester
M60 1QD

Monica Lucas
Pragma Strategic Marketing Consultants
32 York Street
Twickenham
Middlesex
TW2 3LJ

Professor Peter J. McGoldrick
Littlewoods Professor of Retailing in the Manchester Business School
and the Manchester School of Management
UMIST
PO Box 88
Manchester
M60 1QD

Mr Roy Palmer
Director
Pragma Strategic Marketing Consultants
32 York Street
Twickenham
Middlesex
TW2 3LJ

INTRODUCTION

Peter J. McGoldrick

The past decade has been a time of unprecedented change within the personal financial services sector, with the removal of many barriers to competition. As financial and other institutions seek opportunities to diversify their activities, the traditional boundaries have been rapidly eroded. It is increasingly relevant to regard financial services outlets as a form of retailing, and the services themselves as their product ranges. While accepting the important differences between the retailing of goods and services, it is clear that many similar problems are faced in the formulation of retailing strategy, the utilization of the marketing mix and in the evaluation of marketing performance.

Financial institutions are keen to embrace retail marketing concepts and many valuable lessons can be learnt from their counterparts in the consumer goods sector. For example, some of the less successful diversifications by some food stores in the later 1970s, selling high risk, ego intensive merchandise alongside basic groceries, bear a certain resemblance to the concept of 'financial supermarkets'. Parallels can also be drawn with the positioning problems encountered by many product retailers. As retailers of financial services become less differentiated in terms of their product offerings, branch environments, advertising messages and customer service levels, increasingly blurred images may be the result.

THE RETAILING ANALOGY

The term retailing has now become firmly established to distinguish 'small quantity' activities from the corporate side of financial services. The concepts and techniques of retail marketing have been readily adopted by most types of financial institution that have a direct interface with the consumer market. The propensity to refer to financial services as 'products' may be seen as further evidence of a desire to align with mainstream, consumer goods marketing. As traditional retailers, such as Marks and Spencer, increasingly see themselves as offering products and related services, the distinctions between retail outlets and financial services outlets are eroded from both sides (Worthington, 1994).

There are, of course, particular characteristics which distinguish product marketing from services marketing. Intangibility of the service and the inseparability of production from consumption are frequently cited (e.g., Cowell, 1984, p. 23). Yet it is easy to overstate even these important distinguishing characteristics. Many financial services do contain small but important tangible elements, such as the physical properties of the plastic card, the building society 'pass book' or the certificate of insurance. One should also ask whether production and consumption are truly simultaneous; when is an insurance policy or a savings account actually 'consumed'? These services typically provide long term peace of mind and payments at some point in the future. Is this world so remote from the retailing of 'tangibles' such as lawn mowers or washing machines, which also are bought to provide longer term services, namely, grass cutting and home laundry?

The similarity and difference between the retailing of financial services and the retailing of fast moving consumer goods (FMCG) were discussed by Hill (1990). Table 1 summarizes the

Table 1   Characteristics of FMCG and financial services retailing

Typical characteristics of the FMCG sector

Impulse purchasing or rapid decision making
Tangible products
The prospect of instant gratification
Low unit prices and regular special offers
Price sensitivity
Often high levels of trial purchasing
Frequent repeat purchasing
Individual decision making
Well defined and structured product categories
'Repertoire purchasing', rather than single brand loyalty
Simple, easy to understand products

Typical characteristics of the financial services sector

Planned purchasing, with a gestation period of several weeks or even months, e.g., if purchasing a pension
Intangible products
Absence of instant gratification, except in the case of loan products
Often a high price of entry, e.g., minimum investment
High loyalty, e.g., to bank
Generally low levels of trial
Single, as opposed to repeat purchasing activity
Sometimes joint decision making involving spouse or partner
Low consumer interest
Lack of product homogeneity
Complex products

Characteristics generally shared between FMCG and financial services

Branding
Dependence on product positioning
Packaging
Segmentation of markets
Increasing interest in niche products
Importance of advertising
Some evidence of price sensitivity, e.g., on car insurance premiums or interest rates
Increasing use of special offers and other promotional activity
A desire to offer added value, e.g., via service

Source: Hill, P. (1990) From dairy desserts to debit cards—new product research in consumer and financial markets, in ESOMAR (eds) *How to Market Financial Services in an Increasing Competitive Environment*, ESOMAR, Amsterdam, 71–85

characteristics that are most typical of FMCG, those most typical of financial services and those characteristics which are generally shared. There is more than sufficient common ground to justify the pursuit of the retailing analogy, provided that its limits are clearly recognized.

THE RETAILING MIX

The elements of the marketing mix utilized by financial services retailers have much in common with those used by product retailers, although the emphasis tends to be different. It is appropriate to look briefly at seven elements of the mix, noting some of the key marketing issues for retailers of financial services and using a typology presented by McGoldrick and Greenland (1992):

1. *Product range* In spite of recent diversifications, it is notoriously difficult for financial institutions to differentiate their product ranges (Rothwell and Jowett, 1988, p. 23). Given the nature of their 'products', they are very easy to imitate if seen to be successful. The range also tends to be relatively small; accordingly, Watkins and Wright (1986, p. 119) expressed some doubts about the validity of the 'financial supermarket' analogy.

2. *Pricing* Consumers tend to have low awareness of and/or sensitivity towards credit card APRs, largely because over half in the UK settle their accounts in full (King, 1988). Fundamental changes in pricing structure, such as the introduction of an annual fee by Barclaycard, can provoke a sharp response. Whereas product retailers have generally worked hard through the 1980s to shift consumer attention away from price (McGoldrick, 1990, p. 212), pricing is being given increased attention by financial services retailers. Most now offer interest-bearing cheque accounts, following a trend started in 1981 within the United States (Channon, 1986, p. 122).

3. *Promotion* Financial services retailers are now making intensive use of media advertising, which is regarded as a major weapon in their attempts to achieve distinctive positioning. The campaign by TSB to link its name to 'yes' and the 'innovator' theme by Barclays represent major marketing expenditures. In contrast, many product retailers have scaled down their advertising expenditures, in real terms (McGoldrick, 1990, p. 262). In line with a general trend in consumer goods marketing, some financial institutions have diverted funds from media advertising to publicity and sponsorships (Mintel, 1987).

4. *Personal selling* While selling is becoming almost a 'lost art' in many forms of retailing, its importance is largely undiminished within the financial services sector. The complexity of many services, plus high levels of perceived risk, necessitate a high level of personal selling. As financial institutions increase the pressure to 'cross-sell' services (Weinberg, 1987, p. 5) to existing customers, the need for well informed and well trained staff increases.

5. *Service* This broad area embraces many types of personal and electronic services, such as EFTPoS, ATMs and telebanking. As in the consumer goods sector, many retailers are giving great emphasis to service levels in their quest for competitive advantage. One problem is to identify the services most relevant to target customers; as Bateson (1985) found, some customers prefer to use ATMs, whereas others prefer personal service.

6. *Environment* From a situation where many branches were individually designed along very traditional lines, most financial institutions are placing far more emphasis upon the use of integrated designs. Kotler (1973) defined atmospherics as 'the conscious designing of space to create certain effects in buyers'. Branch design is now regarded as part of the selling/service function, playing a major role in helping to differentiate the image of the organization. A major task has been to make their environments appear more 'user-friendly' (Corporate Intelligence Group, 1991).

7. *Location* Many managers and researchers have testified to the critical importance of location for product retailers. This is equally true for financial services retailers, especially in respect of transaction services, typically associated with regular branch contact. Large

numbers of customers are gained and lost, primarily on the basis of branch locations. Given the high cost of maintaining a well located and extensive branch network, many institutions hope that developments such as ATMs and telebanking will help to overcome the constraints of existing locations.

This typology of the mix differs slightly from the frequently cited '7 Ps' of services marketing, namely, the traditional '4 Ps' of product, price, place and promotion, with the addition of people, physical evidence and process. As Cowell (1984) points out, the '4 Ps' were developed with reference primarily to manufacturing companies and are not sufficiently comprehensive for services marketing contexts. It should, however, be recalled that the original concept of the mix (Borden, 1965) comprised some 12 major elements; the much abridged '4 Ps' framework is generally attributed to McCarthy (e.g., 1978).

There is clearly no universally adopted framework for the services marketing mix, although the '7 Ps' (Booms and Bitner, 1981; Cowell, 1984) have gained some popularity. The above typology uses this as a starting point but attempts to distinguish more clearly between the elements of most importance within the context of financial services retailing. The terms 'product range' and 'pricing' are considered preferable to 'product' and 'price', giving due emphasis to the multiproduct character of most forms of retailing. The term 'location' is used rather than 'place', which attempts to shift emphasis towards the accessibility and other key aspects of the branch locations.

At a more fundamental level, there is concern about the diversity of attributes that tends to be included within the category of 'physical evidence'. As discussed earlier, it is felt that many of these are integral components of the 'products' within the range; this typology therefore identifies more specifically the 'environment' within the branch or other point of contact. There are also inevitably many areas of overlap between the 'people' and 'process' attributes. In adopting the alternative headings of 'personal selling' and 'services', an attempt is made to focus rather more upon the two main functions to be achieved by the people and the processes that are employed. It must be accepted, however, that any such typology of the mix can only be a much simplified framework within which to consider a very wide range of strategy variables, many of which are closely interrelated.

CHANNELS OF DISTRIBUTION

The retailing of financial services includes a wide range of 'products' and 'channels of distribution'. These form an increasingly large and complex set of product-channel combinations, as financial institutions continue to diversify into new and related financial services. These diversifications are most likely to succeed when there is a 'common thread' with existing products. For example, Allied Dunbar achieved encouraging results when diversifying from their life assurance and pensions base into unit trusts, health insurance and mortgages; their move into personal banking, however, met a poor response (Weinberg, 1987). Traditional retailers are also expanding into other forms of financial services, having established a bridge-head through their store cards and other credit systems (Worthington, 1994). Other developments have included Debenhams Share Centres, Harrods Trust banking facilities and Harrods Estate Agency.

Figure 1 depicts the major components of financial services retailing, illustrating the scope for product/channel combinations. The financial products are grouped within four main categories, first, those providing the basic cash/cheque/credit/debit services, secondly, house ownership and protection, thirdly, financial provisions for the future and, fourthly, financial investments. To an extent, these categories form a continuum, from the products which are basic and used by most

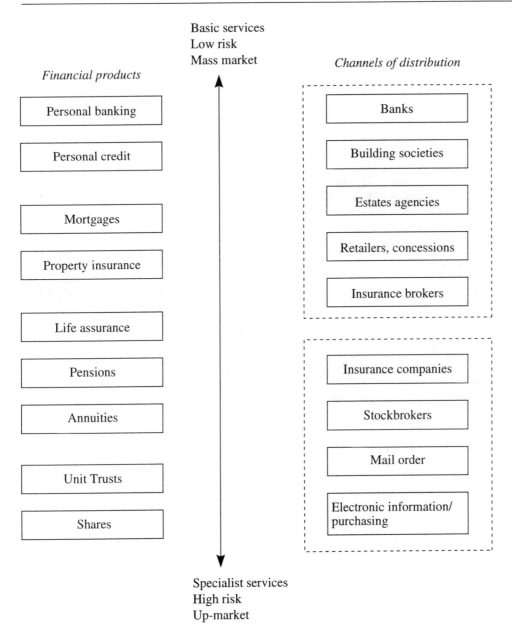

Figure 1   Financial products and channels of distribution

of the market to those which represent more specialized services, with an up-market bias. At the one end of the scale, the services involve little risk, real or perceived; at the other end, the risks to the consumer are obviously greater and the decision process in selecting a supplier of these services is therefore more complex.

The existing channels of distribution are depicted within two main groups, the first typically involving personal contact with the consumer, usually through a 'High Street' branch. The second group comprises the channels which may either interact directly with the consumer, by non-personal means, or operate through various intermediaries. Although it is impossible to maintain rigid distinctions within either the products or the channels, it is felt that some form of classification is helpful in understanding the process of diversification within these channels. Buyer behaviour and the choice of channels is given detailed consideration in Chapter 2. Firstly, Chapter 1 sets the scene by examining the key characteristics of the financial services environment.

REFERENCES

Bateson, J.E.G. (1985) 'Self-service consumer: an exploratory study', *Journal of Retailing,* **61**(3), 47–76.
Booms, B.H. and M.J. Bitner (1981) 'Marketing strategies and organisation structures for service firms', in J. Donnelly and W.R. George (eds) *Marketing of Services*, American Marketing Association, Chicago, 47–51.
Borden, N.H. (1965) 'The concept of the marketing mix', in G. Schwartz (ed.) *Science in Marketing*, J. Wiley, New York, 386–97.
Channon, D.F. (1986) *Bank Strategic Management and Marketing*, John Wiley, Chichester.
Corporate Intelligence Group (1991) 'Banks', *The Retail Services Rankings*, January, 4–13.
Cowell, D. (1984) *The Marketing of Services*, Heinemann, Oxford.
Hill, P. (1990) 'From dairy desserts to debit cards—new product research in consumer and financial markets', in ESOMAR (eds) *How to Market Financial Services in an Increasingly Competitive Environment*, ESOMAR, Amsterdam, 71–85.
King, D. (1988) 'Competition hots up for the card of your choice', *Times*, 16 May, 34.
Kotler, P. (1973) 'Atmospherics as a marketing tool', *Journal of Retailing,* **49**, 4, 48–64.
McCarthy, E.J. (1978) *Basic Marketing: a Managerial Approach*, Richard D. Irwin, Homewood, Ill.
McGoldrick, P.J. (1990) *Retail Marketing*, McGraw-Hill, London.
McGoldrick, P.J. and S.J. Greenland (1992) 'Competition between banks and building societies in the retailing of financial services', *British Journal of Management*, **3**, 169–179.
Mintel (1987) *Opportunities in Sponsorships*, Mintel, London.
Rothwell, M. and P. Jowett (1988) *Rivalry in Retail Financial Services,* Macmillan Press, Basingstoke.
Watkins, T. and M. Wright (1986) *Marketing Financial Services*, Butterworths, London.
Weinberg, M. (1987) 'Does integration of financial services work?', *Proceedings of the Sixth Annual International Banking Conference*, Lafferty Conferences, London.
Worthington, S. (1994) Marks and Spencer Financial Services, in P.J. McGoldrick (ed.) *Cases in Retail Management*, Pitman, London, 293–300.

ONE

DEVELOPING A RETAIL STRATEGY

CHAPTER ONE

THE FINANCIAL ENVIRONMENT

John Hughes   Bradford and Bingley Building Society

INTRODUCTION

The development of an effective retailing strategy which enables an institution to meet its corporate objectives and performance targets must be rooted in a systematic analysis of the external environment in which the company operates. Clearly, a thorough understanding of the external factors which affect the demand for a company's products must be complemented by a realistic appraisal of its internal strengths and weaknesses. However, a failure to recognize external opportunities and threats will have significant ramifications for the long-term survival of any institution. This chapter concentrates on the external factors which influence the behaviour of consumers and suppliers in the retail financial services marketplace. As the balance of factors operating changes over time, it has been necessary to restrict the scope of the material to a review of recent trends. Broadly, analysis has been limited to the period since 1981. In the same way that the exact combination of external factors shaping demand varies with time, so the impact of these factors varies between different groups of institutions. Effort has therefore been made to highlight examples of this phenomenon throughout the chapter. Many external factors have influenced the demand for financial services over the last decade. However, five merit particular attention. First, personal income and wealth play an important part in determining which financial services people can buy. In recent years significant changes have occurred in the distribution of income and the concentration of wealth. These trends are detailed in Section 1.1.

Socio-economic, political and demographic trends have also evolved quite radically since 1981. The impacts of these changes on the mortgage, savings, current account, investment, life, pensions and credit markets are discussed in Section 1.2. Section 1.3 documents the central role regulation has played in shaping the behaviour of consumers and suppliers. In particular, it focuses on the deregulation of the financial services industry since 1986. Market structures have altered fundamentally over the last ten years. The nature and consequences of these changes are presented in Section 1.4. In Section 1.5 attention turns to the changing role of technology. Without doubt, IT has become a crucial area for financial institutions. Some even regard the exploitation of IT as the key to long term success. Finally, the chapter closes with a summary of the key points and a number of review questions to challenge and develop the reader's understanding of the external environment facing financial institutions.

Table 1.1 Profile of UK income distribution 1991/2

Income range £'000	Amount and % of income £m		Number and % of taxpayers in millions	
	Amount	%	No.	%
3—5	9,120	2.5	2.2	8.8
5—7.5	24,190	6.6	3.8	15.1
7.5—10	36,730	10.0	4.2	16.7
10—15	79,980	21.7	6.5	25.9
15—20	68,760	18.7	4.0	15.9
20—30	69,310	18.8	2.9	11.6
30—40	27,080	7.4	0.8	3.2
Over 40	52,580	14.3	0.7	2.8
Total	367,750	100.0	25.1	100.0

Average income per taxpayer = £14,600.

Notes: 1. Income includes earned and investment income.

2. Figures are based on a projection of the 1989/90 Survey of Personal Income by Inland Revenue.

Source: CSO 1992, *Social Trends 22*, p. 95

1.1 PERSONAL INCOME AND WEALTH

1.1.1 Personal incomes

In the financial services marketplace a crucial factor influencing demand is the amount people earn. How much individuals or households have available to spend will affect their capacity to save, to raise and service loans and their attitude to investment risk and insurance. For individuals with relatively low incomes, basic household consumption (food, clothing, heating, etc.) may leave little over to purchase financial services. By contrast, more wealthy households will have significantly more resources to acquire financial products.

The scale of income variation across the population is considerable (see Table 1.1). At the end of the tax year 1991/2 the top 6 per cent of taxpayers earning over £30,000 per annum account for over one-sixth of total income earned. By contrast, those earning under £10,000 per annum (approximately 40 per cent of all taxpayers) accounted for less than 20 per cent of total income.

Since 1971 real personal disposable incomes have risen by over 75 per cent. However, as Table 1.2 shows, much of this improvement occurred during the second half of the 1980s when year on year increases averaged 4.5 per cent. The major factors underpinning this escalation were falling inflation rates, increasing employment, a rising economy and strong business confidence.

In general terms, people have become better-off, particularly over the last decade. However, the rising trend of prosperity revealed in Table 1.2 fails to show how the relative position of different regions of the country and sections of the population have changed. For example, in 1989 (the most recent year for which statistics are available), real disposable incomes per head

Table 1.2 Real household disposable income per head 1971–1990

	Index (1985 = 100)	Annual change %
1971	73	0.3
1976	81	− 1.0
1981	92	− 1.1
1984	96	2.8
1985	100	4.2
1986	106	5.6
1987	110	3.9
1988	115	4.7
1989	122	5.8
1990	128	5.2

Note: 1. Real disposable income adjusts nominal incomes to take account of inflation.
Source: CSO 1992, *Social Trends 22*, p. 89–90

Table 1.3 Gap between highest and lowest paid earners 1971–1990

	Male earners			Female earners		
	Top 10% Index	Bottom 10% Index	Ratio Top/ Bottom	Top 10% Index	Bottom 10% Index	Ratio Top/ Bottom
1971	162	65	2.49	165	66	2.50
1981	168	64	2.63	172	68	2.53
1986	173	60	2.88	170	65	2.62
1989	180	59	5.05	181	63	2.87
1990	181	58	3.12	179	63	2.84

Notes: The index scores given in the table are computed by dividing the average earnings of each decile group by the median earnings for all workers.
Source: CSO 1992, *Social Trends 22*, p. 92

in the South East were on average 14.3 per cent greater than for the country as a whole, and 30.3 per cent higher than for the poorest region of Northern Ireland (Board of Inland Revenue, 1991, p. 32–34). Table 1.3 collates figures which indicate that the gap between the top 10 per cent and bottom 10 per cent of earners has widened progressively over the last 20 years.

One important factor which has contributed to this widening gap has been changes to the income tax system. As Table 1.4 shows, the proportion of gross income paid out as income tax has fallen for all groups. However, the largest reductions in absolute terms have occurred for those earning the most. It is no surprise, therefore, that their disposable incomes have risen by more than that for lower income groups.

Table 1.4   Percentage of income paid in tax by level of earnings and marital status

	half average earnings	Single person on: average earnings	twice average earnings
1981/82	17.5	23.7	27.3
1986/87	14.4	21.7	25.4
1989/90	13.7	19.1	22.0
1990/91	13.3	19.1	23.3
1991/92	13.1	19.1	22.4
Fall in tax burden % 1981/82	4.4	4.6	4.9
	half average earnings	Married men on: average earnings	twice average earnings
1981/82	10.5	20.2	25.1
1986/87	6.2	17.3	23.3
1989/90	6.4	15.7	20.3
1990/91	6.6	15.8	20.5
1991/92	6.9	16.0	20.5
Fall in tax burden % 1981/82	3.6	4.2	4.6

Source: CSO 1992, *Social Trends 22*, p. 96; Board of Inland Revenue 1991, pp. 22–35

1.1.2   Investment income and inherited wealth

For most households, earnings from employment remain the largest and most durable source of income. However, there is significant evidence that investment income and inherited wealth are assuming greater importance as sources of income for some sections of the population. Clearly, investment income and the accumulation of wealth generally result from the consumption of financial services. The underlying factors which drive demand for these instruments will be discussed in Section 1.3. For the moment, consideration of investment and inheritance is restricted to an examination of their role as a potential source of income.

In 1971, 11 per cent of household income came from investments, life insurance policies and pensions. By 1990 the proportion had increased to 18 per cent (CSO 1992, *Social Trends 22*, p. 90). This change reflects many factors including the increasing proportion of the population aged over 60 who use investment and pension income to supplement their state pensions (for a detailed analysis of the current and projected age structure of the population see Ermisch, 1990); the wider ownership of investment products, stock and shares: a shift towards wealth accumulation.

THE FINANCIAL ENVIRONMENT 13

Table 1.5   Value (£b) and percentage of net personal sector wealth by type of holding 1971–90

Type of wealth holding	1971	1976	1981	1990
Dwellings (net of debt)	44.1	257.3	464.9	840.7
	23.0	31.9	31.8	36.6
Other fixed assets	17.8	79.1	96.5	138.9
	9.3	9.8	6.6	6.0
Non-marketable treasury	19.7	92.0	117.0	167.7
	10.3	11.4	8.0	7.3
Consumer durables	17.7	77.4	115.5	160.8
	9.2	9.6	7.9	7.0
Building society deposit	12.1	56.5	115.5	140.1
	6.3	7.0	7.9	6.1
National Savings, bank	22.8	75.0	115.5	190.6
	11.9	9.3	7.9	8.3
Deposits, notes and coins Stocks and shares	38.1	44.4	118.4	186.0
		8.1	8.1	8.1
Other net assets	5.5			
	19.4	125.0	318.7	472.1
	10.1	15.5	21.8	20.6
Total net wealth £b	191.7	806.7	1462.0	2296.9
	100.0	100.0	100.0	100.0

Source: Board of Inland Revenue 1991, p. 100–111

This last point is amply demonstrated by the explosion of personal sector net wealth since 1971 shown in Table 1.5. In nominal terms, personal sector net wealth has gone up over tenfold from £192b in 1971 to £2,296b in 1990. The bulk of this growth has resulted from the appreciation in value of people's homes. Household wealth now accounts for over 36 per cent of the total.

Despite this expansion in personal sector wealth, the concentration of assets in the hands of a small number of people has altered little over recent years. In 1976, 21 per cent of personal net wealth was owned by the most wealthy 1 per cent of the population. By 1989, the figure had slipped slightly to 18 per cent. Over the same period, the share of net wealth held by the most wealthy 25 per cent of the population rose from 71 per cent to 75 per cent (CSO 1992, *Social Trends 22*, p. 101).

It is clear from Table 1.5 that housing wealth constitutes the biggest single source of personal wealth. It is no surprise, therefore, that the bulk of inherited wealth is also locked up in property. Recent research suggests that the inheritance of property wealth has provided an important injection of income for perhaps as many as one in ten households (Hamnett *et al.*, 1991, p. 121). Their work also shows up interesting variations in the use of inherited housing wealth and highlights which sections of the population tend to benefit.

For example, 68 per cent of people inheriting a property either sell it immediately or rent it out for a short period and then sell it. From the housing wealth realized by the sale approximately

31 per cent is then used for direct consumption (holidays, cars, etc.), 42 per cent is used to acquire more liquid financial assets (stock, shares, etc.), while the bulk of the remaining 27 per cent is used to clear an existing mortgage, move upmarket, buy a second home or improve a home.

The research also found that the use of realized housing wealth varied by social class. Tentatively, it suggests that social classes A and B direct relatively more of their windfall gains towards the acquisition of financial assets, and relatively less towards consumption. Inheritors in social classes C1 and C2 tend to use relatively more resources to enhance their own properties (Hamnett *et al.*, 1991, p. 119).

Hamnett *et al.* (1991) also suggest that those in social classes A and B are almost twice as likely to receive inherited wealth as the population generally, and 3.75 times more likely to inherit than social classes D and E. As the average value of property inherited by those in social classes A and B is higher than for the other categories, these differences between sections of the population are in practice even greater.

Over the last decade in particular, variations in personal income and wealth across the country and between different sections of the population have increased. Financial institutions now face a more segmented marketplace which demands more targeted products, dedicated distribution channels and sophisticated retailing strategies.

1.2 SOCIO-ECONOMIC, POLITICAL AND DEMOGRAPHIC TRENDS

Personal income has a bearing on the ability of individuals to purchase all types of financial product. However, socio-economic, political and demographic factors tend to be more product market specific. Accordingly, the material is divided up by product market.

1.2.1 The mortgage market

Between 1981 and 1991 the nominal value of mortgages outstanding with lender institutions rose from £62b to £320b. Discounting the effects of inflation, the value of balances rose threefold. By 1991 lenders held just under 10 million mortgages, a rise over the decade of 3.75 million (CSO 1992, *Financial Statistics 359*, p.104; CML 1992, *Housing Finance 13*, p. 23).

The underlying dynamics of the mortgage market are very complicated. A detailed treatment of the issues involved can be found in Merrett (1982) and Boleat and Coles (1987). Attention in this section focuses on the key factors which have driven the mortgage market since 1981. They are:

- The rate of household formation and the number of first time buyers.
- Government policy and attitudes towards owner-occupation.
- The level of house prices; the availability and affordability of housing finance.

Over the last decade the total number of households in the UK rose by 2 million to 22.8 million, an annual increase of approximately 1 per cent. A significant underlying change has been the growth of single person households. In 1981 22 per cent of households contained one person. In 1991, the figure was 26 per cent (CSO 1992, *Social Trends 22*, p. 40).

A further major driver of mortgage demand is the number of first time buyers entering the market. Unlike existing owner-occupiers, first time buyers provide entirely new demand. Table 1.6 shows that approximately 50 per cent of demand by volume is provided by first time buyers. The figures in the table also reveal a significant down-turn in the fortunes of the mortgage market after 1988. This will be examined later.

Since the early 1950s there has been a growing political commitment to owner-occupation via

Table 1.6   Number and proportion of first time buyers 1981–1991

	000s No. of loans to FTBs	000s Total no. of loans	% FTB to total loans
1981	441	824	53.5
1982	587	988	54.4
1983	624	1,209	51.6
1984	651	1,284	50.7
1985	651	1,315	49.5
1986	727	1,651	44.1
1987	676	1,547	43.7
1988	828	1,820	45.5
1989	642	1,279	50.2
1990	581	1,189	48.9
1991	524	1,120	46.8

Source: CML 1992, *Housing Finance 13*, p. 21–25; BSA research

subsidies (e.g., mortgage interest tax relief) and more recently through direct policy initiatives such as 'right to buy' legislation. In 1981, 57 per cent of households were owner-occupiers, by 1989 the figure was 67 per cent (CSO 1992, *Regional Trends 26*, p. 100). Between regions owner-occupation rates in 1991 varied from 74 per cent in the South East to 49 per cent in Scotland.

Changes in house prices reflect wider movements in the balance of supply and demand factors. It is also the case that the exact combination of factors influencing prices varies over time. During the 1980s, the rate of increase in house prices outstripped the growth in earnings, effectively causing individuals to borrow more (see Table 1.7).

Between 1981 and 1991, average house prices almost trebled in nominal terms from £24,500 to £64,700 (in real terms the rise was approximately 50 per cent) (CML, 1992, *Housing Finance 13*, p.26). Over the same period the ratio of average house prices to earnings increased from 3.31 in 1981 to 4.34 in 1991 (see Table 1.7).

Until the 1980s building societies enjoyed a privileged position as the pre-eminent providers of mortgage finance. Under the 'recommended rate' system of fixing prices, societies were able to adopt an interest rate regime which failed to provide all those who could afford a loan with mortgage finance. This shortage meant that mortgage rationing was a feature of the market throughout the 1970s (Meen, 1986).

Since then, changes in the tax treatment of building society savings (under the Composite Tax arrangements), the removal of credit controls from the banks (commonly known as 'corset' controls) the equalization of corporation tax rules between societies and other institutions and the abandonment of the societies' price fixing arrangements have reduced the societies' competitive advantage and increased the range of institutions selling mortgage finance. Today, access to a mortgage is governed more by the ability of the borrower to pay than by willingness of the supplier to lend.

The intensification of competition, particularly during the second half of the 1980s, certainly increased the availability of mortgage finance; it also caused institutions to adopt more relaxed lending policies in order to win new business. House purchasers were permitted to borrow higher and higher proportions of the value of their home (up to 100 per cent for first time buyers) and to

Table 1.7 Summary of key trends in the mortgage market 1981–1990

	Mortage repayments as % of earnings (all buyers)	Average house price to earnings ratio	Average house price (all houses) £	Average mortgage advance £	Average loan to value ratio
1981	19.0	3.31	24,810	15,165	61.9
1982	18.0	3.13	25,553	16,685	67.9
1983	16.3	3.29	28,593	18,350	67.5
1984	17.5	3.26	30,812	20,345	68.6
1985	20.7	3.30	33,188	22,058	69.2
1986	20.0	3.53	38,121	25,629	69.5
1987	21.0	3.80	44,220	28,593	67.2
1988	22.5	4.25	54,280	34,811	66.1
1989	29.1	4.43	52,135	38,777	65.8
1990	31.7	4.34	66,695	43,337	67.0

Source: CML 1991, *Housing Finance 11*; CML 1992, *Housing Finance 13*

raise loans based on more generous income multiples (three and four times first income plus the whole of a second income became commonplace). The result of these developments was that the proportion of average earnings committed to mortgage repayments rose during the 1980s from 19.0 per cent in 1981 to 31.7 per cent in 1990 (see Table 1.7).

This upward spiral was certainly affected by a rapid escalation in house prices, the removal of multiple borrower tax relief in August 1988 and more general movements in interest rates. However, the effects of increased competition and deregulation cannot be overstated.

The overheating of the housing market in the late 1980s was a significant factor leading to the housing slump of the early 1990s, though the impact of the recession, increased unemployment and rising interest rates should not be ignored. As Table 1.6 showed, the number of loans made in 1991 was the lowest since 1982.

The over-eager lending policies of financial institutions during the late 1980s have now shown up in the repossession statistics. In 1982 lenders repossessed just under 6,500 properties, 0.1 per cent of the stock of loans outstanding. In 1991 repossessions rocketed to over 75,000 (0.8 per cent of loans outstanding) (UBS Phillips and Drew, 1992).

1.2.2 The deposit savings market

The value of personal sector liquid assets held on deposit with financial institutions totalled £123b in 1981. At the end of 1991 the figure was £379b. Despite this significant nominal increase the actual proportion of disposable income saved, as measured by the saving ratio, fell back after 1984 before recovering in 1991 (see Table 1.8).

A number of factors influenced this pattern of change including house price movements, changes in taxation and government initiatives, competition and interest rates, and changing attitudes to risk. As Table 1.7 illustrated, the scale of house price changes in the second half of the 1980s increased the amount of income spent on debt servicing. This naturally depressed the amount available to save.

Table 1.8 UK saving ratio per cent 1984–91

	Saving ratio	Personal sector liquid financial assets £b
1984	10.8	178
1985	10.1	198
1986	8.5	220
1987	6.9	244
1988	5.4	283
1989	7.1	321
1990	8.9	356
1991	10.4	379

Source: CSO 1992, *Financial Statistics 359*, p. 101–105

Table 1.9 Change in deposit interest rates and house price inflation

	Building society average interest rate %	Bank base rate %	Annual change in house prices %
1981	13.13	13.27	0.8
1982	12.57	11.93	3.0
1983	10.39	9.83	11.9
1984	11.06	9.68	7.8
1985	12.41	12.25	7.7
1986	10.92	10.90	14.9
1987	10.16	9.74	16.0
1988	9.16	10.09	22.7
1989	12.04	13.85	14.5
1990	14.11	14.77	7.3
1991	11.03	11.50	na

Note: 1991 figures are for first three quarters only.
Source: CML 1992, *Housing Finance 13*, p. 31

It can also be argued that borrowing to acquire a house was in fact a far more profitable way to accumulate financial wealth during the second half of the 1980s than by direct saving. Table 1.9 compares prevailing interest rates on savings accounts with the annual percentage rise in average house prices.

Looking to the future, it is unlikely that this situation will persist as house price inflation is not forecast to outstrip deposit savings rates (UBS Phillips and Drew 1992, p. 22–25).

Over the last decade the tax treatment of deposit savings has altered in several ways. At the start of the decade the tax payable by an individual depended more on where the money was placed than on how much interest was received. At one extreme, instruments such as National Savings certificates were tax exempt. At the other, interest accrued on deposits placed with banks

Table 1.10   Value of TESSA balances outstanding £m by institution

	Building societies	Banks	Total
1991 Q1	3,487	1,654	5,142
1991 Q2	4,222	2,025	6,247
1991 Q3	4,634	2,189	6,823
1991 Q4	5,010	2,317	73,271

Source: Board of Inland Revenue 1991, *Inland Revenue Statistics 1991*, p. 64–65

was liable to tax at the marginal rate of the account holder. In between these two extremes, building society depositors all paid a reduced rate of tax called composite tax instead of basic rate tax (though higher rate tax payers remained liable for tax on interest at their marginal rate). In 1981 the basic rate of tax was 30 per cent while the Composite Rate was 22.5 per cent.

In 1984 the government, following recommendations made by the Wilson Committee (1980), extended the composite tax regime to registered deposit takers with the exception of National Savings. In 1990 the government removed the composite tax arrangements altogether and depositors became liable for tax at their own marginal rate. In effect, the abolition of composite tax raised the amount of tax payable.

Changes in the tax regime were largely intended to remove differences between institutions. The government has also attempted to stimulate deposit saving more directly through the Tax Exempt Special Savings Account Scheme or TESSA. TESSAs were introduced in 1991 as a tax free deposit instrument, provided savers left their money invested for five years. The popularity of TESSAs is shown in Table 1.10.

It is estimated that at the end of 1991, 2.8 million individuals owned a TESSA (Board of Inland Revenue, 1991, p. 65). While the growth of TESSA deposits has been significant, doubts exist over the extent to which the scheme has actually stimulated individuals to save more. Many now believe that the introduction of the scheme simply allowed savers to switch money out of tax liable accounts, and that the proportion of 'new' money savers was low.

The deposit savings market embraces a range of different products from instant access accounts, generally offering relatively lower rates of interest, to notice accounts requiring advance notification before money can be withdrawn. Interest rates also vary by balance with many accounts offering a tiered interest rate structure which pays higher interest as the deposit balance increases.

It is important to recognize that deposit taking institutions are not only in competition with each other, but with other product markets as well (e.g., stock market, unit trusts, PEPs—see Section 1.3.4). Therefore, the relative attractiveness and accessibility of deposit based savings versus equity based products are important determinants of demand.

Before the harmonization of tax rules governing the treatment of interest accrued on savings accounts in 1984, building societies maintained a competitive edge in the savings market and were able to offer attractive interest rates. Also, access to alternative forms of investment during the early 1980s remained the preserve of the well-off. Since then, however, equity based saving has burgeoned on the back of a bull stock market, government privatizations and PEPS (see Section 1.3.4). Consequently, the deposit savings market has experienced increasing competition from other types of investment.

Another aspect of competition for deposit savings relates to the role of National Savings. The involvement of National Savings in the market is largely determined by government borrowing requirements. During the 1980s, the government ran either neutral or surplus budgets which did not require substantial public sector borrowing via National Savings. National Savings products were therefore not priced so aggressively and were targeted at non-tax payers.

More recently, the government has changed its stance on public sector borrowing, by announcing in March 1992 that it intended to raise £28b in the fiscal year 1992/3. This will involve the launch of a drive to raise funds via National Savings which will have significant impact on other deposit takers.

1.2.3   The current account market

The current account market is one of the most mature in the financial services sector. Statistics covering the major banking groups indicate that in 1981 there were 24.5 million current accounts. By 1991, this figure had increased to 49.2 million of which 18.9 million were non-interest bearing and 30.3 were interest bearing (BBA, 1992, p. 58).

The major driver behind the generation of new business is the number of young people. The scale of existing account ownership means that scope for increasing sales by further market penetration is somewhat limited. Recently, providers of current accounts have sought to capture customers from each other using technology and card based services (see Section 1.6).

Until 1987, current accounts were the preserve of banks. The introduction of the Building Societies Act in 1986 enabled societies to offer money transmission services, including cheque books. By the end of the 1980s, most of the largest societies had entered the market place. The intensification of competition for current accounts could do little to boost demand, although market research suggests that a growing number of people now hold more than one account (FRS, 1992).

A major challenge to the banks posed by the entry of building societies was the payment of interest. Previously, current account holders had not received interest on their balances. Since 1987, the introduction of interest bearing cheque accounts has put significant pressure on the banks' profit margins as they seek to offer attractive enough rates to anchor their customer base.

1.2.4   The equity based investment market

Short-term investment in the stock market can be direct in the form of company shares, or indirect via investment or unit trusts. Traditionally, access to these investment instruments has involved stockbrokers and the personal market has been dominated by the wealthy.

During the 1980s, the demand for stock market related investment products has grown massively. The three major drivers of this have been government-led product innovation and privatization, developments in the distribution of investment products and changing attitudes to risk. The government has played a significant role in promoting investment in the stock market through the launch of Personal Equity Plans (PEPs). PEPs were launched in 1987 to provide investors with an opportunity to place money directly into UK quoted companies. As an incentive to investors, all dividend payments are free of income tax.

Since 1987, the range of eligible stockmarkets has increased, and funds can now be placed in unit and investment trusts. Initially, individuals could acquire one PEP per calendar year. Since 1989 this has been changed to one PEP per fiscal year. The ceiling on the maximum investment has also changed over recent years. Table 1.11 shows the number and value of PEPs bought since 1987.

The government has also played an active role in promoting wider share ownership through its privatization issues. According to a Treasury/Stock Exchange survey one in four adults owned

Table 1.11 Number and value of PEPs bought between 1987 and 1991

	Number of PEPs taken out ('000s)	Value of PEPs taken out £m	Average value of PEP £
1987	270	480	1,800
1988	120	200	1,650
1989 and Q1 1990	580	1,600	2,750
Q2 1990 to Q1 1991	500	1,600	3,200
Q2 1991 to Q3 1991	300	1,000	3,330

Source: Board of Inland Revenue, 1991, *Inland Revenue Statistics 1991*, p. 64–65

shares in 1990, compared with only one in thirteen in 1981. The survey also found that three-sixths of those holding shares in 1990 held privatization issues and that half of shareholders held shares in only one company (*Social Trends 22*, p. 103).

The 1986 Building Society and Financial Services Acts opened up new markets to financial retailers. In particular, building societies were empowered to offer either their own or another company's investment products. The availability of PEPs and unit trusts on the high street provided further momentum for a growing level of demand.

The momentum built up by government action and the availability of investment products on the high street have certainly raised consumer awareness. Also, the strong performance of the stock market during the 1980s (notwithstanding the crash on Black Monday in October 1987) has served to promote share ownership. More generally, it is now widely accepted that consumers are becoming more sophisticated purchasers of financial services. The demand for financial planning advice, for example, has grown over recent years according to market research commissioned by the Bradford and Bingley Building Society (Bradford and Bingley, 1992).

1.2.5 The life and pensions market

Life insurance is a complex area spanning a range of products from simple protection policies to more sophisticated investment instruments. A useful distinction can be made between single (one-off) premium business and regular (monthly or annual) premium business. Pensions will be dealt with a little later.

Although not universally true, the following three generalizations may help unravel some of the complexities of the insurance business: first, the majority of single premium business comprises unit-linked life contracts and annuities. 'Unit-linked' simply means that the policy is connected to a fund which is itself made up of investments in equities, property and unit trusts, fixed interest securities, bank and building society deposit accounts. Typically, such policies are 'open-ended' which means that it is up to the policyholder when the contract is terminated. Annuities are instruments which yield a regular income to the policyholder. Single premium business is essentially made up of investment-oriented life policies where gains accrue over the longer term. Second, the bulk of regular premium business comprises life policies taken out by property owners wishing to purchase their home. The majority of these policies are endowment contracts. Regular premium business is therefore more protection-oriented, though endowments do offer some investment gain as well. Third, within the regular premium area an important

Table 1.12 Premium income £000s for life and annuities

	Single premium life OB	Regular premium life OB	Regular premium life IB	Single premium annuities	Regular premium annuities
1982	1,004	652	227	404	0.7
1983	1,611	1,122	235	494	1.4
1984	2,071	997	230	483	1.2
1985	2,577	882	232	379	3.9
1986	4,395	1,304	233	461	3.5
1987	5,360	1,485	241	365	4.0
1988	3,084	1,745	213	481	6.0
1989	3,659	1,546	224	523	8.0
1990	3,989	1,687	235	727	7.3
1991	5,226	1,741	233	1,114	3.5

Source: ABI 1986, *Insurance Statistics 1982–1986*, p. 4–10; ABI 1991, *Insurance Statistics 1991*, p. 4–10

Table 1.13 Number of life and annuities (millions)

	OB life	IB life	Annuities '000s
1982	3.73	3.70	103
1983	4.72	3.55	103
1984	4.90	3.59	81
1985	5.03	3.35	65
1986	6.42	3.12	66
1987	7.44	3.84	52
1988	6.06	2.08	67
1989	5.58	1.95	76
1990	5.32	1.99	90
1991	4.37	1.79	126

Source: ABI 1986, *Insurance Statistics, 1982–86*, p. 4–10; ABI 1991, *Insurance Statistics 1991*, p. 4–10

distinction can be drawn between policies taken out with companies that collect subscriptions on the doorstep via a 'home service' division, and business which is handled directly with the insurer. These two categories are termed 'industrial branch' (IB) and 'ordinary branch' (OB) respectively. Mortgage related life cover is normally written in the OB class. IB business has generally focused on less well-off households which pay small weekly or monthly premiums for life cover.

Table 1.12 shows the volume of premium business written between 1982 and 1991 for each of the main categories of business. Table 1.13 summarizes the number of new policies sold over the

Table 1.14   Trends in stock market performance and interest rates

	FT all share index	FT all share % change	3 month Interbank rates
1982	342	11.1	10.63
1983	435	27.0	9.31
1984	516	18.6	10.13
1985	632	22.5	11.94
1986	782	23.8	11.31
1987	1,025	31.1	8.88
1988	932	− 9.1	13.19
1989	1,110	19.2	15.03
1990	1,092	− 1.6	13.94
1991	1,187	8.7	10.94

Note: Three month Local Authority rates are US prevailing moneymarket rates. Although they may not carry quite the same risk as other moneymarket instruments, they give a good overall guide of the prevailing interest rate environment.
Source: CSO 1992, *Financial Statistics 359*, p. 140–146

same period. (Note: ABI does not provide separate volume figures for regular and single premium business.)

The factors driving the insurance business vary between categories, though changes in real disposable income affect all classes of business. Not surprisingly, activity in the housing market is a major element influencing mortgage related regular premium OB business. By contrast, the more investment-oriented classes of business (i.e., single premium OB and annuities) become more attractive as general interest rates rise and insurance companies offer high yielding (often fixed rate) bonds. Another powerful factor stimulating this class of business is the strength of the stock market. Bearing in mind that investors in this product area typically take the longer term view, a strongly rising or undervalued market will tend to draw in increased volumes of single premium business.

The association between the general level of interest rates, the state of the stock market and the single premium categories of business can be seen by comparing the data in Tables 1.12 and 1.14.

Before leaving life insurance, it is worth noting the relative decline of the IB sector. Although the annual premiums written under this class remained stable between 1982 and 1991 (though obviously falling in real terms), the number of new policies sold each year fell dramatically from 3.7 million to 1.77 million.

One major factor which has caused this change has been the growing use of bank accounts to pay single or annual premiums direct to the insurer using direct debits and standing orders. A second has been that the economics of running a 'home service' division have become less favourable as IT, centralized marketing and high street distribution have allowed insurance business to be written without the heavy overheads of a 'home service' salesforce.

Since mid-1988, the companies which traditionally relied on IB business have been able to counter the declining life business with a significant growth in personal pensions business. This was possible because many of their policyholders were not covered by occupational schemes. Table 1.15 highlights the scale of the change in demand after 1988.

Table 1.15 Growth in personal pensions business

	Single premium £m	Annual premium £m	DSS rebate £m	Number of new policies (000s)
1982	224	164	0	416
1983	298	181	0	431
1984	434	297	0	660
1985	564	451	0	1,024
1986	592	332	0	734
1987	813	414	0	913
1988	816	830	417	2,614
1989	1,804	1,084	1,472	4,380
1990	3,085	1,052	765	2,809
1991	4,164	1,133	476	1,436

Source: ABI 1986, *Insurance Statistics 1982–86*, p. 4–10; ABI 1991, *Insurance Statistics 1991*, p. 4–10

Prior to 1988, personal pensions were restricted to the self-employed and those in non-pensionable employment (e.g., where companies did not operate occupational schemes). The impetus behind the boom shown in Table 1.15 was led by the government, though there was a widespread feeling that the pensions business required an overhaul.

The government's launch of personal pensions in 1988 was partly a response to the forecast escalation in the costs of the state earnings related pension scheme (SERPS) due to the growing number of older people in the population, and partly due to an ideological commitment to the promotion of self-reliance.

Under the new rules, individuals were allowed to set up a personal pension to contract out of SERPS or to replace an occupational scheme. SERPS rebates are dealt with by the DSS. The government incentivized SERPS transfers by offering a 2 per cent bonus for the period between the tax years 1987/88 and 1992/93. Those contracting out before the end of the tax year 1988/89 had their bonuses back-dated to 1987. Under these circumstances the explosion in contracting out and personal pensions in 1988 and 1989 is hardly surprising. Over the longer term, however, the future growth of this business will hinge crucially on the extent to which individuals can be persuaded to supplement their pensions with additional contributions as the volume of new DSS transfers will diminish.

Alongside the revamping of personal pensions, the government also changed the rules governing the payment contributions by individuals already in occupational schemes. Before 1987, individuals were not permitted to make additional voluntary contributions (AVCs) outside their company scheme. After 1987, individuals in occupational schemes were permitted to set up free standing AVCs (FSAVCs) outside their company scheme. From October 1987 it became illegal for companies operating occupational schemes to compel individuals either to join the scheme or to make extra contributions only via company AVCs. The introduction of free-standing AVCs has played a major part in boosting pensions' premiums since 1988. The trend has also been supported by a growing awareness of the need to plan for retirement as more people look forward to a long and active 'third age'.

Table 1.16 Net advances of personal loans (£m) 1982–91

	Banks	Finance houses	Building societies	Insurance companies	Retailers	Total
1982	2,344	125	–	19	127	2,615
1983	2,583	525	–	40	132	3,280
1984	2,604	362	–	12	116	3,094
1985	2,937	611	–	62	195	3,805
1986	3,476	894	–	59	94	4,523
1987	4,931	746	70	100	248	8,095
1988	5,582	352	214	76	190	6,414
1989	5,139	607	303	32	5	6,086
1990	3,201	254	198	119	64	3,836
1991	1,198	−417	−44	100	60	897

Source: CSO 1992, *Financial Statistics 359*, p. 103

1.2.6 The consumer credit market

Consumer credit includes bank overdrafts, personal loans, retail store and credit cards. The market for personal credit has changed significantly since 1981 (see Table 1.16). Measured by the amount of net advances (i.e., gross lending minus redemptions) the market for personal credit experienced a massive increase in demand between 1987 and 1989, followed by a sharp fall after 1990.

Although the 1986 Building Societies Act enabled societies to enter the personal loans market in 1987, the bulk of the consumer credit market (over 75 per cent of net advances) remains with the banks.

Typically, people raise short-term loans to finance consumption (e.g., holidays, a car, household goods). To a significant degree, people's willingness to borrow reflects their confidence in the economy. As economic prospects rise, so the risk of unemployment falls and disposable incomes tend to increase. People therefore feel better equipped to raise and service the additional debt used to expand consumption. Also, during phases of economic growth lending institutions too feel more confident that consumers will be able to repay the money they borrow. Conversely, during periods of economic slowdown, rising unemployment and tighter pay deals, institutional misgivings tend to reduce the ready availability of personal credit.

It is no surprise, therefore, that a strong correlation exists between general economic prosperity and the demand for consumer credit. Table 1.17 shows movements in a number of general economic indicators which influence the demand for consumer credit.

People's desire to borrow is also affected by the price they have to pay. Taking finance house interest rates as a general guide, it is evident from Table 1.18 that the cost of borrowing was relatively lower during the mid 1980s than it was during the recessionary periods of 1981–2 and 1990–91. It is no surprise, therefore, that demand expanded in the mid 1980s and contracted after 1990.

Since the credit boom of the late 1980s, institutions have reviewed their lending policies. Many now use credit screening techniques to filter out high risk business. Within the credit card sector most issuing institutions now levy an annual fee to off-set some of their operating costs.

Table 1.17 Economic indicators associated with the demand for consumer credit 1981–91

	Registrations of new cars '000s	Retail sales of household goods per week Index 1980 = 100	Unemployment rate %
1981	1,500	102	8.5
1982	1,584	106	9.9
1983	1,800	118	10.8
1984	1,764	126	11.1
1985	1,848	135	10.9
1986	1,872	150	11.1
1987	2,016	183	10.0
1988	2,210	204	8.1
1989	2,304	209	6.3
1990	2,005	205	5.8
1991	1,600	204	8.1

Note: Unemployment is a lagging indicator which is generally 2–3 years behind the economic cycle. Thus, after the 1981/2 recession, unemployment worsened until 1984 though recovery had started two years earlier. The same lag is apparent for the emerging 1990/1 recession.
Source: CSO 1992, *Economic Trends 406*, p. 14 and 22; CSO 1987, *Economic Trends 406*, p. 12 and 36

Table 1.18 Finance house interest rates 1981–91

	%
1981	14.5
1982	15.5
1983	10.5
1984	9.5
1985	10.0
1986	12.5
1987	11.5
1988	9.0
1989	13.0
1990	15.0
1991	14.0

Note: Rates are those prevailing on 1st January of each year listed.
Source: CSO 1992, *Financial Statistics 359*, p. 144

1.3 THE REGULATORY ENVIRONMENT

The regulatory environment plays an important part in governing what institutions can and cannot do. Over the past 10 years the financial services regulatory environment in the UK has been altered quite radically. The two most fundamental pieces of UK legislation affecting the financial services environment were the Building Societies Act and the Financial Services Act, both enacted in 1986. From a European perspective, progress towards the integration of the market for financial services, and new rules governing the solvency and capital strength of financial institutions, have also been influential. The main feature of these regulatory developments and their impacts on the financial services industry are explored in the following sections.

1.3.1 The 1986 Building Societies Act

The 1986 Building Societies Act radically altered the basis on which societies operate (for a full review of the Act, see Drake, 1989). Before the Act, societies were restricted to the savings and mortgage markets. After it they were empowered to offer current accounts and foreign exchange, to sell insurance and investment products, to diversify into estate agency and to set up subsidiaries (e.g., to manufacture insurance and investment products).

The Act also introduced new rules governing the structure and composition of building society assets and liabilities, widened the source of funds available to societies, provided a mechanism by which societies could raise new forms of capital (e.g., subordinated debt and permanent interest bearing shares) and offered a route to conversion to plc status (which the Abbey National took in 1989) (Reid, 1991). It also created the Building Societies Commission to oversee its operation and to supervise the industry.

Pressure to deregulate the building societies was spearheaded by the industry itself. Between 1980 and 1986, societies had experienced increasing competition in their traditional markets, particularly the mortgage market. They felt severely constrained by a legislative framework which had its roots in an Act of 1892. The primary stimulus to the intensification of competition was a series of regulatory changes aimed at reducing the comparative advantage of societies over banks (see Section 1.2.2.). Most societies viewed the introduction of new legislation in 1986 as a major victory, and many moved quickly to use their new powers to enter new markets.

A number of societies, including most of the largest, set up estate agency operations. The rationale behind this move was twofold: first, it was a means of vertically integrating an important source of mortgage origination; second, it provided an opportunity to gain commission fees from the sale of mortgage related insurance and, of course of houses.

In the main, entry into the market was achieved via acquisition, though some societies (e.g., the Woolwich) used cold start and redeployment of redundant branches. The housing market slump after 1989 left many estate agency subsidiaries in serious difficulty. Most societies which operate estate agencies have restructured and rationalized their operations as a result. By the start of 1992, only the Cheltenham and Gloucester had actually sold on its estate agency business, though the Prudential (the UK's largest insurer) withdrew in 1991, writing off over £300 million in the process.

Two other major areas of diversification were entry into retail banking and the provision of insurance and investment services. This latter point will be covered in Section 1.3.2. The first society to offer a current account was the Nationwide. Launched ln 1987, 'Flexaccount' rapidly built up a significant customer base. By 1991, over one million people held a Flexaccount. Between 1987 and 1990, most of the other major societies entered the money transmission marketplace.

Entry into the retail banking market is expensive. First, the market place is already well-served by the traditional suppliers. Second, the infrastructural costs of cheque clearing, transactions processing and account administration are high. Third, to establish a competitive edge societies were obliged to add more cost by offering interest on current account balances.

Off-set against these costs, societies had certain advantages. First, they had lower branch overheads because their branch networks were smaller (the four major clearers support networks of over 2,000 outlets, while the largest societies maintain networks less than half the size). Second, they were able to use state-of-the-art technology to handle the transaction processing and administration of accounts. Third, they were able to promote retail banking products and services by cross-selling to savers and borrowers with whom they already maintained a relationship.

A major motivation behind societies' move into retail banking was the view that in order to be a serious retailer of financial services it was vital to have a current account as the primary product relationship with a consumer. While this rationale may have been correct for the banks, the logic was perhaps less clear cut for building societies which already maintained a mortgage relationship with many millions of households, and a savings relationship with many millions of individuals.

1.3.2 The 1986 Financial Services Act

The 1986 Financial Services Act (FSA) was prompted by a desire to tighten up regulatory procedures relating to the sale of investment products in order to protect consumers from the adverse effects of financial deregulation (Gower, 1984). Prior to the Act, the investment industry had been self-regulating and somewhat secretive. Since 1986, the consequences of the FSA have been far-reaching, affecting how banks, building societies, brokers and insurance companies operate.

The FSA created a two tier system of regulation: the first tier contains the Securities and Investment Board (SIB) which is a statutory authority charged with operating the FSA. (SIB began operating in 1987); the second tier of regulation involves self-regulating organizations (SROs). SROs are authorized by SIB to control the conduct and business procedures of specific groups within the investment industry (e.g., unit trust companies). It was envisaged that SROs would handle the bulk of the regulation, and that SIB would operate largely as a policing agency.

In 1987, SIB produced its 'Conduct of Business Rules'. These rules effectively set out the key principles by which the SROs had to govern their own members. The four key components were:

1. *Know your customer* – find out the key facts describing the position of each potential customer.
2. *Suitability* – only make recommendations which are consistent with the known facts.
3. *Best advice* – firms should be equipped with sufficient information to ensure that they are recommending the best product on the market for each individual customer.
4. *Disclosure* – disclosure of the capacity in which a seller is acting (company representative, independent adviser, etc.), all relevant commissions and fees, and full product information.

Under these guiding principles institutions selling investment products and services must declare whether they are an appointed representative of one manufacturer (a tied agent) or an independent intermediary offering advice across a range of products provided by different manufacturers.

Since 1987 the number of independent insurance brokers and financial advisers has declined from over 12,200 to under 11,000 (estimated from the Financial Investment Managers and

Brokers Regulatory Authority, FIMBRA, and the Insurance Brokers Registration Council, IBRC). In addition, many major financial retailing institutions which initially opted to stay independent have now become tied, e.g., National Westminster Bank.

Several factors have been influential in causing this shift, but two stand out. First, only independent intermediaries were required to disclose the scale of commissions they received. Second, the larger banks and building societies used their market strength to tie their branch network to an insurance company, while also establishing separate independent advice subsidiaries. Several institutions also developed their own manufacturing capacity. These developments will be examined more fully in Section 1.4.

Until the end of 1990, the disclosure of commissions for independents was covered by the 'maximum commissions agreement'. This stipulated that commissions need only be disclosed if they were higher than the agreed maximum. The agreement effectively placed a ceiling on the level of commissions paid to independent intermediaries. As the agreement did not apply to tied agents the scale of commissions offered by the product manufacturers spiralled upwards. From a manufacturer's viewpoint, a tied agent offers a much more stable and secure outlet for its products than an independent intermediary. Manufacturers were therefore keen to 'buy' this more reliable channel of distribution. Many insurance companies carried the costs of installing IT infrastructure in the branches of their tied agents, and of training their agents' staff to sell investment products. The economics of tying were also favoured by the lower costs of compliance.

At the start of 1991, the maximum agreement was ruled uncompetitive by the Office of Fair Trading and the EC Commission, and was promptly abandoned. SIB was given until the middle of 1992 to consult with the industry in order to draw up new disclosure rules. Though new rules have not yet been adopted, it is likely that the SIB consultation papers issued in March 1992 will form the basis of the new regime. With regard to disclosure, SIB recommends that commissions and expenses should be fully disclosed in a manner which customers can understand. In addition, tied agents and independent intermediaries alike will be bound by the new rules. It is highly likely that the clearer disclosure of these costs will encourage more competition as price will become an even more potent competitive weapon.

1.3.3 The impact of European regulation

Moves towards the creation of a single European market after 1992 have set in train several important regulatory changes which have already affected UK institutions. The second European Banking Directive (adopted in December 1989 for implementation by 1993) introduced three important principles to guide the integration of European banking services: the principle of mutual recognition, the principle of home country control and the principle of an essential minimum level of harmonization (for a detailed review of these points see Barnett 1992; Dixon 1991; DTI 1991).

By establishing the idea of a single banking licence, the Directive provides a simple mechanism for authorized banks to provide the whole range of financial services in all member states. A major strength of such a licence is that it will be universally recognized. At present, a company carrying out banking services in several EC countries must obtain a separate licence for each operation. Alongside the single banking licence, the Directive also advanced the case for home country control, sometimes referred to as 'home jurisdiction'. This means that the regulatory regime operating in the home country where an institution is registered will apply to all its foreign operations across the EC. Thus, any subsidiary of a UK bank offering banking services elsewhere within the EC will be regulated by the Bank of England. Institutions will, of course, continue to be bound by local laws and regulations intended to protect 'the general good' (e.g., consumer protection legislation).

Although the Directive does not seek to harmonize every aspect of banking regulation across the EC, it was recognized that a minimum essential level of harmonization was necessary to safeguard consumers and to support fair competition. An important component of the minimum harmonization rules relates to the capital and solvency position of European financial institutions (Ruiz and Smith, 1991).

The internationalization of capital markets over the past few years has placed the spotlight on capital sourcing and capital strength. Although certain changes have occurred in the UK regarding the nature and availability of capital (for example, only following the 1986 Building Societies Act have societies been able to raise Permanent Interest Bearing Shares, or PIBS, which qualify as tier 1 or core capital), it is necessary to set these developments within a wider international context. In 1988 the Bank of International Settlements put forward guidelines covering the definition of capital and the specification of capital adequacy rules. These guidelines became known as the 'Basle Convergence Agreement'.

Since 1988, two important EC Directives have emerged which further expand the Basle Agreement, the Own Funds Directive and the Solvency Ratio Directive. In the main, the Own Funds Directive is concerned with defining the key features of different forms of capital and determining their relative importance. The Solvency Directive seeks to establish formal rules which specify the amount of capital needed to back different types of asset (e.g., mortgages, personal loans, investments in government stocks, etc.). Assets considered to be higher risk will require more capital backing than assets of lower risk. The basic shape of this risk to asset relationship is that all categories of asset carry an 8 per cent capital requirement. That is to say that 8 per cent of the value of the asset must be covered by capital. However, individual categories of asset can be weighted up or down to reflect their underlying risk. Thus, a weighting factor of, say, 0.5 would mean that the effective capital requirement was reduced to 4 per cent. Alternatively, if the weighting factor were, say, 2.0 then the capital requirement would rise to 16 per cent. The quantification of these weighting factors has been delegated to the regulatory authorities within each EC country. Therefore, the extent to which individual states adopt different weighting systems may generate complications in view of the home jurisdiction rule which will guide integration after 1992.

With regard to the life insurance sector, the three principles set out above relating to the banking sector have been codified in the proposed Third Life Assurance Directive. At present this Directive has not been fully ratified, and it is unlikely to come into universal effect until 1995. Until the Third Directive is adopted insurers will have to abide by the regulatory regimes operating in each country.

From a UK perspective, the integration of financial services after 1992 probably creates more opportunities than it does threats. Certainly, the arrival of the single market will enable foreign companies to enter the UK financial services marketplace more readily. However, the UK already enjoys a highly competitive and mature financial services market which may appear attractive, but offers few opportunities for new entrants. This may not be the case in areas where significant differences persist between home country rules. For example, the UK life insurance sector will be bound by the new SIB rules on disclosure. In so far as these rules are much tougher than those operating in some other EC countries, foreign companies may be able to shelter from full disclosure under the home jurisdiction principle.

Turning to the opportunities, UK institutions are probably as well equipped as those of any other country to develop business abroad. Many are already doing so (e.g., Norwich Union in Spain with Plus Ultra, Barclays in France with Européenne de Banque, and Woolwich Building

Society with Banque Immobille du Credit in France), but the Directive may facilitate further expansion, particularly into fast growing financial services marketplaces such as Spain and Portugal.

The mode of entry used by UK institutions to expand into Europe will depend on many factors including the maturity of the market, the level of existing competition, the scope for product innovation, the extent to which profit lies in manufacture or distribution, and the availability of capital and labour. Current evidence suggests that cross-border agreements and joint ventures will be a favoured strategy for expanding into Europe (see Section 1.4).

1.4 THE EVOLUTION OF MARKET STRUCTURE

Most retail financial markets are oligopolistic in structure, that is, they contain a significant number of suppliers of varying size. Economists regard oligopolies as a particularly common type of market structure, and a substantial body of literature has been constructed to explain the behaviour of oligopolistic firms. A central proposition underpinning oligopoly theory is that individual firms are wary of provoking their rivals because this creates uncertainty and risk. Firms therefore prefer to avoid highly aggressive price competition as this tends to precipitate cut throat and ultimately ruinous price wars. Many markets are therefore arranged around some form of coordinated pricing arrangement. The precise mechanism used to coordinate pricing varies, but typical examples include price leadership, focal point pricing and cartels (Scherer, 1980).

Stable price coordination tends to persist where entry barriers to a market are high (perhaps because capital set up costs are substantial). The competitive threat posed by new entrants is therefore diminished. High exit barriers may also afford the same protection as any potential new entrant will be concerned over the high costs of withdrawal. Coordinated pricing is also promoted where firms share common cost structures and maintain recognizably similar products. Under stable coordinated pricing regimes, competitive pressures tend to be displaced into non-price areas such as distribution and marketing. Rapid product development may also emerge as a means of competing with rivals.

The stability of coordinated pricing can, however, be severely tested where entry and exit barriers are low. Other factors too may undermine the strength of coordinated pricing. For example, where the cost structures of individual firms begin to diverge markedly, perhaps due to the use of IT to develop economies of scale, scope for going it alone increases. Also, the greater the scale of product diversity, the less practicable coordinated pricing becomes. More generally, pressures to abandon agreed pricing will increase during periods of slump where demand is weak.

Over the last decade, retailers of financial services have moved from a position where clear boundaries existed between different types of institution, to the current situation where demarcation lines are hardly visible. In the past, specific product markets tended to be the preserve of one particular group of institutions. For example, building societies sold mortgages, banks sold current accounts and insurance companies sold life policies. Today, financial institutions move between product markets much more readily. The stable coordinated pricing arrangements and non-price methods of competition which typified the cosy single product/single supplier relationships up to the early 1980s have been abandoned, and overt price competition has intensified. The principal cause of this change was financial deregulation in the mid-1980s, and the removal of provisions which favoured specific groups of institutions. This change reduced and in some cases removed the entry barriers faced by institutions wishing to move into new markets (e.g., building societies' entry into current account banking in 1987). As a result, traditional markets were raided by new players. The opening up of financial markets also created a situation in which consumers became much more aware of a wider range of products and services (e.g., bank current account versus building society interest bearing instant access account). This process was aided by government-led product innovation which tended to be market specific, but not supplier specific – e.g., PEPs and TESSAs. These developments further undermined scope for coordinated pricing as the range of products, which were close but not perfect substitutes for each other, increased.

By widening the range of suppliers operating in particular financial markets, deregulation enabled industry groupings with radically different cost structures to compete directly with each other. For example, retail banks typically maintain a cost to income ratio (i.e., the costs of running the business as a percentage of the income generated) of around 65 per cent. Building societies, by contrast, typically enjoy a lower ratio of around 50 per cent. This cost advantage clearly gives societies an edge over the banks, and partially explains why they were able to offer interest on their current accounts. It also helps illustrate the shift towards price-oriented competition which followed deregulation.

For insurance companies, deregulation and the collapse of traditional product market divisions posed a problem. Before the Building Societies and Financial Services Acts, insurance companies distributed their products largely via direct sales forces and independent brokers. High street retailing of insurance products alone was not considered economically viable. However, with deregulation, insurance companies found they were able to strike up distribution agreements with banks and building societies, thereby making their products available on the high street.

Although these associations certainly yielded substantial volumes of business for the insurance companies, they also revealed a fundamental weakness in the position of the insurers, namely a lack of direct control over their distribution (for example, in 1990 the Alliance and Leicester Building Society generated £42.5m of new premium income, or 10 per cent of all new business, for its insurance partner Scottish Amicable (*Annual Report of Scottish Amicable 1990*). The changing pattern of business sourcing for insurers is shown in Table 1.19. The data show the rise of the tied agent, largely at the expense of the independent intermediary.

Tied insurers are clearly vulnerable to the actions of their distributing partners. One solution is to tie to a range of distributors, though the costs of administration and of quality control can make this position onerous. Recently, Legal and General has taken steps to reduce the size of its tied agency network because of these problems.

The precarious position of the insurer reliant on distribution agreements was highlighted in 1991 by Abbey National's decision not to renew its agreement with Friends Provident. The lost income to Friends was in the region of 10–15 per cent of new business.

The evolution of market structure in the financial services sector has had many consequences, but three merit particular attention: first, the intensification of competition has increased the need to cooperate efficiently, to compete on price and to cut out unproductive costs; second, it has stimulated concentration within particular industry groupings via merger; third, it has stimulated the emergence of retail financial service conglomerates.

1.4.1. The rise of the efficient producer

Without the shelter of coordinated pricing, firms must strive for profitability and efficiency or go to the wall. Larger firms tend to have an intrinsic advantage in this regard as they can exploit economies of scale. For example, recent evidence suggests that the larger building societies are beginning to operate more efficiently than their smaller counterparts. (See Table 1.20.)

Table 1.19   % of new long term insurance premiums by distribution channel

Year	IFAs	Tied agent	Company salesforce	Other
1986	70	0	26	4
1987	72	0	23	5
1988	65	10	21	4
1989	67	11	20	2
1990	62	12	22	3

Source: ABI 1991, 'Sources of premium income', *Statistics Bulletin* 1991

Table 1.20   Building society efficiency by size of society

Year	Efficiency index			
	Large	Medium	Small	Very small
1989	98	100	114	120
1990	97	106	121	127

Notes: Efficiency is measured by management expenses to mean assets of each group indexed against the industry as a whole. Size is determined by the proportion of industry assets held by each society. Large societies, for example, include institutions holding more than 2.5 per cent of the whole industry's assets. The very small category includes societies with less than 0.1 per cent of total industry assets.
Source: Building Societies Commission 1991, p. 16

Perhaps more strikingly, the average amount of income consumed by the largest eight banks to run their businesses in 1990 averaged 64 per cent (the highest was Midland at 76 per cent and the lowest Abbey National, an ex-building society, at 44 per cent). The equivalent figure for the top eight building societies was 46 per cent, with a range from 60 per cent down to 28 per cent (UBS Phillips and Drew 1991, p. 75).

To overcome this cost uncompetitiveness the banks have undertaken measures to reduce their operating expenses. All the major clearers have announced substantial reductions in the size of their labour force, and many have reduced the number of branches they operate. In 1990 Midland set in place a programme to axe 4,000 jobs. Barclays announced a 5,000 job reduction in 1991 and aims to contract by a further 15 per cent over the next five years. National Westminster Bank initiated a 15,000 job reduction programme in 1991 which it estimates will save £100m in 1991 rising to £400m by 1993. Between 1985 and 1991 the number of high street branches operated by the clearing banks declined by 10 per cent from 14,300 to under 13,000. Over the same period the number of building society branches fell by less than 3 per cent to stand at approximately 6,000 in 1991 (all figures exclude Abbey National which converted from a building society to a bank in 1989). In May 1992, Midland announced proposals to close 500 outlets. In the current climate further cost cutting is inevitable and efforts to streamline business using IT, particularly at the point of sale, can only gather momentum.

Table 1.21   Concentration ratios for the building society industry: per cent of total assets

Year	Largest 5	Largest 10	Largest 20
1986	56.8	76.6	89.2
1987	60.8	79.3	89.9
1988	62.5	80.7	90.8
1989	61.0	79.1	89.9
1990	59.9	79.7	91.2

Note: The conversion of Abbey National to a bank in 1989 results in a break in the time series data.
Source: Building Societies Commission 1991, p. 46

1.4.2   Industry concentration

During the late 1960s and early 1970s, the banks went through a period of concentration during which the number of individual institutions fell rapidly, and a small number of large organizations emerged. Since then, the four major clearing banks (Barclays, National Westminster, Midland and Lloyds) have consolidated their market position and now control over 60 per cent of the retail banking market (market share measured either in terms of numbers of current accounts or branches (*BBA, 1992*)).

Deregulation has done little to concentrate market power further in this sector, though scope for doing so is limited by government competition policy. As Lloyds' bid for Midland Bank in 1992 demonstrated, the government felt obliged to refer the proposed acquisition to the Monopolies and Mergers Commission on the grounds that the new bank would control over 20 per cent of the market and would thereby weaken competition by leaving the UK with only three main clearing banks. For the banks and, to a significant extent, for the insurance sector, the concentration of market power has taken the form of integration via conglomeration. This is discussed further below.

For the building society industry, the increasing concentration of market power in the hands of the largest institutions since the mid-1980s has been more marked. Before deregulation in 1986 there were 150 societies. By the start of 1991 the figure had fallen to 116 (Building Societies Commission 1991, p. 51). Over the same period the proportion of total assets held by the largest organizations rose. (See Table 1.21.)

Since the start of 1991 the trend has continued with several major mergers increasing further the proportion of industry assets held by the top ten, e.g., acquisition of Portsmouth Building Society by the Cheltenham and Gloucester, the Leamington Spa by the Bradford and Bingley and the Town and Country by the Woolwich. Some forecasters argue that this trend can only accelerate, and that the building society industry will contain fewer than 30 organizations by the end of the century (Morgan Grenfell 1991; Morgan 1988).

1.4.3   Financial conglomeration

The intensification of price competition since 1986 has stimulated the appearance of financial service conglomerates. These organizations combine different institutions under one holding

Table 1.22   Models of bancassurance in the UK 1991

Bank	Insurance company	Relationship
Barclays	Barclays Life	Barclays Bank 100% owned subsidiary
Bank of Scotland	Standard Life	33% Standard Life
Lloyds	Black Horse Life (100% owned by Lloyds Abbey Life)	60% Lloyds Bank
Midland	Midland Life	65% Midland Bank 35% Commercial Union
Royal Bank of Scotland	Royal Scottish Assurance	51% Royal Bank
TSB	TSB Trust Co.	100% TSB Bank

Source: Morgan Grenfell 1991, p. 23

company umbrella. In the UK, the link up between Lloyds Bank and Abbey Life Insurance, and the relationship between TSB Bank and TSB Trust Company are examples of this phenomenon, commonly described as 'bancassurance'. The basic rationale behind the bancassurance model is that it brings together the more sophisticated selling skill of the insurance operators and the stronger customer orientation and loyalty of the banks. Harnessed together, the potential for highly profitable and cost-effective cross-selling of insurance and investment product is substantial. It is estimated that a good insurance salesman can increase his productivity as much as three or four times working within a bancassurance regime compared to the traditional cold calling insurance company representative.

Bancassurance is similar to the distribution agreements which operate between banks and building societies, and the insurance sector. It differs from tied agency arrangements in three key respects: first, bancassurance is enduring and cannot be dissolved quickly; second, it can improve profitability by retaining all commissions within the group structure and by reducing some of the administrative costs involved in distributing via a third party; third, it allows the group to coordinate its approaches to customers and to establish multi-product links with them.

The dominant party in most of the models of bancassurance in the UK is a bank. (See Table 1.22.) No insurance company has yet acquired a controlling interest in a bank, though Standard Life owns one-third of the Bank of Scotland. This reflects the point raised earlier concerning the distribution problem created for insurance companies by deregulation. Since 1987, manufacturers have found it difficult to establish strong control over their own distribution. By contrast, distributors have found no difficulty in signing up suppliers. Distributors have therefore been better placed to pursue backward integration than manufacturers have been in achieving forward integration.

In the building society sector similar connections between distributor and manufacturer have begun to emerge. To date, only the Britannia has gone down the route of outright acquisition, buying FS Assurance (now Britannia Life) in 1990. However, the Woolwich and National and Provincial have both established their own insurance subsidiaries via joint ventures with major insurers. No society has yet been acquired by an insurance company, though Eagle Star has invested £50m in the Bristol and West Building Society, and Prudential has attempted to interest the Skipton Building Society in a takeover. For the medium size societies, acquisition by an insurer (UK or even foreign) may offer a last route to long-term survival as market pressure continues to increase.

On the continent bancassurance is widespread, and in some cases crosses frontiers (e.g., Allianz of Germany and Banco Popular of Spain (see Salomon Brothers 1990)). To date, foreign banks and insurance companies have concentrated on acquiring within their own industry in the UK. For example, Compagnie du Midi acquired Equity and Law in 1987 and Groupe des Assurances Nationales purchased General Portfolio in 1989. In the banking sphere, National Bank Australia acquired Clydesdale Bank, and Hongkong Shanghai Bank has bought Midland Bank. If the European experience is any gauge, the advent of the single European market in 1992 may well herald the appearance of a major trans-national link up between either a UK insurer and a foreign bank, or a UK bank and a European insurer.

1.5   THE CHANGING ROLE OF TECHNOLOGY

Financial products and services differ from most other retail goods in two respects. First, they generally take the form of a contract with obligations which can endure for years. These contracts generate ongoing servicing costs for the supplier, as well as future income. Second, financial products are 'manufactured' within computer systems. Product innovation can be made by changing a few parameters within a computer program literally in a matter of minutes. The speed with which rivals can copy products by modifying computer software mean that product innovation, particularly within established markets, rarely yields a sustainable competitive advantage.

IT can, however, provide a competitive edge where it is used to realize economies of scale perhaps via the automation of routine tasks or by increasing the speed with which management information is communicated around an organization. (For a recent survey of building society IT development see Watkins and Wickrama-Sekera 1991.) IT can offer an edge where computer software, hardware, market research and business development combine to generate new forms of financial services such as debit cards and new ways of providing financial services such as telephone banking and database marketing.

1.5.1   IT and efficiency

Before computers were available, financial institutions were paper based, updating accounts or policies by hand. The advent of mainframe computers enabled this process to be automated, and has made it possible for institutions to cope with many more products and customers. Automation has also increased the speed with which transactions can be handled, and improved the quality and consistency of account administration. Some institutions have moved a long way down this road and now operate mainframe systems which are connected to their branches. This allows staff to key in sales information and account transaction data directly to the computer, obviating the need for logging data centrally.

IT has also been used to encourage customers to take transactions away from branch counters, freeing up branch staff to concentrate on selling. The prime example of this is the introduction of automated teller machines (ATMs) during the 1980s. ATMs allow customers to make cash withdrawals, deposit money, pay bills and keep up-to-date with their account balance. Many institutions encouraged customers to use ATMs by introducing special accounts and by placing charges on counter transactions. In 1985, the banks and building societies supported around 8,800 ATMs. At the end of 1990, the total had reached 16,900.

The extent to which ATMs have succeeded in releasing branch resources to devote more time to selling is unclear. Evidence is sketchy, but many institutions report that ATMs simply stimulate a higher volume of transactions per account, and may not therefore reduce the effective costs of servicing accounts. Between 1985 and 1991, the average value of ATM cash withdrawals rose from £28 to £45 (BBA, 1992, p. 20), barely holding its value in real terms.

Over the last two decades rival computer companies have sought to invent bigger and faster machines capable of handling larger volumes of business more and more quickly. For institutions purchasing these systems, a major concern has been to avoid being locked into one type of technology. No institution wants to be at a competitive disadvantage through misplaced faith in just one system or just one supplier. In recent years, the development of 'open systems' technology has reduced this problem as software is now available which allows machines manufactured by different suppliers with different operating systems to communicate with each other. Also, financial organizations are much clearer about the purpose of IT and are more aware of the need to build in flexibility. IT infrastructure can improve efficiency by allowing information to circulate around organizations more quickly. Electronic mail speeds up communication between different parts of an organization. Satellite technology now enables executives to discuss issues face-to-face though they may be sitting in different countries.

In most cases, information technology is equally accessible to all sizes of institution. However, the largest tend to have more negotiating power than the smaller ones and can therefore secure a better price. Also, larger systems tend to offer better value for money in so far as any fixed cost elements within the price are outweighed by variable costs. Larger organizations therefore tend to benefit more from the efficiencies offered by IT than smaller ones.

The degree of technological sophistication reached by some financial institutions has actually allowed them to sell their software or to sell a technology-based service to other organizations. For example, Skipton Building Society has been very successful in selling its mortgage administration system to other lenders. Midland Bank and the Britannia Building Society have jointly developed 'Stasis', a facility which can give financial organizations a gateway into the debit card business.

1.5.2 IT and market development

Since the mid-1980s, the UK financial service market has experienced three innovations which rely heavily on technology. The first is the introduction of direct (telephone) financial services retailing; the second is the launch of point-of-sale debit cards and the third is the advent of database marketing.

The first major home-based or telephone banking system was introduced jointly by the Bank of Scotland and Nottingham Building Society. Their home and office banking system (HOBS) was launched in 1986. This was shortly followed by TSB's Speedlink system in 1987, and Midland's First Direct in 1989. National Westminster has recently developed telephone banking services for its business customers ('Bankline'), and two systems for its personal customers, Actionline and Primeline. On the insurance side, Royal Bank of Scotland has established Direct Line Insurance to sell motor, home and credit insurance over the phone.

Evidence of the potential of this mode of selling is the steady rise of Midland's First Direct. At the start of 1991, First Direct had secured in the region of 100,000 accounts, only 25 per cent of whom were 'cannibalized' from Midland itself. The bank had therefore acquired 75,000 new customers within a mature market. First Direct's chief executive stated that at the end of the first quarter in 1992 the bank was acquiring 2,500 new customers a week (*Retail Banker International* 1992, p. 6). He suggests this figure is equivalent to the number of new accounts a new branch would secure in a year. At this rate, First Direct is effectively recruiting a customer base which would require 52 offices to secure. Moreover, it would require a much greater cost outlay to set up 52 offices with the necessary managers and staff. The key feature of all these operations is that they have enabled the institutions concerned to target specific segments of the population and to win new customers. Generally speaking, telephone banking has been geared to younger, more affluent individuals who are technologically literate and willing to conduct their business away from branches.

For the institutions, the advantages of telephone retailing include the acquisition of new customers, the reduction of overheads, and the freeing up of other distribution channels (i.e., branches) to develop services for other customer segments which require face-to-face contact.

The institutions which have so far established direct banking operations have enjoyed two further advantages: first, they have been able to attack selectively an existing customer base and, via targeting, migrate certain types of customer across to the new service; second, they have had the benefit of being first into the market.

The second major IT-led market development has been the launch of debit cards. Debit cards allow customers to pay for goods and services with a plastic card at the point of sale with the payment debited directly from their account. Funds are transferred electronically from the customer's account directly to the retailer's bank. For high street retailers and financial institutions alike, debit cards are less cumbersome than cheques, less paper intensive and transactions can be validated and processed more quickly thereby decreasing the risk of fraud. For the customer, debit cards overcome the problems of having no ready cash, running out of cheques or reaching credit card limits. Instead, the only constraint is that the customer has the money in his account.

The first debit card introduced into the UK was launched by Barclays Bank in 1987 under the 'Connect' brand name. Uptake of the card was hampered by high transaction charges and strong resistance from food retailers who felt that the Visa Connect card was too much like a credit card. In 1988 a consortium of three banks, Midland, National Westminster and Royal Bank of Scotland, introduced 'Switch'. Retailers were offered a flat transaction fee rather than the percentage fee charged by Connect. Also, Switch was entirely free of credit card connotations. These factors enabled Switch to establish itself as the market leader. Visa responded in 1989 by launching its 'Electron' card, though this failed to take off. It rebranded the card in 1991 under the 'Visa Delta' brand name.

By the end of 1991, Switch claimed to have over 12 million cardholders, executing over 70 million transactions per annum, in 35,000 outlets equipped with over 100,000 electronic terminals. Visa Delta claimed a cardholding base of 10 million, making 120 million transactions a year across 145,000 outlets, 75,000 of which have electronic terminals. Currently, around one person in four has a debit card, though approximately one-third of these are thought not to use the facility at all. Protections by APACS (Automated Payments and Clearing Systems) suggest that the total number of debit card transactions by the year 2000 will exceed three billion, more than ATM withdrawals and credit card payments combined.

The third major market oriented IT innovation has been the emergence of marketing databases or customer information files (CIFs). The rationale behind a CIF is that by properly organizing customer information describing what products people buy and how they use them, institutions can track changing patterns of behaviour and consumption and can spot opportunities to target specific products to particular individuals. A marketing database effectively allows an organization to set up an internal market of its own customers in order to prospect for new business via cross-selling (often via direct mail or lead generation for a salesforce) and to define the profile of customer segments for further recruitment.

The ease with which the basic concept of a CIF can be described contrasts sharply with the difficulty financial institutions have experienced in actually creating a viable marketing database. A key problem has been the fact that most institutions have traditionally arranged their administration systems around products and accounts, and not customers. Also, few organizations set up procedures to ensure that customer details were recorded in the same format across different administration systems. As a result, financial organizations, particularly in the insurance sector, have struggled to build up a clear view of their customers' consumption of financial products.

As product files turn over and old accounts are replaced by new customers, so the quality and constancy of customer data will improve. Further, open systems software will overcome the problem of having product administration files held on different machines. In time, therefore, the incompatibility of data will diminish, and customer based files will improve.

Despite these difficulties, many institutions have embarked on bold CIF projects—some are even going through the process for a second time! Barclays, National Westminster, Royal Bank of Scotland, as well as a number of leading building societies and major insurers have all initiated the construction of an integrated CIF.

So far, many hundreds of millions of pounds have been spent creating CIFs. The crucial question is will the payback justify the investment? Currently, that question is hard to answer. However, the chances of success will be increased where institutions can convince consumers that having a multi-product relationship with them is worth paying a little extra for. If, however, the current trend for consumers to become ever more sophisticated and less loyal continues, then it may take some time for institutions to get a return on their CIF investment.

SUMMARY

Since 1981, the retail financial service market has changed fundamentally. Deregulation has been a particularly potent force, initiating significant market restructuring and breaking down traditional market boundaries. Out of deregulation, new worms of organization have emerged based upon alliance and joint ventures. These new modes of operation offer the prospect of combining the best skills of different types of institution to exploit the potential of profitable business growth. In parallel with these developments, major structural changes have occurred in the social, economic, political and demographic character of consumers. There is strong evidence that financial markets are no longer homogeneous with all consumers willing to accept the same product, price or quality of service. Today, retail financial markets are better characterized as segmented markets with different sections of the population demanding different forms of financial service provision.

Information technology has become an integral part of the response made by financial institution to market segmentation. IT not only offers internal efficiency improvements, but also provides opportunities to manufacture, market and distribute new forms of financial services to targeted groups of consumers.

Looking to the future, it is likely that the number of financial institutions in the UK will decrease further and that market power will continue to concentrate in the hands of the larger companies (as far as the Monopolies and Mergers Commission and EC Competition Policy permit). The single European market and the integration of financial services may increase the proportion of UK institutions owned by foreign companies, though this is likely to happen only slowly. It is more likely that UK institutions will look to the continent to launch new ventures, probably in collaboration with foreign institutions.

In the UK the mortgage, deposit savings, pensions and retail banking markets are all reaching mature levels. This indicates that the fight for market share can only intensify as demand becomes more reliant on the turnover of existing business rather than the addition of entirely new business. For the investment market and some areas of insurance, the prospects for strong underlying growth are better. At present, penetration rates for unit trusts, private medical insurance, and permanent health care insurance are low. However, the trend is a rising one, and demand is forecast to accelerate.

It is highly likely that for certain sections of the population at least, inherited wealth will become increasingly significant. As those who entered the housing market in the 1950s and 1960s die, so the appreciated value locked up in their homes will be bequeathed to their relatives. The first to gain will be those in the higher social classes.

Over the coming decade, retailers of financial institutions will need to become more responsive to the needs of customers. They will have to define more accurately which sections of the population they wish to recruit and retain as customers, and they will have to work harder to organize their product manufacturing, marketing, sales and distribution to establish a firm relationship with their customers.

REVIEW QUESTIONS

1. A realistic assessment of a company's internal strengths and weaknesses is a better way of ensuring success than a detailed appraisal of the external opportunities and threats faced by the business. Discuss.
2. Identify three environmental trends which support the view that the retail financial services market place is becoming more segmented.
3. By the year 2001, it is forecast that the UK population will contain an additional one million people aged over 60. What opportunities and threats do you consider this change poses for retailers of financial services?
4. How does the inheritance of housing wealth affect demand in the mortgage market? Why will its importance grow over the next decade?
5. A major building society is weighing up the costs and benefits of entering either the retail banking market or the estate agency business. Based on a review of the recent past, present and future conditions of these markets which diversification would you recommend and why?
6. How has deregulation benefited the consumer?
7. The UK will not be overrun by foreign competition after 1992. What evidence is there to support this view?
8. Bank branches offer a reactive sales environment for retailing financial services. Insurance companies are skilled in hard selling. Does this cultural conflict mean that bancassurance is an inherently unstable mode of operation?
9. The future for financial institutions lies in distribution not manufacturing. Do you agree?
10. To grow and flourish in the future, retailers of financial services must commit resources now to the creation of marketing databases and CIFs. Do you agree?
11. Why should an institution which has developed advanced computer software for handling account administration sell this to its rivals? Outline the risks and rewards of such a strategy.
12. Retailers of financial services are seeking to develop multi-product relationships with consumers. At the same time people are becoming more sophisticated and less loyal to one company. How should financial institutions respond to this challenge?

REFERENCES

Association of British Insurers (1991), *Insurance Statistics 1991*, ABI.

Association of British Insurers (1991), 'Sources of Premium Income', *Statistics Bulletin 1991*, ABI

Association of British Insurers (1986), *Insurance Statistics 1982–86*, ABI.

Barnett M. (1992), 'The parent/subsidiary directive—the first three months', *European Report April 1992*, 3–6.

Board of Inland Revenue (1991), 'Inland Revenue statistics 1991', HMSO

Boleat M. and A. Coles (1987), *The Mortgage Market: Theory and Practice in Housing Finance*, Allen and Unwin.

Bradford and Bingley Building Society (1992), 'The Money Factor' No. 19, Bradford and Bingley Building Society.

British Bankers Association (1992), 'Annual Abstract of Banking Statistics Volume 9', BBA.

Building Societies Commission (1991), 'Annual Report of the Building Societies Commission 1991/2', HMSO.

Central Statistical Office (1992), *Economic Trends*, No. 460, HMSO.

Central Statistical Office (1987), *Economic Trends*, No. 406, HMSO.

Central Statistical Office (1992), *Financial Statistics*, No. 359, HMSO.

Central Statistical Office (1992), *Regional Trends*, No. 26, HMSO.

Central Statistical Office (1992), *Social Trends*, No. 22, HMSO.

Council of Mortgage Lenders (1992), *Housing Finance*, No. 13, CML.

Council of Mortgage Lenders (1991), *Housing Finance*, No. 11, CML.

Department of Trade and Industry (1991), 'The Single Market: Financial Services', DTI.

Dixon R. (1991), 'The effect of the Single European Market on the UK banking industry', *Journal of Management Accounting*, January 1991, 36–38.

Drake L. (1989), *The Building Society Industry in Transition*, Macmillan.

Gower Committee (1984), 'Review of Investor Protection', HMSO Cmnd 9125.

Ermisch J. (1990), *Fewer babies, longer lives*, Joseph Rowntree Foundation.

Financial Research Surveys (1992), Ongoing research for financial institutions—personal communication, N.O.P. London.

Hamnett C., M. Harmer and P. Williams (1991), *Safe as Houses: housing inheritance in Britain*, Paul Chapman Publishing Ltd.

Meen G. (1986), 'Some aspects of mortgage market liberalization in the UK: an econometric analysis', PhD thesis, London School of Economics.

Merret S. (1982), *Owner-occupation in Britain*, Routledge and Kegan Paul Ltd.

Morgan V. (1988), 'The role of Building Societies in a changing environment', report prepared for the Britannia Building Society.

Morgan Grenfell (1991), 'The Future of Medium Sized Building Societies', Morgan Grenfell.

Reid M. (1991), *Abbey National: Conversion to PLC*, Pencorp Books Ltd.

Retail Banker International (1992), *Direct banking rings death-knell for branches*, April 29th, Lafferty Publications Ltd.

Ruiz E. and S. Smith (1991), 'Implementation of the Own Funds and Solvency Ratio Directives in the UK', *Journal of International Banking Law* No. 1, 5–10.

Salomon Brothers (1990), 'Multinational Money Centre Banking: The Evolution of a Single European Banking Market', Salomon Brothers.

Scherer F. (1980), *Industrial market structure and economic performance*, Rand McNally.

Scottish Amicable Assurance Society (1990), Annual Report.

UBS Phillips and Drew (1992), 'Housing Market: Economic Time Bomb?', UBS Phillips and Drew.

UBS Phillips and Drew (1991), 'Building Societies Research: the Major Players', UBS Phillips and Drew.

Watkins J. and U. Wickrama-Sekera (1991), 'Focusing on Business Success: A comprehensive study of the changing use of Information Technology in the Building Society sector 1991', University of Bristol.

Wilson Committee (1980), 'Review of the functioning of financial institutions', HMSO Cmnd 7937.

UNDERSTANDING THE FINANCIAL CONSUMER

Erica Betts   Manchester School of Management

INTRODUCTION

Financial service institutions have long been criticized for their belated and rather reluctant adoption of the marketing concept, persevering instead with their largely 'product led' strategies. This disinclination is ironic according to Cowell (1992), when the hazards of such 'marketing myopia' (Levitt, 1960) were in fact originally illustrated using two services, transportation and energy. The banks probably stand most audibly chastised, painted as smugly complacent (Watson, 1982), and more attuned to the technicalities and intricacies of financial systems than attending to customers' needs (Turnbull, 1982). Others, such as stockbrokers and investment companies, frequently conveyed an attitude of professional conceit, making the customer feel ignorant, guileless and incapable of grasping the formidable complexity.

But environmental change has since compelled many to reconsider the role of marketing within financial services, with the need to satisfy customers gradually assuming greater importance: thus Yorkshire Bank commercials mockingly recall the irritating custom of bank staff adjourning for lunch, whilst the TSB began to like to say 'Yes', and with further refining, progressed to wanting the customer to say 'Yes', too. Understanding customers is no longer simply a marketing requirement either, with the 1986 Financial Services Act came legal obligations to 'know your customer' and provide the 'best advice'. Investment companies were in effect being forced to credit consumers with a modicum of intelligence, or a least treat them in such a manner—some still viewed the new regulations as being about as attractive as the proverbial 'hole in the head'. Yet understanding customers lies at the heart of any successful retail strategy. Ultimately, getting the customer to say 'Yes' demands an understanding of consumer psychology: not simply consumer needs, but also their motives, perceptions, attitudes and decision processes. These psychological processes are not observable, only inferable, and the intangible nature of financial services compounds the problems of inference. Customers who are themselves unaware of what they want until they do not get it (Lovelock, 1983; Lewis and Booms, 1983) cannot be the easiest to satisfy.

Understanding how 'services marketing is different' has all too often been approached from the perspective of the supplier, with a particularly introverted focus on the problems they encounter due to the four 'distinguishing features' of services (Berry, 1980). As a consequence, extending our understanding of consumer behaviour has taken a back seat to improving the efficiency of the service provider. Thus, the chapter begins by looking at the general ways in which these distinctive characteristics are likely to affect the behaviour of financial consumers.

On a more fundamental level, some writers are sceptical about whether 'services marketing' should make any difference, arguing that the 'consumer benefit concept' should be central to all goods and services. All strategies should be based around formulating the bundle of benefits which produces buyer satisfaction, those 'bundles', however intangible, being the 'product' (Bateson, 1977; Enis and Roering, 1981). Section 2.2 of this chapter, therefore, examines the financial consumers' needs and the benefits they seek, in conjunction with the principles of motivation. Section 2.3 proceeds to focus on how effectively some segmentation variables are able to indicate likely differences in consumer needs.

Motivation exerts only a very general influence on behaviour, directing it towards generic product types rather than specific brands or suppliers; it is the other psychological processes, namely learning and perception, which are the more critical determinants here. In Section 2.4, the cognitive map is examined, with the importance of perception being underlined in terms of retail image and positioning. Consumers have traditionally had considerable difficulty distinguishing between 'faceless' financial institutions, a problem purported to have increased since the deregulation of financial markets. Understanding how images are shaped has therefore become topical as well as critical. Also under perception, more than a cursory mention is given to the rather neglected notion of perceived risk, which, as we shall see, is hypothesized to increase with intangibility.

Attitudes towards credit, mortgage debt and accepting responsibility for our own financial security have changed dramatically in recent years. Attitudes and how they are structured are covered in Section 2.6. They form the basis of many so called 'limited' buyer behaviour models, the response hierarchies, one of which has been expressly adapted for complex financial services on the basis of knowledge from a number of privatization share issues. The traditional comprehensive buyer behaviour models are described in Section 2.7, although many writers doubt the validity of their assumptions of rationality and sequential information processing. Being primarily concerned with one-off purchases, they also fail to acknowledge the importance of long-term relationships. Instead it is proposed that organizational buying models may make a better contribution to understanding the financial consumer. The implications for customer loyalty, the holy grail of many financial service organizations, are discussed along with the related concept of relationship marketing.

2.1 CHARACTERISTICS OF FINANCIAL SERVICES: IMPLICATIONS FOR BUYER BEHAVIOUR

That 'services marketing is different' to goods marketing (Berry, 1980) has been generally acknowledged and the subject of a flourishing body of literature for two decades. Yet, despite the use of the term services 'marketing', somewhat paradoxically, the effects of the differences on understanding consumer behaviour have been of rather less interest than the problems posed for the service providers (McKechnie, 1992). In addition, the work on understanding the service consumer is neither generalizable across services *per se* or even all financial services (Lovelock, 1983; Zeithaml, Parasuraman and Berry, 1985). Services, as well as services marketing, are different. Financial services require varying amounts of customer participation, they range from highly standardized to bespoke and can entail high or low customer involvement.

The four characteristics typically cited as distinguishing services from goods marketing, and the ways in which they affect buyer behaviour, are:

1. *Intangible*   In the words of Berry (1980), a good is 'an object, a device, a thing' whereas a service is 'a deed, a performance, an effort', an absence of physical substance which makes services more difficult to grasp mentally and evaluate (Bateson, 1977). Pre-purchase evaluation

of alternative services is hampered by a paucity of 'search qualities', i.e., tangible indications or clues as to the quality or features of the service.

Intangibility is, however, a matter of degree rather than an absolute notion, as illustrated by the continuum proposed by Shostack (1977). Many financial services contain significant tangible elements on which they can be evaluated or judged, such as ATM cards, statements, share and insurance certificates, etc. It has long been recognized that these tangible clues or items of 'physical evidence' are eagerly latched onto by consumers and are often central to their evaluation processes (Shostack, 1977; Berry, 1980; Booms and Bitner, 1981). Emphasizing these tangible clues or items of 'physical evidence' gives the consumer more concrete bases on which to make their choice and decreases uncertainty.

2. *Inseparability* Services are said to be high in 'experience qualities', which as the name implies, suggests that they have attributes which can be evaluated only after purchase or during consumption. Thus they cannot be sampled or returned, only cancelled in some instances although irreversible damage may already have been done, for example in the cases of bad investment advice or taking out inadequate insurance cover.

In some respects, inseparability holds true for a limited range of financial services. At what point are insurance policies or savings accounts actually 'consumed'? (McGoldrick and Greenland, 1992). Adding to the uncertainty, pension recommendations and other investment advice cannot even be evaluated until maturity, whereas insurance cannot be fully evaluated unless the occasion for a claim arises. When services cannot be evaluated even after purchase they are said to be high in 'credence qualities'. The difficulty associated with evaluating service options leads consumers to rely extremely heavily on word of mouth communication, from friends, family and other reference groups.

3. *Heterogeneity* Inseparability leads to some services being more prone to variation in quality, which further exacerbates the consumer's uncertainty over the outcome. Production and consumption being an interactive process (Gronroos, 1978), quality becomes dependent upon the consumer's ability to articulate what is required, as well as the uneven temperaments of both front line staff and computer technology. Some financial services have greater potential for variation than others; technology can be employed in some to 'industrialize' (Levitt, 1981) the service and improve consistency, but the standard of financial advice, for example, is far more vulnerable to the shortcomings of human nature.

4. *Perishability* It is not only the service providers who are inconvenienced by the fact that services cannot be stored. Consumers can only pay a bill when it arrives and when they have time. They want cash when they run out, regardless of whether the bank is closed, or the ATM empty. Just as they want to 'strike while the iron's hot' when speculating on shares or bonds. Supplier's must synchronize supply and demand, not simply with respect to the number of tellers or staff on duty, but also by offering convenient trading hours—convenient for the customer that is. Until quite recently, what read 'convenience' to the banks read 'intensely irritating' to everyone else: denoting 3.30pm closing and no Saturday morning opening.

McKechnie (1992) supplements these four general goods-services distinctions with two further distinguishing features relevant to buying behaviour in financial services:

5. *Fiduciary responsibility* Ultimately the financial consumer is buying a set of promises, to the effect that the supplier takes responsibility for looking after the buyer's funds and welfare. However, so rarely are there sufficient dependable search qualities to validate promises that trust and confidence in the institution and its personnel are imperative. In addition to trust and personal sources of information, consumers rely on cues such as the size, image and

longevity of the organization to indicate whether the promises are likely to be fulfilled. The development of trust can bring about a degree of inertia in customer supplier relationships, as buyers have no wish to repeat the arduous process of seeking out and evaluating alternative suppliers.

6. *Two-way information flows* Not simply concerned with one-off purchases, financial services may involve a series of regular two-way transactions, usually over an extended period of time. The wealth of confidential information captured as a result can be used to influence behaviour through both customer retention and customer acquisition programmes.

However, having noted these differences, a cautionary proviso should be heeded:

The existing literature is replete with unsubstantiated principles about service excellence, service quality and related topics. Yet too little evidence exists to substantiate whether these principles result in outcomes such as long-term customer satisfaction and profitability. (Fisk, Brown and Bitner, 1993)

2.2 NEEDS AND MOTIVES

The first aim is to readdress the fundamental question of what motivates or drives consumers to acquire financial products at all? Purchase is not typically cause for any great excitement and most of us could, hopefully, imagine more enjoyable pastimes than evaluating complex pension plans or sweating over the legal implications of signing a credit agreement.

Motivation describes the forces acting on a consumer which initiate and direct behaviour towards the attainment of specific goals. Goals are the result of needs which cause a state of tension in an individual, which may be physiological (e.g., a need for food), psychological (e.g., a need for self-esteem) or sociological (e.g., a need for social interaction). It is the state of tension which acts as a cue for goal orientated behaviour; achieving the goal releases the tension. For example, the prospect of a burglar finding an individual's life savings under their mattress causes worry (tension). Typically the worry would be removed by depositing the money in a savings account of some description, restoring equilibrium. A simple model of the motivation process is shown in Figure 2.1.

2.2.1 Needs and solutions

Equally however, the consumer could remove the money and spend it on a car, give it to charity, buy premium bonds or hide it somewhere else. All the options would reduce tension; the individual wanted peace of mind not a bank account. All the options are solutions, or means to the same ends (albeit not all very sensible or particularly satisfactory). Needs should not be confused with solutions as this invariably produces a product orientation (McGoldrick, 1990). A cheque book is a solution not a need, consumers do not 'need' cheque books. Cheques have traditionally been used to transfer money between accounts, but many more convenient 'money transfer' solutions are now available: debit cards, as Barclays Bank notes, are 'the cheque you don't have to write', whereas the direct debit is a series of payments for which only one 'cheque' has to be written which assist with budgeting too.

In a similar vein, Yorke (1982) urged companies to consider which 'business' they were in Banks, he concluded, were in the businesses of supplying:

1. *Cash accessibility* Customers need to have access to cash at frequent intervals in order to purchase goods and services where cash is the specified medium of exchange (e.g., ATM card, credit card, cash cheque).

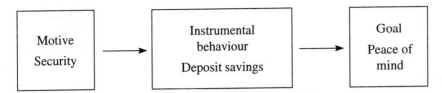

Figure 2.1   A simple model of the motivation process

2. *Asset security*   Covering both physical security (from theft) and security against depreciation (e.g., credit cards, safe deposit boxes, interest bearing accounts).
3. *Money transfer*   Where cash is not stipulated, it is safer to reconcile debts through transferring sums across accounts (e.g., cheque book, debit and credit cards).
3. *Deferred payment*   Customers wish to delay repayments at a reasonable cost (e.g., credit card, personal loan, overdraft, mortgage).
5. *Financial advice*   Not a solution in itself, but instrumental to finding one. Consumers want advice concerning the increasing number and complexity of financial services.

Financial service institutions may be in the same broadly defined industry sector, but they are clearly not in the *business* of satisfying a homogeneous set of needs. The consumer benefit concept would define insurance companies as being in the business of risk transfer, while insurance brokers provide advice in addition to facilitating risk transfer. Not all the benefits are as easy to locate however.

The constant task of the service marketer is to try to come to terms with what benefits customers seek; benefits which are so central to the success of the service marketing operation, but so elusive to define. (Cowell, 1992)

2.2.2   Motive classification schemes

Motives are drives which exist due to unfulfilled needs. Some classifications simply name motives after the object which will satisfy the need, such as 'insurance needs', but this again falls into the same myopic trap described above. Greater explanatory power is afforded by categorizing motives, for which there are many classification schemes.

Physiological and psychological needs   Motives are usually divided into physiological and psychological. Physiological or primary needs concern the innate, unlearned bodily requirements for food, water, sleep, shelter, etc.; when activated they typically demand immediate attention. Highly though we may regard this elemental commodity, money is not an innate need. The link between physiological needs and financial services is a tenuous one, in themselves they obviously cannot satisfy any of them—although custom has it that money is instrumental to acquiring products which will. While purchases are usually a means to an end, in the case of physiological needs, all financial services are but a means to a means to an end.

The relevance of basic primary needs to consumer behaviour *per se* has, in any event, been largely dismissed; not only are they largely satisfied in western societies but also:

...allowing for such ideas as the concept of individual differences and man's widened imagination, it is fruitless and even nonsensical to talk about man's basic needs. (Markin, 1969)

Thus basic needs are subject to modification by psychological factors. Consumers do not want water, but Perrier, Coke, coffee syrups and branded beers. Similarly, we are no longer content

	Need	*Example*	*'Typical' tolerated satisfaction*
5	Self-actualization Personal, fulfilment, self-development, need to learn and understand.	Mastering the principles and practicalities of investment schemes or the stock exchange.	10%
4	Ego/esteem Prestige, success, recognition, status.	Lloyds Gold Card—'a card which recognizes your achievements' (Lloyds, 1993). —American Express —Coutts bank account	40%
3	Social/belongingness Affiliation, companionship and affection.	'Club membership' events for cardholders, personal service can be appealing for social contact.	50%
2	Safety and security Future satisfaction of physiological needs on a permanent basis and physical safety.	All types of insurance, from holiday to life assurance, cardholder protection plans, mortgages, physical safety of cash and other assets.	70%
1	Physiological Biological drives for food, drink, shelter and exercise.	Financial services are only instrumental to satisfaction.	85%

Figure 2.2 Maslow's 'Hierarchy of Needs'

with a roof over our heads, but want a warehouse flat by a marina and/or a cottage in the country. On a slightly different level, neither do we simply want cash accessibility, perhaps coveting a Halifax 'Cardcash' to make a statement about our warehouse apartment or our aspirations to own one.

For a suitable definition of psychological or secondary needs we turn to Bayton (1958), who describes them as those based 'upon tension systems existing in the individual's subjective psychological state and in his relations with others.' Psychological needs are thus terms used to describe a large number of mainly extrinsic, socially acquired and learned motivations. Financial services are purely psychological in the satisfactions they give, being central to self-maintenance (security) and enhancement (speculative achievements and excitement).

The issue of speculation brings to the fore the assumption that all behaviour is motivated by the desire to reduce tension. Cognitive psychologists reject this idea, with mental stimulation being a basic need of the personality, individuals must actively seek drive intensification in order to maintain an optimal stimulation level. The 'general incongruity adaptation level' (GIAL) suggests that an optimal level of stimulation or tension exists for each individual, below which intensification will generally be sought and above which reduction will be the objective (Streufert and Driver, 1971). However, although the GIAL optimum is stable, consumers grow accustomed to certain levels of incongruity or stimulation and become bored with daily routines, interests and habitually bought products. Risky, adventurous or variety seeking buying behaviour is a means of heightening stimulation and incongruity.

Maslow's hierarchy of needs   'Man is a perpetually wanting animal—as soon as one of his needs is satisfied, another appears in its place'. (Maslow, 1943) One of the most popular theories of motivation is Maslow's 'hierarchy of needs', which proposes that needs are organized in a sequence of priorities, as shown in Figure 2.2.

As 'Man lives for bread alone, when there is no bread' his lower order physiological needs must be tolerably satisfied before others can emerge, such that paying the food or gas bill assumes priority over starting a personal equity plan.

Clearly, many financial services are related to level two: safety needs, or motives relating to security, protection and stability in life. Thus home contents insurance protects a certain standard of living from the ravages of fire or burglary while pensions secure an income into old age, needs which should take precedence over the desire for a sun-soaked family holiday, a prestigious car or other luxury goods. Should, perhaps, but Maslow proposed that consumers have their own subjective 'tolerated' levels of satisfaction so that needs do not have to be 100% satisfied before progressing to the next level. Maslow declared that they 'averaged' at the magnitudes shown in Figure 2.2, although critics are wont to see them as reckless generalizations (Gibson *et al.*, 1985). Thus the propensity to go on holiday with the mortgage money or similar acts of 'irresponsible' spending are not sufficient grounds for dismissing the model, although they do weaken the model's explanatory power somewhat.

The hierarchy can also work in reverse, for example, high mortgage rates, the fear of unemployment and house repossession reactivated safety needs, with noticeable increases in the savings ratio (the proportion of personal disposable income saved) since the onset of recession in the late 1980s (Figure 2.3) (NOP, 1992). Thus, the hierarchy is intuitively appealing and employs elements of sound common sense, although in reality, scant empirical evidence exists to support it (Louden and Della Bitta, 1988).

Primary versus selective influences and basic orientations   Motives have only a very general influence on behaviour, they are usually *primary* influences which initiate behaviour and direct it towards generic product classes (pensions, savings accounts). It is the *selective* influences of learning, perception, attitudes and personality which ultimately guide choice between brands.

The 'basic orientation' of consumers, predisposing them to respond favourably to certain types of appeal, is a selective influence although it appears frequently in motive classifications. Of those listed, only prestige can be seen as a 'motive' as such, the others rarely initiate behaviour in themselves.

- 'Prestige' where status is a driving concern.
- 'Value', obtaining the best quality for the cost.
- 'Economy' where cheap is the major criteria.
- 'Convenience', when 'time poor' or apathetic consumers demand an easily accessible, nearby and/or swift service.

Hence basic orientations will tend to be useful predictors of 'selective' evaluation criteria (e.g., rate of return—'value', no annual credit card fee—'economy') and thus brand choice.

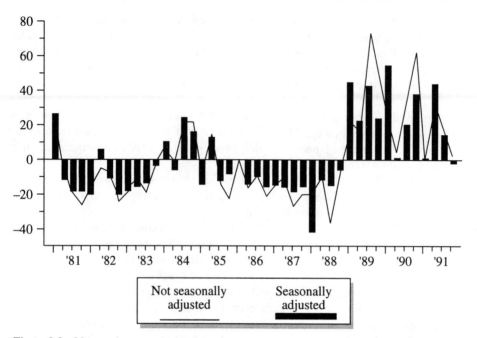

Figure 2.3 New real personal savings per quarter: Year-on-year percentage change
Source: NOP (1992), *The Financial Consumer*, NTC Publications Ltd, Henley-on-Thames

Herzberg's (1966) 'two factor' theory of motivation can also be applied to considering selective influences. Making the distinction between 'extrinsic' and 'intrinsic' attributes of a product or service, only the intrinsic elements can actually provide satisfaction. Extrinsic 'hygiene' factors are conspicuous only by their absence, when the outcome is one of active dissatisfaction. The implications for the evaluation of alternatives are considered in Section 2.7.2.

2.2.3 A multidimensional model of motivation

Motives are not mutually exclusive, hence all the classifications thus far have been limited in terms of their practical use by their use of only one characteristic. Acknowledging this, McGuire (1976) offers a series of two pole motive tendency schemes to gauge the relative strengths of different types of motives in force. His distinctions recognized that drives range from extremes of emotional/cognitive ('rational' reasoning to emotional responses), preservation/growth (maintenance of equilibrium versus self-development), active/passive (self-initiated versus reactive) and internal/external (driven by need for internal change or driven by environmental change).

Motive 'bundling' Compounding the complexity, a single product frequently attends to a number of needs simultaneously. The number of 'businesses' addressed by the credit card (Section 2.2.1) makes it a case in point; the lure of 'buy now, pay later' being but one of the reasons for subscribing. 'Motive bundling' can make it critical to ascertain which motives are strongest in target customers, as often the difference will only be a matter of degree. Vendors can appeal to the need for safety (less cash handling), belongingness ('club' membership), esteem (prestige) or power (additional entitlements) (McGoldrick, 1990).

American Express unashamedly promotes its services as being for the better heeled among society, creating an up-market image for its products (prestige). But more concrete benefits are needed too. Thus, American Express and the Royal Bank of Scotland (1991) announce:

The Gold Card is more than simply the most prestigious charge card ... As a Gold Cardmember, you have the flexibility of a current account together with an immediate unsecured overdraft facility ...

The American Express Card also offers prestigious 'club' benefits which ...

enhancing your lifestyle. As a Cardmember you'll receive invitations to exclusive events such as the opportunity to shop at Harrods out-of-hours ... Apply today and receive a set of personalised luggage tags with our compliments.

The economical yet artfully conceived introductory gift means that even though the cardmembers' new status symbol cannot be worn on their sleeve, it will at least be fully visible on their suitcases!

Home ownership also satisfies many needs, as a more secure form of tenure than rented accommodation ('safety needs'), with status attached ('esteem needs'), as well as bestowing a sense of belonging and providing for the family ('social needs'). Similarly, the preoccupation with moving up the 'housing ladder' to ever larger properties in 'nicer' neighbourhoods could be an interest in safety, making a more comfortable home for the family and/or the prestige attached to the new post code.

British culture is noted for the high value attached to owner occupation, in other countries people are far more favourably disposed towards renting accommodation. The influence of cultural values, ideas, beliefs and norms has a pervasive influence on our perceptions of needs and how they should be satisfied. Odih (1991) noted that the economist Duesenberry was one of the first writers to recognize the importance of culture:

In every case the kinds of activities in which people engage are culturally determined; nearly all purchases of goods are ... either to provide physical comfort or implement the activities which make up the life of our culture.

The processes of opening bank accounts, taking out insurance, saving for retirement as well as actually retiring are facets of Western culture. Examining cultural values and characteristic ways of living in societies is required to understand what is bought, when, through which channels and how it is paid for. Acceptable solutions, as well as the needs, may vary considerably.

Polarity of motives and the 'fear appeal'   Needs drive motivated behaviour in a specific direction; positive goals are those which a person strives to attain, such as a satisfying career, fun and excitement, good health, etc., and involve 'approach' objects (Lewin, 1935). Conversely, negative goals involve 'avoidance' objects, caused by fears and aversions to such states as poverty, pain and physical injury and social embarrassment.

Avoidance objects are the *raison d'être* of most financial services, protecting against the unpleasant financial consequences of theft, ill-health, an impoverished old age, a motor accident, unemployment, etc. Hence it is difficult to motivate consumers without using the 'fear appeal' to draw attention to the benefits on offer:

Critical Illness Benefit: 'For some people there really is a fate worse than death. They suffer a critical illness—and survive ... and the last thing you need on top of a health crisis is a cash crisis. Unfortunately, you can't rely on conventional life assurance policies because they are only designed to pay out on death ...' (Barclays Bank, 1993)

Royal Scottish Personal Pension Plan: 'When you left that last job did you leave something valuable behind? Your pension!' (Royal Scottish Assurance, 1992)

(i) *Approach-Approach Conflict*

| Take out a personal pension plan | $+ve \rightarrow$ Consumer $\leftarrow +ve$ | Buy a new car |

Consumer must make a choice between two desirable alternatives.

(ii) *Avoidance-Avoidance Conflict*

| Paying insurance premium | $+ve \rightarrow$ Consumer $\leftarrow -ve$ | Losing possessions with no compensation |

Consumer must make a choice between two unpleasant alternatives.

(iii) *Approach-Avoidance Conflict*

| Use credit card | $+ve \rightarrow$ Consumer $\leftarrow -ve$ | Paying back debt |

Consumer wants to make a purchase—but must ultimately pay for it.

Figure 2.4   A typology of motive conflict situations
Source: Adapted from Louden and Della Bitta, (1988), *Consumer Behaviour: Concepts and Applications*, 3rd edn, McGraw Hill, New York

Pensions: 'Most people dream about retirement. They believe that at last they will have the time to do the things they really want to. Up to a point, they're right. They'll have all the time they need. But will they have the money? The sad truth is that only a very small percentage of people retire on the maximum amount available to them....' (Royal Bank of Scotland, 1993)

Life Assurance: 'The chance of suffering a long-term illness or disability is 7 times higher than the likelihood of dying before retirement...... Protecting your income through permanent health insurance and starting a pension early begin to look like good ideas.' (National Westminster Bank)

However, care should be exercised when using fear appeals. Empirical research, not to mention common sense and experience, warn that selective deafness can be exercised at will to protect ourselves from information too unpleasant or alarming to accept. In one of the earliest studies of this type, on the harmful effects of smoking, Janis and Feshbach (1953) found the effectiveness of fear appeals to be inversely related to the strength of the warning.

Goal Conflict   Examples of conflicting motivations are illustrated in Figure 2.4. Differences in goal polarity, either attracting or repelling forces, combined with 'motive bundling' results in three types of goal conflict (Lewin, 1935). The corollary can be prolonged indecision (tension) if the consumer does not reestablish his priorities.

2.3   CONSUMER NEEDS AND BASES FOR SEGMENTATION

That no supplier can be all things to all people is one of the guiding principles of marketing, meaning that most organizations must design strategies which 'focus' on appealing to and satisfying smaller groups of customers with relatively homogeneous needs (see Chapter 3 for a discussion of Porter's generic strategies). Being aware of how needs differ among consumers is only the first step, suppliers must also know on what *actionable* bases these needs vary if they are to design appropriate marketing mixes for target segments.

There is no single way to segment a market, but the desired result will possess three qualities (Kotler, 1991). Segments should be:

1. '*Measurable*'—thus traditional geographic, demographic or socio-economic bases are easier and cheaper to use than psychographic or behavioural bases such as attitudes, personality, lifestyle or the benefits sought.
2. '*Accessible*'—the seller must be able to communicate with target segments cost-effectively.
3. '*Substantial*'—it must be of sufficient size and value to be profitable. Economically 'viable' is probably a more appropriate term (Yorke, 1982).

Thus needs and motives are generally unactionable and so proxy variables must be found. The bases for segmentation have traditionally been classified as geographic, demographic, psychographic and behavioural, which are discussed more fully in the specific context of marketing strategy in Chapter 3. Here it suffices to consider how a select few bases rise to the challenge of approximating to consumer needs.

2.3.1   Traditional, single variable bases

Sex   Women have traditionally assumed a less active role in familial financial matters for a multitude of reasons, most arising from their status as society's homemakers rather than breadwinners. In a 1976 NOP survey of unbanked households, women felt apprehensive about becoming overdrawn and uneasy about coping with cheque books, also presuming that they would make them more susceptible to bouts of impulse buying (Lewis, 1982a). Davis and Riguax (1974) examined marital roles in purchase decisions, confirming that financial services were exceptionally 'husband dominant'.

Now more women are employed and thus in possession of their own income (NOP, 1992). Furthermore with the demise of the nuclear family, due to one in three marriages ending in divorce and the growing propensity for young singles to live alone, an increasing number of women are head of household with all the commensurate financial responsibilities. But despite sexual equality having improved manifestly since the original surveys, women still feel significantly less confident with personal investment options than men (Key Note, 1992). Asked whether they knew enough to consider investing in a scheme, the greatest discrepancies were apparent in the more complex schemes such as personal equity plans (PEPs) (Table 2.1) and unit trusts (19 per cent men, 9 per cent women).

Whether or not they are actually less knowledgeable is, of course, open to doubt. Men may be reluctant to admit their lack of knowledge, due to cultural pressures which have asserted that it is a man's role to take care of family financial matters. Women may actually know as much as men but not be convinced that it is sufficient to make a prudent decision. But while there are gender differences, they are few, declining and insufficiently explicit to use as a basis for segmentation in themselves.

Table 2.1   Awareness of personal equity plans

Socio-economic group (%)	Age (%)	Sex (%)
AB—21	16–24—6	Male—17
C1—16	25–34—14	Female—5
C2—7	35–44—13	
DE—4	45–64—13	
	65+—8	

Source: Adapted from *Personal Finance in the UK*, Key Note Publications Ltd 1992, Middlesex, pp. 9–11

Base: all who do not own their own home

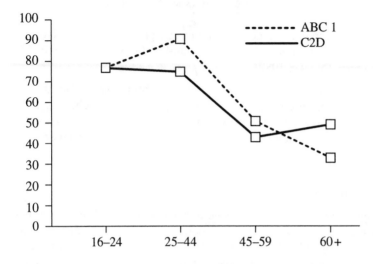

Figure 2.5   Ideal of owner occupation still strong
Source: The Henley Centre (1993) *Metamorphosis in Marketing*, London

Social class   Using social class as a method of segmentation is conceptually complicated, philosophically upsetting and methodologically challenging (Coleman, 1983), yet it continues to be used in its various guises as a predictor of consumer behaviour. According to Engel, Blackwell and Minniard (1986), class is still the predominant method of social stratification in industrialized nations because classes are the basis for social interaction and separation from other members of society. People of similar class (a sub-culture) learn and share similar values which influence their attitudes towards issues such as home ownership (Figure 2.5) and credit. Borrowing and credit are undoubtedly viewed in a far less positive light now than they were during the mid-1980s, but C1C2s have had the most striking change of heart towards purchasing on the 'never-never'. Reverting back to old style values, many are now reluctant to admit ever having bought on credit.

'It's not a credit, it's a debt—they twist your words . . . "your flexible friend", they never make out you've got to pay it back in these adverts' and 'I don't believe in credit, never have done. If we can't afford it we don't get it or we save. It's the only way to be.' (C1C2 interview respondents, The Henley Centre, 1993)

Key Note (1992) suggests that it should come as no revelation that the best informed socio-economic groups are those likely to have the most to invest. However, while awareness of investment schemes, particularly PEPs (see Table 2.1), did rise with socio-economic standing (typically class is determined by the occupation of the head of household), expecting this to be a good predictor of buyer behaviour is fraught with difficulties (Coleman,1983):

● The social grade attributed to certain occupations is not always reflected in salaries, hence blue collar workers having 'more brass than class'.
● It does not account for low salaries due to the age earnings cycle.
● Divorce and bereavement often leave households with an income below their class average, just as a mother returning to work will cause the household income to rise but invariably without a change in class.

Income   The above perhaps suggests that income would be a more reliable predictor of behaviour, which would doubtless delight many financial services organizations having customers' private pecuniary particulars at their fingertips. However:

- Disposable income should not be confused with discretionary income. The mortgage, a dependent spouse and children can leave high earners with little room for manoeuvre.
- Income in itself gives precious little indication as to what people actually need and want—only whether they will be able to afford it (not to be dismissed too readily).

Nevertheless, the continuing polarization of income is set to increase the unequal distribution of consumer spending power, with a concomitant fragmentation of markets (Henley Centre, 1993). According to the Henley Centre, the top 60 per cent of households will see their incomes rise by around 12 per cent, whereas the real income growth in the bottom 40 per cent will average a meagre 1 per cent. More niches will emerge in the higher bands as the income distribution stretches, with the affluent two-thirds becoming increasingly accustomed to paying for services previously sustained by the state. These consumers will need to plan or at least budget to meet the considerable expense of education and healthcare, providing windows of opportunity for financial advisors, life assurance firms and many others:

You go to school ... It costs about £139,000 to educate a child to age 18 at boarding school, £55,000 at day school. Paying for education out of income is becoming almost impossible.

A regular savings plan, taken out now with the benefit of professional investment expertise, can provide the extra money when you need it ... (National Westminster Bank)

2.3.2   Hybrid, multivariate bases

The family life-cycle (FLC)   The wisdom of this hybrid segmentation concept is rooted in behavioural science and particularly family sociology (Odih, 1991). It charts the reasonably predictable progression of stages through which most families pass, starting with the young single 'bachelor', to newly-wed (and the creation of the basic family unit), to family growth (with the birth of children), to family reduction (as they become independent), before the family unit dissolves with the death of one spouse.

As families progress through the FLC both their financial circumstances and needs clearly change substantially. Of the multitude of FLC classifications available, Table 2.2 uses Wells and Gubar's (1966) version to detail some of the typical courses and directions of change. The FLC is a composite of many demographic variables, systematically combining marital status, size of family, age of family members and employment status. Age of the parents and likely disposable income are inferred from the stage in the cycle. Traditionally, the most affluent sector has been the 'empty nest I', with peak pre-retirement salaries, paid-up mortgages, no dependent children to drain the coffers and possible inheritances as well. Families with children of pre-school age are characteristically those with the heaviest financial axe to grind. Figure 2.6 shows that their substantial outgoings coupled with only one income make the burden of debt particularly disturbing for this group to live with.

The profusion of life-stage/lifestyle acronyms during the 1980s showed how the concept captured the nation's imagination. So easy were the stages to recognize and identify with, not only did we have the now burnt-out 'yuppies' (young urban professionals), but also delightful expressions for childless couples 'dinkies' and 'oinks' (dual/one income no kids), celebrated old 'woopies' (well off older people) as well as many not so acclaimed variants, such as the 'manillas' (middle aged no income lonely lay-abouts).

Table 2.2 Life-cycle stages

Life-cycle stage	Typical characteristics and products sought
Bachelor phase	Highly mobile, few financial burdens or assets. Leisure and fashion orientated. Loans for car/holiday, overdrafts, student loans, credit cards.
Newly married couples (young no children)	Dual income, although careers may not be particularly well established, lack of financial planning fairly typical. Mortgage, loans for home improvements, life insurance.
Full nest I (youngest under 6)	Highly dissatisfied with financial position: many new financial outgoings coincide with possible loss of one wage. Financial advice, family health plans, concern over pending school fees.
Full nest II (youngest over 6)	Some families may return to dual income, plus more established careers improve finances too, although outgoings still heavy. May start planning/saving for retirement, move to larger house.
Empty nest I (older married couples)	Head of household still working and, with no dependent children, are likely to be in best financial position. Saving for retirement, housing assets may be realized with move to smaller house.
Empty nest II	Retirement and a large fall in income. Health insurance, financial advice on avoiding inheritance tax.
Solitary survivor (in work)	Income probably good, but likely to sell home. As with 'empty nest I' above.
Solitary survivor (retired)	As with 'empty nest II', but pension income likely to be lower.

Source: Adapted from Wells, W. D and G. Gruber (1966) 'Life cycle concept in marketing research, *Journal of Marketing Research* (Nov.), pp. 355–63

However, the FLC does have its critics. Most focus on the demise of the traditional family unit, the most notable cause being the one in three marriages which end in divorce. But others break the mould too: single parents, childless couples, middle-aged couples who marry late in life, those starting families in their thirties, unmarried couples, homosexual couples, extended families, etc. Stampfl (1978) accommodates contemporary trends by adding a further 'single parenthood' category into his consumer life cycle. Although likely to be less affluent on the whole, single parents' needs will still be subject to similar stages as those characterizing conventional family units. Acknowledging a myriad of possible variants in their updated version, Murphy and Staples (1979) all but 're-invent the cycle'.

Nevertheless, financial services organizations appear to agree that the multivariate FLC gives a constructive, practical insight into how needs, priorities and resources are likely to be distributed and change over time. Thus Midland Bank has its 'Navigator' (1993) service:

Helping you map out your future—Do you have sufficient savings to meet both short term and long term needs? Will you have enough to live on when you retire? Have you recently changed jobs, got married or started a family?

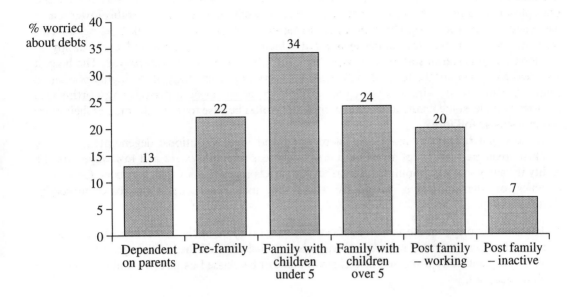

Figure 2.6   Concern about debts in the family life cycle
Source: The Henley Centre (1993) *Metamorphosis in Marketing*, London

The National Westminster's 'Life Map' illustrates how life assurance policies are ideally suited to use the basic concept of 'life stages', a slight variation on the FLC as it begins with birth rather than bachelorhood—useful when trying to recruit young savers and students. The excerpt below also acknowledges the likelihood of a less than faithful reconstruction of the rather idealistic FLC:

The Map: You're born. You lie in a cot. Then you're walking. And talking. You go to school. Maybe college. You fall in love. You get a job. You get a flat. You get married. You start a family. You change your job. You buy a house. You go on holiday. You take time off. To have a baby. To improve your career. You start a business. You work all hours. You save for your daughter's wedding. Perhaps get divorced. You may start another family. You think about retiring. You retire. You find you're worth more than you think.

You notice that the words 'life assurance, pensions and investments' are not mentioned. And yet you need them for nearly every one of these events. And dozens more of the things that make up life ...' (National Westminster Bank)

Life assurance policies have adapted their products to give holders the opportunity to increase or decrease contributions as their financial fortunes fluctuate through the life stages:

Lifestages—the Life Protection Plan that evolves as you do ... At each stage of your life—when you are single, setting up home, bringing up children or looking forward to grandchildren—your responsibilities, and therefore your protection needs, change. Any solution needs to be flexible, capable of changing with you throughout your life. (Barclays, 1992)

Geodemographics   The social injustice created by the north–south divide has been a matter of concern for decades. Again in the 1980s, the extent of the economic disparity was put under the spotlight, as the south's service economy prospered while the north's heavy industrial base continued its steady decline. Property prices boomed in the south, earnings were higher and unemployment, among the predominantly white collar workforce, was considerably lower. Or so the general story went until the turn of the decade when deep recession took hold again. This time the downturn was less discerning about which sectors it ravaged and quite happy to overlook the managerial status of those it threw into the ranks of the unemployed. The biggest and wealthiest also fall the hardest, with most noise coming from many of the highly populated southern counties. If, with recovery, the reality does prove to be a diminishing north-south economic divide, some financial services companies would be wise to write off some of their basic assumptions as folklore.

But any generalizations mask critical regional and local variations: degenerated, poverty stricken areas are features of all modern cities, whereas unemployment and low wages are the reality in many sparsely populated agricultural districts regardless of their location. Geodemographics, or 'the analysis of people by where they live', works upon two basic principles (Mitchell, 1989, 1992):

1. That two people from the same neighbourhood are far more likely to share similar characteristics than two randomly selected individuals; or 'birds of a feather flock together'.
2. That geographically dispersed neighbourhoods can be classed as having similar population characteristics.

ACORN (A Classification of Residential Neighbourhoods) was the first geodemographic system, which, like its modern day rivals, used cluster analysis on Census of Population information to classify enumeration and postcode districts into neighbourhood types. The 'new detached houses, young families', 'unimproved terraces with old people', 'multi-let big old houses and flats', 'villages with wealthy older commuters', etc., provided useful approximations to family life stages.

Progress since the 1981 Census has been impressive, especially so with respect to financial services applications, where a number of suppliers now vie for custom using the likes of 'affluence rankings' (SuperProfiles) and 'wealth indicators' (PiN). FiNPiN was designed expressly to identify prospects for financial products and services, matching census data with behavioural information from NOP's 'Financial Research Survey' (such as the use of bank and building society accounts, ownership of stocks and shares, mortgage and pension arrangements, holding/use of credit and store cards) with other discriminating variables to categorize financial consumers by their attitudes towards personal finance as well as their behaviour. Designed with direct marketing applications firmly in mind, credit checking features can reduce the risk of targeting potential bad debtors. Two of the three levels of FiNPiN analysis are shown in Table 2.3, for details of the third, highly suited for use in location analysis, see Chapter 4.

2.4 THE COGNITIVE MAP

Cognition refers to the mental processes of knowing, perceiving and judging which enable individuals to interpret the world around them. Both learning and perception are central to the production of the individual's world view or cognitive map.

Learning is closely related to perception. Both involve the individual's responses to environmental and psycho-social stimuli; both can be explained theoretically in terms of either a stimulus response or a Gestalt paradigm, both processes are intimately connected with and shaped by the individual's attitudes, personality and motives. Learning influences perception and, in turn, depends on it. (Foxall, 1980)

Table 2.3 FiNPiN 93: Classification summary labels (levels 4 and 10)

(A)	Financially active (24.3)	i	Most active (12.2)
		ii	Financially secure savers (12.1)
(I)	Financially informed (41.1)	iii	Multiproduct savers and investors (19.7)
		iv	Traditional multiproduct users (7.5)
		v	Nett savers (13.9)
(C)	Financially conscious (18.7)	vi	Average users (9.7)
		vii	Uncommitted investors (1.2)
		viii	Basic product (7.9)
(P)	Financially passive (15.8)	ix	Inactive borrowers (9.5)
		x	Least active (6.3)

Note: Figures in brackets show the size of each FiNPiN type as a percentage of all United Kingdom Households (excluding Northern Ireland).
Source: Pinpoint Analysis Ltd, London

2.4.1 The learning process

For these purposes, consumer learning can be described as the 'process by which they acquire the purchase and consumption knowledge and experience they apply to future related behaviour' (Schiffman and Kanuk, 1991). Psychologists do not agree on how individuals learn. Theories range from the simple, conditioned responses advocated by behavioural theorists, to the active information searching and problem solving approach of the cognitivist school.

Behavioural Conditioning Theories Classical conditioning is the automatic response to a stimulus acquired through repeated associations with a reward. 'When consumption or utilization of the goal-object leads to gratification of the initiating needs there is (positive) "reinforcement"' (Bayton,1958). Just as Pavlov's dogs learned to salivate at the sound of a bell signalling the forthcoming reward of meat, so customers would see a bank and withdraw money. The notion of a bank being a conditioned stimulus provoking an impulsive act is not especially useful: classical conditioning is more commonly used to explain simple behaviours.

Instrumental conditioning is somewhat more relevant to financial services. According to Skinner, most learning occurs on a trial and error basis, whereby the individual actively seeks stronger, positive reinforcements, and in doing so will learn which behaviours and service suppliers produce the most gratifying rewards and thus encourage repetition of that behaviour. Negative reinforcement is an unpleasant outcome which also encourages behaviour, for example a tourist losing his wallet encourages him to buy travellers' cheques in future.

Cognitive learning theory Cognitivists reject the premise that all behaviour is learnt through stimulus-response and reinforcement, as it ignores the powerful influence of observation and conscious problem solving. The cognitivist school believes that learning is the result of mental activity which restructures the cognitive map. Chisnall (1985) cites Asch on the subject:

Human actions, even the most lowly, are marked by a quality of intelligence or insight . . . Our actions are permeated with inferences . . . we may fumble and engage in trial and error, but it almost never has the blind character that associationistic doctrines impute to it.

Behavioural and cognitive theories have been unified by introducing cognition as an intervening

Table 2.4 FiNPiN profiles: classification level 4, 1981 and 1991 census data

FiNPiN Profile	1981	1991	Change
Financially active	18%	24.3%	+ 6.3%
Financially informed	23%	41.1%	+18.1%
Financially conscious	23%	18.7%	− 4.3%
Financially passive	28%	15.8%	−12.2%

Source: Derived from FiNPiN Classification Summary Labels (1983, 1993), Pinpoint Analysis Ltd, London

organizing force between the stimulus and the response. Continued reinforcement can be seen as decreasing the amount of cognitive or mental activity required for a decision, leading to habit or loyalty. This learning process is the key to profitability in many financial services, as acquiring customers typically entails costs (advertising, selling effort, administration, pass books, etc.) which can only be recouped if custom is retained. Loyalty and habit are discussed further in Section 2.8.1.

The unification of the two learning concepts is well demonstrated in the growing number of individuals owning shares. Consumers often have their first dealings with equity via shares in new privatization issues (Guirdhan, 1987), positive reinforcement occuring when the value of shares rises. These rewards encourage new shareholders to *repeat the behaviour* by investing in subsequent flotations, occasionally progressing onto regular non-privatization issues. However, it is rather doubtful that this can all be done in a subconscious haze, *cognitive processing* is involved too. The degree of cognitive effort will vary with involvement, which in turn depends upon both the nature of the product and the characteristics of the individual.

Consumers have regularly been credited with elevated levels of financial literacy and sophistication in recent times. Newspaper publicity, the threat of a less supportive state system of benefits and increasing cash conciousness are said to be amongst the factors responsible. But the Chartered Institute of Banking (1991) found such claims extremely difficult to substantiate, the evidence being confined to greater awareness of extremely high APRs on some store and credit cards. However, data from the 1991 Census has since become available and Pinpoint Analysis have updated their FiNPiN classification of financial consumers (see Section 2.3.2). Comparing the composition of their four major profile groups (Table 2.4) does intimate a conspicuous degree of consumer learning during the intervening ten year period.

Everyone complains of his memory, nobody of his judgement. (La Rochefoucauld)

Memory Cognitive learning requires memory, both short- and long-term. Information passing the individual's perceptual screen is rehearsed in the short-term memory, before being encoded into 'Gestalts', or chunks, for perceptual organization in the long-term memory. Motives are important determinants of what is selectively stored, as it is widely believed that consumers retrieve product benefits or shortcomings rather than attributes (Schiffman and Kanuk, 1991).

Through experience and reinforcement, learning encourages consumers to discriminate between services and organizations formerly seen as being similar. But despite two people being exposed to the same advertisements, literature, conversations and experiences, what is actually learnt from them will invariably be quite different—largely due to judgement, interpretation and perception.

2.4.2 Perception

The cognitive map of the individual is not, then, a photographic representation of the physical world; it is, rather, a partial personal construction in which certain objects, selected out for a major role, are perceived in an individual manner. Every perceiver is, as it were, to some degree a nonrepresentational artist, painting a picture of the world that expresses his individual view of reality. (Krech *et al.*, 1962)

Consumers interpret advertisements, evaluate products and make decisions on basis of incomplete knowledge and their subjective interpretation of 'reality'. Perception can be described as 'the process by which an individual selects, organizes, and interprets stimuli into a meaningful and coherent picture of the world' (Schiffman and Kanuk, 1991). Each of these three central constructs is considered in turn:

1. *Selective perception* occurs in three main ways
Selective attention and selective exposure   In our 'overcommunicated society' (Ries and Trout, 1982) consumers are incapable of attending to the millions of stimuli they are bombarded with every day. 'Attention filters' screen out most stimuli in order to preserve some semblance of sanity in most of us. Attention usually follows:

(a) Relevance to current motives, needs, interests etc.
(b) A preference for pleasant information which fits comfortably with existing beliefs.
(c) Expectations: people usually perceive what they expect to see, based on familiarity and previous experience. Alternatively, stimuli which are in sharp contrast with existing beliefs may be too incongruous to ignore. This 'contrast' effect also holds for:
(d) The nature of the stimulus: those which are large in relation to, or in marked contrast to, normal are more likely to penetrate the consumer's perceptual screen. Television commercials demand our attention by being louder than the programmes they follow.

Perceptual defence: selective distortion and selective blocking   In addition to seeing what is expected, consumers are also apt to see what they want to. Filtering out, blocking or distorting messages which are painful, threatening or harmful to the ego, they defend themselves against information which is not consistent with their needs, values and beliefs. This *perceptual defence* has an important role to play in reducing post purchase dissonance. BCCI customers may have ignored indications of bad practices, wishing to concentrate on the high rates of return instead, just as new home owners would not be overly receptive to news of falling house prices.

Selective retention   People forget much of what they learn, 'conveniently' tending to retain information which supports or reinforces existing attitudes and beliefs.

2. *Interpretation*   Sensory stimuli are interpreted selectively through a process of comparison with information stored in the memory. Thus, there are two main facets of perception (Foxall, 1980): the stimulus (e.g., a queue) and its interpretation (e.g., long or short/slow or fast moving etc). Interpretation of stimuli is a function of:

(a) Their clarity: ambiguous messages are obviously open to variable interpretation. For this reason commercials and politicians are often vague as interpretation also depends upon:
(b) Needs and motives: interpretation is likely to be related to satisfying current needs.
(c) Frame of reference: past experience and learning influence interpretation. Lindquist (1974) adds that interpretation is likely to be over simplified, cognitive limitations leading consumers to abstract only a few meanings which appear salient.

3. *Perceptual organization*   Gestalt theory describes the principle of perceptual organization, the way individuals need to mentally arrange discrete and often unrelated stimuli to give a complete picture. Lack of information or cognitive limitations call for 'closure': consciously or subconsciously filling in gaps by making inferences from other cues (or through pure fabrication). Judgements about the overall quality of a service product are often determined by a small number of tangible cues (Shostack, 1977) due to 'stimulus discrimination' or 'stimulus generalization'. Consumers are apt to generalize about products and companies on the basis of a limited number of observations, or *discriminations* (Nystrom, 1970). Thus, a particular insurance company may be 'extortionate' on the basis of one quotation, a bank 'totally unreliable' on failing to dispense a new cheque book. One such complete picture is the image a consumer has of a particular retailer. Given the fundamental importance of perceptual positioning to targeting and the success of a retail strategy, image formation and related issues are addressed in Section 2.5.

2.4.3   Perceived risk

Almost by definition, financial services involve risk. Even regular current and savings accounts carry risk: banks do fold and a number of small building societies have been perilously close to a similar fate in recent years. Nothing, even houses, are 'as safe as houses'. Profit is, after all, the reward for risk taking. Consumer behaviour research, however, is only concerned with subjective or 'perceived risk'. If consumers are unaware of the objective risk it cannot influence behaviour.

Consumer behaviour involves risk in the sense that any action of a consumer will produce consequences which he cannot anticipate with anything approximating certainty, and some of which at least are likely to be unpleasant. (Bauer, 1967)

Perceived risk contains two structural dimensions: uncertainty over the outcome and the seriousness of the consequences. While the significance of the consequences will vary enormously, as functions of the particular financial product under consideration or the amount at stake (e.g., investing in a personal pension plan versus opening a current account), research suggests that the uncertainty component of perceived risk increases with intangibility:

After a day of buying services, the consumer still has an empty market basket ... consumers perceive services as compared to goods, to be characterized by higher prices, less consistent quality, less reputable brands, a lower overall satisfaction. (George, 1977)

Types of perceived risk   As suggested above, the very term financial services suggests that financial risk will be an intrinsic element, although it is but one of four categories of possible loss or 'unpleasant consequences' studied by Mitchell and Greatorex (1993). These are:

1. *Physical risk*—this represents the danger of physical injury as a result of using the product. Financial services are not usually associated with this type of loss, but using a bank with badly lit or dangerously located ATMs may increase concern over mugging.
2. *Psychosocial risk*—the failure of a product can cause embarrassment, a bruised ego or damage the consumer's self-esteem. Many local authority finance directors lost professional credibility by depositing money with the corrupt Bank of Credit and Commerce International (BCCI) forced to cease trading by bank regulators in 1991. Similarly, some Barlow Clowes' investors possibly felt that they should have been more discerning over their choice of

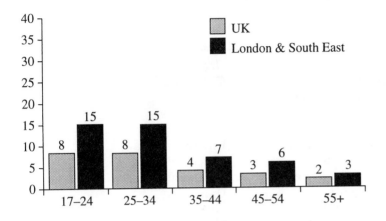

Figure 2.7   The fear of falling house prices—the negative equity trap
Source: The Henley Centre (1993) *Metamorphosis in Marketing,* London

supplier (although this would have abated with the compensation paid from the public purse).
Having been fooled or deceived in the full glare of the public eye, the social element of the loss
is arguably greater than a discreet loss on the stock exchange.

3. *Financial risk*—Hapless Lloyds' 'Names' are perhaps one of the most striking examples of
financial loss in recent years, heightening perceptions of the financial risk surrounding
insurance syndicates. Similarly, the notion that property investment warranted the 'safe as
houses' conviction has received a direct hit, although perceptions of risk are still moderate
considering the scale of house repossessions, mortgage arrears and the 11 per cent of
homeowners caught in the 'negative equity trap' (houses worth less than originally paid—see
Figure 2.7). With 50 per cent of the adult population still believing housing to be a good
short-term investment (Henley Centre, 1993), the British mind-set is still clearly devoted to
the ideal of home ownership (an idea returned to in Section 2.6.1).

On a somewhat smaller scale, incidences of banks overcharging small business customers
and inaccurate ATM withdrawal records are financial risks causing great angst among
customers and consumer groups.

4. *Time risk*—pertains to the amount of time which can be lost as a result of product failure
and/or the additional time required to rectify the failure. Service failures could be an unsatis-
factory length of time spent in a queue, or the time consuming correspondence which must be
entered into to resolve a problem.

Mitchell and Greatorex (1993) examined the risk perceived by students when considering
acquiring various goods and services, banking services being among them. Their findings
confirmed that services were perceived as involving more risk than goods, principally due to the
uncertainty component. The average seriousness of the consequences was also high among the
bank services; being without money has serious implications, not least for a student's social life.

Of all the services, banking was perceived to involve highest time loss risk, the need for
convenience and time-saving devices or procedures being something the banks are only too
aware of. Banks were not seen to be as variable as the other services, probably due to the high
degree of automation and the fairly routine services students generally demand of their banks.

Table 2.5 Risk reliever usefulness ratings for banking services

Rank	Risk relieving strategy	Reduce consequence or uncertainty
1	Shop around	Uncertainty
2	Buy cheap	Consequence
3	Read product information	Both
4	Brand loyalty	Uncertainty
5	Special offers	Consequence
6	Ask family or friends	Uncertainty
7	Read buyer's guides	Uncertainty
8	Image	Uncertainty
9	Buy well-knowns	Uncertainty
10	Guarantee	Both
11	Trial	Uncertainty
12	Salesperson's advice	Both
13	Celebrity endorsements	Uncertainty
14	Buy expensive	Uncertainty

Source: Adapted from Mitchell, V.W. and M. Greatorex (1993) 'Risk perception and reduction in the purchase of consumer services', *The Services Industries Journal*, **13**(4), pp. 179–200

2.4.4 Risk tolerance and risk reducing strategies (RRS)

Perceptions of risk obviously vary, not only across products and services, but also according to the individual's character, financial situation, whether the service is being bought direct or through a retail outlet, personal experience, etc. High risk perceivers, sometimes described as narrow categorizers, often limit the size of their 'evoked set' of alternatives to a few 'safe' options: the major clearing banks may be the only considered savings institutions, despite the lower interest rates offered. Conversely, the broad categorizers or low risk perceivers would rather make a bad choice than restrict their choice set unduly (Schiffman and Kanuk, 1991).

Restricting choice of financial institutions to well-known suppliers or brands is just one of the many 'risk relieving strategies' used to reduce risk to a subjectively 'tolerable level'. Given the high level of perceived risk in financial services, recognizing the variety of ways in which consumers try to reduce it can have valuable practical applications. Levels of risk can logically be reduced by either lessening the severity of the consequences or the uncertainty surrounding the outcome—as is the case in supplier loyalty. Similarly, buying 'blue chip' equity reduces uncertainty whereas speculating on a few 'penny shares' reduces the consequences. The comprehensive range of risk relievers (see Roselius, 1971) examined in the banking study are shown in rank order of usefulness in Table 2.5. It should be noted that the lowest ranking risk relievers may not actually be applicable to banking services.

While the results would provide useful guidelines to banks looking to target notoriously precarious student finances, findings are not generalizable across segments. Students may, for example, be more deal prone (special offers) and unable to 'buy expensive'.

With respect to other financial products, consulting buyer's guides could be a more effective

RRS when choosing a pension plan, an expensive stockbroker might be viewed as offering better advice than cheaper competitors, whereas succumbing to retailers' expensive extended warranties on electrical appliances reduces the risk of financial loss.

2.4.5   Cognitive dissonance

Bauer (1967) also saw the explanatory power of perceived risk theory extending to post-purchase decision processes, describing Festinger's cognitive dissonance theory as involving the tendency to seek out information which confirms the wisdom of their original choice. This 'postpurchase dissonance' can be illustrated by recent house buyers swallowing the self-interested reports of recovery by estate agents and building societies—they are reducing the perceived risk of buying property *after* the event.

Dissonance arises through the need for 'cognitive consistency' between thoughts and behaviour. When consumers perceive incongruity they may tackle the discomfort in a number of ways (Kassarjian and Cohen, 1968):

1. By dissociating control or responsibility for the act or decision. Consumers frequently think of their decisions as having been inevitable, unavoidable or even sensible because other people behaved in the same way. Apportioning blame in this manner is a relatively painless method of dissonance reduction:

    It's the credit card company's/building society's own fault that I can't pay them—they should not have lent me so much or everyone was buying at those high prices: we had to get on the 'housing ladder' before it was out of reach.

2. Dissonance can be reduced by perceptual elimination or distortion of one of the conflicting cognitive elements. Advice given prior to purchase can be conveniently forgotten: having taken out a barely affordable loan, the consumer may choose to forget warnings that interest rates can rise.
3. Perceptual selection and retention of information which supports their beliefs. Being reassuring, advertisements for the products/brands purchased have a far higher propensity to penetrate the perceptual screen. Competitors' adverts, only serving to draw attention to the limitations of the chosen product, are 'selectively ignored'.
4. Lessening the perceived significance of the decision will also reduce dissonance. Small stakes warrant little search or evaluation effort, while more pressing concerns may 'distract' the individual from making an optimal decision. Thus, the poor decision will be due to a lack or interest or effort, rather than personal ineptitude.

Watkins (1990) points out that the potential for dissonance could have been reduced by the compulsory 14 day 'cooling off period' laid down in the 1986 Financial Services Act. This allows buyers to reconsider the wisdom of their investment decision away from possible high pressure selling situations. How postpurchase dissonance fits into the 'grand scheme' of consumer decision making is detailed in Section 2.7.2.

Perceived control   Although dissociating control for the decision was cited as a method of dissonance reduction, psychologists have long asserted that the need to feel personally in control of a situation is a major influence on human behaviour—to the extent that feelings to the contrary are a primary source of stress in everyday life. Bateson (1985) suggests that 'perceived control' can be used to increase overall customer satisfaction levels in some services. Simply making the service encounter more predictable can be effective, which is viable even in services where actual control cannot be relinquished.

2.5 IMAGE AND POSITIONING

'Cheap and nasty', 'over-priced rubbish' or simply 'different', unsurprisingly, the concept of image is often portrayed as being an abstract, vague something. Retailers have an inextricable web of cognitive processes to thank for being 'credited' with such images, primarily those discussed above: learning, stimulus discrimination, generalization and perceptual closure. While the following discussion of image refers primarily to retail stores, one need look no further than Direct Line Insurance and Midland Bank's 'First Direct' to find exemplary models of what a clear and favourable image can do for non-store retailers.

Store image was initially defined by Martineaux (1958) as:

the way in which the store is defined in the shopper's mind, partly by its functional qualities and partly by an aura of psychological attributes.

However, this definition has been criticized as bestowing an unnecessary aura of mystique on the intangible components (Doyle and Fenwick, 1974; McGoldrick, 1990). The psychological or intangible components, such as the branch atmosphere, can in fact be studied reasonably objectively by measuring each of its more tangible elements, such as the layout, colours, lighting and appearance of staff, etc. (McGoldrick, 1990) (see Chapter 6). Neither should attributes actually be classed as tangible/intangible, or emotional/rational, as some dimensions are influenced by both. Prices and location are both tangible, but overall subjective images of price levels, value for money and locational convenience will be influenced by the intangible too.

Just as images can be formed on limited information, through stimulus generalization or discrimination, they are equally apt to change on it too. While many writers describe image in terms of attitudes (Mazursky and Jacoby, 1986), which implies that they will be reasonably enduring, Kunkel and Berry's (1968) behavioural perspective applies learning theory to image, describing it as 'the total conceptualized or expected reinforcement'. Hence, even the small things—be it a rude receptionist or tales of the nightmare service scenario suffered by a friend of a friend's neighbour—can make a difference.

2.5.1 Components of image

If a service provider can determine which dimensions are instrumental to creating a favourable image, resources can be concentrated in these areas. The importance of identifying the salient components of store image cannot be overstated and are not always as obvious as we may think; according to Oxenfeldt (1974), images are often formed on 'largely irrelevant' information, people relying heavily on cues (both tangible and intangible) rather than on direct observation of what they presumably want to know.

Which components are critical will clearly vary considerably between customer segments (economy-oriented will attach more weight to prices than convenience), the particular financial product (convenience will be more important when choosing a bank than a financial adviser or stockbroker) and also the competitive situation (a standardized branch design may be highly rated in one area but 'scruffy' in relation to competitors in another district).

Some academics have sub-divided image constructs into categories, such as the Hansen and Deutscher (1977) classification:

1. *Attribute*—the narrowest, most specific constructs (e.g., access).
2. *Component*—aggregation of similar attributes (e.g., locational convenience).
3. *Dimensions*—the most general constructs (e.g., convenience).

The justification for such a system becomes quite apparent when the potential for overlooking critical features is recognized. For example, convenience is often a critical factor in the choice of bank, but within an overall 'convenience' rating the respondent could be referring to any of the following:

1. *Locational convenience:*
   (a) Distance from work
   (b) Distance from home
   (c) Proximity/convenience for other stores and services
   (d) Access
   (e) ATM network (convenience of using other banks)
2. *Other convenience factors:*
   (a) Parking
   (b) Opening hours
   (c) Branch layout
   (d) Telephone banking facilities
   (e) Convenience (in general)

Source: Adapted from: Kunkel and Berry (1968), 'A behavioural concept of retail images', *Journal of Marketing*, **32**(4), p. 26

2.5.2   Image measurement techniques

A study by Pathak *et al.* (1974) concluded that retail managers were prone to overrate their stores on all dimensions of image, a finding corroborated by May (1974) who observed not only sharp contrasts between the perceptions of customers and managers, but also between managers. Clearly, granting store managers a free reign over retail image without the benefit of systematic research could have dire consequences.

Image research involves assessing attitudes rather than amassing objective, factual data. All attitude measurement is riddled with problems of reliability and validity. Firstly, identifying the salient components is crucial to avoid forcing consumers to judge attributes which do not feature in their image of the service (Kunkel and Berry, 1968). This points towards the use of open-ended techniques, such as focus groups and interviews, to isolate the critical image components prior to the use of any rigid scaling techniques such as the semantic differential. For a thorough review of attitude research techniques see Tull and Hawkins (1990) or Chisnall (1992). McGoldrick (1990) specifically addresses applications of these techniques in the context of retail image measurement, with one extremely important addition—multidimensional scaling techniques.

Multidimensional scaling   Using a combination of both scaling and open-ended techniques, multi-dimensional scaling investigates the extent of perceived similarities and contrasts between different retailers' images. Dots placed on a grid represent specific attributes such as 'deal with claims rapidly' and 'well informed staff' in insurance. Retailers are then located on the map according to how relevant or strongly consumers believe the attribute relates to that store. The result is a perceptual positioning map illustrating each retailer's total 'image space' in the minds of consumers (Davies, 1987).

2.5.3 Positioning

Although the regulatory environment now allows an extremely wide range of product offerings, profitability dictates that a selective offering must be positioned to appeal to specific markets (Laroche and Taylor, 1988). Ries and Trout (1982) captured the fundamental importance of perception to positioning in their 'battle for your mind':

Positioning starts with a product. A piece of merchandise, a service, a company, an institution or even a person.
But positioning is not what you do to a product. Positioning is what you do to the mind of the prospect. That is, you position the product in the mind of the prospect. (Ries and Trout, 1982)

Branding and the Gestalt phenomena facilitate positioning by promoting stimulus discrimination, giving the brand a unique organized whole which differentiates it from competitors. However, it is notoriously difficult for consumers to differentiate between brands in financial services, be they individual product, family or corporate brands. Not only are the characteristics of generic products essentially quite similar, with bright new service concepts easily copied (see Chapter 7), but historically many financial institutions have had little interest in differentiation.

The challenge confronting the banks is to differentiate themselves from one another, ... But that is easier said than done, after decades in which they have all been content to present the same image of respectability and trustworthiness. (Kay, 1987)

The banks were not even projecting consistent images across their own branches, the traditional, granite pillared 'miniature versions of the Bank of England' contrasting sharply with their modern designs.

Deregulation added urgency to Kay's 'challenge'. The banks were keen to stir the building societies' comfortable near monopoly on mortgages, also moving into estate agencies and in-house share shops; meanwhile the building societies moved into retail banking, unsecured loans, tied insurance and investment services and also bought up chains of estate agents (as detailed in Chapter 1). This widespread diversification was instrumental in blurring the traditional images of financial institutions, overlapping product ranges bringing service personalities closer together. Moving into estate agencies also had other unanticipated consequences for the building societies, their carefully preserved caring image being threatened by the incessant wrangling and arguing which characterizes the customer agent relationship (Kay, 1987).

Escalating the identity crisis, not only have financial institutions become less differentiated, but traditional retailers have muddied the waters too. Recognizing how favourably placed they were to achieve a clean sweep, stores now market their merchandise alongside the money to pay for it. Further discussion on the relevance of positioning in product range development is contained in Chapter 7.

Such was the extent of the diversification by building societies and banks that the analogy with modern one-stop grocery shopping in 'financial supermarkets' generated earnest consideration. The relative positioning of these two types of institutions is therefore a highly topical theme for demonstrating a practical example of positioning research. McGoldrick and Greenland (1992) amassed comparative ratings on image components found to be relevant to the banks and building societies, finding significant differences in 13 out of the 22 components. The banks compared favourably in only two dimensions: 'offer a range of related services' and 'convenience of bank location'; thus, any assumption that their trustworthy image would do them any great favours in the competitive struggle would have been unfounded: in 'established/trusty institution' and 'confidentiality of details' both scored equally highly. A full list of the components examined, together with how each type of institution fared, is shown in Table 2.6.

Table 2.6 Banks and building societies: comparative study of image components

Aspects of service	Banks mean ratings—ranked	Building societies mean ratings—ranked	Level of significance from T-tests (p)
Sympathetic understanding	16	14	0.000
Helpful friendly staff	9	3	0.000
Not too pushy	12	8	0.003
Time for decisions	6	5	0.028
Efficient staff	8	7	0.000
Range of related services	4	11	0.000
Convenient branch location	3	9	0.000
Modern up-to-date attitude	7	4	0.017
Explain terms fully	11	10	0.003
Clearly explains costs	17	13	0.000
Confidentiality of details	1	1	NS
Branch manager availability	18	18	0.090
Branch manager personality	13	15	NS
Established trusty institution	2	2	NS
Comfortable branch surroundings	15	17	NS
Expert advice	10	12	NS
Independent advice	21	21	NS
Flexibility to needs	19	19	NS
Flexible charges conditions	22	22	0.001
Willingness to renegotiate	20	20	0.063
Ease of transfer	14	16	NS
Efficient businesslike service	8	6	NS

NS = not significant

Source: McGoldrick, P.J. and S.J. Greenland (1992) 'Competition between banks and building societies in the retailing of financial services', *British Journal of Management*, **3**, 175

Clearly, despite their diversification, there are still some strongly held beliefs regarding the relative strengths of the banks and building societies. However, the warning against diversification on the grounds of competitive reaction and short-term profit projections are clear:

Repositioning should be the outcome of careful research and strategic planning not the by-product of a lemming-like rush towards one 'ideal' format. (McGoldrick and Greenland, 1992)

As Pierre Martineau (1958) noted:

It is high time that we retailers recognize that we cannot be all things to all people. When we do that, we end up with no particular appeal to anybody.

2.6 ATTITUDES

Issues such as the social acceptability of credit, faith in a recovery of the housing market and the level of consumer confidence, each involve attitudes. They are expressions of inner beliefs and emotions which reflect whether an individual is favourably or unfavourably predisposed to some object (a service, a brand, an organization). As this rather modest, unadorned description of attitude will probably cause social psychologists some considerable distress, a more scientific alternative is:

an enduring organization of motivational, emotional, perceptual, and cognitive process with respect to some aspect of the individual's world. (Krech and Crutchfeld, 1948)

Thus attitudes are an unobservable outcome of all the psychological processes described thus far. All attitudes share four common properties (Louden and Della Bitta, 1988):

1. Attitudes have objects; the objects can be abstract, such as consumerism, or material such as an ATM.
2. Attitudes have direction, intensity and degree; they express how an individual feels towards an object:
   (a) direction—either favourable or unfavourable. Older people tend to dislike ATMs.
   (b) degree—how favourable or unfavourable the individual feels.
   (c) intensity—the level of confidence or conviction the individual has in their belief. While related to degree, intensity is not the same. An individual may think that unit trusts offer a *very* attractive investment opportunity, but still not have enormous strength in this conviction.
3. Attitudes have structure; they have a core comprising the individual's most important values and self-concept and, as all other peripheral attitudes are related to these in some way, they must display a reasonable level of consistency. Attitudes are also generalizable, so that a person's opinion of a particular service may be generalized to include all the institution's services.
4. Finally, attitudes are learned; from personal experience, family, other peer groups, the media and many other influential sources. Further, because they are learned, attitudes tend to become stronger, or at least more resistant to change, the longer they are held: hence the 'set in their ways' adage, which could be applied to the reluctance of the over 60s age group to accept more relaxed social attitudes towards credit and borrowing (Henley Centre, 1993).

2.6.1 Attitudes towards credit and debt

The deregulation of financial markets in the 1980s allowed consumers to borrow more money than ever before. However, the unparalleled increases in personal debt (see Figure 2.8) could not have taken place without more *favourable* attitudes towards debt, or rather, credit, to use its socially acceptable new name. Thus we saw shopping and conspicuous consumption become a national sport: collecting designer labels, electronic gadgetry, a perpetual stream of home improvements and of course a vast range of store and credit cards with which to 'pay' for the spoils.

Borrowing is no longer seen to be shameful, an admission of weakness, and evidence of a lack of restraint; most people do not believe that it is wrong to want goods before one has the money to pay for them. With present inflation, more people are content to borrow in order to buy at today's prices and pay back in tomorrow's devalued money. Also, the fear of not being able to repay loans has decreased due to greater personal security made available by state intervention in unemployment pay, sickness benefits and allowances, and by pensions and life assurance. (Lewis, 1982b)

However, attitudes towards buying on the 'never never' appear to have swung yet again, although the social stigma may not be as biting as it once was. Instead, it is the worry concerning

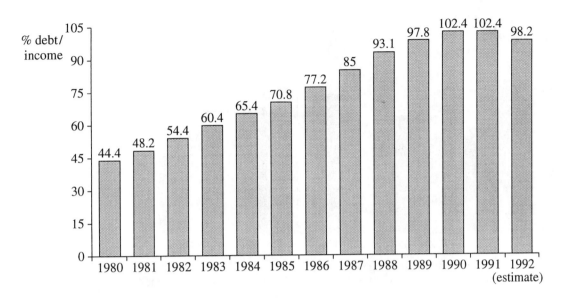

Figure 2.8 The indebted society
Source: The Henley Centre (1993) *Metamorphosis in Marketing*, London

borrowings, which has spurred some consumers to repay a small amount of debt, notably consumer credit (Figure 2.9). While sweeping statements to this effect are quite common, this change of heart could be ascribed to any number of factors, including:

1. A severe recession, which once again saw unemployment pass the three million mark, crushed consumer confidence. The strength of the fear of unemployment has prevented many people from making major purchases (Figure 2.10), particularly the lower socio-economic classes who are perhaps less likely to have adequate reserves, or, being less skilled, may be less confident about obtaining new employment (see class as a segmentation variable in Section 2.3.1). The Henley Centre suggests that high unemployment will be the major motivation to strengthen personal balance sheets, forecasting subdued lending growth over the next few years.
2. Levels of inflation over the last three years have been at their lowest for almost three decades, lessening the appeal of paying back with 'tomorrow's devalued money'. But while attitudes towards the principle of credit may be less favourable, this dislike has been tempered by the lower costs of servicing debt, i.e., the dramatic fall in interest rates.
3. The feeling of personal wealth increased with escalating house prices. Consumers not only felt affluent, but lending institutions were falling over themselves to encourage people to spend their paper gains. With house prices having fallen, the practise of borrowing on the back of housing assets has been severely curbed ('the disposable capital syndrome': Poyner, 1987). Attitudinally, consumers no longer feel as wealthy, with the more cautious lending policies adopted by banks and building societies having dampened enthusiasm for borrowing further.

Mortgage debt Mortgages have long been viewed far less as a debt than an investment. Despite the crash in property prices, this attitude is still prevalent. As indicated earlier, 50 per cent of people believe that housing will prove a good investment in the short term, which increases to two-thirds over the medium to long-term (Henley Centre, 1993). This may be a case of the

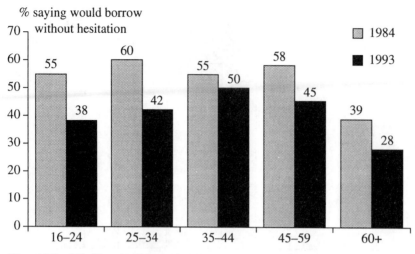

Figure 2.9 Likelihood of borrowing money
Source: The Henley Centre (1993) *Metamorphosis in Marketing*, London

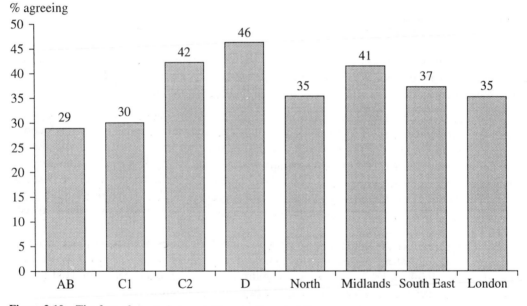

Figure 2.10 The fear of unemployment. Base = all work full or part time
Source: The Henley Centre (1993) *Metamorphosis in Marketing*, London

ego-defensive function of attitude, or 'wishful thinking' (see Section 2.4.2), but the overall attitude towards home ownership in the UK is still very favourable and remains very much a part of the British consumer psyche.

2.6.2 Attitudes towards savings and investment

There have been few changes in social attitudes towards wealth, either earned or unearned, since those characterizing Conservative Britain in the 1980s. The once dirty words of 'profit' and

Table 2.7   Awareness of investment schemes

	Awareness of investment schemes by age (%) *April 1992*				
	16–24	25–34	35–44	45–64	65+
Backing interest-paying current account	42	53	48	30	28
Bank deposit account	40	50	49	48	43
Building society account	58	75	68	71	61
National Savings	27	35	31	29	25
TESSAs	17	24	24	25	18
Personal equity plans (PEPs)	6	14	13	13	8
Shares	17	27	21	22	18
Units trusts	9	13	19	19	9
Investment trusts	4	8	10	11	6
Personal pension	35	45	44	34	14
None of these	22	15	9	13	22

Source: Key Note (1992), *Personal Finance in the UK*, Key Note Publications, London

'money' are still perfectly acceptable in most social circles even in these, the 'nicer' 1990s. The savings ratio has increased over the course of the recession, but this has been principally to reduce debt, rather than being symptomatic of a new savings mentality; in fact, the recession has had remarkably little effect on attitudes towards saving (Henley Centre, 1993).

The government's determination to make people accept responsibility for their own financial security, through inducements to contract out of the state earnings related pension scheme (SERPS) and proposals for the likes of compulsory unemployment insurance, do appear to be instrumental in increasing awareness of money schemes. In 1993, falling rates of interest paid to savings account holders were also a factor behind rising interest in investment plans, as people extended the search for higher yields.

A recent survey by Key Note (1992) suggests that those in the 25–34 age group are generally most aware of 'money' schemes, described as knowing enough to consider investing in them. Table 2.7 also reveals that the notion of a more sophisticated financial consumer (see Section 2.4.1) is not generalizable across generations. The over 65s were notably uninformed about personal pensions in addition to the relatively simple financial services, the ideal of self-sufficiency coming too late to affect their attitudes towards investment. The 16–24s were not particularly knowledgeable either. In keeping with the family life cycle concept, the need to plan for long-term financial security into old age may seem too distant to pose any serious threat to partying, buying a car or a home, etc.

2.7   MODELS OF BUYER BEHAVIOUR

2.7.1   Attitude models in financial services

The Krech and Crutchfield definition of attitude forms the basis of the 'tri-component' approach utilized in marketing 'response hierarchy' models. These portray the consumer progressing through a series of attitude changes, initially acquiring knowledge of the product

Movement towards purchase	Related behavioural dimension

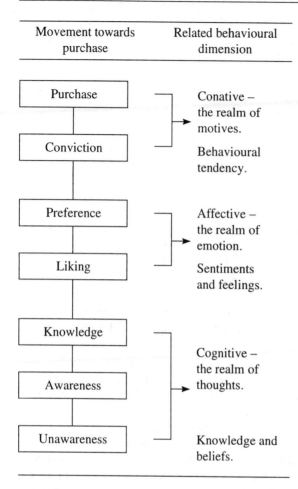

Figure 2.11 The 'hierarchy of effects'
Source: Adapted from Lavidge, R.J. and G.A. Steiner (1961), 'A model for predicative measurements of advertising effectiveness' in *Marketing Classics* (1988) 6th edn, B.M. Enis and K.K. Cox (eds.), Allyn and Bacon (Massachusetts), 493.

(cognitive component), then developing liking (affect), taking them closer to the conative act of purchase. The response hierarchy models include 'AIDA' which characterizes the stages as awareness, interest, desire and action; Roger's 'innovation-adoption' model for new products (Kotler, 1991) and Lavidge and Steiner's (1961) 'hierarchy of effects', shown in Figure 2.11.

Rarely can a single communication move a prospect from unawareness through to 'conviction' and 'purchase.' The series of attitude changes required to effect a purchase require different marketing approaches. However, research on the BT, TSB and British Gas flotations led to Guirdham (1987) redrawing the four stage awareness-interest-desire-action hierarchy to relate more closely to complex financial products such as PEPs, shares and unit trusts (see Figure 2.12). Some of the more notable points and differences are:

1. Firstly as Table 2.1 suggested, lack of knowledge hampers further penetration of PEPs, but with complex financial products 'knowledge' should read 'know how' (or know how to buy),

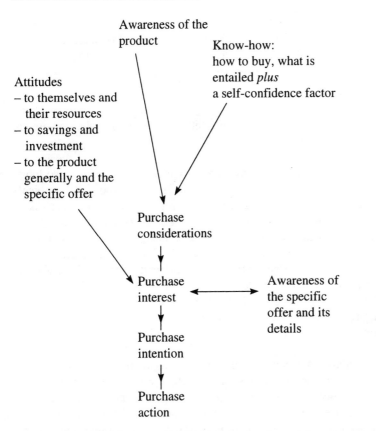

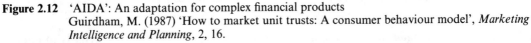

Figure 2.12   'AIDA': An adaptation for complex financial products
Guirdham, M. (1987) 'How to market unit trusts: A consumer behaviour model', *Marketing Intelligence and Planning*, 2, 16.

and be accompanied by adequate self-confidence to buy—both critical factors for the first time buyer (Guirdham, 1987).
2. 'Awareness' comes in two stages: spanning both the product category (e.g., shares, unit trusts) and at a later stage, the specific offer or brand details.
3. 'Interest' still reflects the affective or emotional component of attitudes, but attempting to change those conveyed in statements such as 'I can't afford to invest in anything' or 'public utilities belong to everyone—privatization is wrong' represent wasted marketing effort.
4. That 'intention' replaces 'desire' may be a result of the inability of the typical financial product to stir the emotion implied, but it also reflects the fact that consumers rarely evaluate financial products without the intention to act on their findings. This can be contrasted with luxury goods or products with leisure appeal, such as cars, sports and stereo equipment which can be investigated simply as a matter of interest.

2.7.2   Comprehensive models

The 'comprehensive' models of consumer buyer behaviour provide a framework for analysing all the factors known to influence consumer behaviour, unlike the 'limited' models such as the response hierarchies which simply look at attitudes. Most depict a buying process broken into a

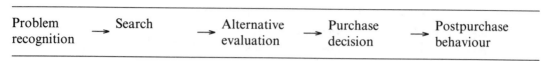

Figure 2.13   Five stage model of the buying process

sequence of stages, such as the Engel–Kollat–Blackwell model (1968) in which the consumer passes through five discrete stages (see Figure 2.13).

Problem recognition is the initial point at which the consumer recognizes the need for a product. As discussed in Section 2.2, needs are driven by a range of physical, social and psychological factors. In some cases the 'recognition' can be involuntary, as in motor insurance, which is a legal requirement for all drivers. Searching entails an internal search of the consumer's memory, revealing whether sufficient is known about alternatives to make a decision without having to expend further time and effort on an external search. Experience of a financial institution is an obvious internal source, which may encourage loyalty to a supplier because services lack search qualities (see Section 2.1). When a service is high in 'experience qualities', personal sources or 'word of mouth' recommendations become particularly credible external sources of information (Zeithaml, 1981). Thus, despite their typically banal humdrum content, the grounds for using conversational style/endorsement advertising are actually quite rational.

Decision rules in alternative evaluations   Alternative evaluation leads to the formation of, or change in, beliefs, attitudes and the intention to purchase (Engel, Blackwell and Miniard, 1986). It is often suggested that consumers employ decision rules, or heuristics, in the evaluation stage which enable them to assess relative strengths and come to a final decision. Consumer decision rules have been broadly categorized into two groups, compensatory and non-compensatory models.

1. *Compensatory decision rules,* or the linear additive choice strategy, assign weights to reflect the perceived importance of each relevant attribute. Each alternative then receives a score on each attribute dimension. The service with the highest sum total will be preferred. It is known as the compensatory model because a low rating on one dimension can be compensated for by a high score on another. Therefore a very expensive financial adviser may still be chosen for experience and trustworthiness.

2. *Non-compensatory decision rules.* This range of models includes:
   (a)   Conjunctive rule: the consumer sets minimum acceptable standards for each attribute and any falling below this level are rejected. As a consequence, the financial adviser above may prove prohibitively expensive. The consumer may only achieve a smaller choice set with this method, requiring a further decision rule.
   (b)   Lexicographic choice strategy: the consumer first ranks the attributes according to their relative importance. The alternative scoring most highly on the most important criterion will be selected, but in the event of no clear winner emerging, the process is repeated using the second most important attribute. Table 2.6 shows that banks and building societies ranked equally highly on the first two attributes, meaning that if consumers felt these to be the most important factors, they would have to stretch to using their third factor.
      Strong inferences about consumers' general 'shopping' motivations can be made from this model. If the top ranked attribute for a credit card is 'low APR' the consumer is likely to be economy-oriented, if the attribute is 'exclusive' the basic orientation would be prestige.

Table 2.8   Importance of factors when selecting a financial services supplier

Aspect of service	Major loan	Importance rank mortgage	Life policy	Pension
Clearly explain costs	1	1	2	2
Expert advice	2	4	3	3
Confidentiality of details	3	3	4	5
Explain terms fully	4	2	1	1
Established/trusty institution	5	5	5	4
Efficient staff	6	6	6	6
Time for decision	7	10	7	8
Efficient/businesslike service	8	11	10	10
Flexibility to needs	9	7	9	9
Willingness to renegotiate	10	8	17	17
Flexible charges/conditions	11	12	13	16
Independent advice	12	14	8	7
Ease of transfer	13	13	12	12
Sympathetic/understanding	14	9	15	11
Modern, up-to-date attitude	15	16	14	13
Helpful/friendly staff	16	15	16	15
Branch manager availability	17	18	18	18
Not too pushy	18	17	11	14
Branch manager personality	19	20	20	20
Range of related services	20	19	19	19
Convenient branch location	21	21	21	21
Comfortable branch surroundings	22	22	22	22

Source: Adapted from McGoldrick, P.J. and S.J. Greenland (1992) 'Competition between banks and building societies in the retailing of financial services', *British Journal of Management*, **3**, 176

Obviously it would be unrealistic to suggest that consumers undertake such deliberate, painstaking calculations every time they need to make a decision. However, the models are valuable if used to focus on and understand consumers' priorities. For instance, if a lexicographic model is roughly adhered to by target prospects, embellishing a service with a host of added extras may increase costs more than the chances of making a sale, whereas this would not be the case in the compensatory model. Recognizing elements of the conjunctive model in action may prevent the loss of further sales by improving on one or two weak attributes.

Another angle taken in the image study by McGoldrick and Greenland (1992) (Section 2.4.3), entailed examining the importance of evaluation criteria. The same 22 aspects of services were ranked by respondents according to their significance when selecting a supplier for four financial products: a major loan, a mortgage, a life policy and a pension plan. The results are shown in Table 2.8. Although enlightening, the authors recorded important differences between subgroups of respondents, urging that the rankings be treated as guidelines, as opposed to universally applicable hierarchies. They also noted the potential for distortion inherent with self-reported importance ratings. For example, the lowly standing of 'comfortable branch surroundings' does not acknowledge the likely impact of tangible clues on the evaluation process. The consumer may deduce that a scruffy environment denotes an old fashioned, slovenly attitude. It may be appropriate to return to Herzberg's two factor theory at this point (discussed in Section 2.2.2): a sumptuous environment may not be intrinsically satisfying, but as a 'hygiene' factor, removing it may have distinctly negative consequences (see Chapter 6).

Advertising is frequently used to influence which criteria become the 'preferred product attributes'. For example, Barclaycard stress the attribute 'accepted at over 10 million places worldwide', whereas the Bradford and Bingley Building Society emphasizes impartiality and a wide range of mortgage policies for recommendation. Others put the accent on an extensive branch or ATM network, a long history (inferring stability of the organization). All are effectively drawing attention to particular strengths hoping to increase the attribute's perceived importance.

However, the intangibility of financial services arguably makes attributes more difficult to assess in a rational manner:

The greater the degree of subjectivity involved in the interpretation of phenomena (. . . the greater the valence of intangibility) the greater the potential for more idiosyncratic processing. (Klein and Lewis, 1985)

Purchase decisions logically follow alternative evaluation. However, if the salesperson is unhelpful, the forms perceived to be unnecessarily complex, the queues too long or the telephone left unanswered, the purchase decision could be postponed or altered. 'Decisions' are not irreversible.

It is worth noting that some people delegate purchase decisions to financial advisers, particularly more complex investment products. This will almost certainly have repercussions on the search and evaluation stages, although agents should ensure that they are sufficiently well briefed on critical features (how much to invest, risk tolerance, likely duration of investment, tax position, etc.). To a lesser extent, using an insurance broker is also a case of delegation, although a limited number of alternatives may be advanced from which a final decision can be made.

Post-purchase behaviour involves the natural comparison of the actual purchase outcomes with the results anticipated; they need to confirm that they did in fact make the right choice. The very existence of alternatives presents the opportunity to make a bad choice or a wrong decision, since even the worst alternative often has some positive qualities. Recognizing these qualities, as well as the limitations of the choice made, leads to postpurchase doubt and 'cognitive dissonance' (see Section 2.4.5). Some service marketer's suggest under-promising to avoid creating unrealistically high expectations and one of the 'service quality gaps' (see Chapter 10).

Meidan (1984) uses this sequential approach to decision making to illustrate the insurance policy buying process (see Figure 2.14).

2.7.3 Alternative models of decision making for financial services

However, not all financial services require consumers to embark upon 'extensive problem solving' using such 'comprehensive' models of consumer behaviour. Low involvement or routinely purchased services, where few differences are perceived between brands, rarely warrant the use of extensive problem solving. Limited problem solving is usually sufficient for services providing basic cash, cheque, credit and debit services—or those services typically in the latter stages of their product life cycle (Cockrell and Dickenson, 1980).

Neither is there agreement on whether or not the financial consumer does progress through an orderly sequence of stages at all—even for complex, high involvement service products. That

Step	Action
1.	Decide on the 'best' type of insurance
2.	Estimate the amount of cover required
3.	Specify important insurer attributes: eg reputation/reliability, policy benefits and quality of policy
4.	Evaluate the various insurers on each of the attributes identified
5.	Buy a certain policy

Figure 2.14 Insurance buying behaviour:
Source: Adapted from Meidan, A. (1984) *Insurance Marketing*, Graham Burn, Leighton Buzzard, 23

comprehensive models fail to consider the special characteristics of services, approaching services in the same manner as consumer products (Cowell, 1992; Zeithaml, Parasuraman and Berry, 1985; McKechnie, 1992), is a source of growing disquiet. McKechnie (1992) summarizes the main criticisms as follows:

1. They assume an infeasibly rational decision making process.
2. Evidence suggests that the orderly discrete stages can in fact take place both out of sequence and overlap in some buying situations.
3. There are no empirically testable hypotheses.
4. They consider one-off purchase decisions rather than ongoing, repeat purchases.

Similarly disparaging, Cowell (1992) suggested that a model was needed which specifically acknowledged:

- The role consumers play in the actual production of services.
- The model should incorporate the sequence of interactions taking place during the service production/consumption process.

Drawing on Fisk's 'consumption/evaluation' model, Zeithaml, Parasuraman and Berry (1985) note that simultaneous production and consumption make the post-choice evaluation process dynamic, cumulative and ongoing. This contradicts the notion that post-choice evaluation will occur only after use. They, therefore, see the purchase process for services as having only two complex stages: (1) pre-purchase choice and (2) post-purchase/evaluation and consumption, often dubbed 'the service experience'.

The neglect of the buyer-seller interface led Yorke (1982) to suggest a radical departure from the sequential information processing models, by substituting them for the IMP Group's (1982) organizational buying model—the 'interaction approach' (McKechnie, 1992). Deemed particularly appropriate to financial services, the interaction approach emphasizes the *active participation of both parties* and the propensity for *long-term relationships* to become unquestioned or *inertia ridden*.

The interaction approach considers broad categories of factors that influence the character of long-term relationships. A series of 'episodes' both take place within and create the 'atmosphere' which pervades the relationship. Episodes can be of four types, exchanges of:

1. Information: the quantity, quality and tone or formality of the information exchanged will influence the relationship.

2. Product/service: satisfaction in the exchange is likely to be affected by the characteristics of the product itself.
3. Financial: this involves all monetary payments, their timing (speed, promptness), accuracy and reliability. When dealing with financial services it is rather more difficult to divorce these exchanges from the service product exchanges.
4. Social: not simply referring to dinner with the bank manager, front line service delivery staff engage in many social exchanges with customers, as do insurance sales people and financial advisors.

In turn, the atmosphere develops within the context of broad environmental influences, including behavioural norms from the social system and the firm's position in the distribution channel. The structure of the market (e.g., number, nature of alternative suppliers, rate of change since deregulation) is another environmental factor, clearly influencing the options open to consumers (IMP Group, 1982).

Thus the notion of buying behaviour being a rigid, orderly sequence is abandoned in favour of a more flexible conceptual framework, unconstrained by the nuances characterizing particular product-market areas.

To draw this section to a suitable conclusion, Baker (1983) offers some useful cautionary advice on the subject of buyer behaviour models. First, he suggested that all models demand the knowledge and experience of an authority in the particular product-market space and secondly, due to the complex and dynamic nature of buyer behaviour he dismissed demands for an all encompassing model as lacking realism (McKechnie, 1992).

2.8 LOYALTY AND RELATIONSHIP MARKETING

2.8.1 Consumer loyalty

Loyalty is brought about by satisfaction, or positive reinforcement, which leads to repeat purchasing. However, as we have seen, supplier 'loyalty' also reduces perceived risk, which is behavioural 'loyalty' arising from decidedly less flattering processes—habit and inertia. Inertia can be attributed to two main factors:

1. *'Better the devil you know'* Having established a certain level of trust in an institution, valuable time and effort have been expended gathering the information needed to assess the service (McKechnie, 1992). It is also difficult to actually acquire the information necessary to compare brands and suppliers. Therefore, if remotely satisfied, the customer is less likely to be willing to repeat the process. Automatically renewing insurance policies is an obvious example, although Cockrell and Dickenson (1980) maintain that personal and situational factors also affect the propensity to renew. A stable income and the absence of premium increases are often associated with re-purchase, the latter factor being particularly noteworthy in this era of soaring insurance premiums.
2. *No decision required* In the case of continuous, ongoing services, there may be no actual decision to make a repeat-purchase. Writing another cheque, making another pension contribution, do not amount to purchase 'decisions' as such, in effect they are 'non-decisions'.

While there is no agreement on what actually constitutes loyalty, most agree that it requires not only a high degree of repeat purchasing (the behavioural component), but also a favourable or positive attitude towards the supplier or product. Marketers should be wary of assuming long-standing customers are loyal patrons: customers without the favourable attitude will be more prone to switching suppliers. The interaction approach highlights the potential for high 'switching costs' to sustain barely tolerable customer supplier relationships. There can, however, be convincing arguments for 'divided loyalty' in financial services as a means to diversify risk. Here the behaviour is not undividedly loyal, but it does not preclude the existence of favourable attitudes.

2.8.2   Relationship marketing—loyalty and profitability

While developing loyal customers is not a new marketing objective, the realization that markets do not contain an infinite number of new customers has penetrated most financial services organizations. Retaining customers and maximizing their lifetime value through relationship marketing is based on the supposition that it is more cost-effective to repeat sell to an existing customer than to acquire a new one.

There is a growing interest in customer retention instead of just customer acquisition. This means determining the worth of each customer. (Kotler, 1991a)

By implication, establishing the probable 'worth' of customers also determines whether or not they are actually worth acquiring in the first instance. All customers are not necessarily profitable to all organizations. Relationship marketing aims to realize the full 'worth' or profit potential of those customers who should be profitable, seizing opportunities to cross sell other products and upgrade customers to superior versions. The insurance company selling a third party motor policy to a proud teenager with a first moped may ultimately be able to provide a home contents policy (cross selling) in addition to upgrading the motor insurance to cover four wheels, fully comprehensive.

Relationship marketing is attracting, maintaining and ... enhancing customer relationships ... The marketing mind-set is that the attraction of new customers is merely *the first step* in the marketing process. (Berry, 1983)

Although more commonly associated with dazzling cash prize draws, mounds of 'junk mail' and intrusive telesales operators attempting to sell fitted kitchens, direct marketing is actually an approach which has the 'customer lifetime value' at its very core. As initially touched upon in Section 2.4.1, acquiring new customers is an expense which should represent a profitable long-term investment. Initially many will be unprofitable, absorbing considerable account time or holding very low account balances; the skill lies in isolating those with the potential to be profitable in the greater scheme of things—the lifetime. Reaping their full lifetime value will, of course, be contingent upon the ability to retain their loyalty; but financial institutions with their rich sources of customer and transaction details should find this a far less onerous task than many others. They have greater potential to, and fewer excuses not to, 'know the customer'.

Loyalty and lifetime values in banking   Recognizing these principles, the banks have long endeavoured to 'catch them young': National Westminster excels in this with its Piggy Bank Account, recruiting children on the condition that they are over a year old. School-leavers progressing onto college or university have been particularly sought after, on the premise that while highly unprofitable when studying, their future earnings potential would eventually more than compensate for the cost of offering not only free railcards, record tokens, radios and sums of cash, but also free banking and overdrafts.

However, the strategy has not been as profitable as may have been anticipated, being based on the overly simplistic assumption that students, probably one of the most mobile segments of society, rarely switch their accounts from one bank to another (Watkins, 1990). The emphasis is now firmly on retention, hence the 'Students—For this term, next term and the long-term' from Barclays Bank:

Graduation and Beyond—At Barclays we have a Graduate Package which won't leave you stranded when your final term ends ... You may find your finances are overstretched whilst you're waiting for your first salary cheque. If you need to buy new clothes or pay rent in advance you can apply for a loan ... at a preferential rate, providing you have a firm job offer. (Barclays Bank, 1993)

The banks now give more attention to school-leavers in general, particularly those going into immediate employment. While they may not have the same earnings potential as graduates, they are at least immediately profitable and, being less mobile, have a higher propensity to remain 'loyal' (Lewis, 1982b), in body, if not always in soul.

SUMMARY

Financial services should be defined in terms of the 'bundle of consumer benefits' which satisfy consumer needs and thus motivate behaviour. In this sense, the extensively chronicled distinguishing features of services are irrelevant, financial services being no different to goods.

The chapter concentrates primarily on understanding the financial consumers' psychological processes. From a marketing perspective, it is logical to commence with motivation, as it actually initiates behaviour and directs it towards goal 'objects', the generic product categories. Financial services are psychological in the benefits they provide, most relating to needs for safety and security. Maslow's hierarchy proposes that needs are organized into a series of priorities; but while intuitively appealing, the notion has not been empirically substantiated.

Motives having guided behaviour towards generic product types, learning and perception have more influence over which brands and suppliers are selected. Learning theories are central to the ideas of increasing financial sophistication and customer loyalty; it is important to distinguish between behavioural and attitudinal 'loyalty'.

Bauer's (1967) perceived risk theory is concerned with subjective interpretations of risk, as unrecognized objective risk does not affect behaviour. The intangibility of services increases the uncertainty component of perceived risk, although obviously the financial stakes can be extremely high. Similar is the notion of perceived control, the degree of objective control being as immaterial as objective risk, if it goes unrecognized.

Perceptual processes are key to the formation of consumer images of service providers, that is, where they 'position' them in a given market. Critical to the success of a retail strategy, store (and non-store) images can be formed on 'largely irrelevant' cues, although store images and retail personalities do not warrant the mystical qualities often ascribed to them.

Attitudes are an outcome of all these psychological processes. Despite being reasonably enduring, some attitudes towards personal finances have changed dramatically in recent years, the product of recession, deregulation of financial markets, a changing political mood, feckless borrowing records and the collapse of property prices.

Models of buyer behaviour should be treated as basic blue-prints for adaptation to fit particular product market areas. A 'limited response hierarchy' model of attitudes was adapted for complex financial products, showing that whereas 'knowledge' may be sufficient to progress to the next stage in some product areas, buying shares requires 'know-how' and self-confidence.

The comprehensive models were criticized for their multitude of sins, i.e., assuming rationality, a sequential process, being concerned with one-off purchases etc. The appeal of the 'interaction approach', an organizational buying behaviour framework, centred upon its ability to trace the development of long-term relationships and the propensity for them to become unquestioned or inertia bound. Relationship marketing was described in the context of direct marketing 'lifetime values': acquiring a customer is only the first stage, ultimately profitability can be contingent upon the supplier retaining their custom and developing the relationship.

REVIEW QUESTIONS

1. What are the factors said to make financial services marketing different? Review the relevance of each of these factors to:

   (a)   Insurance bought through the post.
   (b)   Unit trusts.
   (c)   Making an ATM withdrawal.

   In what respect(s) should 'services marketing' not make a difference?
2. What is a motive? Review the concept of motive bundling with specific reference to the possible motivations to acquire:

   (a)   Home contents insurance.
   (b)   A credit card.

3. Why are 'fear appeals' so prevalent in financial services?
4. Assuming the role of the following financial service providers, anticipate consumer needs using the family life cycle:

   (a)   A bank.
   (b)   A stock broker.

5. What is customer loyalty and how do learning theories aid understanding of customer 'loyalty' as opposed to habit and inertia?
6. As the provider of a financial service of your choice, which would you consider to be the most important types of perceived risk and how would you attempt to reduce them?
7. What implications do perceptual closure, stimulus generalization and discrimination have for the development of retailers' images?
8. Recall the effects of the deregulation of financial markets on the image and positioning of financial institutions. Would they have been well advised to resist diversification and 'stick to the knitting' instead?
9. What are the four characteristics of an attitude? Why and in what ways do you think attitudes towards credit, borrowing and investment have changed among sections of society in recent years?
10. How do the differences between goods and complex financial services affect the suitability of 'response hierarchy' models?
11. Describe the decision rules used in the attribute evaluation stage of the consumer's decision-making process. Drawing on your own experience with financial services, what contribution do you believe they can make to understanding the consumer's decision-making process?
12. Why have the comprehensive, sequential models of buyer behaviour been treated with such reproach by writers on financial services? How does the 'interaction approach' overcome some of their criticisms?
13. Why are financial service organizations being urged to put less effort into finding new customers?

REFERENCES

Baker, M.J. (1983) *Market Development*, Penguin, Harmondsworth.

Bateson, J. (1977) 'Do we need service marketing?', *Marketing Consumer Services: New Insights*, Report 77–115, Marketing Science Institute, Boston.

Bateson, J. E. G. (1985) 'Perceived control and the service encounter' in *Managing Services Marketing: Text and Readings*, Bateson, J. E. G. (ed.), The Dryden Press, pp. 112–121.

Bauer, R.A. (1967) 'Consumer behaviour as risk taking' in Cox, D.F. (ed.) *Risk Taking and Information Handling in Consumer Behaviour*, Harvard University Press, Boston.

Bayton, J.A. (1958) 'Motivation, cognition and learning—basic factors in consumer behaviour' in *Consumer Behaviour: Selected Readings* (1968) Engel, J.F. (ed.), Richard D. Irwin, Illinois, pp. 20–29.

Berry. L.L. (1980) 'Services marketing is different' in *Marketing Classics*, 6th edn, B.M. Enis and K.K. Cox (eds.) Allyn and Bacon, Massachusetts.

Berry (1983) 'Relationship marketing' in *Emerging Perspectives on Services Marketing*, L. Berry, G.L. Shostack and G. Upah (eds), American Marketing Association, Chicago, pp. 25–28.

Booms, B.H. and M.J. Bitner (1981) 'Marketing strategies and organization structures for service firms' in *Marketing of Services*, Donnelly, J.H. and W.R George (eds), American Marketing Association, Chicago, pp. 47–51.

Chartered Institute of Banking (1991) *CIB Study Text: Marketing*, BPP Publishing, London.

Chisnall, P.M. (1985) *Marketing: A Behavioural Analysis*, McGraw-Hill, London.

Chisnall, P.M. (1992) *Marketing Research*, 4th edn, McGraw-Hill, London.

Cockrell, H.A.L. and G.M. Dickenson, (1980) *Motor Insurance and the Consumer*, Woodhead-Faulkner.

Coleman, R.P. (1983) 'The continuing significance of social class to marketing', *Journal of Consumer Research*, **10** (Dec), 265–280.

Cowell, D. (1992) *The Marketing of Services*, 2nd edn, Butterworth Heinemann.

Davies, G. (1987) 'Monitoring retail strategy by measuring customer perception', in G. Johnson (ed.), *Business Strategy and Retailing*, John Wiley, Chichester, 133–152.

Davis, H.L. and B.P. Riguax (1974) 'Perception of marital roles in decision processes', *Journal of Consumer Research*, **1** (Jun), 5–14.

Doyle, P. and I. Fenwick (1974) 'How store image affects shopping habits in grocery chains', *Journal of Retailing*, **50**(4), 39–52.

Engel, J.F., R.D. Blackwell and P.W. Miniard (1986) *Consumer Behaviour*, 5th edn, Dryden Press, Chicago.

Engel, J.F., D.T. Kollat and R.D. Blackwell (1968) *Consumer Behaviour*, Holt, Reinhart and Winston, New York.

Enis, B.M. and K.J. Roering (1981) 'Services marketing: different products, similar strategy' in *Marketing of Services*, Donnelly, J.H. and W.R George (eds), American Marketing Association, Chicago, 1–4.

Fisk, R.P., S.W. Brown and M.J. Bitner (1993) 'Tracking the evolution of the services marketing literature', *Journal of Retailing*, **69**(1), 61–103.

Foxall, G. (1980) *Consumer Behaviour: A Practical Guide*, Croom Helm, London, 29–43.

George, W.R. (1977) 'The retailing of services—a challenging future', *Journal of Retailing*, **53**(3), 86–93.

Gibson, J.L., L.M. Ivancevich and J.H. Donnelly (1985) *Organisations*, 5th edn, Business Publications, Texas, 54–58, 60–67, 102, 114–119.

Gronroos, C. (1978) 'A service orientated approach to marketing of services', *European Journal of Marketing*, **12**(8), 588–601.

Guirdham, M. (1987) 'How to market unit trusts: a consumer behaviour model', *Marketing Intelligence and Planning*, **2**, 15–19.

Guseman, D.S. (1981) 'Risk perception and risk reduction in consumer services' in *Marketing of Services*, Donnelly, J.H. and W.R George (eds), American Marketing Association, Chicago,

Hansen, R. and T. Deutscher (1977) 'An empirical investigation of attribute importance in retail store selection', *Journal of Retailing*, **53**(4) 59–73.

Henley Centre (1993) *Metamporphosis in Marketing*, London.

Herzberg, F. (1966) *Work and the Nature of Man*, Staples Press, London.

IMP Group (1982) 'An interaction approach' in *International Purchasing of Industrial Goods*, Wiley, Chichester, 10–27.

Janis, I. L. and S. Feshbach (1953) 'Effects of fear-arousing communications', *Journal of Abnormal Social Psychology*, **48** (Jan), 78–92.

Kassarjian, H.H. and J.B. Cohen (1968) 'Cognitive dissonance and consumer behaviour' in *Perspectives in Consumer Behaviour*, H.H Kassarjian and T.S. Robertson (eds), Scott, Foresman and Co., Illinois, 171–180.

Kay, W. (1987) *The Battle for the High Street*, Judy Piatkus, London, 151–166.

Key Note (1992) *Personal Finance in the UK*, Key Note Publications, London.

Klein, D.M. and R.C. Lewis (1985) 'Personal construct theory: a foundation for deriving tangible surrogates in services marketing' in *Services Marketing in a Changing Environment*, Bloch, T.M, G.D. Upah and V.A. Zeithaml (eds), American Marketing Association, Chicago.

Kotler, P. (1991) *Marketing Management*, 7th edn, Prentice-Hall, London.

Kotler, P. (1991a) 'Silent satisfaction' in *Marketing Business*, December 91/January 92.

Krech, D. and R. Crutchfeld (1948) *Theory and Problems in Social Psychology*, McGraw-Hill, New York.

Krech, D., R.S. Crutchfield and E.L. Ballachey (1962) *Individual Society*, McGraw-Hill, New York.

Kunkel, J.H. and L.L. Berry (1968) 'A behavioural concept of retail images', *Journal of Marketing*, **32**(4), 21–27.

Lavidge, R.J. and G.A. Steiner (1961), 'A model for predicative measurements of advertising effectiveness', in *Marketing Classics* (1988), 6th edn, B.M. Ellis and K.K. Cox (eds), Allyn and Bacon, Boston.

Laroche, M. and T. Taylor (1988) 'An empirical study of major segmentation issues in retail banking', *International Journal of Bank Marketing*', **6**(1), 3–18.

Levitt, T. (1960) 'Marketing myopia', *Harvard Business Review*, July/August.

Levitt, T. (1981) 'Marketing intangible products and product intangibles', *Harvard Business Review*, 94–102.

Lewin, K. (1935) *A Dynamic Theory of Personality*, McGraw-Hill, New York.

Lewis, B.R. (1982a) 'The personal account sector', *European Journal of Marketing*, **16**(3).

Lewis, B.R. (1982b) 'Student accounts—a profitable segment?' *European Journal of Marketing*, **16**(3).

Lewis, R.C. and B.H. Booms (1983) 'The marketing aspects of service quality' in *Emerging Perspectives on Services Marketing*, L.L. Berry, G.L. Shostack and G. Upah (eds), American Marketing Association, Chicago, 99–104.

Lindquist, J.D. (1974) 'Meaning of image: a survey of empirical and hypothetical evidence' *Journal of Retailing*, **50**(4), 29–38, 116.

Louden, D.L. and A.J. Della Bitta (1988) *Consumer Behaviour: Concepts and Applications*, 3rd edn, McGraw Hill, New York.

Lovelock, C.H. (1983) 'Think before you leap in services marketing' in *Emerging Perspectives on Services Marketing*, L.L. Berry, G.L. Shostack and G. Upah (eds), American Marketing Association, Chicago, 115–119.

Markin, R.J. (1969) *The Psychology of Consumer Behaviour*, Prentice-Hall, New Jersey, 8–14, 20, 52–53.

Martineaux, P. (1958) 'The personality of the retail store', *Harvard Business Review*, **36**(1), 47–55.

Maslow, A.H. (1943) 'A theory of human motivation', *Psychological Review*, **50**, 370–396.

May, E.G. (1974) 'Practical applications of recent image research', *Journal of Retailing*, **50**(4), 15–20, 116.

Mazursky, D. and J. Jacoby (1986) 'Exploring the development of store images', *Journal of Retailing*, **62**(2), 145–165.

McGoldrick, P.J. (1990) *Retail Marketing*, McGraw-Hill, London.

McGoldrick, P.J. and S.J. Greenland (1992) 'Competition between banks and building societies in the retailing of financial services', *British Journal of Management*, **3**, 169–179.

McGuire, W.J (1976) 'Some internal psychological factors influencing consumer choice', *Journal of Consumer Research*, **2**, 302–319.

McKechnie, S. (1992) 'Consumer buying behaviour in financial services: an overview', *International Journal of Bank Marketing*, **19**(5), 4–12.

Meidan, A. (1984) *Insurance Marketing*, Graham Burn, Leighton Buzzard.

Mitchell, V.W. (1989) 'Geo-demographics—a look at new developments', *Proceedings of 22nd MEG Conference*, Glasgow, 1056–73.

Mitchell, V.W. (1992) 'The future of geodemographic information handling', *Logistics Information Management*, **5**(3), 23–28.

Mitchell, V.W. and M. Greatorex (1993) 'Risk perception and reduction in the purchase of consumer services', *The Services Industries Journal*, **13**(4), 179–200.

Morgan, N. and N. Piercy (1990) 'Marketing in financial services organisations: policy and practice' in *Managing and Marketing Services in the 1990s*, Teare, R. (ed.), Cassel Education, London.

Murphy, P.E. and W.A. Staples (1979) 'A modernised family life cycle', *Journal of Consumer Research*, **6**, 12–22.

NOP (1992) *The Financial Consumer 1992/93*, NTC Publications, Henley-on-Thames.

Nystrom, H. (1970) 'Retail pricing: an integrated economic and psychological approach', Economic Research Unit, Stockholm School of Economics.

Odih, P. (1991) *Financial Decision Making in a Changing Social Environment*, Working Paper, F.S.R.C., Manchester School of Management, UMIST.

Oxenfeldt, A.R. (1974) 'Developing a favourable price-quality image', *Journal of Retailing*, **50**(4), 8–14, 115.

Pathak, D.S., W.J. Crissy and R.W. Sweitzer (1974) 'Customer image versus the retailer's anticipated image', *Journal of Retailing*, **56**(1), 94–106.

Poyner, M. (1987) 'The changing consumer' in *The Changing Face of British Retailing*, Newman, London.

Ries, A. and J. Trout (1982) *The Battle for Your Mind*, Warner Books, New York.

Roselius, T. (1971) 'Consumer rankings of risk reduction methods', *Journal of Marketing*, **35**.

Schiffman, L.G. and L.L. Kanuk (1991) *Consumer Behaviour*, 4th edn, Prentice-Hall International, New Jersey.

Shostack, G.L. (1977) 'Breaking free from product marketing', *Journal of Marketing*, **41**(2), 73–80.

Stampfl, R.W. (1978) 'The consumer life-cycle', *Journal of Consumer Affairs*, **12**.

Streufert, S. and M.J. Driver (1971) 'The general incongruity adaptation level (GIAL)', *Technical Report 32*, Dorsey Press, Homewood, Illinois.

Tull, D.S. and D.I. Hawkins (1990) *Marketing Research: Measurement and Method*, 5th edn, Macmillan Publishing, New York.

Turnbull, P.W. (1982) 'The role of the bank branch manager in the marketing of bank services', *European Journal of Marketing*, **16**(3), 31–36.

Turnbull, P.W. (1991) 'Organisational buying behaviour' in *The Marketing Book*, M.J. Baker (ed.) 2nd edn, Butterworth-Heinemann, Oxford.

Walters and Bergiel (1989) *Consumer Behaviour*, South Western Publishing, Ohio.

Watkins, T. (1990) 'The demand for financial services' in *Marketing Financial Services*, Ennew, C., T. Watkins and M. Wright (eds), Heinemann, Oxford.

Watson, I. (1982) 'The adoption of marketing by the English clearing banks', *European Journal of Marketing*, **16**(3), 23–30.

Wells, W.D and G. Gruber (1966) 'Life cycle concept in marketing research, *Journal of Marketing Research*, November, 355–63.

Yorke, D.A. (1982) 'The definition of market segments for banking services', *European Journal of Marketing*, **16**(3), 14–22.

Zeithaml, V.A. (1981) 'How consumer evaluation processes differ between goods and services' in *Marketing of Services*, Donnelly, J.H. and W.R George (eds), American Marketing Association, Chicago, 186–189.

Zeithaml, V.A., A. Parasuraman and L. Berry (1985) 'Problems and strategies in services marketing', *Journal of Marketing*, **49**(1) 33–46.

FORMULATING RETAIL STRATEGY

Roy A. Palmer and Monica Lucas   Pragma Marketing Consultants

INTRODUCTION

The retail financial services industry is characterized by a history of almost complete absence of any formal approach to the strategic planning or marketing function. Indeed, as Catherine Smith (1991) pointed out, strategic marketing in this sector really only came into being in the late 1980s or early 1990s. Traditionally, financial service providers in the UK have been constrained by regulations, a focus on a narrow range of unexciting products, a poor recognition of customer needs, an offer which is delivery and transaction oriented, and by a lack of effective management with the necessary long-term vision and strategic marketing skills. The traditional senior executive will have come up through the seniority grades, starting at branch management level and working through the many management layers that lie between the branches and the board. Only very recently, in the early 1990s, has there been more evidence of a widespread move to recruit senior executives from backgrounds outside the financial sector, who have board responsibility for planning the future strategic direction and growth of the business. The background experiences of these new entrants include product retailing, leisure and consumer goods marketing. The application of this new wave of analytical, customer-focused, strategic marketing expertise is clearly having a considerable impact on the retail financial services sector, as organizations focus much more upon the provision of products and services based upon an understanding of customers' needs, as discussed in the previous chapter.

Michael Bon (1987) identified three main forces that were instrumental in driving the revolution in grocery retailing in the 1960s, and that are now evident in shaping the market for financial service products in the 1990s.

1. *Self-service*   The customer serves him or herself. This required careful product selection and better presentation systems.
2. *Comprehensive supply*   Also known as 'one-stop-shopping'. A wide range of complementary products is found under one roof, obviating the need to shop elsewhere.
3. *Discount selling*   The growth of supermarkets offered the opportunity to compete both on range and price. The same focus on lower distribution costs and hence lower pricing is clearly evident in the financial services sector today.

This theme was reflected by Ellwood (1989), who commented that: 'The wind of change is not coming from within the banking sector. I believe it is coming from the retail sector where competition has raised customers' expectation of service.'

In this book's sister publication, *Retail Marketing*, McGoldrick (1990) points out that even in the retail sector, formal structures and processes for strategic planning have had a very short history of success—and much of retail planning has tended to be *reactive* rather than *strategic* in its development.

This chapter therefore sets out to propose and explore a number of the more formal models of planning that are suitable and appropriate for the retail financial services sector today. The concept of developing a mission statement which succinctly sums up the key objective of the organization is discussed. In developing such a planning framework, the use of techniques such as SWOT analysis, and the formal evaluation of areas that offer opportunities for developing sustainable competitive advantage, are explored. The factors forcing change in the financial services sector are identified, and the need for focus and differentiation are highlighted.

The crucial role of segmentation and targeting, discussed initially in Chapter 2, is developed further here, with examples given of their importance in the design of products and delivery systems. The use of more complex customer scoring techniques to provide more effective targeting is contrasted with that of a more mass-market branded approach, with particular reference to differential strategies in distribution and selling. The importance of key areas of competitive strategy are highlighted, drawing upon discussions with senior executives in the financial services industry, setting the scene for the more detailed discussions of competitive weapons in the chapters that follow. The chapter concludes with some possible implications for the financial services market over the next decade.

3.1 RETAIL STRATEGY FRAMEWORKS

3.1.1 Frameworks and models

The fundamental goal of business strategy was summarized by Alfred P. Sloan Jr (1963), who masterminded the development of General Motors:

The strategic aim of a business is to earn a return on capital, and if in any particular case the return in the long run is not satisfactory, then the deficiencies should be corrected, or the activity abandoned for a more favourable one

In the last 25 years, since the formative early work by Ansoff (1988), much has been written in the area of the development of analytical frameworks and modelling techniques to assist organizations with defining and evaluating relevant business development strategies.

Robert M. Grant (1991), in defining strategy, referred to the military distinction between strategy and tactics:

- *Strategy* is the overall plan for deploying resources to establish a favourable position.
- A *tactic* is a scheme for a specific action.

He went on to identify four ingredients of successful business strategies:

1. Clear objectives
2. An understanding of the external environment
3. An appreciation of internal strengths and weaknesses
4. Effective implementation

Porter (1980), in his definitive work on competitive strategy, stressed that the essence of formulating a successful competitive strategy lies in relating a business to its environment—the two key aspects of a firm's environment being the nature and the intensity of competition in the industry within which the firm competes. He defined five basic competitive forces, summarized in

Source of competition	Nature of competition
Potential entrants	Threat of new entrants to industry
Industry competition	Rivalry among firms already in the industry
Substitutes	Threat of substitute products or services
Buyers	Bargaining power of buyers
Suppliers	Bargaining power of supplier

Figure 3.1   Basic competitive forces
Source: Porter (1980), *Competitive Strategy. Techniques for Analysing Industries and Competitors*, MacMillan, New York

Figure 3.1, which determine and influence the profit potential measured in terms of the rate of return on invested capital (ROI) in any given industry. These five competitive forces are:

- Potential new entrants
- Threat of substitution
- Bargaining power of suppliers
- Bargaining power of buyers
- Rivalry amongst current competitors

Porter (1980) identifies a number of structural determinants that influence the strength of each of these five competitive forces. This model can be related to the area of financial services, in order to identify some of the challenges facing the banks and other providers of financial services as they compete for market share and profitable growth in the late 1990s and beyond.

Threat from potential new entrants   Success in the consumer financial services sector requires access to a customer base, competitive products, investment capital, good retailing skills, and effective marketing.

Recent competitors to the established, previously dominant providers of financial services have come from such diverse players as:

- The deregulated building societies, with their expanding range of products and services, coupled to rapidly growing ATM and branch distribution networks.
- High street retailers offering extended credit facilities and, more recently, cash withdrawal facilities at point-of-sale ('cash back').
- National retail chains such as Marks and Spencer in the UK, or Sears Roebuck in the USA, offering a wide range of specialist financial services to their retail customer charge card base, including loans, investment products such as unit trusts, pensions, insurance, etc.
- Institutions such as motoring organizations (AA and RAC) offering personal loans and insurance facilities to their membership, using to a large extent direct mail and telephone sales.

In each case, the traditional barriers to entry are reduced because of the ability, to a greater or lesser degree, of the new entrants to:

- Exploit economies of scale by utilizing existing distribution channels.
- Utilize the power of existing corporate brand names and brand strength images.
- 'Cherry-pick' the most profitable product lines and offer products that are relatively easy to tailor to the current needs of the market.

• Target customers by cost-effective direct (in store) or indirect (mail order address-lists) means.

The relative ease of entry of non-traditional players is further facilitated by the low cost to buyers of switching from one supplier to another. However, this potential customer drain is to some extent mitigated in that customers rarely switch the *whole* of their financial service relationship from one supplier to another, due to a desire to transact certain types of business with 'specialist providers', and by the ingrained consumer inertia which is manifest in this sector. Nevertheless, significant barriers to entry do exist for new entrants who wish to do more than 'cherry-pick' and where the objective is to build a substantial broadly-based retail financial services business. These barriers are concerned primarily with developing cost-effective distribution strengths—and the associated investment in technology that is necessary to target, to manage, to service, and to cross-sell effectively to a large customer base. It is in the two areas of distribution and effective customer service where we see major opportunities for developing competitive advantage in financial services over the next decade.

Industry competition   To date, the retail financial services industry in the UK has been characterized by short bursts of competitive activity, where one of the major players, or groups of players, has developed a relatively short-term competitive advantage. For example, the payment of interest on bank current accounts, which was first offered by Midland Bank in response to competition from building societies in the mid-1980s, has been rapidly adopted by the other UK clearing banks. If they had not responded quickly, then they would have suffered a significant loss of customers to the more attractive Midland offer. Barclaycard, which spearheaded the rapid growth of credit cards in the UK in the 1960s and 1970s, was rapidly followed by the launch of Access. This highlights one of the most challenging aspects of the retail financial services market in general, which is that products and new marketing initiatives tend to be relatively easy to replicate by competitors. The result is a constant stream of new products onto the market, which often differ only marginally from what has gone before. Indeed, one of the classic routes to managing bank and building society profitability has been to introduce lodgement products on terms which are initially attractive to depositors, but then to replace these products within one to two years by others that offer more attractive rates for initial investors, meanwhile quietly allowing the terms of the original products to worsen while not explicitly encouraging customers to switch to the new product. This relies on the inertia or constraint imposed on the original borrower to continue to leave money on deposit at marginal rates, a situation which is clearly very attractive to the banking institution. Under such circumstances, it is hardly surprising that, with a few notable exceptions such as Midland's branded Orchard and Meridian accounts, little has been done to try to build long-term brand strengths within product ranges. The brand values associated with financial service products certainly do not have the strengths, nor the investment money behind them, that are to be found in the portfolio of consumer product brands of companies such as Mars, Procter and Gamble, or Unilever.

   Channon (1988), in examining innovative product strategies, highlighted the dramatic success that Merrill Lynch scored when they launched their Cash Management Account (CMA) in late 1978. This product (which took 100 man years of systems work to develop) was designed to appeal to the moderately well-off customer segment of the mass market. To open a CMA, investors had to have $20,000 of cash or marketable securities to place in the account. For a small annual fee, account holders received a cheque book, Visa card, a comprehensive itemized monthly statement of all transactions including sales and purchases of securities and an automatic sweep of all cash into a money market fund that paid interest daily. The appeal to the investor was that it concentrated most of the financial services into one comprehensive, simple to run, cheap, very convenient account that offered the automatic conversion of assets into cash, a limited loan facility for short-term cash demands, and an automatic sweep facility of surplus cash into an interest paying fund.

By mid-1982, Merrill Lynch's Cash Management Account had attracted 680,000 account holders and was adding new ones at the rate of 1,000 per day. By 1984, there were over one million CMA holders with an average balance of $70,000 per account, 30 per cent of whom were new customers to Merrill Lynch.

The impact of the CMA on the banking and financial services sector in the USA was considerable. Previously the traditional approach had been to separate accounts between current accounts, on which no interest was paid, and deposit accounts, on which low rates of interest were paid. The new systems-driven CMA approach allowed customers to optimize a full range of personal financial services through the medium of just one single account. It took Citibank until 1984 to develop the advanced system architecture that allowed them to launch a range of similar competing products.

Pressure from substitute products or services The role of substitute products or services in threatening the existing position of competitors in financial services is less easy to identify than for other industries. In many ways, all similar financial service products can be viewed as substitutes, in whole or in part, one for another.

Where structural substitutes in the retail sector could occur would be, for example, if Smart Cards were developed to the point where card-holders could draw out as much of their salary as they wished from their employer on their card, and this was then drawn down directly off the card by retailers when making purchases. Interest on any monies left with the employee's company would then automatically be credited to the employee's account. Bills such as to public utilities could be paid by direct debit via a Smart Card number down a telephone link, thus obviating the need for separate credit cards, debit cards, or current or investment account facilities. The technology and infrastructure to provide such a substitute product could come from the computer industry, the telecommunications industry or other large national or multinational corporations with skills and resources in advanced data processing and communications.

Bargaining power of buyers The role that important buying groups can have in influencing corporate development strategies in the financial services sector was evident in the dispute between the banking sector and the retail stores sector over the level of charges for debit card processing through EFTPoS systems. Here the retailers as buyers of the customer-related transaction-processing service are, as a group, unwilling to pay the level of charges which the banks are claiming they need to provide and support the service. This is a rare example of buyer power being consolidated in the hands of a few very powerful organizations who have the collective strength and will to influence the financial retailers' strategy. In the case of the individual consumer, who is buying personal financial products and services, transactions are conducted on a one-to-one basis, and any switching between one supplier and another tends to be at individual account level, rather than mass market level. Hence the threat of losing an individual personal account is, in itself, rarely seen as significant. However, this is almost certainly because the current level of appreciation of the value of the discounted net cash flow of the future stream of income from any one personal customer is low, if not non-existent, in many financial institutions in the UK today. Hence it is difficult, if not impossible today, for a financial institution to respond appropriately to the potential loss of a customer relationship, should that customer decide to switch to a competitive offer.

Bargaining power of suppliers The role of suppliers in influencing strategy and profitability in the financial services industry can be recognized by the massive investments being made by banks, building societies and insurance companies in hardware and software in an effort to drive down long-term processing costs and raise standards of customer service. Such programs, aimed at replacing the manually based back-office functions of a branch by centralized remote processing and on-line customer databases, have been costing individual high street banks in the UK sums of anything from £500 million to £1000 million, as they struggle to cope with the sheer size and complexity of the problem. The influence on banking strategies of specialist suppliers such as IT consultants, system providers, computer and communications hardware suppliers is therefore considerable. This is not only in terms of the basic cost and configuration of the systems, but also in the degree to which these systems in practice do or do not actually achieve the projected benefits on which the feasibility of the projects was based in the first place.

3.1.2   The corporate mission

Frameworks such as those outlined above are helpful in providing an organization with a structured approach to analysing and defining its strategic options and objectives. However, before such a task can be undertaken, it is important that an organization defines clearly what its overall role or mission is—or is to become. This is frequently communicated by way of a 'mission statement', which is an attempt to encapsulate and communicate inside and outside the organization the objectives, values, directions and increasingly today—the social responsibilities and ethics of the business entity. Some examples:

American Express's mission is simple: to be the best at what it does. This means a never-ending search for excellence by attracting outstanding people who embrace entrepreneurship and flexibility in management change; creating premium products with strong brand names that are provided through carefully targeted marketing channels; an individual and corporate commitment to community involvement and citizenship; and, above all, commitment and uncompromising quality in all we do. (*American Express Company, 1988 Annual Report* p.6.)

We will supply financial services to the retail public which embody the values of quality, value and service implicit in the name Marks and Spencer. (*Marks and Spencer, 1987*)

We will strengthen our lead in UK housing finance and personal savings. We will offer personal financial services where they can be delivered profitably and well to meet customer needs. (*Halifax Building Society, 1992 Annual Report*)

Mission statements clearly do not necessarily have to be long and complicated to be an effective communication of the primary purpose and goals of the enterprise. As LL Bean, a highly successful North American speciality retailer, once put it:

The Golden Rule of LL Bean: Sell good merchandise at a reasonable profit, treat your customers like human beings, and they will always come back for more. (Source: LL Bean Inc magazine advertisement)

Perhaps there are some lessons in this for the financial services industry!

  The definition of a corporate mission requires that the organization asks itself some very basic yet important questions:

Who and what are we?   How do our customers see us?   Where have we come from?   What are our strengths and weaknesses?   Where do we want to go?   How might we get there?

In answering such questions, there are clearly many ways in which an organization can view its activities, its relationship and role in respect to its customers, and hence its possible development directions. For example, a retail bank could take a number of possible definitions of its primary purpose, from a spectrum ranging from a basic functional activity to something much more complex and all-embracing:

1. Helping people to transact their day by day monetary affairs.
2. Providing a secure haven for surplus personal funds.
3. Assisting with long-term bridge funding for the acquisition of major assets.
4. Offering advice and counselling on personal financial matters.
5. Helping take the stress out of modern living.
6. Helping people realize their ambitions in life.

Interestingly, the progression in such a table is from function/product through to lifestage/lifestyle servicing. From discussions held with many financial institutions in the UK over the course of the past year, it is clear that the collective vision for the year 2000 is that customers will increasingly develop more symbiotic and complex personal relationships with their bank or other financial institution through a more careful matching of the product/service offer with identified customer needs. To achieve this, will require a considerable investment by the financial services sector in the collection and analysis of customer information related to such complex factors as the customers' attitudes, their behaviour, their lifestyle, their particular circumstances and requirements at key stages in their life, their personal goals and objectives, etc.

   At the time of writing, this remains at best a much desired long-term objective throughout the whole of the industry.

3.1.3   Strategic audit—SWOT analysis

In developing the framework for an appropriate plan to achieve the defined corporate goals, it is frequently beneficial to conduct an audit or review of the existing status of the organization, and of the opportunities and possible threats that it may need to respond to. A formal way of doing this is to carry out a SWOT analysis of the strengths, weaknesses, opportunities and threats facing the company. Figure 3.2. gives an example of such an analysis for a traditional retail high street bank as it might be configured today.

   This is by no means an exhaustive list, but illustrates the kinds of issues that need to be considered in examining where the organization is today, and the possible ways forward. Having identified the key issues, each of the subject headings in Figure 3.2. can then be studied in some level of detail. For example, while the traditional branch network can be seen as a strength, it also carries the penalty of an associated high fixed cost structure. So the financial institution must identify strategies that will reduce costs while at the same time not impair the distribution capability provided by a retail high street branch presence. In so doing, the organization is responding to the opportunity to improve profitability by reducing costs, while at the same time developing innovative delivery systems to meet the possible threat from other competitive suppliers.

   It is important to maintain a level of objectivity and focus in such an evaluation process, as there is a risk of making assumptions about business potential that are not delivered in practice. For example, it might at first sight seem that a travel agency chain with a high profile brand name in the travellers cheques and currency exchange business would be a logical fit with a banking business, and thereby represent a business opportunity. However, Midland Bank's acquisition of Thomas Cook never produced the synergies and returns anticipated, as the opportunities for cross-selling to the two customer bases were in practice virtually non-existent. Hence Midland

Strengths	*Weaknesses*
Traditional family-based relationships	High level of fixed costs
Customer inertia	Poor levels of customer service
Branch network	Lack of customer information
Product range	Product, not market, focus
Management skills/resources	Lacks brand strength
Processing technology	Lack of flexibility to respond
Communication network	Traditional management practices
Brand image	Complexity of operations
Trustworthy reputation	
Opportunities	*Threats*
Develop enhanced customer service	New market entry competitors
Develop effective marketing systems	New technologies
Reduced cost structures	Product innovations
New distribution opportunities	Changing customer attitudes/needs
Market/product/customer segmentation	Innovative delivery systems
Product innovation	Legislation
Social changes	
Brand positioning/strengthening	

Figure 3.2 SWOT Analysis
Source: Pragma Consulting

Bank eventually sold Thomas Cook to a larger international travel operator whose fundamental business and markets were much more attuned to that of Thomas Cook's core activities.

Another strategic audit approach that can be useful is that of identifying key success factors. Grant (1991) emphasized that for a firm to survive and prosper, it needs to meet two criteria: First it must supply what customers want to buy, and secondly it must survive competition. Hence to identify the key factors for success, it is necessary to answer two fundamental questions:

1. What do our customers want?
2. What does the firm need to do to survive competition?

Grant's basic framework for identifying key success factors is shown in Figure 3.3.

3.1.4 Product—market strategy

The personal financial service sectors, like many other areas of retailing, are characterized increasingly by shortening product lifecycles and rapidly changing, innovative delivery systems. Any company wishing to survive must therefore evaluate carefully the changing market place, decide in which areas it wishes to compete—and hence what products and marketing strengths it needs to develop or acquire. Ansoff (1988) advocated a product-mission matrix, which identified alternative option routes for expanding the business depending on which directions it decided to move in (Figure 3.4). Ansoff's 'sales gap' represented the increasing difference between what could be achieved through the normal process of product/market development and new directions which necessitate business expansion or diversification.

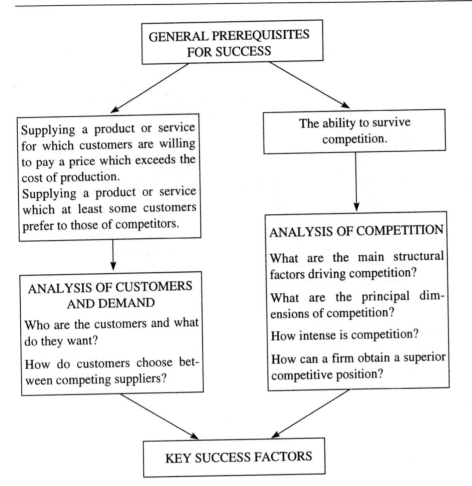

Figure 3.3.   Identifying key success factors
Source: Grant, R.M. (1991), *Contemporary Strategy Analysis*, Blackwell, Oxford

Mission	Product	Strategy
Present	Present	Expansion by market penetration
Present	New	Expansion by product development
New	Present	Expansion by market development
New	New	Diversification

Figure 3.4   Alternative routes to business expansion
Source: Ansoff, H. I. (1988), *New Corporate Strategy: an analytical approach to business policy for growth and expansion*, Wiley, New York

Ansoff's original product mission matrix can be adapted and applied to segment products and markets to help identify growth strategies in financial services. Figure 3.5 looks at the opportunities for a building society to develop business with existing customers and with new customers.

Product markets	Existing product areas	New product areas
Existing building society customers	*Market penetration*: Increase market share by more effective marketing and cross-selling of existing products	*Product development*: Development of new products and services such as cheque accounts, ATM card-based services
New building society customers	*Expand market*: Develop marketing campaigns to attract new customers e.g., students first time home buyers	*Diversify*: Enter new business sectors by start-up/ acquisition e.g., estate agency insurance broking home banking

Figure 3.5 Product market strategy alternatives
Source: Pragma Consulting

3.1.5 Competitive advantage and differentiation

Having first determined the objectives of the business organization and secondly defined the target markets or segments within which the business wishes to compete, it is relevant to consider some of those factors that lead to success in practice. Porter (1980) identified three potentially successful generic strategies whereby firms can achieve long-term sustainable competitive advantages over their rivals in an industry:

1. Overall cost leadership
2. Differentiation
3. Focus

In most industries, Porter observes that it is rare for a firm to be ultimately fully successful by pursuing more than one strategy as its primary objective. In discussions with companies in the financial services sector, however, it was found that there may be some overlap between these three alternatives.

Overall cost leadership Cost leadership in financial services clearly implies developing a low cost distribution system, a range of products that is efficient to support and service, and heavy investment in technology to keep processing costs down. It also implies the need to improve branch network profitability by closing or relocating branches, and targeting branches carefully to the needs of their local market. It also raises questions about staff sales productivity, and the qualities needed for effective interpersonal selling. Synonymous with all of this is the constant requirement to examine new cost-efficient methods of providing customers with the three main services they require, namely:

- Cash transactions (money in, money out)
- Account manipulation and enquiries
- Financial services advice and sales

None of these today necessarily need to be branch related, as we will see later in this chapter.

While it is clear that there are considerable opportunities for organizations in the financial services sector to adopt a low-cost leadership strategy, this may only be achievable in practice with a level of concentration, or focus, on specific segments of the market. It is clear, for example, that the Cheltenham and Gloucester Building Society has decided that its strategy will not be to target the mass market with an extensive national branch network, but will be focused on providing a highly efficient service to the upper sector of the market by way of remote (telephone, postal) banking. This cuts down the need to invest in expensive processing and on-line facilities within the branch, leaving the branches free to act more as sales outlets in carefully selected locations. This strategy does not, of course, preclude generating new non-branch business through carefully targeting prospective customers by direct marketing methods, particularly where the branch low-cost structure makes funds otherwise locked up in premises available for use more productively elsewhere.

Differentiation   Porter (1980) stresses that in adopting this strategic route it is necessary to differentiate the product or service offered, such that it is perceived industry-wide as being unique. Ideally, the firm will differentiate itself on several dimensions.

Examples of successful product differentiation in the UK financial services sector are as yet hard to identify. Where attempts have been made to try to break out of the conventional traditional banking offer, these have not necessarily met with success. The Midland Bank's development of a branded, segmented range of carefully targeted accounts (Meridian, Orchard) has been watched with interest by the rest of the industry. There is scant evidence, though, to suggest that this attempt to brand differentiate the offer to the customer has, in practice, either been understood by the prospective buyer, or been successful in positioning the Midland Bank at the forefront of the market.

In terms of differentiation in delivery systems, this is clearly an area where there has been significant investment recently by the banking and building society industry. This is most obvious in the new branch format designs that have adopted retail display and merchandising principles, and have applied them to transform radically the traditional branch design and layout. These are considered further in Section 3.3.3 and in Chapter 6. Notable among these are the new designs by the Midland Bank (with an emphasis on technology), Lloyds Bank, and new open-plan retail branch concepts by the Halifax, Bristol and West and Abbey National. Also, of course, there is the relatively new branded remote banking service, First Direct, which was launched by the Midland with an advertising campaign that no one could argue was not differentiated from the usual financial services advertising at the time. While First Direct has been relatively slow to build up its customer base (to in excess of 200,000 at the time of writing) and may only just be moving into profitability after some three years, nevertheless it does represent an area of innovative differentiation which competitors are watching very carefully. Again, the nature of the financial services market is such that, at its current stage of evolution, experimental formats such as First Direct are relatively easy to replicate by competitors.

Another area for competitive advantage, however, that may not be so easy to replicate is that of *time*. This issue is explored by Stalk and Hout (1990), who point out that delays in, for example, obtaining a personal loan or a mortgage can materially influence consumers' decisions as to where to build a financial service relationship. Recognizing this, CitiCorp produced a new packaged funding programme in 1986 called MortgagePower that operated through a 37 state sales network of tied estate agents (who paid an annual fee of $2,500 to join the programme). As a result CitiCorp was able to reduce the time to approve a mortgage loan from an average of 45 days to the promise of a decision within 15 days. The reduction in time was achieved by using a combination of electronic mail, lowering the requirement for customer status evidence, restricting loans to a maximum of 80 per cent of the property value, and making a final confirmation dependent upon a subsequent CitiCorp-approved appraisal. As a result, CitiCorp's mortgage lending grew from $5.5 billion in 1986 to $14.8 billion in 1987, putting it at the top of the mortgage origination league. Seven years earlier CitiCorp was not even in the top 100. In truth, however, time is only one of several factors in the whole area of competitive advantage which originates from focusing on giving the customer a superior level of appropriate total service.

Focus   The third area for developing competitive advantage identified by Porter is that of focus. This involves concentrating the business' activities on a particular buyer group, product segment, geographic area, etc. The concept is to serve a particular sector of the market exceptionally well, thus allowing the supplying firm to achieve levels of service and costs that are hard for other more widely-based competitors to achieve.

In financial services in the UK, there is a number of examples where, for example, building societies have decided not to offer a broad portfolio of products to match the major clearing banks offer. Instead, they have focused on doing what they are traditionally strong at, which is offering mortgages, together with convenient and friendly deposit account facilities. Similarly, the TSB has little intention of expanding outside its core customer of mass market BClC2 consumers. This is where it has been traditionally strong—and by focusing on providing appropriate levels of service (including carefully targeted delivery systems and products) the TSB sees little benefit in, for example, chasing after the high net worth customer.

Other clearers have adopted different strategies, and are focusing their marketing and product efforts on addressing the specific needs of narrowly defined target customer segments. Lloyds Bank, for example, has an Asset Management Service for high net worth customers. This offers a comprehensive range of account management and investment services targeted at customers who have an asset value of £50,000. The delivery is through a personal account executive operating from a separate network of Asset Management Service offices.

In deciding whether or not to adopt one of the three generic strategies, Porter stresses that it is important to recognize that each one carries a certain level of risk, and strategies need to be regularly reviewed. For example, cost leadership is vulnerable to:

- Technological change that may negate or reduce the cost advantage.
- Low entry costs of competitors as the markets/technology matures and becomes more widely available.
- An inability for the firm to recognize market shifts because of the single-minded emphasis on cost reduction.
- Inflation which narrows the scope for competitive advantage.

The risks inherent in a differentiated strategy involve:

- Buyers becoming less susceptible to the need for differentiation as they become more sophisticated.
- Price competition from low cost producers erodes customer loyalty based on brand image or service.
- Product imitation narrows the scope for perceived differentiation.

The risks in a focused strategy are that:

- The relative cost of the focuser may increase and either narrow the scope for cost advantage or offset the differentiation achieved.
- The market changes so as to narrow the required differences in products or services between the broad-based and focused suppliers.

- Competitors find sub-markets to exploit, and out-focus the focuser (Porter 1980).

3.1.6   Competing on capabilities

Stalk, Evans and Shulman (1992) put forward a new concept of corporate strategy called 'capabilities-based competition'. They cite a number of instances where established competitors in an industry are being out-manoeuvred and overtaken by more dynamic rivals. Because markets fragment and evolve with increasing speed, and because technology erodes established market sector positions, it is those organizations who have the capabilities to respond and change rapidly to meet identified customer needs who will win.

The five essential dimensions on which a successful capabilities-based company is able to out-perform its competitors are:

1. *Speed* of response to changing market or customer needs.
2. *Consistency* in an ability to produce products or services that unfailingly satisfy customer expectations.
3. *Acuity* in an ability to see the competitive environment clearly and thus anticipate and respond to customers' evolving needs.
4. *Agility* to adapt simultaneously to many different environments.
5. *Innovativeness* in generating new ideas and in combining existing elements to create new sources of value (Stalk, Evans and Shulman, 1992).

In evaluating a company on these dimensions, it is critical to recognize the key role played by the CEO of a successful capabilities-based organization in focusing and directing the company's efforts. Stalk, Evans and Shulman (1992) give two examples of banks in the USA, both of which compete on capabilities but in very different ways, namely Banc One, and Wachovia Corporation. The latter competes through having 600 or so 'personal bankers' who provide its customers with a level of personalized service which approaches that only previously available to private banking clients. In order to achieve this, the company has invested heavily in specialist support systems which include an integrated customer file, simplified work processes that facilitate a response to a customer request by the end of business the same day, and a five year personal banker training programme. Wachovia's focus is on business processes that facilitate the transfer of customer specific information across numerous points of customer contact (each personal banker services and supports some 1,200 customers). However, because the company relies on a very high level of management training, it cannot easily and quickly transfer its specific capability skills to, for example, growth by acquisitions outside its core markets in North Carolina and Atlanta. Nevertheless, it has superior returns and increasing market share in those markets in which it operates.

Banc One, in contrast, has been able to develop its business rapidly by acquisitions, and out-perform its competitors by developing an ability to understand and respond to the needs of entire local communities. Banc One scores by structuring its operations such that it is able to offer the same level of professional expertise, state-of-the-art products, and the competitive cost structure of a large national bank such as Citicorp, as well as maintaining a high level of involvement with each local community. It achieves this by combining decentralized local decision making with group wide guidance and advice. Managers in the 58 separate banks in the Banc One network are encouraged to learn from best practice throughout the network and adopt it to their own markets and operations. Hence, while the individual banks share common management systems and product portfolios, they are relatively free to design and personalize their own pricing strategies and local marketing programmes. Between 1991 and 1992 this policy enabled Banc One to grow its network by a combination of acquisition and internal growth from 587 to 1,328 branches, and its total assets from $30 billion to more than $75 billion.

Only four other US banks—Bank of America, JP Morgan, Chase Manhattan and Bankers Trust—earned more than Banc One's $529.5m of net profit in 1991. In the words of one company slogan, Banc One 'Out-locals the national banks and out-nationals the local banks.'

Both of these banks compete on capabilities by:

1. Focusing on key business processes as the building blocks of corporate strategy.
2. Providing superior value to their customers.
3. Investing in the necessary support infrastructure to deliver the desired standard and quality of service.
4. Vesting decision-making authority at CEO or equivalent local level.

3.2   SEGMENTATION AND TARGETING

Until relatively recently the traditional financial services offer to the consumer was simple both in its concept and in the way it was delivered. Broadly speaking, the main high street suppliers and their core products were:

Banks	Building societies
1. Current account	1. Mortgages
2. Deposit account	2. Savings account
3. Lending	

Delivery was through a network of branches located in the traditional centres of cities, towns and conurbations. New customers were acquired mainly through recommendation (friend or family), through convenience of location or through local long-standing reputation. There was little or no overt marketing, nor was there any understanding of the potentially differing needs of different customers. Products were simple and inflexible, and hence sophisticated segmentation of customers into differing categories with different user requirements was neither recognized as an opportunity for competitive advantage, nor considered desirable or necessary.

This all started to change in the UK in the 1960s, when it clearly emerged in the general retail sector that the more successful high street retailers were beginning to understand the effectiveness of targeting specific customer groups with specific retail formats. For example, Habitat was a huge success in the early 1960s when Terence Conran (later to become Sir Terence Conran) created a total lifestyle concept in home furnishing that had enormous appeal to the younger, more affluent, more independent first time home-makers, and which was far removed from the traditional over-designed unimaginative offer in existing furniture shops and department stores. By targeting that specific group of consumers with a design of retail store and a product range carefully sourced and merchandised to match the customers' needs and expectations, Habitat totally transformed the furniture sector and became a model for other retailers to adopt similar segmented marketing strategies throughout the 1960s and 1970s.

Some of the basic and more complex systems of market segmentation were discussed in Chapter 2. It is clearly important that the variables used for segmentation must be indicative—directly or indirectly—of the target customers' relevant needs, preferences, conceptions or behaviour patterns. The segments thus defined must also be measurable, economically viable and accessible if they are to form the basis for effective targeting. In this section, a number of examples of effective market segmentation are presented, followed by discussion of alternative approaches to targeting.

3.2.1 Examples of effective segmentation

In the area of customer segmentation, the financial services industry has an enormous in-built advantage over other providers of consumer or retail products or services. In theory, a financial retailer has the capability to establish, at the point at which a new customer opens an account, a mass of extremely valuable background data on what kind of person that customer is. For example, information can be sought on:

- Age
- Education
- Income level
- Type of job, company
- Family circumstances
- Leisure pursuits/interests
- Car/home ownership
- Pension/life insurance
- General level of assets
- Where live, type of house etc.

Furthermore, it should then be possible to track that customer's behaviour in relationship to their pattern of account usage and identify key opportunities to sell him or her an extended range of carefully targeted products or services. The key, as will be discussed later, is in matching customer needs to product type, and then being able also to match the delivery system to deliver the product to customers in the way they prefer or find most convenient.

Simple demographic information such as age, sex, income, social class is both reliable and useful in terms of segmenting consumers into broad target market segments. For example, taking age as a segmentation variable allows a range of products and offers to be developed to attract new customers at key points in their potential banking relationship. Age clearly has a close link with lifestage, which is also emerging as a possibly interesting and effective way of segmenting the financial services market. With the opportunity being available to track customer account behaviour over years, it should be possible to identify key points in people's lifestages for products such as home loans, insurances and pension plans as individuals get married, raise families, finance education, and plan retirement. For example, possible segmented lifestages could be:

- Children
- Younger singles
- Independent adults
- Young families
- Better-off established families
- High net worth older couples
- Pensioners

Each of these consumer segments will have different financial product needs for that stage of their lives—depending on each target customer's personal circumstances at that time. Attitudinal segmentation also has attractiveness in the financial services market. This is where customers and potential customers are classified according to their attitude or behaviour when faced with a particular situation. Classifying people into groups based on psychographic segmentation techniques can help develop a better understanding of their needs, wants, concerns and likely behaviour and hence facilitate tailoring an offer specifically to address these issues.

For example, in research that Pragma Consulting has carried out in the area of segmentation of mortgage customers, we identified three main different behavioural customer types. These we called:

1. The New Thinkers, who comprised 40 per cent of mortgage holders
2. The Sophisticates, who comprised 28 per cent of mortgage holders
3. The Traditionalists, who comprised 32 per cent of mortgage holders

The New Thinkers tended to be typical of the new generation of home owners—more down market, lower income, least educated, and at the lower end of the housing market in price. They were most likely to have a building society mortgage. Interestingly, they were characterized as responding warmly to personal contact and were most likely to have been influenced by a personal recommendation. They had the highest level of mortgages obtained through intermediaries.

The Sophisticates we found to be diametrically opposed to The New Thinkers, being up-market and sophisticated. They moved house most frequently, had more cars, travelled abroad for holidays, read quality papers (*The Times*), and were most likely to have their mortgage with a bank. They tended to shop around, rather than go direct to the mortgage provider.

The Traditionalists were Mr and Mrs Average. They were the slowest movers and tended to read the *Daily Express* and the *Sun*.

In our research, we established that there were two principal factors that sharply divided each group's attitudes towards their uptake of mortgage products. These were:

1. *Conservatism/loyalty* the degree to which people are prepared to depart from conventional practice and established previous habits.
2. *Attitudes* towards working through intermediaries as opposed to a direct relationship with a mortgage supplier.

A closer examination of these customer groups revealed a very different set of attitudes between the three cluster types when asked for their views in respect of mortgage behaviour. In Figure 3.6, the New Thinkers and the Traditionalists showed very similar levels of response (measured in terms of mean scores) to statements relating to conservatism or loyalty factors. The Sophisticates, however, were clearly less committed to the more conventional established mortgage providers, and shopped around for the best deal for themselves. Figure 3.7, on the other hand, shows that in respect of the use of intermediaries for advice and sourcing of a mortgage there was a sharp difference between the attitude of the New Thinkers (who subscribed to the benefits of using intermediaries for mortgage advice) and the Traditionalists who clearly preferred to go direct to the mortgage provider.

We were then able to combine the results of this attitudinal analysis to develop a behavioural map showing the different positioning of the three target market customer groups in relationship to the two factors of conservatism/loyalty, and interest in using intermediaries. This is shown in the mortgage cluster positioning map in Figure 3.8. By understanding customer behaviour and attitudes in this way, the supplier is able to target the offer much more precisely and effectively in terms of both product and method of delivery. For example, the New Thinkers welcome personal advice, and prefer the security of a large established bank or building society. Hence they represent a good potential prospect for a traditional supplier.

The Sophisticates, however, are more aware and more able to value the offer, so they look for the best terms and will shop around. Hence they are perhaps less easy to market to through conventional means of distribution. A direct sales approach or telephone selling might be more effective.

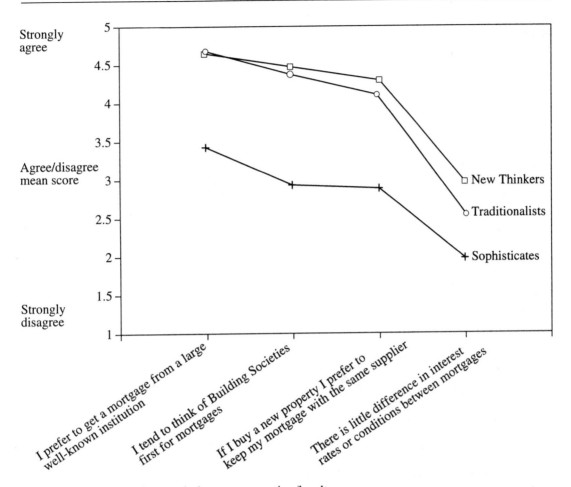

Figure 3.6   Mortgage cluster solutions—conservatism/loyalty
Source: Pragma Consulting

The Traditionalists, on the other hand, are unlikely to represent a hot prospect in new business generation terms as they tend to be hard to convert from their existing supplier.

Campbell-Keegan and Consensus Research have used a similar approach to classifying general users of financial services into five types of borrower. These are shown in Table 3.1.

Another approach to segmentation which has received wide usage by the financial services sector recently is that of geodemographics, which is based on a combination of demographic, geographic and lifestyle characteristics. One major system is ACORN, which stands for 'A Classification Of Residential Neighbourhoods'. The system was developed by CACI Information Services. Table 3.2 shows ACORN's 38 neighbourhood types, the 11 groups they form, and their share of the GB population of 54,841,359 in 1992. ACORN is based on the government's Census of Great Britain, conducted in 1981. Census neighbourhoods are updates derived from CACI's proprietary demographic model of Great Britain.

These groupings, with their 38 neighbourhood type sub-groupings, have the advantage of being very easy to measure and relate to. In particular, it has been possible to give each postcode in the UK an ACORN classification which is a descriptor of the predominant type of household to be found in that postcode. By relating financial services behaviour to type of household, the

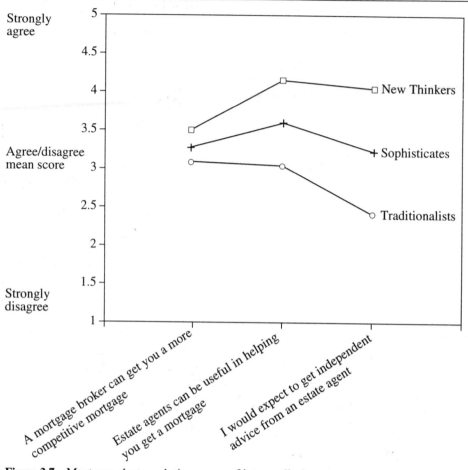

Figure 3.7   Mortgage cluster solutions – use of intermediaries
Source: Pragma Consulting

Table 3.1   Consumer segmentation in UK retail finance

Suggested types of borrower

Traditionalist	Conservative in approach to money. Savers rather than spenders. Loyal to institutions. Suspicious of change and financial innovations (26% of population).
Anxious	Derive no pleasure in finances and regard institutions as threatening. Respond well to personal relationships with account managers. (21% of population)
Connoisseur	Informed and sophisticated, though not necessarily in high finance bracket. (19% of population)
Carefree	Money as a means to an end, the route to fun. Tend to have variable relationships with the bank mangers. Interested in credit. (19% of population)
Pragmatist	Confident about money matters. Balanced and practical view of money. (14% of population)

Source: Based on survey of 2,000 adults undertaken for Consumer Finance Segmentation. Campbell-Keegan and Consensus. Reported in the *Financial Times*, 23 April 1987

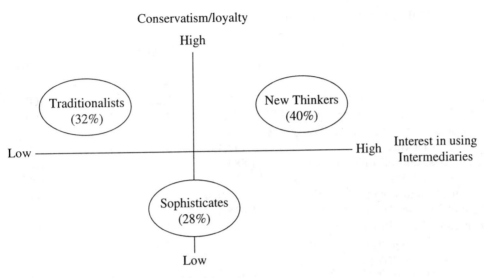

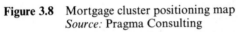

Figure 3.8   Mortgage cluster positioning map
Source: Pragma Consulting

Table 3.2   CACI ACORN profile of Great Britain

			1992 population		
		1992 pop	*%*	*Base %*	*Index*
	ACORN Groups				
A	Agricultural areas	1,808,289	3.3	3.3	100
B	Modern family housing, higher incomes	9,729,155	17.7	17.7	100
C	Older housing of intermediate status	9,853,739	18.0	18.0	100
D	Older terraced housing	2,278,829	4.2	4.2	100
E	Council estates – category I	7,244,456	13.2	13.3	100
F	Council estates – category II	4,780,317	8.7	8.7	100
G	Council estates – category II	3,786,994	6.9	6.9	100
H	Mixed inner metropolitan areas	2,084,520	3.8	3.8	100
I	High status non-family areas	2,236,048	4.1	4.1	100
J	Affluent suburban house	8,667,293	15.8	15.8	100
K	Better-off retirement areas	2,079,121	3.8	3.8	100
	ACORN Types				
A1	Agricultural villages	1,412,501	2.6	2.6	100
A2	Areas of farms and smallholdings	395,788	0.7	0.7	100
B3	Post-war functional private housing	2,421,013	4.4	4.4	100
B4	Modern private housing, young families	2,025,081	3.7	3.7	100
B5	Established private family housing	3,324,090	6.1	6.1	100
B6	New detached houses, young families	1,593,510	2.9	2.9	100
B7	Military bases	365,461	0.7	0.7	100
C8	Mixed owner-occupied and council estates	1,917,117	3.5	3.5	100
C9	Small town centres and flats above shops	2,256,713	4.1	4.1	100
C10	Villages with non-farm employment	2,669,426	4.9	4.9	100

Continued

Table 3.2 CACI ACORN profile of Great Britain (*continued*)

	1992 pop	1992 population %	Base %	Index
C11 Older-private housing, skilled workers	3,010,483	5.5	5.5	100
D12 Unmodernized terraces, older people	1,340,565	2.4	2.4	100
D13 Older terraces, lower income families	740,773	1.4	1.4	100
D14 Tenement flats lacking amenities	197,491	0.4	0.4	100
E15 Council estates, well-off older workers	1,885,515	3.4	3.4	100
E16 Recent council estates	1,570,548	2.9	2.9	100
E17 Better council estates, younger workers	2,752,924	5.0	5.0	100
E18 Small council house, often Scottish	1,035,459	1.9	1.9	100
F19 Low rise estates in industrial towns	2,495,409	4.6	4.6	100
F20 Inter-war council estates, older people	1,545,665	2.8	2.8	100
F21 Council housing, elderly people	739,243	1.3	1.3	100
G22 New council estates in inner cities	1,066,907	1.9	1.9	100
G23 Overspill estates, higher unemployment	1,605,080	2.9	2.9	100
G24 Council estates with some overcrowding	813,935	1.5	1.5	100
G25 Council estates with greatest hardship	301,072	0.5	0.5	100
H26 Multi-occupied older housing	201,147	0.4	0.4	100
H27 Cosmopolitan owner-occupied terraces	572,500	1.0	1.0	100
H28 Multi-let housing in cosmopolitan areas	384,880	0.7	0.7	100
H29 Better-off cosmopolitan areas	925,993	1.7	1.7	100
I30 High status non-family area	1,137,812	2.1	2.1	100
I31 Multi-let big old houses and flats	817,869	1.5	1.5	100
I32 Furnished flats, mostly single people	280,367	0.5	0.5	100
J33 Inter-war semis, white collar workers	3,114,205	5.7	5.7	100
J34 Spacious inter-war semis, big gardens	2,740,714	5.0	5.0	100
J35 Villages with wealthy older commuters	1,563,183	2.9	2.9	100
J36 Detached houses, exclusive suburbs	1,249,191	2.3	2.3	100
K37 Private house, well-off older residents	1,246,536	2.3	2.3	100
K38 Private flats, older single people	832,585	1.5	1.5	100
U39 Unclassified	292,598	0.5	0.5	100
AREA TOTAL	54,841,359	100.0	100.0	

propensity of each postcode to respond to a given financial services offer can be, in part, determined. Clearly, in practice, some of the classifications are shown to be better predictors than others.

Other developments in this area of geodemographic segmentation include FiNPiN coding (Pinpoint Analysis) and MOSAIC (CCN). In both cases, the approach was to cross-reference other research-based data on the uptake of financial services to the original geodemographic descriptor. For example, Pinpoint Analysis cross-tabulated their PiN code against the usage pattern of financial services established by the Financial Research Survey (FRS is a national regular survey of respondents' usage of financial products). From this cross-tabulation, a more industry specific classification was produced of FiNPiN types, as described in Chapter 2.

As database-held information on customer behaviour becomes more comprehensive and competitor analysis techniques become more advanced, we are seeing more sophisticated statistically-based segmentation models being developed. One area that looks promising in terms of its long-term potential is that of behavioural scoring or profiling. For example, this technique could be used to build up a score card which could predict the likelihood of future bad debt in existing credit card holding accounts by analysing the current payment patterns of account holders.

Field (1992) gives an insight into the future potential of applying artificial intelligence techniques, in particular neural networks and rule induction, in combination with statistical modelling to predict and model credit card holders' future pattern of behaviour. Such analysis allows each card holder to be allocated to a particular behaviour profile group. Different groups with clearly identified different behaviour patterns can be targeted with specific product offers to stimulate card usage, thus boosting that group's profitability. Such an approach also has the added advantage of allowing the user to respond more quickly to identified changes in card holder needs. These can be triggered by changes in card usage patterns that could indicate, for example, either a marketing opportunity, or perhaps the need to reduce credit limits or levy payment charges if a card holder's account balance starts to exceed certain pre-determined limits.

3.2.2 Method of targeting

In researching this chapter, discussions were held with a number of senior executives within banks, building societies and insurance companies. Although much consensus emerged from these discussions, there were interesting contrasts of opinion in the area of customer focus and targeting. Some of the respondents considered that the way forward lay in very careful analysis and modelling of the customer database, with each customer being given a score based either on lifestage, lifestyle or behavioural modelling. These segmented customers would then be sold to by way of carefully focused branded products, using direct selling methods such as mail, telephone or one-to-one salesperson.

Other respondents considered that the solution lay with investing in building a long-term customer relationship based on the overall brand image of the business, and then offering a wide range of unbranded products, simple to understand, delivered through a multi-channel delivery system. To deliver this successfully means establishing a high level of overall consumer awareness, and national or at least strong regional branch coverage. This approach means that it is then less necessary to identify and sell to individual customers by complex segmentation processes, relying instead on each customer automatically including that supplier in his or her repertoire of providers to visit when shopping around. The difference between these two approaches, described as micro-targeting and global targeting, is illustrated schematically in Figures 3.9 and 3.10.

By adopting the micro-targeting approach illustrated in Figure 3.9, the implication is the need to have dedicated products delivered down a dedicated distribution system focused on a specific target customer or group of customers. The global targeting strategy in Figure 3.10 has the advantage of needing less investment in target marketing techniques, but more investment in overall brand image marketing. The level of investment in distribution is probably not too dissimilar, though the facilities themselves will differ in their functions, needs and degree of customer focus.

Target customer segment by lifestyle

	Student	First-time buyer	Family	Retired	High net worth
Student loan					
Mortgage					
Product Insurance					
Pension					
Asset management					

Figure 3.9   Micro-targeting

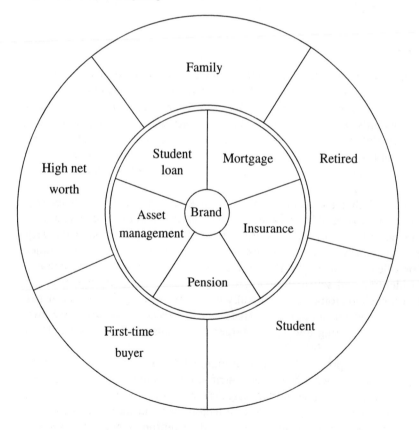

Figure 3.10   Global targeting

Micro-targeting requires a dedicated support team to deliver the product message appropriately to the customer group on a one-to-one basis. But this approach should as a consequence benefit from a high level of credibility at the point of sale. Global targeting, on the other hand, relies on convincing a wider group of customers with differing needs that the supplier has the right product for them, delivered at the right price and in the most convenient way. Hence the key barriers to be overcome in marketing such a proposition are those of credibility and capability. Is the offer itself credible to the consumer, and does the financial retailer have the apparent capability to deliver the product and support that the customer is looking for?

The Halifax Building Society, for example, together with the Abbey National, has taken the view that the overall brand approach will probably be the most cost-effective method of building profitable sales. Hence all the Halifax marketing efforts are aimed at reinforcing the core values of the Halifax brand. These are that the Halifax stands for:

1. *Size*   No.1 building society in the UK, secure, reliable, solid, stable, safe, trustworthy.
2. *Approachability and accessibility*   by emphasizing people and interpersonal relationships in the Halifax advertising.
3. *Professionalism*   especially in the area of new products, by stressing the level of professional expertise and support.

Hence the Halifax is seeking to build a 'cradle-to-grave' relationship with its customers, convincing them through its brand image and its offer of a 'lifetime portfolio' of products that it can meet their needs at any stage in their lives.

On the other hand, the Cheltenham and Gloucester, not having the same national coverage as the Halifax, has sharply focused its offer and carefully targeted its customer base. It concentrates more on investment products, and has not opted for mass market card-based products or ATM networks. The product range is smaller; the target customer has higher balances to invest; and at branch level there is an emphasis on reducing costs by focusing on personal selling, rather than on offering cash deposits, withdrawals and account enquiry facilities where the relationship is postal and telephone based.

The Leeds Building Society has also focused its offer by not offering money transmission, but instead giving high levels of added value customer service. One such packaged product is the Leeds Home Arranger service, which offers the customer not only a mortgage and the associated insurance products when buying a house, but the backup of a dedicated support team who will progress-chase the actual house purchase and sale transaction so as to anticipate and overcome any problem that may arise in such areas as surveys, title searches, drawing up the legal contracts, etc.

These are examples of different approaches to customer marketing and selling. Nevertheless, the problem that the industry to date has yet to solve is how to identify the 'trigger point' at which any given customer is motivated to shop for and buy a financial service product. As discussed in Chapter 2, much more research into customer behaviour is needed to understand those factors that contribute to customers' level of awareness, their decision to include a particular supplier on their list, the comparative shopping process involved, and the actual buying decision itself.

3.3   KEY ELEMENTS OF STRATEGIC IMPLEMENTATION

The importance of customer segmentation is that it enables suppliers of the product or service to focus their marketing efforts on those sectors of the target market which are considered either to be the most commercially rewarding, or to have a particularly good fit with a supplier's product or distribution strengths. This need to focus the marketing efforts of the organization is particularly important, given the increases in competition analysed in Chapter 1, and the more complex patterns of buyer behaviour discussed in Chapter 2.

This section considers six key elements of strategic implementation, forming a prelude for the more detailed treatments within the chapters that follow:

1. Customer/non-customer definition
2. Product specification
3. Delivery system specification
4. Marketing and point of sale promotion
5. Customer service
6. Back office support functions

Unless the provider of the financial service has successfully addressed each of these areas it is unlikely that the full market sector opportunity will be realized. Each of these will be discussed in turn.

3.3.1 Customer/non-customer definition

We have seen earlier in Section 3.2 that there is a number of ways in which the consumer market for financial services can be segmented. However, this is simply the external aspect of defining the target market. What is also needed in determining an effective strategy is information relating to the actual profitability of that segment to the bank or financial institution concerned. As matters stand today, there is still much further work needed in the UK market to understand and quantify the current and potential profitability of a given customer of a bank or of a building society.

Traditionally, banks and building societies maintained their customer records at branch level and held them by account type. Hence there was no effective data held by customer name (other than the manager's own perception) to indicate the current or potential profitability of any given customer to the bank. This situation arose because the mentality and *modus operandi* of a bank has been that of a product provider, and the operational culture has been product-driven rather than customer-need driven. Today, huge investments are being made by all the traditional clearing banks and building societies to reorganize their customer data and behavioural information into file structures that will allow real marketing opportunities to be identified and capitalized on.

As a result of such efforts—focused firstly on determining product profitability and secondly on identifying actual customer profitability—banks and building societies are today in a better position to be able to implement programmes designed to increase the return, or reduce the losses, from key sections of their customer base. Hence the decision in 1991 by Lloyds Bank, Barclays and others to impose annual fees of £12–£15 on credit card users where previously the card was provided free. The reason for this change in strategy was simply that more sophisticated users were carefully operating their accounts so that they could enjoy up to 60 days free credit—hence reducing their profitability to the banks to unacceptably low levels.

Similar analysis by the Halifax Building Society recently identified segments of its customer base where the account balances were maintained at very low levels, and the account activity was also low. The conclusion was reached that the cost of maintaining such accounts would be uneconomic unless additional charges were made to those customers. It was felt that the potential risk of losing some customers by imposing such charges was worthwhile in strict short-term commercial terms. (This does, however, raise key questions of how such policies should be implemented such as to reduce the risk of customer backlash.)

One of the real problems of such focused short-term profit-segmentation policies at present is that the true nature of an individual's *total* relationship with the bank or building society is not fully understood, nor taken account of. For example, without additional information on a particular customer that supports the premise that their account relationship is not in the bank's best interest, there is a risk of alienating customers who may have the underlying potential to be highly profitable to the bank in the longer term. This clearly shows the need for more sophisticated total customer management programmes based around behavioural scoring techniques. The opportunities that could be generated by the application of such data driven marketing systems to focus marketing efforts more effectively is highlighted by Swanson and Walker (1991).

3.3.2   Product specification

The development of a range of products which is appropriate for the target customers' identified needs is critical to generating and sustaining sales. However, again this is only one half of the story, since the product range must also have the potential both to be profit-earning for the financial service supplier and to be deliverable through an appropriate distribution system.

In studying the options available to, say, a bank as a traditional full-service provider, Figure 3.11 highlights the need to consider products in terms of both profit margin and sales volume. Clearly, in the past it has been just as attractive for a bank to sell a large number of home loans at relatively low margins as it was to operate (at least until the recent trend to offer interest on current accounts) a current or deposit account that had higher net margins to the bank. However, as Figure 3.11 shows, the goal of achieving a high profit contribution by having a portfolio of high margin accounts that also sell in high volumes is subject to the competitive market pressures that force margins down and increase the competition for customer account acquisition.

Figure 3.11 shows several routes that can be followed in product development, range extension and marketing. Low contribution, low margin products should be seen as providing account support to ensure that customers are more favourably disposed towards, and hence 'locked into', their main current account or other key account relationship. Low margin products need very effective mass marketing, but provide the opportunity to cross-sell other products to the customer that are not merely interest-related (e.g., life insurance, house insurance).

Current accounts, which used to be highly profitable to banks, need to be regarded more as a 'hanger' on which to position a wide range of personal products and services. This can be seen in the Midland's development of packaged branded accounts such as Orchard and Meridian, which offer specific target customer groups a range of complementary linked services based around the traditional current account (see Table 3.3). Further, detailed discussion of product development and the management of the product range is contained within Chapter 7.

3.3.3   Delivery system specification

An area which is receiving considerable attention throughout the whole of the financial service sector is that of effective product delivery and distribution. Traditionally, customers banked locally, and their account relationship was with a particular local branch. Their account records were maintained and kept by that branch, and day-by-day transactions were usually conducted

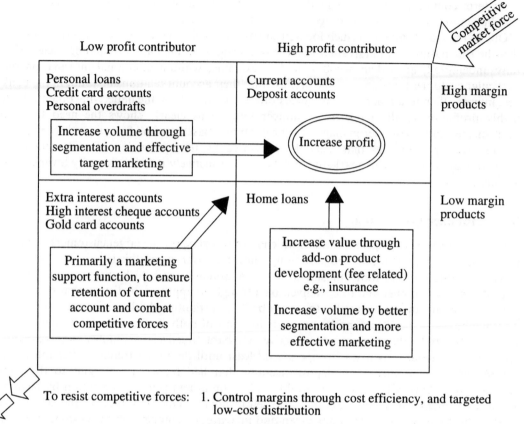

Figure 3.11   Product profit/contribution matrix
Source: Pragma

Table 3.3   Differentiated current accounts: Midland Bank

Orchard	*Meridian*
• Current account	• Current account with interest
• Requirement—£400 p.m. income	• Monthly credit/debit balance of £1000 (or £10 fee per month)
• Cheque book	
• Autocheque card	• £250 Autocheque card
- Switch	• High interest savings account with sweep facility
- Cashflow ATM	
- £50 cheque card	
• Standing orders	• Standing orders
• Monthly statement	• Fully itemized statement on current account and balance on savings account

at the branch itself. Clearly, several developments have made this behaviour pattern obsolete, primarily driven by the fact that the customer is seeking maximum flexibility and convenience in their day-to-day banking arrangements. Delivery systems now include:

- The branch network as a whole
- Other organizations' ATMs with reciprocity
- Lobby services
- ATMs at non-branch locations
- Intermediaries
- Direct sales forces
- Telephone banking
- Postal banking

The clearest evidence of change in the basic role of the branch can be seen in the many 'retail concept' branches that have been developed over the last five years in the UK. These new designs were the outcome of a belated recognition that the traditional product-focused, transaction-related, branch design was wholly inappropriate as a vehicle for selling the wider range of products and services to the more sophisticated retail customer of the 1990s. The key design elements of the move from the traditional product-focused branch format to the new retail customer-focused format are shown in Figure 3.12. The most significant changes here were to open up the branch, take away the barriers between staff and customers, separate processing from selling functions (locating the former eventually in a remote location), and change the balance of space from 30 per cent customer/70 per cent staff to 70 per cent customer/30 per cent staff. This then allowed much more customer/staff interaction and enhanced the opportunity for the branch to communicate with and sell to customers.

The application of communications and computer technology has allowed the traditional account management back-office functions of a branch to be relocated away from the actual branch itself. This has had two benefits: first it has enabled the branch to make more effective use of its space for selling purposes; secondly, it has increased the overall efficiency of the branch network through cost reduction and economies of scale that result from centralizing the processing functions of a number of branches. This has resulted in the concept of network design known as 'hub and spoke'. This was described more fully by Channon (1988) and is discussed within the context of network hierarchies within Chapter 4.

The objective that many banks and building societies in the UK are seeking today is that of *transparency*. This is where, from the customer point of view, there is no obvious barrier at any stage between him or her and their banking relationship or transaction. In practice, this means that the customer can access his or her account, and obtain the full range of services provided by the bank at any branch in the network that they might visit. In order to deliver this successfully, each individual customer's record, personal history file and value to/relationship with the bank needs to be available and accessible on-line at any time in all branches or as appropriate through the telephone or, to a more limited extent, through the ATM network. Not only is this a considerable task to achieve in practice, given the complex current account handling and processing functions in most banks, but it also has major implications for customer service and selling at branch level. Clearly, to deliver effective service means being able to respond to customer enquiries across the product range, either face-to-face, in branches, direct or remotely such as over the telephone. This demands investment in sales staff with good selling and interpersonal skills, backed up by a simplified rather than a more complex range of products, with access to the appropriate product information and signing-on procedures at the point of sale. All of this is as yet in its infancy in the current state of the development of financial services in the UK today.

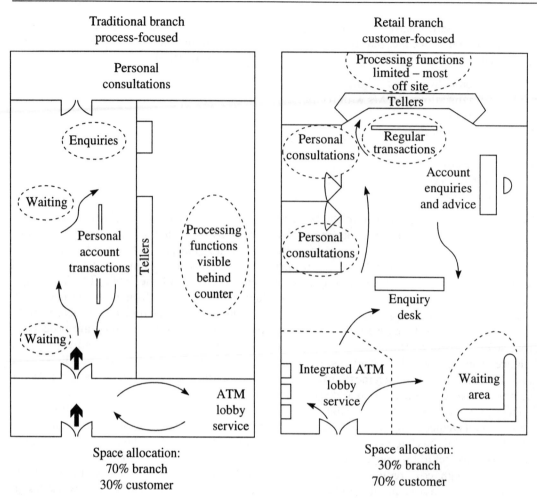

Figure 3.12   Changes in retail branch focus

One of the most interesting developments in the UK recently has been the Midland Bank's launch of First Direct; a branded 24 hours a day telephone banking service. This got off to a somewhat slow start, as the concept was both unfamiliar and the advertising (featuring surrealist scenes), while thought-provoking, lacked focus and clarity. Some two years into the project, the number of First Direct accounts opened was stated to be in excess of 200,000. This was by no means a dramatic success, but it is a clear indication of the opportunity, even in a highly conservative market characterized by huge customer inertia, to build sales with an innovative targeted and differentiated product.

First Direct's advertising is now much more specific, and the key facilities of the product that are being promoted are:

- A remote, telephone banking relationship
- 24 hours service, 365 days of the year
- A full range of banking services, based around a current account structure
- Trained staff dedicated to customer service and response

- Current account interest rates higher than other clearing banks (due to lower overheads and no branch costs)
- A £100 standard cheque guarantee card, which is also a debit card on the Switch network
- A £500 per day cash withdrawal facility, which can be made from Midland, NatWest, TSB, Northern or Clydesdale bank cash machines
- Free banking if in credit, with no transaction charges, and an agreed overdraft at time of opening the account

The appeal of First Direct is to a specific target customer group, who wish either to conduct all their banking in such a manner, or to have the opportunity so to do, hence opening a First Direct account in addition to their more traditional branch-based account relationship. First Direct encourage this in their advertising, stressing to new customers that they do not need to close their existing account but that they should simply compare the difference between the two over time and make their own minds up as to which is better.

The development of non-branch remote banking has raised concern that the lack of personal contact could mean that the opportunity to sell a wider range of personal finance products is lost. These concerns are unquestionably legitimate, as experience shows that the more complex financial services do need to be *sold*. To do this effectively usually implies some form of interpersonal, face-to-face relationship. The success of selling insurance products through the branch network—known as bancassurance—illustrates the opportunity to generate revenues that are profit and commission related rather than interest or account transaction fee related. Not only can such sales be effected through the branch network to the one-third or so of customers who regularly visit their branch, it is also possible, as Lloyds Bank has shown by its investment in Abbey Life and the development of the Black Horse Financial Services Division, to capitalize on the customer/bank relationship by offering other services delivered through non-bank branch distribution methods. The strategy here is to maximize the sale of products to current customers by offering, for example, insurance sold by a direct sales force through Lloyds Abbey Life, house purchase or sale through a national estate agency network branded as Black Horse Agencies, other personal financial and insurance products through Black Horse Financial Services and Lloyds Bank Insurance Services, with Lloyds Bowmaker providing specialist skills in the area of leasing.

One of the interesting aspects of the First Direct offer of remote telephone banking is that it implicitly should allow a higher level of skilled response to be provided. By centralizing the operation and taking it away from a branch network of hundreds of branches, it then becomes feasible and economical to recruit and train a core of customer service executives with all the skills needed to deliver and support the service. By 1992, for example, the TSB had some 1,400 branches, 2,100 ATMs, and 57 remote customer service centres. The objective by the late 1990s is to rationalize the branches to perhaps half that number, with a carefully designed network to ensure that the branches that do remain are carefully targeted and sized for their local market. A more extensive and sophisticated ATM network, positioned where customers most need to have access (i.e., not necessarily at a branch location) will help provide the day-to-day money transaction needs. Additional service and advice will be provided by telephone linking to the service centres which might eventually be rationalized down to just half-a-dozen that will be focused on providing a full remote banking and account enquiry service to address the 20–30 per cent of customer business which TSB currently estimates could be telephone-based. The reduction in cost then allows investment to be put into providing enhanced customer services, reducing account charges, increasing rates on investment products, and investing in further cost-reduction programmes. It becomes a virtuous circle of lower costs and improved service.

Nevertheless, the importance of the branch is not to be overlooked—even if its role changes. To quote David Pirrie, Director of UK Retail Banking, Lloyds Bank:

We must respect the needs of our customer and meet their rising expectations. In achieving this, we must recognize the reality of the professional relationship with the customer. This should be viewed more like that of a doctor or lawyer than a retailer or shop keeper. The branch should be like a consulting room where customers come for advice, rather than a shop where they just come in, 'buy' and leave. Lloyds Bank believes that this relationship deepens at each stage in a customer's life—for as the life cycle progresses, new sales opportunities appear. At each stage advice is required, and as the professional relationship evolves, links with the customer's branch are strengthened. (Pirrie, 1990)

The Alliance and Leicester is an interesting example of a forward-thinking building society that is moving increasingly into becoming a full banking service provider. The most significant step in this direction was taken in the late 1980s with the acquisition of Girobank, the UK post office-based banking service. The initial three key objectives of this acquisition were:

1. To acquire an on-going current account business
2. To acquire a credit card
3. To have access to the 2.5 million Girobank customers

What Girobank also provided, though, was a fully developed telephone and postal banking system, together with a highly efficient cash-handling service for customers in retailing, operating through a branch network of 20,000 post offices at relatively low cost. Alliance and Leicester regard Girobank as effectively the bank of the future, with all the communication and database technology in place, and already delivering a full non-branch based service through five regional centres. The opportunity to reposition the Alliance and Leicester local branch network with an emphasis on selling an enhanced range of products, with Girobank providing the basic banking service together with an enhanced telephone sales service is clear and appealing. In many ways, the Alliance and Leicester is an excellent example of a financial service provider in the UK, that is starting to understand how it can compete on its capabilities.

Another interesting experiment which has proved very successful is the Royal Bank of Scotland's 'Direct Line' telephone insurance operation. This was set up to challenge the traditional approach of selling insurance through a broker network with high commissions and relatively high delivery costs compared to the volume of business transacted. Direct Line is a telephone-based insurance provider set up to quote and transact business over the telephone. It is a highly successful example of:

- A new distribution channel
- A new entrant (though backed by an established bank)
- A highly cost-effective approach
- A focus on low operational costs which has introduced a new pricing structure to the market
- Excellent levels of service based on convenience, speed and value

Other developments in distribution have focused on providing self-service branch banking through fully automated high street branches. There have been a number of such moves across Europe, often driven by different requirements in specific countries. In Italy, Banca Commerciala Italiana has plans to expand its 500 branch network by a further 200 'Banca Non Stop' outlets throughout the country. Italy is fundamentally under-branched with 2.4 branches per 10,000 population compared with 6.5 in France and Germany, and 4.3 in Britain; this development is seen as a more cost-effective way of opening up hundreds of local branches in towns where a full service branch simply would not be economical.

In Portugal, the country's second largest bank, Banco Portugues do Atlantico, developed its fully automated branches 'Los Automatica' as a response to the control by the central banking system on branch openings. The authorization that is needed to open a full service manned branch could take over a year, but this restriction has not applied to automated branches—hence self-service banking is one of the more obvious routes to rapid network expansion. Typical services offered in such fully automated branches include terminals for:

- Cash dispensing
- Cheque issuing
- Foreign exchange
- Account transfers
- Insurance quotes
- Interactive videos for information
- Credit (using on-line credit scoring)
- Ticket ordering (football in Italy)
- Night safe depositing for small businesses

While the initial investment in technology is high, the lower costs in staff, together with the need for less space resulting in site cost savings, means that the projected payback period for such automated branches can be under three years.

3.3.4 Marketing and point of sale promotion

Retail marketing involves more than simply advertising and promotional activity to support and sell a branded product or service. In financial services it encompasses factors that include:

- The corporate brand
- Media advertising
- The premises themselves (internal, external, location etc.)
- The product range offered
- The level and type of personal service
- Point of sale information

The role of *corporate branding* in financial services is to convey trust and integrity in the customer's perception of the financial institution concerned. This clearly is even more important, given the recent adverse publicity which surrounded such situations as the worldwide collapse of the Bank of Credit and Commerce International, and the impact of unforeseen levels of claims on the members of Lloyds of London insurance market.

Hence much of bank *media advertising* has, in the past, tended to stress the traditional role of banks, and has been aimed at communicating images of solidity and reliability. Lloyds Bank's Leo McKern advertising of the 1980s was developed both to communicate these brand strengths as well as provide a bridge to a more customer-friendly responsive image. In many ways, the original mid 1960s campaign of 'The Bank Manager in the Cupboard' was in advance of its time when it was developed, jointly by the banks, as a response to the then perceived threat from National Giro.

Certainly, the difference between the collective image of the banks in the UK and that of the building societies is very marked, and represents a real challenge for the banks. The building societies' image tends to be much more customer-friendly and service-related (see Chapter 2), and they have capitalized on this in the corporate image advertising. The function of premises is that, apart from their key role as part of the delivery system, they act as a focus for the corporate brand on the high street. Hence the image of the branch, from outside and in its internal environmental treatment, is critical.

In detailed research that Pragma Consulting undertook in 1990 into those factors that motivate customers to choose a particular branch at which to open an account, we identified a number of key influencing factors. These included:

- The exact location of the branch in relation to the competition and its local town centre
- The external treatment of the building; was it traditional, or did it look more like a shop?
- Its external signage
- The proportion of the exterior that was glazed
- Its length of frontage
- The number and visibility of external ATMs
- Whether it had a lobby service
- The standard and type of interior design
- The total floor area
- The number of teller positions etc.

We established that some of these factors were more important than others in influencing people's decision of choice of branch. Hence it was necessary to develop weighting factors such that any given branch could be scored on a common set of criteria. In this way, each branch could be compared both with its immediate local competitor branches and with the total portfolio of 1,000 branches in the UK network. By utilizing such an approach and combining it with catchment analysis, branch trading performance analysis and further specific consumer research, it was possible to develop strategies to focus each branch on that specific combination of premises design, location and local marketing effort which had the capability of generating the most new account business.

3.3.5 Customer service

Customer service has been expounded by nearly all retail customer-focused businesses, including banks, building societies and other financial service providers, as *the* single most important area for developing a long-term sustainable competitive advantage. While much has undoubtedly been achieved since service became fully recognized as an issue in the late 1980s, we are still far from the Japanese city banks where the response is that 'the customer is always right'. In a recent article, Arnold (1991) referred to the training guidelines produced by an Australian bank during a project entitled 'Project People—Getting Along with People'. Two of the guidelines related to 'Understanding People' and to 'Customer Contact'.

1. *Understanding people:* The first step in getting along with others is to develop an understanding of them. You will be better able to do this if you remember that there are two sides to every relationship and consider how you would feel in the other person's position. Showing a person that you are genuinely interested in him/her is only treating him/her as you yourself would like to be treated.
2. *Customer contact:* In respect of 'customer contact', staff were trained to recognize that:

- A customer is not an interruption to our work—he or she is the whole purpose for it.
- She or he is not dependent upon the bank—the bank is dependent upon him or her.
- She or he is not just a transaction—she or he is a person; in fact she or he is the most important person in the branch.
- It is up to each of us to see that she or he gets the best and friendliest service.

Customer service in banking in the UK has to move a long way before it starts to address such issues satisfactorily. Simply providing longer opening hours and weekend opening, while helpful in transactions, does not in the end compensate for lack of service in other areas such as accurate basic account maintenance and effective face-to-face communication.

An area of concern, as the market for financial services becomes ever more complex and more competitive, it that of the quality and effectiveness of front-line customer-focused staff. The real goal—that still remains elusive today—is simply that of providing a good quality *basic* error-free banking service. This means simply running the standard day-by-day account and service activities at a level of service that all bank and building society customers wish to receive. There is little point in developing sophisticated segmented targeted products if the basic day-to-day account activities cannot be delivered with 100 per cent reliability. This not only implies developing and investing in fool-proof systems, but also necessitates a complete rethinking of the calibre of staff needed at each level in the customer-focused operation. The challenge is to provide an exceptional level of basic service at branch level with the existing staff resources. As the majority of bank staff were not recruited when such customer-handling skills were considered necessary, it is becoming increasingly doubtful that the required level of one-to-one service can be provided within the staff resources of existing networks. Two clear needs emerge:

1. To redesign the banking process such that it is simple to operate, and simple to deliver and support.
2. To redesign the people so that they have the skills and capabilities to deliver the product.

The current emphasis within many organizations is for staff to achieve performance targets at each level in the organization. This is based on the end objective of meeting earnings per share and return on capital targets. The fact that such targets are achieved at each level, and hence the end result in the short-term is good for the share price, masks the fact that along the way no account has been taken of the long-term impact on customer attitudes and customer satisfaction. Simply putting up charges to reflect the true costs of running accounts, or weeding out 'unprofitable' accounts, can clearly have a short-term beneficial impact on profit ratios and is easy to measure. But it does not take account of the longer term implications of customers becoming alienated by such a hard-edged, performance-driven approach.

3.3.6   Back office support functions

Clearly, the massive levels of investment that have recently been directed by the industry at premises design, marketing campaigns, and staff selection and training will not in themselves achieve the desired twin goals of enhanced customer service and reduced cost. These key components of the marketing mix rely to a large extent on the effectiveness of the back office support functions that are necessary to process transactions and to keep customer account records and personal files up to date.

The development of hub and spoke branch networks is an attempt both to improve standards of service and to reduce the cost of providing this at branch level. To do this effectively means major investment in branch re-design, systems technology, communication and data processing links, and customer databases. These all involve a high level of costs and the danger is that the result of providing such facilities and information remote from the branch (but accessible to it) may result in an inflexible and impersonal offer to the customer. Nevertheless, the freeing-off of staff for redeploying in customer-focused selling and communication areas should help considerably in the banks' and building societies' objectives of increasing their effective personal marketing and selling capabilities in the later 1990s.

The chairmen, chief executive and directors interviewed confirmed that there will continue to be acute pressure to reduce costs in the network and across the whole delivery system. This will be achieved by adopting more cost-effective distribution techniques and by a combination of more effective customer acquisition programmes and cross-selling based on improved potential customer selection criteria. The investment in technology and in databases will be considerable, with some observers in the industry beginning to question the degree to which such investment will turn out in practice to be successful. The concern is that such information-driven systems may be found to be inflexible and unable to respond to innovative changes in both product, distribution and customer service. Such changes may not necessarily emerge from the other traditional financial service providers, but could impact the industry from outside.

3.4 THE MAJOR CHALLENGES AHEAD

3.4.1 General pressures on the industry

The financial services industry in the UK is today undergoing a radical change from its traditional structure and function. Some of the factors that are contributing to this change include:

- Deregulation
- Overcapacity
- Technology
- Capital availability and cost
- New entrants
- Changing consumer requirements

The impact of these external forces has been heightened by traditional fixed cost infrastructures, restrictive practices, ingrained management practices, cultures that are out-of-tune with current modern day requirements, and an emphasis on products and delivery systems rather than on customer needs.

Llewellyn and Drake (1990) focused on the impact on the sector in the 1990s of the combined and related effects of competition, profitability and capital. At the centre of all institutions, strategic planning has to be a recognition of the implications of these three factors on the retail financial service sector.

Impact of competition   The potential impact of competition in the financial services industry is summarized in Table 3.4. In particular, there will be considerable pressure to contain costs and to eliminate cross-subsidies in setting product pricing strategies. The result will be to encourage moves towards concentration in the industry by way of mergers and joint ventures—particularly where, for example, certain building societies find themselves neither focused enough on a local area, nor large enough to compete efficiently nationally or regionally.

Profitability   Llewellyn and Drake go on to point out that it is likely that the average cost of retail funds (compared to market rates) will rise. As banks will find it difficult to offset this by increasing the relative rates of interest earned on assets, the net effect will be adversely to impact underlying profitability. Hence the intense effort being made today by the banks and others to find alternative sources of profitable revenue such as insurance, which are not interest or transaction based. The banks particularly may find this pressure considerable as they start to lose current account business to competitive offers from building societies. In their traditional area of lending products, more stringent criteria for credit approval is reducing the level of credit

Table 3.4   Impact of competition in financial services

1.   Efficient firms become more efficient, and overall sector efficiency rises.
2.   Product pricing adjusts so as to eliminate excess demand.
3.   Internal cross-subsidies and price structures not based on cost or risk considerations disappear.
4.   Mergers and acquisitions occur as less efficient or smaller players find competition too intense.
5.   Competitive pressures eliminate any possible cartels in fixing prices and charges.
6.   Restrictive practices are eliminated through competitive circumvention.
7.   Overall profitability of the sector declines.
8.   Risk characteristics of sector increase.
9.   Major players seek to diversify.
10.   Some firms exit the sector as a response to over-capacity

Source: Llewellyn and Drake (1990)

uptake, which is being exacerbated by the impact of the recession forces on consumers' attitudes towards loans and mortgages.

Capital constraints   Lewellyn and Drake particularly stress that the expansion of bank balance sheets in the 1980s was as a result of banks being able to expand their assets by way of increasing subordinated debt capital without having to raise equity capital. As the cost of debt capital is lower than the effective cost of equity capital, this was a relatively cost-effective way of raising funds. In the 1990s, with pressures on the banks' profits and balance sheets as a result of the decline in the economy, the overall cost of capital may be significantly higher than in the previous decade. With little scope for expanding debt capital, as debt-equity capital limits are reached, the result is likely to be the need to raise equity capital by rights issues. In a depressed stock market this could prove both difficult and expensive.

Other possible moves to raise capital may include the sale of those parts of the business that do not fit with core focused activities. For example, the Midland sold its Northern and Clydesdale banks, and sold the Thomas Cook travel business to a continental specialist. Lloyds Bank disposed of part of its US operations to Japanese banks, and Yorkshire Bank (jointly owned by three of the clearing banks) was sold to an Australian bank. It is interesting that the battle for control of the Midland between the successful bidder, Hongkong and Shanghai, and Lloyds had much to do with the potential benefits of combining the Lloyds and Midland branch networks and improving profits through the implementation of cost-cutting strategies. This was something that Lloyds had achieved very successfully in the period 1989 to 1992 in its own business, as it set itself singlemindedly to increase the return on its shareholders funds to a target of at least 10 per cent. From the Midland point of view, having suffered badly from poor investment decisions in the 1980s (including the ill-advised and ill-timed disastrous purchase of the Crocker banking operation in the USA), having access to the greater resources and capital base of the Hongkong and Shanghai Banking Corporation was critical if it was to rebuild its battered UK business.

3.4.2   Which will be the winning strategies?

The three key areas in which banks, building societies and other financial service providers will seek to gain sustainable competitive advantages in the years ahead are clearly:

1. Cost
2. Delivery systems
3. Customer service

No single strategy will emerge as being the most likely to succeed. However, competing on cost alone is unlikely in the end to deliver the full offer of convenience, value, service and support that will be essential to retain current customers, sell them a wider range of products, and attract new long term personal banking business.

The area of delivery systems appears to be the current focus of many financial services providers. Undoubtedly, there have been a number of innovative approaches to offering a higher level of convenience and service through a new distribution channel, First Direct and Direct Line being interesting examples. This will continue, with the ultimate goal of a number of service providers being to deliver transparent banking where the response to the customer has virtually nothing to do with the actual medium of contact at that moment in time. The customer relationship and response to his or her needs is the same whether it is being delivered at their own branch, a branch elsewhere, over the telephone, or through some form of direct personal banker interface.

The area that offers the most opportunity for developing a real competitive advantage, and at the same time offers the most challenge, will undoubtedly be that of customer service. Few people claim or attribute much demonstrable success in this area to date. In many ways, much of the focus on costs, rationalization of the branch-based delivery systems, and margin enhancement through increased charges and fees has had a negative impact on customer service and satisfaction. The techniques considered earlier for more effective targeting, segmentation and behavioural scoring may facilitate the development and delivery of a higher level of service to individual customers based on a perception of their particular needs. However, the solution does appear to lie in simplifying the relationship with the customer and delivering a simple but highly appropriate level of service with easily understandable products. This may not necessarily be the cheapest, but any price disadvantage can be compensated for by the added-value service level. To do this effectively, though, means developing a much greater understanding of what the consumer needs actually are in the area of financial services, and what it is that they want out of the relationship.

The statement by banking ombudsman Lawrence Shurman to the Franks Committee sums up the problem and the opportunity for the banks and other financial institutions in the years ahead.

Customers do not use banks because they want to, but because they are a necessary evil. The customer who savours a good wine, derives no pleasure from the plastic card used to buy it. His pride in his home will not extend to the mortgage with which it is acquired, let alone to the bank which made the advance. Primarily what a bank has to offer is a service, and it is on service not product that the emphasis should be.

REVIEW QUESTIONS

1. Using relevant examples, distinguish between business strategies and tactics.
2. What are the five basic competitive forces, as defined by Michael Porter? Illustrate the likely nature of these forces for a credit card company.
3. You have been asked to prepare a mission statement for a leading provider of general and life insurance products. Describe how you arrived at the final version of your mission statement. To whom would you wish to communicate this statement?
4. Draw up a list of the factors that a building society should consider in conducting a strategic audit.

5. Using Ansoff's product-mission framework, how could this help a retail bank to identify ways of filling its planning gap?

6. Provide examples of financial services retailers that have pursued each of the following primary strategies:
   (a) Cost leadership
   (b) Differentiation
   (c) Focus
   You may select your examples from any area of financial services retailing but justify your choices.

7. What information about clients will typically be collected by a motor insurance company or broker? Illustrate how some of this information can be utilized to help define the more profitable market segments.

8. Explain the difference between micro-targeting and global targeting. For which types of organization does each of these offer the more appropriate form of targeting.

9. Show how the development of the product portfolio can be assisted by analysis of relative margins and profit contributions.

10. First Direct offered an innovative form of delivery of banking services. What factors were of greatest appeal to its customers, and what factors may have retarded its more widespread adoption?

11. Taking a financial services retailer of your choice, what attributes of its products or services should be given particular attention within its promotional strategy?

12. Outline a strategy to ensure that branch staff not only meet their profit criteria but also provide an excellent service to customers.

REFERENCES

Ansoff, H.I. (1988) *New Corporate Strategy: An Analytical Approach to Business Policy for Growth and Expansion*, John Wiley & Sons, New York.

Arnold, S. (1991) 'Do the Banks Care?', *Banking World*, December.

Bon, M. (1987) *Europe and the Future of Financial Services*, Symposium paper 5–7 November 1986, Lafferty Publications, London.

Channon, D. (1988) *Global Banking Strategy*, John Wiley & Sons, New York.

Ellwood, P. (1989) 'Lessons from the Retailers', *Banking World*, December.

Field, S. (1992) *Credit Management*, May, pp. 24–25, Institution of Credit Managers.

Grant, R.M. (1991) *Contemporary Strategy Analysis*, Blackwell Publishers, Oxford.

Llewellyn, D. and L. Drake, (1990) 'Profitability: A view of the 1990s', *Chartered Building Society Institutes Journal*, March.

McGoldrick, P.J. (1990) *Retail Marketing*, McGraw-Hill, London.

Pirrie, D. (1990) 'Service and Costs', *Banking World*, December.

Porter, M.E. (1980) *Competitive Strategy, Techniques for Analysing Industries and Competitors*, MacMillan, New York.

Sloan, A.P. (1963) *My Years with General Motors*, Sedgwick and Jackson, London.

Smith, C. (1991) *Retail Banking Rethink*, Dolca Ltd, Braco, Dunblane, Perthshire, Scotland.

Stalk, G., P. Evans, and L.E. Schulman (1992) 'Competing on Capabilities: The New Rules of Corporate Strategy', *Harvard Business Review*, March-April, pp. 57–69.

Stalk, G. and T.M. Hout (1990) *Competing Against Time: How Time-based Competition is Reshaping Global Markets*, The Free Press, MacMillan, New York, pp. 98–102.

Swanson, Ward and M. Walker (1991) 'Customer Service—Time for Change', *Montague Finance Gazette*, November/December.

TWO

THE BRANCH NETWORK

FOUR

BRANCH LOCATION, NETWORK STRATEGY AND THE HIGH STREET

Steven Greenland   Manchester School of Management

INTRODUCTION

Players in the financial services industry have traditionally viewed branch location as a major influence on potential customers' choice of bank (National Consumer Council 1983; Lanphear 1989; Gwin and Lindgren 1986). While service, in terms of quality, efficiency, friendliness, helpfulness and confidentiality, might be considered the key to maintaining a substantial customer base, it is location that is perhaps the most important single variable influencing the initial selection of a financial service outlet (McGoldrick and Greenland 1992). This factor along with the substantial, long-term capital investment involved means that the location decision is one of the most significant in the marketing mix strategies of institutions.

Developments and changes in the UK market have resulted in problems arising with branch networks that have had to be addressed. For instance, the stereotyped bank branch was described, by the deputy managing director of a leading UK bank, as being; 'big, grim, unwelcoming, wrongly sited and has nowhere to park' (Buchan 1992). Financial institutions have developed strategies to overcome these difficulties and provide a more efficient and cost-effective system of delivery. This chapter discusses current developments in branch networks, examines the influences upon branch location decisions and details the procedures used to evaluate sites. The importance of town planning on the shape of branch networks is also assessed.

4.1   OUTLET LOCATION AND THE BRANCH NETWORK

Three main requirements must be fulfilled by a branch's location in order for it to be successful, and these fall into area and site specific categories. First, the branch must be located in a customer catchment area that has a market capability large enough to sustain levels of branch profitability. Secondly, within this area the branch must receive substantial levels of exposure and visibility, i.e., situated where pedestrian activity is high, so that it is convenient for public use. Thirdly, the premises itself must be suitable, in terms of costs, as well as appropriate size and layout, for the efficient functioning of the branch. During the last decade, both the area and site specific details of location have become the foci of financial institutions' attention, as attempts to review their entire branch networks have been made. These reviews have been brought about by a complexity of events and issues involving the dynamic nature of towns' retailing cores, fluctuating economy, increased industry competition, changing industry structure, technology developments, different premises requirements, and re-evaluation of the branch as a channel of distribution.

4.1.1 Factors shaping the branch network strategy

Increase in competition due to deregulation, the practices of certain retailers (Bliss 1988), as well as recession have made it all the more crucial for institutions to maximize the effectiveness of their marketing activities in order to gain strategic advantages over competitors. As a direct result, the function of branch siting and location has come under close scrutiny and branch network strategies as a whole are being reassessed in the search for other more economic and effective solutions. For example, one of the major UK institutions recently (May 1992) seconded some 80 managers into a new branch development team, its function being to evaluate site performance and potential and develop the national branch strategy. As a result of these new strategies, major changes in the UK branch networks can be observed.

4.1.2 Developments in telephone banking

Recent efforts have been made to introduce branchless telephone banking into the UK. However, the market response has so far been slower than anticipated. First Direct, for instance, was launched in 1989 by Midland. Its market research predicted a market of six million customers in Britain for telephone banking. It took three years to attract only 250,000 customers. Midland does, however, expect this number to rise to two million by the end of the 1990s (Buchan 1992). Other banks have also been pursuing this track; NatWest is offering a trial service ActionLine and recent disclosures indicate that Barclays is about to launch a full telephone banking service (Thomson 1992). This type of service provides banking facilities by telephone 24 hours a day, 365 days of the year, customers use ATMs for cash and only need to visit a branch to deposit cash. Such a distribution method, provided it attracts a certain level of use, creates a service delivery system with greatly reduced costs and overheads, when compared to those of traditional branch banking. Developments in telephone banking will undoubtedly continue in the future and these may to some degree, actually diminish the importance of traditional branches:

Nonetheless, branches do remain anchors of distribution strategies since 40% of bank customers regularly make visitations to brick-and-mortar facilities. (Duffy 1991)

4.1.3 Changes in UK networks and high street retailing

The networks of financial service retail outlets are dynamic and continuously evolving, accordingly their management is a complex and difficult process. Historically, banks served business needs and distribution followed patterns of commercial rather than social developments. As the importance of the personal sector was recognized, this emphasis shifted to the present predominance of numerous high street locations, convenient for both personal and business customers. In the 1970s and early 1980s the encroachment of this non-product retailing activity into traditional shopping areas was recognized as a significant element of urban change in Britain (Fernie and Carrick 1983). In fact, in some areas, it is arguable that communities have actually become 'overbanked'. The dynamism found in many core retail areas, especially with the spate of new shopping centre developments in the 1980s and early 1990s resulted in many branches now finding themselves in less than optimum locations. Consequently, many institutions are involved in relocating branches to sites closer to the shifted retail core and its high levels of pedestrian traffic flow. Where large, out of town shopping centres have been developed, some institutions have felt it necessary to acquire new branch sites. These units, however, tend to be small, heavily automated and marginal, if profitable at all. While they serve a banking function for the centres' retailers, shoppers visiting the sites are usually there for recreation and only require cash withdrawal services. A branch in such a centre is frequently there as a show piece giving the institution a higher profile. As one UK institution senior manager put it: 'we are really thinking of the costs of not being there'.

4.1.4   Branch numbers

Some building societies and certain smaller banks such as Abbey National and the Yorkshire Bank have actually been expanding their branch and ATM networks, in certain regions, to be more geographically representative. The Yorkshire Bank is currently gaining approximately five branches per year in its effort to expand the network further south, from its traditionally northern roots. The TSB suffers from a similar problem and is also reviewing its network, deleting branches at some locations while acquiring in others, in an attempt to strengthen its presence in the south.

The main overall trend in the UK financial service industry has, however, been widespread branch closure. The major institutions, without exception, are rationalizing their networks, reconsidering both the number and geographical spread of branches. Figure 4.1 shows that during the past ten years the number of branches belonging to the major banks has steadily declined. They have been actively reviewing their patterns of distribution closing down or relocating unprofitable, unnecessary and unsuitable branches in continuing efforts to optimize network potential, while minimizing costs. Another benefit experienced from this process of rationalization is that property investment capital is released. However, the potential proceeds from surplus premises have deteriorated in a declining market. Despite this set-back, branch rationalization will continue until 'ideal' size and network patterns have been achieved and even then constant monitoring and adjustment will be required.

A number of the leading institutions have also been involved in merger/acquisition activity; Martins by Barclays, Williams and Glyn by Royal Bank of Scotland. These have resulted in an over-representation of the bank in certain areas and created the need for still further rationalization.

The number of building society branches is, after a dramatic increase in the 1970s and early 1980s beginning to fall. The network growth rate during this period was enormous, with an increase of some 3,668 in the total number of society branches between 1970–1980 and 1,278 branches from 1980–1987 (BSA and CML 1993). The number of building society outlets has shown decline though since 1987 (see Figure 4.2). This decline, as with the banks has been partly due to mergers and acquisitions, but is also due to the closure of smaller institutions less able to survive in recession; the total number of societies has in fact more than halved in the past ten years (BSA and CML 1993). As a result, some of the building societies are also in positions to rationalize parts of their networks.

These continuing rationalization programmes can only exacerbate the current problems of empty premises in the primary and secondary retail cores of many towns and cities. The consequences for the traditional high street retail areas and their planning authorities are quite considerable and will add to the ongoing debate surrounding the vitality and viability of high street retailing (Greenland 1993; McGoldrick and Thompson 1992; Jones 1991; Hillman 1990;

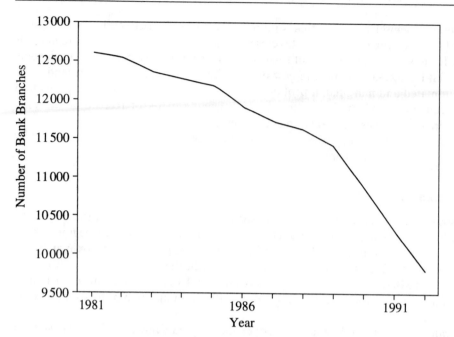

Figure 4.1   The changing branch networks of the leading five UK banks
Source: Calculated from figures in Table 6.05, Annual Abstract of Banking Statistics, Volume 10, Statistical Unit, British Bankers' Association 1993.

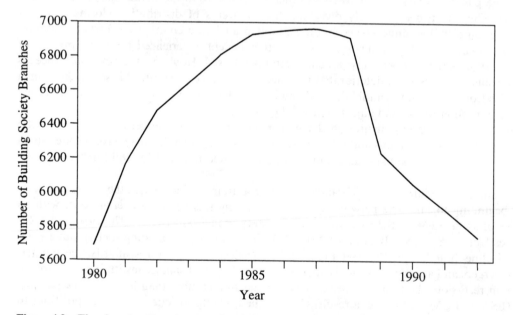

Figure 4.2   The changing branch networks of the UK Building Societies
Note: Figures from 1989 exclude the 667 branches of Abbey National plc, which became a bank in 1988.
Source: Based on figures in Table 24, Housing Finance No. 19, 1993

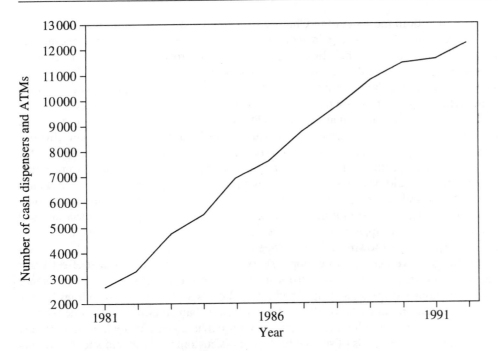

Figure 4.3   The changing ATM networks of the leading five UK banks
Source: Calculated from figures in Table 6.07, Annual Abstract of Banking Statistics, Volume 10, Statistical Unit, British Bankers' Association, 1993

McDonald 1987; Schiller, 1987, etc.). Further issues regarding town planning and branch networks are covered in greater detail later in this chapter.

4.1.5   ATM numbers

The rationalization process has been facilitated by the massive growth in automated banking which provides 24 hour access, seven days a week to services. Cash 'points' are now a familiar feature of retail areas and machines have been developed which offer full 'touch screen' banking facilities and far more than simple cash withdrawal. During the past ten years the number of cash dispensers/automated teller machines and their usage has increased enormously (see Figure 4.3). For fuller details on the usage of ATMs, consult Chapter 6 on the branch environment. Many ATMs are associated with branch outlets, but a more recent growth area has been with isolated service machines that form the 'remote' ATM network, operating from transport centres, retail and service outlets and non-branch high street sites. The availability of ATMs and sharing arrangements, giving card holders of one institution the ability to use the cash machines of several others has reduced the customer demand for such extensive branch networks. Several managers interviewed, involved with branch network development felt the national ATM network was approaching saturation point and was itself in need of some rationalization.

4.1.6   Branch specifications and appearance

Several other key developments have influenced network review and rationalization strategies. The characteristics of units required as premises have changed considerably over the past five years. (This is dealt with in more detail in Chapter 6). Due to enabling technologies, the major banks have been able to cut costs and gain economies of scale by removing both processing and telephone enquiry functions from their branches to centralized processing and enquiry centres. As a result, a large proportion of the network's branch staff, having been freed from these duties, are no longer necessary, enabling considerable savings to be made in employee costs. Both the premises and remaining staff of such branches have been reoriented from account-based activities to a more retail function, their goals being to attract, sell to and serve customers. The traditional style bank sites do not generally present the desired retail image or an effective cross-selling environment. In many cases, this type of premises simply does not satisfy the modern branch and so acquiring more suitable premises has been another stimulant to rational-ization programmes. The old branch designs are being replaced by open plan designs that have large glass frontages and more of a retail appearance about them. The traditional, stone-architectured, large, closed plan, multifloored bank units typically occupying uneconomical corner sites are gradually disappearing and represent an important element of change in the historic urban morphology of towns and cities. (See Figure 6.4 in Chapter 6.)

Several institutions have been putting emphasis on the fact that it is not cost-effective or necessary to offer uniform levels of service across much of their branch networks. The emergence of processing and enquiry centres has helped reduce staff costs and created possibilities for the downgrading of certain branches, especially in urban or suburban situations with other outlets nearby. Networks with more of a hierarchical delivery system have been created, each hierarchy of branch providing different levels of service to the bank's customers. Hub and spoke arrange-ments have evolved; the 'hub' branch providing higher levels of services and support functions to the smaller surrounding 'spoke' branches. Reorganizing and rationalizing the branch network in this manner, upgrading some outlets and downgrading others has also been a considerable cost-cutting exercise, facilitating a further reduction in staff numbers and managerial presence, as well as increasing operational efficiencies. One leading bank, for example, which began its network review early in 1990 estimated the proposed implementation of some 300 closures and the downgrading of a similar number of outlets would bring revenue savings well in excess of £40m p.a. by 1994.

4.1.7 The network hierarchy

When the branch networks are observed as a whole, it is clear that different types of service outlet and administrative centres have evolved. When these are viewed, according to the different levels or order of service that they provide, a hierarchy of representation can be identified. (See Figure 4.4.) All institutions in the UK's financial service industry exhibit at least some of these hierarchical levels; the actual number represented depends upon individual network strategies. The amount of telephone enquiries and volume of processing performed at each branch level also vary between institutions, according to the degree to which these functions have been centralized. The geographical distribution of these different service delivery types and the proportion each contributes to the network as a whole also depends upon the institution and is likely to change over time as efforts to enhance efficiency continue. 'Remote deposit boxes' and 'nominal or automated branches,' for instance, at present form only a small part of networks; they are relatively new developments to the UK and as such tend to be experiments found in out of town shopping centres and transport centres such as airports, they might, therefore, be considered only an annex to the current main network strategies.

Hierarchical level		Facilities provided
LEVEL ONE	Remote ATM Remote deposit box	ATMs/deposit boxes detached from the branch, but usually serviced by a local parent or community branch
LEVEL TWO	Nominal or automated branch	Predominantly 'remote' self-service outlet/kiosk projecting the corporate image; ATM's advanced touch screen banking machines, telephone links with community branches and maybe one or two sales assistants
LEVEL THREE	Sub-branch	Small retail unit; ATM, cash counter, maybe an interview facility, limited service offering and perhaps limited opening hours. They frequently have no managerial presence but are visited by a 'nomadic' sales adviser from a parent/community branch
LEVEL FOUR	(i) Parent branch	Retail/personal branch, typical town/suburban outlet, a more complete range of personal banking services in a retail orientated design
	(ii) Corporate branch	Outlet offering facilities for corporate/business customers only, i.e., no tills/retail area. They frequently comprise management suites with parking areas operating from business park developments that have lower rents
LEVEL FIVE	Community branch	Financial supermarket; banking hall is broken into specific product areas, full service range including personal as well as business corporate services, tele-enquiry/tele-service/telesales support facility for lower level branches and frequently processing and administration assistance too. They tend to be large expensive city centre branches
LEVEL SIX	Regional headquarters	Administration/control centres for the regional network
LEVEL SEVEN	National headquarters	Administrative and management centres determining and implementing a national network policy via the regional headquarters

Figure 4.4 The UK's financial services industry network hierarchy

i
ii

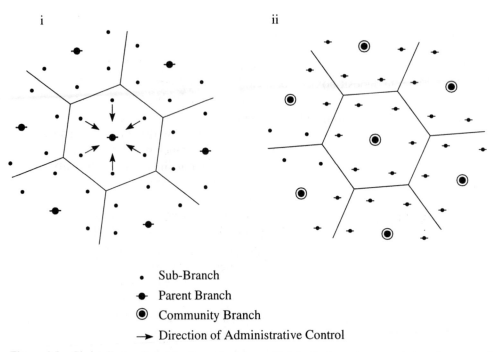

- Sub-Branch
- Parent Branch
- Community Branch
- Direction of Administrative Control

Figure 4.5   Christaller's administrative principle applied to the branch network (i = lower service order pattern, ii = higher service order pattern)

4.1.8   Central place theory and branch networks

The hierarchical nature of the network with its hub and spoke arrangements is reminiscent of Christaller's central place theory, which in part aims to explain and predict the effective geographic distribution of different levels of product and service provision. The theory may help to give explanation to some of the current network strategy objectives. In the past, the traditional financial service institutions tended to have more of a standard level of service offered across their networks. With an expanding range of financial service products on offer and the need for greater efficiency, many institutions are now trying to limit employee and premises costs by providing a more cost-effective and discriminating network. One of their primary objectives being 'to ensure at least a minimum representation in all geographic areas in which the bank is located' (Council on Financial Competition, August 1990). They are achieving this by increasingly differentiating the levels of service provision, limiting levels at certain locations, while providing customer services of a higher order, including cheque processing and telephone enquiry facilities, at others. If a sub-branch is approached by a customer but does not offer the particular level of service required, then that customer is referred or connected to another branch higher up in the hierarchy that does provide services of that order. Christaller's administrative principle is perhaps the most appropriate approach for predicting distribution patterns of financial service networks (illustrated in Figure 4.5). In Figure 4.5, each hexagon represents the administrative area for the higher order branch and encloses six lower order branches to which it provides higher level services. It is much more effective to administer whole centres than parts of them. For instance, if the lower order centres, were spatially distributed equidistant from each higher order centre there would be confusion as to which parent branch each of the sub-branches should report to. This pattern of distribution actually maximizes the ratio of low order to high

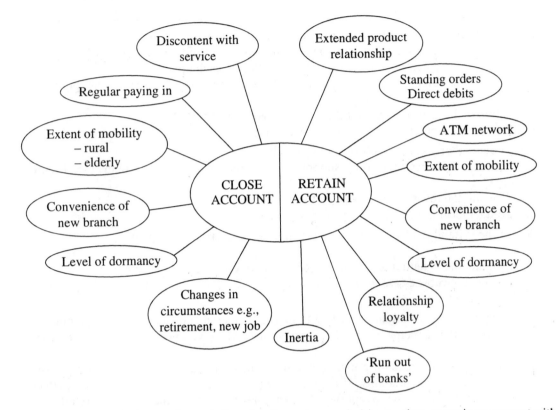

Figure 4.6   Branch closure, factors influencing the customers decision to close or retain an account with the bank at another outlet (supplied by a leading UK bank)

order branches and thus helps to minimize the number of higher order centres across the network as a whole and their associated high overheads.

The central place theory does, however, operate under several idealistic assumptions and therefore represents a system that cannot be totally applicable to settings in the real world. What it does expose though are certain factors and concepts that should be considered when contemplating the ideal size, shape and structure of a branch network.

4.1.9   Closure: customer responses to rationalization and relocation

Financial institutions are anxious for any network modifications to cause as little disruption to their customers as possible. Closing an outlet at any location can have a negative impact on image. They rely on the fact that most relocations and alternative branches are frequently nearby and offer an improved service facility, thus minimizing inconvenience. However, any changes are likely to result in the loss of at least some accounts. Most of these losses will be to competitors in the vicinity of the old site and to those intercepting customers on route to the new one. Some customers may find themselves having to cross main roads or other physical barriers and therefore no longer find the outlet convenient. A number of account losses are likely also to occur as the move will affect the institution's image of stability and familiarity, customers finding themselves in alien environments with unfamiliar tellers. Some might even be unaware of the move.

1. Prepare a 'hitlist' of potential areas to join the branch network
   (a) Identify the geographical urban regions where the institution is under-represented
   (b) Estimate the potential market/revenue for outlets in each area
   (c) Decide the level of branch or branch network required to service the potential market
   (d) Estimate the return on capital that would need to be invested
   (e) Prioritize the potential towns/areas for development
2. View potential areas and establish site availability
   (a) Perform 'desk' research using shopping centre reports e.g. GOAD plans (see Figure 4.10.)
   (b) 'Eyeball' the towns to get a feel for their suitability
   (c) Contact local agents to identify vacant premises
3. Assess the suitability of potential sites/premises for the proposed type of outlet(s) in each area
   (a) Estimate the potential for 'retail performance' offered by each site/premises
   (b) Where applicable assess the likelihood of planning permission being granted for service use/unit redesign
4. Reprioritize specific locations according to market potential and site/premises suitability
   (a) Reassess the anticipated market and return on investment, given site/premises details
   (b) Prioritize the premises for potential purchase, there will be some trade off between area and site/premises suitability. If area priority (stage 1e) is high then a less than perfect site/premises might be acceptable. If area priority is lower then a prime retail site/premises might be conditional
5. Offer made/lease negotiated and planning permission applied for where required (if refused see Figure 4.13)

Figure 4.7 General procedure for identifying suitable locations to expand the network (*based on interviews with relevant bank/building society personnel*)

Research by one leading UK bank into the effects of branch closure on their customer base revealed that the decision to close or retain an account is a complex process involving many factors and not just the physical relocation. Their findings are summarized in Figure 4.6. Branch managers, of course, try to minimize the net losses in customers and might expect to more than compensate with extra local custom from the new branch area. Marketing activity aims to reduce the impact of the move and maximize the selling opportunity at the new site. The main tactics employed are to notify customers prior to the move, by word of mouth and notices in branches, newsletters, local press and personal letters. A potential problem here is keeping to the proposed movement schedule; delays in construction etc. can be detrimental to customer confidence. At the new branch, efforts to maintain regular tellers can help to reduce customer anxiety with the move and grand openings and other reception functions can actually reinforce patronage as well as generate additional local interest. At sites that have been downgraded, institutions frequently avoid/minimize the appearance of change. Customers telephoning enquiry centres or ordering chequebooks etc. by mail are unaware that they are not actually communicating with their regular branch, but with the enquiry/processing centre.

4.2 LOCATION AND BRANCH EVALUATION PROCEDURES AND TECHNIQUES

4.2.1 The location/evaluation process

The previous description of the UK's financial services branch network has revealed several trends. Most institutions are involved, to varying degrees, in expanding their representation in certain areas and rationalizing their networks as a whole. This rationalization entails upgrading or downgrading some branches, closing others and the relocation of some outlets to more suitable sites and premises. The methods and techniques used in the location and site evaluation procedures vary considerably between institutions. Some adopt very systematic approaches, utilizing large databases and sophisticated modelling techniques, others are far more subjective applying little science and relying much more heavily upon secondary data sources and local management knowledge. However, regardless of the differing complexities of techniques used, in most instances the general step-by-step processes are similar for each institution. Figure 4.7 illustrates the general process for identifying new locations once the institution has made a decision to expand its network.

For rationalization, which is more concerned with reducing/optimizing the networks coverage, many of the stages considered in the general location process of Figure 4.6 are equally apt. In this assessment, of course, actual branch performance/profitability data are available. Institutions look at specific branch data concerning sales efficiency, cost to income ratios, percentage of accounts lost compared to accounts gained etc. This information is then examined against the estimated market potential of the branch's hinterland.

4.2.2 Market effectiveness and prioritization

Tandy and Stovel (1989) suggest that market effectiveness ratings should also be calculated for each branch to help direct distribution strategy for the network:

$$\text{Market effectiveness} = \frac{\text{Market share}}{\text{Branch share}}$$

where:

$$\text{Market share} = \frac{\text{The institution's market in a defined area}}{\text{The total market share in that area}}$$

$$\text{Branch share} = \frac{\text{The institution's number of branches in the defined area}}{\text{The total number of branches in that area}}$$

Institutions should be aiming for a market effectiveness of at least 1 or more.

In this way underperforming or unprofitable branches can be identified and accounted for in the rationalization programmes. One UK bank indicated that it selects which branch to close on the basis of:

- Insufficient customers
- Too much competition
- People are not giving them money/not leaving their money there
- Insufficient space/too much space/refurbishment requirements
- Accessibility

Profitability will, of course, be the key determinant for deleting or maintaining a branch in the network. There are, however, certain circumstances when an unprofitable outlet will be kept in the network, these are:

1. In a rural/suburban location where no others are to be found nearby and the outlet is maintained as an exercise in public relations.
2. At sites which provide good advertising and public exposure for the bank's name, such as out of town shopping centres, airports and retail store locations, these tend to be primarily transaction facilities with high rents and low volumes of accounts.
3. In locations where the market potential in the surrounding area is predicted to increase in the future.
4. Where the outlet can be downgraded or other managerial adjustments made to enhance its profitability.

Once branches in the network have been assessed according to actual and potential performance, it has been proposed that strategies directed at improving the network should be categorized in order of priority for implementation:

Priority one: 'No hope branches' with poor market and location; close or relocate.

Priority two: 'Underperforming branches' with the potential to improve with appropriate adjustments in the marketing mix.

Priority three: 'Unlikely performers' with above average performance but unattractive locations. These will be vulnerable to new developments in the market and should be monitored and considered for relocation.

Priority four: 'Solid performers' performing well in areas of high potential. Efforts/resources should be made available to maintain this position.

(Tandy and Stovel 1989)

In an ideal world the four categories should be implemented simultaneously; however, where resources are limited, as they inevitably are, they should be implemented in order of priority.

4.2.3   Location evaluation techniques

As mentioned earlier, it is the sophistication of the methods and techniques used in location and branch evaluation procedures that varies between institutions. In the past, attempts at estimating and predicting site profitability were less scientific than they are today. As banks and building societies have begun to view themselves as financial retailers and their outlets more akin to shops (Riley and Knott 1992; McGoldrick and Greenland 1992), some have started to adopt store location techniques and models. Methods developed in and more typical of the product retailing industry, ranging from the more basic but frequently used location evaluation checklist through to the complex multiple regression models, now have their counterparts in the financial services sector. These techniques when used effectively provide a systematic approach for effective branch location evaluation and rationalization of the network as a whole. The following section details these methods, illustrating with examples and discussion where appropriate.

Checklists   The checklist details factors for consideration in the location decision. It is one of the more qualitative approaches that is frequently used by management to assess both actual and potential branch sites, providing a framework for examining and evaluating specific locations. While certain factors in the checklist are bound to be prioritized, it is important not to disregard performance in others, since they all work in close association to produce overall location quality. The following statement helps to illustrate this view;

If pressed to choose the most important factor I would pick density. All of the factors, however, are tied together. Every site and market area will be different and characteristics will change. You need to examine each factor to determine its impact (Council on Financial Competition, 1989)

The site evaluation team must therefore aim to be aware of both the benefits and impediments that are associated not only with the key elements but also the 'less' critical factors in the checklist.

Fairly exhaustive checklists have been presented in the past (e.g., Reidenbach and Pitts 1986; McGoldrick 1990), but these have, however, focused on the product retailing sector. While many of their elements are applicable to the personal banking sector, especially the demographic details, some factors have not been included that ought to be when considering location evaluation for financial service outlets. Figure 4.8 displays a checklist of location factors for the financial services industry. Four categories appear: geodemographics, branch activity, centre details and premises which represent the general progression from area/macro factors to more site specific or micro detail. Most of the variables listed are dynamic rather than static and so trends should be observed and predicted changes accounted for in the evaluation process. The majority of the checklist factors are self explanatory but some may require further explanation. The following gives some explanation of each of the four checklist categories and discusses some of the data sources that can be exploited by institutions.

Geodemographics	*Branch activity*
Financial activity	Branch density
Population - density	Branch distribution
- structure	Saturation index
- projections	Institutions represented
Lifestyles represented	Level of representation
Social-economic groups represented	Institutions images
Employment trends	Outlets potential
Occupations	Turnover estimates
Disposable incomes	Patronage estimates
Main employers	Territory overlaps
Economic stability	Branch share
Economic forecasts	Market share
Growth potential	Network development activity
Retail attraction	Internal data:
Business attraction	- turnover
Land values	- product performance
Housing density	- accounts opened
Ownership levels	- accounts closed
Cultural/ethnic groups	- customer profiles

Figure 4.8   Checklist of factors for evaluating financial service outlet location

Centre details	Premises
Cumulative attraction	Availability
Commercial zoning	Suitability
Primary/secondary retail areas	Present use class
Primary/secondary business areas	Unit - area
Retail sales	- shape
Shop statistics	- structure
Business statistics	- design
Street statistics	- expansion potential
Prestige of areas	- age
Shifts in cores	Front/rear access
Local authority policy	Security
New developments planned	Parking spaces
Work patterns	Interception potential
Travel patterns	Frontage length
Shopping patterns	Frontage orientation
Pedestrian entry routes	Physical barriers
Public transport details	Elevation topography
Road network details	Exposure
Car ownership	Expected footfall
Drive times	Specific drive times
Parking facilities	Refit needs
	Refit costs
	Building restrictions
	Property costs
	Leasing terms
	Rates
	Maintenance costs
	Operational costs
	Adjacent amenities
	Neighbouring activities

Figure 4.8   Continued

1.   Geodemographics   The majority of geodemographic details will provide information on the market potential of specific areas. By examining population structures, housing structures and economic forecasts the demand for financial services can be predicted and networks planned accordingly. The main population data sources used to acquire such information will be 1991 census data, NOP's financial research services survey, electoral registers, local authorities and classification systems developed by the various agencies operating in the financial services sector such as CCN, CACI and Pinpoint. Pinpoint's FiNPiN system for instance classifies the population into four main categories according to their levels of financial activity. Each group has a predictable behaviour and purchase pattern for the various financial products and services (see Figure 4.9). The FiNPiN data is geographically referenced and so using this system it is relatively straightforward to assess the potential demand for specific product types and services across defined areas. Accurately assessing the market potential of different regions is, of course, absolutely essential when planning the size and structure of the branch network. As Frerichs

(1990a) claims: 'Logic supports the premise that population, demographics and future growth potential in the market would supersede a good location. The relative strength of the market accounts for 70–75% of the facility potential score, i.e., ultimate sales potential.'

In the assessment of market areas, commercial enterprise must also be considered as business and retail activity can contribute significantly to outlet profitability, providing both commercial custom as well as attracting population from the surrounding region to the specific centres of activity.

FiNPiN: Classification summary labels

4 Level FiNPiN types		10 Level FiNPiN types		40 Level FiNPiN types	
Financially active (A)	(20.1)	(i) Most active	(11.6)	1 'Wealthy' families with older children	(2.0)
				2 'Wealthy' families	(2.2)
				3 Families with young children and two working adults	(1.9)
				4 'Wealthy' families with students and older children	(2.7)
				5 Families with growing children and two working adults	(2.8)
		(ii) Financially secure savers	(8.5)	6 'Wealthy' empty-nesters	(2.6)
				7 'Wealthy' retired	(5.9)
Financially informed (I)	(25.9)	(iii) Multiproduct savers and investors	(10.7)	8 Established families with older children	(4.3)
				9 'Wealthy' urban areas with few children	(1.8)
				10 Agricultural families	(0.2)
				11 'Wealthy' rural empty-nesters	(2.2)
				12 Rural or suburban elderly	(2.2)
		(iv) Traditional multiproduct users	(7.1)	13 Suburban families	(1.6)
				14 Established families with two working adults	(3.7)
				15 Army families	(0.3)
				16 'Wealthy' farmers and agricultural workers	(1.4)
		(v) Nett savers	(8.1)	17 'Wealthy' self-employed with older children	(0.2)
				18 Young professional singles and families	(1.9)
				19 Elderly empty-nesters	(2.4)
				20 'Wealthy' in flats	(3.6)
Financially conscious (C)	(27.1)	(vi) Average users	(12.0)	21 Young professional adults, students and ethnic populations in rented accommodation	(2.7)
				22 Families with young children in owner occupied housing	(5.2)
				23 Elderly rural empty-nesters	(2.3)
				24 Young families in council flats in deprived areas	(1.9)

Figure 4.9   (FiNPiN) – financial service users classification courtesy of Pinpoint Analysis

4 Level FiNPiN types		10 Level FiNPiN types		40 Level FiNPiN types	
Financially conscious (C)	(vii)	Uncommitted investors	(3.2)	25 Smallholding and farming families	(0.4)
				26 Young adults and ethnic populations in crowded rented property	(1.0)
				27 Large families in council houses, mothers working part-time	(1.9)
	(viii)	Basic product users	(11.8)	28 Small families in council accommodation with women in part-time work	(5.8)
				29 Deprived areas with few children	(4.6)
				30 Elderly in small council dwellings	(1.4)
Financially passive (P)	(26.9)	(ix) Inactive borrowers	(15.2)	31 Young adults and ethnic populations in bedsits	(3.1)
				32 Established families in council accommodation	(4.6)
				33 Young families and ethnic populations in small inner city dwellings	(1.2)
				34 Empty-nesters in council accommodation	(3.6)
				35 Large young families in council accommodation	(2.7)
	(x)	Least active	(11.8)	36 Large families in crowded council accommodation, mainly in Scotland	(1.7)
				37 Elderly in small council accommodation in ethnic neighbourhoods	(2.7)
				38 Elderly in crowded council neighbourhoods	(4.7)
				39 Families with older children in deprived council neighbourhoods	(2.0)
				40 Crowded council neighbourhoods with ethnic populations	(0.6)

(Figures in brackets show the size of each FiNPiN type as a percentage of all United Kingdom households excluding Northern Ireland)

Figure 4.9 Continued

2. Branch activity Information concerning existing branch activity indicates how well an area is being served. Obviously an area with little activity and a large geodemographic potential is the ideal place for new branches, while an area saturated with branches or with a low geodemographic potential will be the focus of rationalizing and reassessing the network. Information regarding competitor branches can be gained from surveys, local knowledge and area shopping reports which are examined in the next section. Simple trade area mapping of own and competitor network patterns frequently help in identifying areas for consideration in the distribution strategy. A more sophisticated method of examining branch catchment areas using gravity modelling is discussed in the later section on more systematic approaches to branch location evaluation.

The first two checklist categories have encompassed the assessment of an areas market potential, the next two look at some of the smaller scale or micro location details that help to ensure the market is exploited to the full.

3.   Centre details   This checklist category focuses in on specific areas and lists factors to be considered when evaluating centre locations. For an outlet to be productive it must be situated in an area that has a high enough level of community activity. Clearly knowledge of the local population's travel, work and shopping patterns are essential to establish where the most appropriate sites for ATMs and the different branches in the network hierarchy, with the greatest potential for sales are to be found. Local management knowledge should be utilized, with many institutions also relying on agency shopping reports as well as their own market research. Reports can be obtained for all UK towns and cities, providing geodemographic, commercial and retail profiles, pedestrian flow counts, as well as street by street maps and associated photographs detailing the specifics of the units found in them. Statistics are also available concerning floor space areas and the ratio of outlets by activity type, index linked to the national average. Figure 4.10 is an excerpt from such a report illustrating this type of infor-mation. The policies of local authorities will also be a key consideration as the planning department governs land use, imposing restrictions in the core shopping areas where the prime pitches are to be found. To an extent, local authorities actually limit where institutions can locate their premises. This factor is extremely important and is therefore dealt with in greater detail in the later section on town planning and the branch network.

4.   Premises   This category deals with site specific details at the micro scale that determine the effectiveness of each ATM/outlet, as a vehicle for providing/selling services. Other site specific factors that will directly effect profitability are also considered. It is data from this category that can be used to predict profitability at one site using information from analogous branches in the institution's network. The analogue procedure has been detailed by McGoldrick (1990) and has been adapted here for financial service outlets as follows:

1. Identify other branches, preferably of the same institution, which have many essential features in common with the branch location in question.
2. Quantify the key features of these branches and catchment areas, then tabulate and sum-marize these data.
3. Extrapolate from these analogue branches to estimate the likely turnover and profitability of the branch location in question.

Such a technique can reduce the subjectivity that is frequently involved when evaluating specific premises in the branch network.

4.2.4   More systematic approaches to branch location evaluation

The above description of the analogue method leads us onto some of the more scientific location evaluation procedures. The main quantitative methods for optimizing branch location were described by Meidan (1984). Of these, gravity modelling and multiple regression techniques were cited as being more frequently used by interviewed bank personnel and commercial agencies. Agents such as CCN and GMAP are involved with developing more sophisticated location evaluation instruments. A summary of these methods and their applications is given below.

4.2.5   Gravity models

These are spatial interaction models and when applied to financial service networks suggest that branch patronage will exhibit a distance decay relationship with its hinterland. They work on the principle that sphere of influence of a branch will be a function of its size, distance and

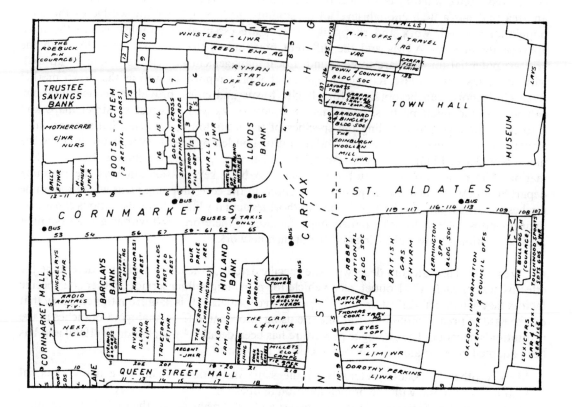

SAMISTAT – MULTIPLE OUTLETS REPORT

======================================

SAMI CENTRE NAME ....REVIEW OUTLETS COUNT FOR MULTIPLE GROUPS..........										
CODE	DATE	6001	6002	6033	6040	6048	6091	6111	6043	6134	6180
30FZ OXFORD	01/92	1	2	1		1	1	1	1	2	1
30FU OXFORD–HEADINGTON	05/91	1									
30JN OXFORD–SUMMERTOWN	05/91	1		1							

SAMI CENTRE NAME ....REVIEW OUTLETS FLORR AREAS (,000 SQ. FT.) FOR MULTIPLE GROUPS..........										
CODE	DATE	6001	6002	6033	6040	6048	6091	6111	6043	6134	6180
30FZ OXFORD	01/92	3.64	1.94	1.40		1.40	1.40	.54	1.40	1.08	.54
30FU OXFORD–HEADINGTON	05/91	1.40									
30JN OXFORD–SUMMERTOWN	05/91	.54		.54							

LIST OF MULTIPLE CODES USED

6001 Abbey National
6002 Alliance and Leicester
6033 Bradfor and Bingley Bldg Soc
6040 Britannia Bldg Soc
6048 Cheltenham and Gloucester Bldg Soc

6091 Halifax Bldg Soc
6111 Leeds Permanent Bldg Soc
6143 National and Provincial Bldg Soc
6134 Nationwide Anglia Bldg Soc
6180 Woolwich Equitable bldg Soc

Figure 4.10 Extracts from GOAD Oxford shopping centre plans and data
Source: SAMI Data from Goad Plans. (Copyright 1992, Chas E Goad Ltd, Salisbury Square, Old Hatfield, Centres: OXON – Oxfordshire)

customers' journey times in relation to other branches in the surrounding area. Their aim is to predict the probability of movement between places. For example, the Reilly model, an early and basic gravity type model predicts that the 'breaking point' or boundary between the trading areas of branches A and B will be equal to:

$$\frac{\text{The distance between branch A and branch B}}{1 + \sqrt{\dfrac{\text{Size of branch A}}{\text{Size of branch B}}}}$$

Since Reilly's model, modified and more complex equations have been developed, involving a greater number of variables and assessing the interaction between more than two places. Using patterns of branch distribution and information concerning road networks, physical features, centre attractiveness values, population densities and area boundaries, complex gravity models have been developed and applied to financial services, their aim being to establish the branch catchment areas. This information can then be used to predict branch performance and, by comparing with actual performance data, help to identify anomalies in the network. Such a system relies heavily on the institution's own customer data. For example, an institution's customer distribution in an area can be geographically assessed using customer postcode data. This information is then mapped out to show customer flows, identify branch catchment areas and reveal any areas of market overlap. In this way, overbanked and underbanked areas can be diagnosed. Investigation of the surrounding areas demographics, roads etc. give a greater understanding of the pattern of custom, providing information on journey times and the perceived attractiveness of centres. Once this information has been ascertained, the gravity models can be used to predict the effects of altering the distribution pattern of branches in the region. In this way, network strategies can be planned to achieve an optimum pattern of distribution, basing decisions on probable usage levels, calculated by the gravity models.

4.2.6   Multiple regression

Multiple regression analysis involves developing equations that represent linear relationships between branch performance indicators (dependent variables) and location attributes (independent variables). Its aim is to identify correlations between the dependent and independent variables. If high levels of correlation exist then the independent variables can be used to predict the dependent variables. The regression analysis identifies the key factors, in the branch catchment and site specific data that determine performance. It does this by assessing the degree of correlation between the dependent and independent variables and developing an equation that represents the relationships. This equation, by incorporating various site data (independent variables) from actual locations, can then be used to forecast performance. To produce such predictive instruments requires massive amounts of data from a large number of outlets, collected over a considerable time period. The variables utilized in the regression analysis are derived from databases constructed using the institution's own customer data as well as factors found in the location evaluation checklist. It is the quality of this database that will determine the reliability and predictive accuracy of the instrument. A reliable data set should allow the effects of various micro site details to be considered, such as the impact of different branch sales floor areas, as well as some of the macro considerations, such as altering the number of branches in an area.

   The use of these sophisticated location evaluation techniques is not widespread in the UK financial services industry, as yet. Many of the major institutions have only recently begun to consider and use them in their network distribution strategies. The potential applications of such approaches to the financial services industry have, however, been realized for a considerable length of time. Bennett (1975), for example, in a publication by the American Bankers Association, wrote of multiple regression analysis, 'because this method considers the impact of many variables, quantifies the impact of those variables and can result in more accurate forecasts; this technique should be used whenever possible'. Financial institutions have very detailed customer information, in most cases vastly superior to that available to major retailers. This information, though, is traditionally account and not customer focused. Before techniques like multiple regression can be widely applied, these data handling difficulties must first be overcome and databases rearranged to provide more customer-oriented information. Many institutions are currently addressing this problem and in the future, the use of systematic approaches to location evaluation will become more commonplace in the financial services sector.

4.3   TOWN PLANNING AND THE BRANCH NETWORK

The branch location evaluation procedures can predict which sites and units are most likely to generate the greatest profits and sales. Shifts in town centre cores, changes in desired premises specifications and the re-evaluation of networks have meant that many existing branches are unlikely to be the most effective, and as a result many institutions are involved in relocating some of their town centre branches. The ideal unit is likely to occupy a ground floor only and be somewhat smaller than the larger traditional corner sites, which stem from towns' historical pasts. The ideal site will be in areas of high retail activity, where traffic flows are at a maximum and there is a greater likelihood of attracting custom off the street. Such premises tend also to be the most expensive and so there may be some trade off between cost and situation in the location decision. However, perhaps potentially the most significant external influence upon institutions' location decisions will be the local authority planning department. Finding a vacant unit satisfying the desired site and premises specifications is only part of the process, obtaining the planning permission for a bank or building society outlet can be an arduous and resource intensive task in itself. This is because local authorities have to look after and protect the health of their shopping centres. Generally they prefer retail usage in prime urban sites and seek to maintain this as the dominant function by restricting the proportion of non-retail activity.

4.3.1   Planning perspectives on financial service outlets

Local planning departments frequently distinguish their centres in terms of size and function. Some towns will have a limited catchment area and a mixed service-retailing role, others will have predominantly a shopping role to play. Where larger towns that serve sub-regional and regional centres are concerned, planning departments will strive to actively promote and improve them as principal shopping centres in an attempt to increase the size of their visitor catchment areas. This is achieved by ensuring such areas remain the focus of provision of shopping facilities and direct investments towards these core areas with this and other complimentary objectives in mind. Consequently, centres that institutions perceive as being the most suitable and providing the most appropriate sites for their branches are frequently the most difficult and sometimes impossible to obtain.

Local authorities view attractive, compact and accessible prime shopping areas as one of the keys to economic and social success, excerpts from borough unitary development plans help to illustrate this:

The Royal Borough contains some of London's finest shopping areas including Kensington High Street,

Knightsbridge, Kings Road and Portobello Road. These shopping areas act as a magnet for visitors in particular and thus make a valuable contribution to the economic vitality of London as a whole. (Kensington and Chelsea UDP—deposited draft 1992).

While centres are the focal point for many aspects of community life, including offices, services and leisure activities, the Council considers a healthy shopping role is the foundation for this. (Sefton UDP—deposit 1991)

While banks and building society branches are seen as providing necessary and complimentary services to the primary shopping areas, land users of a predominantly retail character are considered more favourably by the local planning authorities and high levels of retail use in centres are protected by restricting 'inappropriate' development accordingly.

4.3.2   Government guidelines and local planning restrictions

The government provides local authorities with a considerable degree of autonomy in the policies they adopt in the development of their centres. General guidelines are, however, specified which the planning departments are obliged to adhere to. The Town and Country Planning (Use Classes) Order 1987, No. 764, the Department of the Environment Development Control Policy Note 11 (1985) and Circular 13/87 detail issues and governmental standing on non-retail uses and change of use in shopping areas. The Use Classes Order classifies the premises of shops as class A1, those of financial and professional services class A2, food and drink outlets class A3 and those in class B of a business or industrial nature. In most situations, for the class of use of a premises to be changed, planning permission must first be granted by the local authority. The Department of the Environment recognizes that:

Branches of banks provide the main financial services supporting the shopping and commercial functions of town and district centres. (Paragraph 8 of the Annex to DCPN11 (1985))

and gives planning control to local authorities:

Subject to the provision of local planning policies, therefore, both banks and building society branches may often be acceptable uses in both primary and secondary shopping areas. Local planning authorities may, however, restrict a permission by condition, to prevent a bank or building society office being used for office purposes which would not attract many callers. (Paragraph 10 of the Annex to DCPN11 (1985))

In keeping with Department of Environment guidelines, many authorities divide their larger shopping centres into two types of area; primary areas which are dominated by shops for the retail sales of goods and secondary areas where shopping and service uses are more mixed. When assessing applications for the establishment of new service uses within the different areas, the councils operate each along specific change of use criteria. Each planning authority develops its own individual set of policies, the main caveats of which usually include the following. In the primary shopping streets, change of use from shops to service use will generally not be permitted, with authorities actively resisting the loss of shop units and retail floorspace. In the secondary shopping streets, planning is less restrictive and the establishment of an A2 or A3 use may be permitted provided the proposal will not threaten the character or functioning of the centre.

Different planning authorities have developed different criteria on the basis of which they grant or refuse planning permission for a change of use in the various shopping centre areas. Many have already or are currently developing these criteria. Figure 4.11 details the area types and change of use policies for a district centre in the Metropolitan Borough of Stockport, which aim to protect the attractiveness and viability of the centre as a whole. Another example of policy is provided by the Chelsea and Kensington Borough Planning Department.

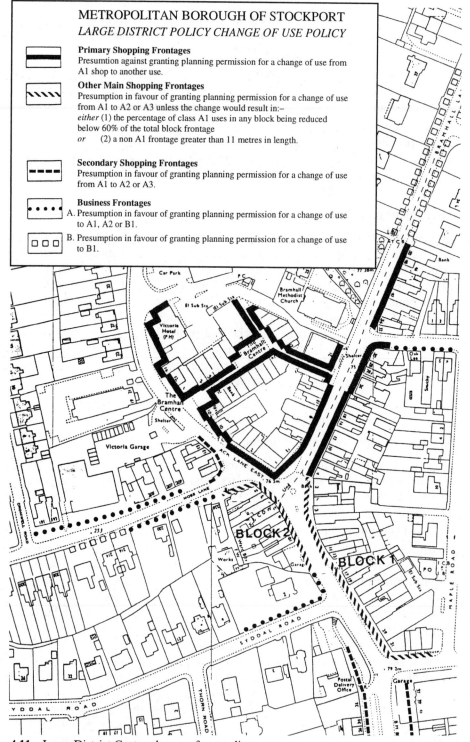

METROPOLITAN BOROUGH OF STOCKPORT
LARGE DISTRICT POLICY CHANGE OF USE POLICY

Primary Shopping Frontages
Presumtion against granting planning permission for a change of use from
A1 shop to another use.

Other Main Shopping Frontages
Presumption in favour of granting planning permission for a change of use
from A1 to A2 or A3 unless the change would result in:–
either (1) the percentage of class A1 uses in any block being reduced
below 60% of the total block frontage
or   (2) a non A1 frontage greater than 11 metres in length.

Secondary Shopping Frontages
Presumption in favour of granting planning permission for a change of use
from A1 to A2 or A3.

Business Frontages
A. Presumption in favour of granting planning permission for a change of use
to A1, A2 or B1.

B. Presumption in favour of granting planning permission for a change of use
to B1.

Figure 4.11   Large District Centre change of use policy
Source: Reproduced with permission from the Metropolitan Borough of Stockport Planning
Department

Policy S1 indicates that they normally resist the loss of shop units and floorspace. In the event they would not normally permit a change from class A1 to class A2 or A3, at ground floor level if the development resulted in any of the following:

1. Less than 75 per cent of the total core ground floor frontage being in shop (A1) use.
2. Less than 65 per cent of the total non-core ground floor frontage being in shop (A1) use.
3. Three or more non-shop uses in adjacent units.
4. Significant increase in traffic and parking problems.
5. Any loss of residential floorspace including ancillary space such as that necessary for access.

(Policy S12 from Kensington and Chelsea UDP (deposited draft 1992))

Waltham Forest planning department, in an effort to maintain the main shopping frontages of Walthamstow and its principal centres insist that, in addition to satisfying criteria similar to those for Kensington and Chelsea, a change of use from A1 will only be permitted provided a shop style window is maintained, 'and that the premises remain open throughout normal shopping hours'. (Waltham Forest UDP (deposit draft) 1992.) This clearly aims to deter banks from opening branches in the primary area and ensures that if they do, a retail image is maintained. Other authorities are less specific about their policies, for example, Chester operates a 'blanket' policy in its core areas, whereby no more non-retail activity is allowed than that which is there from a historical background:

This policy does not seek to remove existing non-retail uses from the primary retail areas but is intended to restrict further intrusion of non-retail users into Chester's main shopping area. In the secondary areas the establishment of A2 use may be permitted where these stimulate pedestrian flow and do not detract from the predominantly retailing function of the area. (Chester Local Plan 1988)

4.3.3   Refusal of branch applications

Many financial institutions find the local authority unitary development plan guidelines on change of class use conflict with their own interests. An extract from a letter to the directorate of planning services for the Royal Borough of Kensington and Chelsea, concerning the 1992 UDP (deposited draft) helps to illustrate this viewpoint;:

The restrictive policy which the Council seeks to adopt in policies S1 and S12 is based upon the outdated concept that uses such as those within class A2 can threaten the vitality and viability of the whole shopping centre or particular core or non-core frontages. It fails to recognise the metamorphosis of the financial and professional service sector and its significant contribution to vitality and viability. (Estates Surveyor, a UK Bank plc April 1992)

Accordingly, and in spite of the local authority UDP guidelines, as potential prime sites for branches are in the restricted core areas, financial institutions submit applications for change of use. The local planning department may reject such proposals, in which case the applicant has the right to appeal against the planning decision under the Town and Country Planning Act 1990, Section 78 and Schedule 6 (Halsbury's Statutes 1990). At these appeals an independent planning inspector from the Department of the Environment decides, upon hearing argument from both parties, whether permission will be granted. Figure 4.12 provides the most common reasons given by local authorities for restricting the development of a bank or building society outlet in their main shopping area.

1. The site could be leased for a more beneficial and attractive product retail use.
2. The proposed length of non-retail frontage, or the ratio of non-retail to retail length of frontage, would fall outside development control specifications and rise to an unacceptable level.
3. Alternative sites are offered in the non-core area, which is the more appropriate sector for non-retail use.
4. Bank/building society use would not be in keeping with the character of main shopping parades changing its essential feel, detracting from the predominantly retailing function.
5. The shopping role of the centre would become fragmented and diluted with an actual reduction in the number of prime retail sites.
6. The removal/reduction of shopping provision in core areas will have a significant social impact, especially for those individuals who are less mobile.
7. Windows of financial service outlets are very uninteresting creating 'dead frontage' on the high streets.
8. The vitality of the frontage would be reduced causing a decrease in pedestrian activity.
9. Opening hours do not conform with those of retail traders.
10. Petitions from neighbouring retail properties and letters from other interested parties confirm that a financial service outlet would make the street less attractive to shoppers.
11. The purchasing power of financial institutions will put up rents in the centre preventing smaller/novelty/boutique shops, which add an important retail element, from locating there.
12. External ATMs are a form of pavement trading disrupting narrow pedestrian links, hindering both the movement and safety of shoppers.
13. Core shopping areas tend to have restricted parking along their road sides. Financial service facilities can create problems with traffic congestion as customers are frequently willing to park on yellow lines to make a quick visit to the branch. This situation is exacerbated if in the vicinity of other A2/A3 sites or near to public transport, or a convenience store.
14. The Council performs consistently within its guidelines, if one institution is seen to have received permission for non-retail use in a core area it will be viewed as a watermark or test case and others will expect/demand the same treatment.

Figure 4.12   Common reasons for restricting bank and building society outlets in primary shopping areas
Source: Based on local authority interviews, UDPs, bank/building society interviews and Planning Inspectorate appeal enquiry reports

4.3.4   Attempts to win planning appeals

Many financial institutions are aware of the bases for planning department rejections and have developed strategies to counter them. Figure 4.13 indicates the arguments and strategies employed by financial institutions to enhance the likelihood of the success of their planning applications. In addition to utilizing these strategies, institutions have the financial and personnel backing to support their applications. At potentially problematic applications, they are sometimes in a position to canvas some local support; in effect 'tapping the old boy network'. Local authorities generally do not have these management or financial resources to perform their own market research in support of their arguments which would enable the presentation of a stronger case at appeal. A certain amount of agitation might therefore be anticipated between

1. The restrictive policy and the classification system grouping banks with offices fail to recognize the metamorphosis of the financial service sector and are outdated. Modern branches have a reduced processing and enquiry role, their designs are more open plan, both looking and functioning more like shops.
2. It is unfair to refuse permission if the proposal keeps within most UDP guidelines.
3. Provision of branch sites must be made somewhere as financial services play an important and necessary role on the high street. (Institutions frequently produce market research figures to illustrate that there is a market for another branch.)
4. Commercial viability depends on locating where pedestrian traffic flows are high.
5. Banks and retailers compliment each other, shoppers cannot buy without the services of banks and retailers need a branch nearby so that takings can be swiftly and safely deposited.
6. Institutions reiterate the pointlessness of locating where they would be detrimental to traffic flows as these are as essential to banks/building societies as they are to retailers.
7. Little evidence exists to show that a financial service outlet causes a reduction in footfall. (Institutions may even produce market research data depicting examples of high street outlets generating 500–1500 customers daily.)
8. Drawings, plans, photographs and even computer aided design images are frequently produced to show how a proposed outlet would appear on the high street, emphasizing that it would in fact enhance the shopping parade.
9. Emphasis might also be made about the proposed branch's conformity to local authority specifications in terms of, ramps, automatic doors and correct ATM and counter heights for disabled people, and appropriate use of signs, facias and illumination in conservation areas and on listed buildings.
10. Branch designs are frequently produced with ATMs in lobby areas to reduce worries about the disruption to pedestrian flows.
11. The ATM lobby areas have 24 hour, card access to give customers banking services outside normal trading hours. Some institutions may even offer to give the proposed branch extended opening hours, including Saturdays.
12. It is anti-competitive if other institutions are represented in the core area.
13. Granting one institution a site in the primary shopping area will not necessarily mean all the others will come in, most institutions will be represented there already.
14. Banks and building societies frequently try and obtain units with parking spaces at the rear, in the basement or at a nearby car park to avoid any traffic/parking congestion.
15. Most institutions are rationalizing their branch networks, this along with merger activity means that further gaps are likely to be left in the parade in the future.
16. Recession and the development of out of town shopping centres will also continue to create gaps in the retail cores, an active branch is better than a vacant premises, with bill stickers.
17. In times of recession and reduced retail activity banks remain busy and can help to prop up a centre's performance during times of economic downturn, as well as providing much needed employment.
18. Institutions with their considerable financial backing may be in a position to trade 'planning gains' or incentives towards getting a favourable decision. Contribution to a local cause such as play equipment for a local park is an example.

Figure 4.13 Financial institution's argument/strategies to enhance the success of planning applications. *Source:* Based on, local authority interviews, UDPs, bank/building society interviews and planning inspectorate appeal enquiry reports

institutions and planning departments. This might, however, be avoided or ameliorated if preliminary discussion, in a less formal atmosphere, first occurs. Indeed, there is some evidence to suggest that an application by an institution is more likely to be successful if there is some initial communication and cooperation between the planner and applicant. It goes without saying that towns need to be planned and planning departments need to control development in order to maintain the structure of shopping centres. This is a mutually important objective and, especially in the current climate of recession, would benefit all the more from an atmosphere of cooperation. If mergers continue to occur within the industry and financial institutions persevere with their strategies of rationalization, selling off the traditional style corner sites which are no longer appropriate in terms of unit requirements, they could actually add to the already depressed nature found in many of the UK's retailing centres. A reduction in the total number of branches will lead to even more vacant units appearing in the town centre. To date many of the large traditional style bank premises have been refitted as fast food outlets and wine bars, but the market for these will become saturated. Careful planning and communication between planners, retailers and service providers might help someway towards preserving retail centres and increase awareness of factors that may become important issues effecting their vitality and viability in the future (Greenland 1993).

SUMMARY

Location and rationalization decisions involve substantial long-term capital investments and have far-reaching effects on network performance. Branch location is a key factor, influencing a customer's choice of financial institution and its area and site specific characteristics are fundamental determinants of potential profitability. During the past ten years, the networks of the UK's banks and building societies have undergone dramatic changes in response to town centre evolution, the economy, increased competition, mergers and acquisitions, new technologies, different premises requirements and the reconsideration of distribution strategies. Despite developments in telephone banking, it is the branch that continues to be the critical channel for financial service provision. Virtually all the institutions are involved in actively increasing the efficiency of their networks through a process of rationalization and relocation. Such strategies have resulted in smaller, more automated and cost-effective networks, many of which exhibit different levels of hierarchies of service offering which help to further minimize overheads. The branches themselves, with the removal of processing and enquiry functions have become more self-service and retail-oriented, being located in smaller shop-like units. In this way the financial institutions are providing a significant element of change in the urban morphology of towns and cities. The familiar traditional looking bank branch with its austere appearance and impressive architecture will be less commonplace and may well become a thing of the past. Such trends and the changes in the high street will continue as institutions strive further towards attaining optimum network efficiency, with the minimum of disruption to their customers.

Site and location assessments are only as reliable and accurate as the evaluation techniques and data upon which they are based. Considerable resources and effort have been expended to enable the most appropriate decisions, in the development of network strategies to be made. A general step by step process for location evaluation and rationalization can be identified for banks and building societies, profitability being the key determinant. The main differences between institutions lie in the sophistication of evaluation techniques adopted. A checklist approach is a frequently used method, the main components of which can be categorized into geodemographics, branch activity, centre details and premises. Data concerning these categories are derived from the institution's own data sources and in some cases relevant commercial agencies provide specialist information. More intricate location evaluation techniques have been developed. These generally involve spatial interaction techniques such as gravity modelling, or multiple regression analysis which aim to calculate and predict network profitability. However, before such techniques can be applied to financial service outlets, traditionally account driven records have to be transformed into customer-oriented databases. The use of these methods is likely to become more widespread in the future as financial institutions further evolve their customer records.

Branch location decisions can be heavily influenced by local authority planning departments, whose role it is to maintain the retail nature of town centres. Government guidelines presented by the Department of the Environment have been adapted by town planners and developed into policies which can restrict the establishment and development of financial service outlets. Planning departments are likely to reject applications for new branches in primary retail centres, but as these tend to be the sites with the greatest potential profitability, institutions still submit proposals for these areas. Once a request for planning permission has been refused the case can be taken to appeal, where a number of strategies can be adopted to increase its likelihood of success. In the 1980s and early 1990s, vacancy rates in town centres have increased in a poor economic climate, some banks and building societies have therefore found it easier to gain planning permission. However, it is in the interest of financial institutions to maintain the retail predominance in centres, as they rely heavily on the high pedestrian flows attracted to such areas. The rationalization and relocation programmes being adopted by some financial service providers actually contribute to the increasing vacancy rates in town centres and thus detract from their attractiveness. As such, increased cooperation should be encouraged between town planning departments and banks and building societies to help in the attainment of mutually beneficial objectives; namely the maintenance of viable and prosperous retail cores.

REVIEW QUESTIONS

1. 'Branch location is perhaps the most significant element in the marketing mix'. Discuss.
2. Why has there been a decline in the size of the branch networks of the main UK financial service providers?
3. What factors should be considered when developing a branch network distribution strategy?
4. Discuss the concept of a branch hierarchy and explain how it can effect network profitability.
5. Explain the value of effective branch evaluation.
6. What are the key factors that should be considered when assessing potential sites for network expansion?
7. How can information from financial institution's customer databases assist in branch location and evaluation?
8. What are the logical stages for rationalizing the branch network?
9. How can gravity models and multiple regression techniques be used to assist location evaluation?
10. Assess the role of the branch location evaluation checklist.
11. How do local and government authorities constrain financial service developments?
12. What approach should an institution adopt to maximize the likelihood of a successful planning application?
13. 'Town planning restrictions protect the financial institutions as much as the product retailers'. Discuss.

REFERENCES

Abler, R., J.S. Adams and P. Gould (1972) *Spatial Organization: The Geographer's View of the World*, Prentice-Hall International Inc., London.

Andrew, K. (1986) *The Bank Marketing Handbook*, Woodhead-Faulkner Limited, Cambridge.

Bennett, R.O. (1975) *Bank Location Analysis Techniques and Methodology*, American Bankers Association, Washington D.C.

Berry, L.L. and L.A. Capaldini (1974) *Marketing for the Bank Executive*, Mason and Lipscomb Publishers Inc, New York.

Bliss, M. (1988) 'The impact of retailers on financial services', *Long Range Planning*, **12**(1), 55–58.

Bradford, M.G. and W.A. Kent (1977) *Human Geography Theories and Their Applications*, Oxford University Press, Oxford.

British Bankers' Association (1993) *Annual Abstract of Banking Statistics*, Vol. 10, May, Statistical Unit, British Bankers' Association.

Buchan, J. (1992) 'Called to account', *The Independent on Sunday*, 7 June, 3–4.

Building Society Association and Council of Mortgage Lenders (1993) 'Building Societies' Section 6, *Housing Finance* No. 19, May, BSA CML Publications, London.

Channon, D.F. (1986) *Bank Strategic Management and Marketing*, John Wiley and Sons, Chichester.

Christaller, W. (1966) *Central Places in Southern Germany*, translated by C.W. Baskin, Prentice Hall, Englewood Cliffs, NJ.

Cowdell, J. and M. McNamara (1992) 'Locating branches', *Banking World*, **10**(5), 52.

Cowell, D.W. (1984) *The Marketing of Services*, Heinemann Professional Publishing Ltd, Oxford.

Council of the City of Chester (1988) *Greater Chester Local Plan*, February, Council of the City of Chester.

Council On Financial Competition (1987) '*The impact of branch relocation*', Council On Financial Competition, November, Washington DC.

Council of Financial Competition (1988) *Organization and usage of branches in transportation centres*, Council On Financial Competition, May, Washington D.C.

Council On Financial Competition (1988) *Criteria for opening branches in shopping malls*, Council On Financial Competition, October, Washington DC.

Council On Financial Competition (1988) *Alternative branch strategies—branches in airports and shopping malls*, Council On Financial Competition, October, Washington DC.

Council On Financial Competition (1989) *Branch site analysis*, Council On Financial Competition, December, Washington DC.

Council On Financial Competition (1990) *Branch network strategies in the United Kingdom*, Council On Financial Competition, August, Washington DC.

Council On Financial Competition (1991) *Branch Site Analysis*, Council On Financial Competition, May, Washington DC.

Department of the Environment (1985) *Development Control Policy Note 11 Service Uses in Shopping Areas*, HMSO, London.

Department of the Environment (1987) *Town and Country Planning (Use Classes) Order*, April, No. 764, HMSO, London.

Department of the Environment (1987) *Changes of use of buildings and other land, the Town and Country Planning (Use Classes) Order Circular 13/87*, 6 May, HMSO, London.

Dixon, M.E. (1987) 'Micro-generated maps guide bank to potential new branch sites' *Bank Systems and Equipment*, February, 64–65.

Duffy, H. (1991), 'Seeking competitive advantage in retail delivery', *Bank Management*, February, 20–26.

Fernie, J. and R.J. Carrick, (1983) 'Quasi-retail activity in Britain: planning issues and policies', *Services Industries Journal*, **3**, 93–104.

Frerichs, G.R. (1990a) 'The decision matrix maps branch profit potential', *Bank Marketing*, November.

Frerichs, G.R. (1990b) 'To know where you're going, you must find out where you are', *American Banker*, Vol. CLV, No. 130, 1–2.

Ghosh, A. and C.S. Craig (1986) 'An approach to determining optimal locations for new services', *Journal of Marketing Research*, **23**(4), 354–62.

Greenland, S.J. (1993) 'Change in the high street: Banks that want planners to say yes'. *Town and Country Planning*, June, **62**(6), 152–153.

Gwin, J.M. and J.H. Lindgren (1986) Bank attribute determinance: Initial findings in the consumer choice process' in *Creativity in Services Marketing*, eds M. Venkatesen, D.M. Schmnalensee and C. Marshall, American Marketing Association, Chicago.

Halsbury's Statutes of England and Wales (1990) Fourth Edition, Volume 46, 1990 Reissue, Butterworths, London.

Hillman, J. (1990) 'The importance of the street', *Town and Country Planning*, February, 42–46.

Jones, P. (1991) 'Regional Shopping centres: the planning issues', *The Service Industries Journal*, April, 171–178.

Lanphear, S. (1989) 'Location is the key to branch success', *Credit Union Magazine* **11**, 5860.

Littlefield, J.E., G. Jackson Burney and W.V. White (1973) *Bank Branch Location A Handbook of Effective Technique and Practice*, Banking Marketing Association, Chicago.

London Borough of Waltham Forest (1992) *Unitary Development Plan* (Deposit Draft), London Borough of Waltham Forest.

McDonald, G. (1987) 'How out-of-town shops help the centre. *Town and Country Planning*, February, 46–47.

McDonell, J.H. (1990) 'Finding the right site', *Credit Union Management*, April, 30–31.

McDonell, E.D. and M.J. Rubin (1991), 'Develop a profitable service delivery strategy', *Profitable Banker* **3**(3), 1–4.

McGoldrick, P.J. (1990) *Retail Marketing*, McGraw-Hill, Maidenhead.

McGoldrick, P.J. and S.J. Greenland (1992) 'Competition between banks and building societies in the retailing of financial services', *British Journal of Management*, **2**(3), Autumn.

McGoldrick, P.J. and M. Thompson (1992) *Out-of-town or In-town shopping*, Avebury, Aldershot.

McIver, C. and G. Naylor (1986) *Marketing Financial Services*, Second edition, The Institution of Bankers, London.

Meidan, A. (1984) *Banking Marketing Management*, MacMillan Publishers Ltd, London.

Metropolitan Borough of Stockport (1992) *Unitary Development Plan* (Second Draft), Metropolitan Borough of Stockport.

National Consumer Council (1983) *Banking Services And The Consumer*, Methven and Co. Ltd, London.

Peck, N.H. (1989) 'The science of selling and purchasing branches', *The Bankers Magazine*, September/October, 59–64.

Reidenbach, E.R. and R.E. Pitts (1986) *Bank Marketing A Guide to Strategic Planning*, Prentice-Hall, Englewood Cliffs, NJ.

Riley, D. and P.A. Knott (1992) 'Through the eyes of the customer: Research into the new look and functioning of bank and building society branches'. Paper presented to the *155th ESOMAR Seminar on Banking and Insurance*, January.

Royal Borough of Kensington and Chelsea (1992) *Unitary Development Plan* (Deposited Draft), Planning Services Royal Borough of Kensington and Chelsea.

Schiller, R. (1987) 'Out-of-town exodus', in *The Changing Face of British Retailing*, ed. E. McFadyen, Newman, London, 64–73.

Sefton Metropolitan Borough Council (1991) '*Unitary Development Plan: Deposit 1991*' The Metropolitan Borough of Sefton.

Simkin, L.P., P. Doyle and J. Saunders (1985) 'How retailers put site location techniques into operation' *Retail and Distribution Management*, May/June, 21–26.

Tandy, G and R. Stovel (1989) 'Are your branches out on a limb?', *Banking Marketing*, November, 26–29.

Thomson, R. (1992) 'Barclays goes to the phones in profit drive', *The Independent on Sunday*, 2 August, 1.

Volk, R. (1987) 'Community banking the basics of branch site selection', *The Bankers Magazine*, September/October, 68–71.

..
FIVE

RETAIL BRANCH SECURITY

Malcolm Hughes   Watermill Consultants

INTRODUCTION

All customers and staff of branched financial services businesses will be familiar with the presence of security measures in those branches. This chapter examines policies, principles and practices in this area, identifies the main methods of protection employed, discusses staff and customer attitudes and surveys current developments in the United Kingdom and overseas.

It is very firmly stressed that the information on which this work is based arises from the public arena and is available from published sources. The writer is critically aware of the sensitivity of information about retail branch security and, having himself been in a branch when an attempted armed robbery took place, will give no help or encouragement, real or imagined, to those who seek to raid banks and building societies.

5.1 THE CONTEXT OF RETAIL BRANCH SECURITY

5.1.1 Scale of the problem

There were around 2,000 armed raids on branches of banks and building societies during 1992 throughout Great Britain. The number of such attacks is rising rapidly and the 1992 figure was more than double the 1989 total. The sharpest increase in armed raids took place in the London area where the incidence appears to be doubling every 12 months. In nearly all these cases, a weapon was involved or a threat of violence to staff or customers or both. (Banking Insurance and Finance Union, 'The Hidden Cost' 1992.)

There are some 36,000 retail financial services branches in the United Kingdom, including Girobank through Post Office Counters, the clearing banks and all building societies. This total continues to decrease steadily because of mergers, takeovers, the 'rationalization' of branch networks in the face of cost pressures and the increasing use of cash dispensers and ATMs. The number of ATMs and staffed branches was analysed in the previous chapter. From a statistical point of view, a branch raid is a rare event—one chance in 13 years on the figures. In fact, it is clear from the published data on raids that they are concentrated in urban areas generally, and in particular districts specifically, like all robbery. Some branches are raided several times each year.

Thankfully, in most attacks, staff and customers are unhurt but this is not to underestimate the intense effects which can be caused by the sheer terror of being threatened with a weapon wielded by a robber whose mental state and emotional stability may be questionable. Branch security systems, therefore, have to be designed to balance a number of, often conflicting, requirements and it is this area that we now examine.

5.2   PRECAUTIONS AND PREVENTATIVE MEASURES

5.2.1   The roles of staff and trades unions in branch security

Most of the trade unions which represent retail workers have an interest in the security of their membership. For example the Union of Shop, Distributive and Allied Workers; National Union of Public Employees; Civil and Public Services Association; National Association of Local Government Officers have all done extensive work in the field of member security, carrying out research, supporting working parties, publishing guidelines and advice, for example, CPSA 'Violence at Work'; NUCPS 'Guidance on violence at work for union representatives'. It is true that there are violent attacks on staff in Job Centres, Social Security Offices, Housing Offices and equally true that public servants such as traffic wardens, rent officers, health visitors are often in circumstances of danger and are attacked. In this latter 'outdoor' category, of course, physical security is not possible but increasingly, staff in local, central government and government agencies' offices have to be protected from claimants and other aggrieved members of the public.

The main burden of staff interest in financial services has fallen to the Banking Insurance and Finance Union (BIFU). BIFU has published widely in this area, sponsored independent research, supported numerous working parties and worked tirelessly on behalf of its membership in the retail financial services industry. Indeed, it has established something of a reputation on an European and international scale for its expertise in this area and its representatives' views are sought on all important working parties and conferences of which there are many.

The publication in 1992 of the Piper-Hastings management consultancy report, commissioned by BIFU on behalf of the health and safety executive financial services working group marks a watershed in the move to accept that the majority of staff victims of raids face long-term distress and trauma, which need to be counselled for after the event and trained for before the event. The Report also makes recommendations of the need to:

- Develop a policy which is integrated in terms of training and post-raid provision for victims; consistent across the organization; takes account of all available management information.
- Introduce effective training for staff to increase security awareness and develop effective support systems for the victims of raids.
- Evaluate and share information about the pioneering work being done on post-raid counselling.
- Gain management support for the implementation of policy and for an input to the post-raid recovery process.
- Monitor and evaluate staff who experience raids, counsellors, staff who offer ideas on security improvements, departments who interface with victims.

The BIFU report focuses on the effect on staff of being raid victims and goes to considerable lengths to establish the fact that mental and emotional injury is as traumatic as physical injury and in some cases significantly longer lasting. The report shows that 60 per cent of staff in affected institutions 'worried occasionally' about being involved in a raid and that this level of concern is rising as incidents increase. One key area is the difference between staff attitudes depending on the investigative method. For example, using a written questionnaire, 55 per cent of staff involved with incidents described their reactions as 'shock, shaken, shaking' and 21 per cent as 'fear, terrified, frightened'. In personal interviews with trained moderators, these figures increased to 75 per cent and 65 per cent respectively. Most of the descriptions of emotional response showed similar large increases in measurement. Since most banks and building societies rely upon (usually) standardized questionnaire replies to evaluate staff attitudes to raids and security measures, then it would seem that such dispositions are not being accurately determined and this in turn could be leading to faulty policy on post-raid management and security planning.

It is clear from this work, and the results of other similar investigations, that 'post-traumatic stress disorder' or in lay terms, the lasting emotional and physical effects of exposure to violent or disturbing events, is a tangible outcome for staff, but that this is not universally recognized by employers. For example, it is indicated that absenteeism normally increases after a raid and that employees undergo serious changes in their attitude to their employer, including wanting to leave or relocate. It is also clear that employers have a vital responsibility to staff who have been victims and that this responsibility includes post-traumatic stress disorder counselling and a sensitive and interactive approach to emotional attitudes and responses.

However, post-raid event management is only part of the requirement for staff as victims. Staff also need to be trained and educated in how to respond to a raid. The surveys showed that pre-raid training made staff feel more in control, better cared for by the organization and able to recover faster from a raid event. However, exposing staff generally to issues relating to raids was found to be less appropriate since it raises anxiety levels unnecessarily. Three-quarters of financial sector staff 'never or hardly ever' thought about raids; this ties in with the fact that the vast majority of staff will never experience an event. But it was also found that most staff wanted more training in the form of videos, group discussions, response practice. There are some natural conflicts within these responses which are in line with other areas of stress. For example, virtually all adults agree that it is important to have a current will; less than 25 per cent actually do so. It is understandable that financial services retail staff agree with the need for more information and training; yet are made more anxious by such efforts.

BIFU will, quite rightly, express no views in public as to the effectiveness of the various security systems that are available on the market to protect its members. It is known from other research sources that staff attitudes to security devices (screens, alarms, cameras etc.) are ambivalent. This is to say that staff are trained to provide customer service in an ambience which is appropriate to the customer feeling welcome and relaxed. Staff realize that security is necessary for their own protection and that of their customers, but naturally want it to be as unobtrusive as possible. It is difficult to carry out a discussion of a confidential financial matter with a customer on the other side of a glazed security screen, even with a modern sound system, particularly if the customer is elderly. To develop the discussion into a properly structured sales interview is next to impossible. In a contemporary open plan branch, much more effective use can be made of selling techniques.

One unusual feature of the financial services business is the existence of staff unions, often wrongly referred to as staff 'associations'. Quite why such organizations should be so prevalent in this sector is unknown; but it is most likely to date from the strong resistance that the banks and building societies put up in the 1970s to the recruitment efforts of BIFU. This resistance took the form of encouraging the growth of the staff association and its application for certification under the 1972 Employment Act. This Act, among other provisions, set out the framework for bargaining rights and banks and building societies were understandably keen to have their own staff union with sole bargaining rights, rather than BIFU. In fact, since then, BIFU has made significant recruitment inroads against staff unions in almost all the institutions. Staff unions are, of course, fully accredited trades unions and any suggestion that they are in some senses 'tools' of the management of the business is quite wrong. It is true to say that staff unions are very conscious of the charge that they are less aggressive in the service of their members than say BIFU or USDAW and will often go to lengths to show it as false. In the area of staff security, therefore, the staff unions have been as active as any other representative body.

So, at the core of the branch security issue exist a number of conflicts. Heavy branch security gets in the way of good quality customer service and presents the staff with great difficulties in making the branch a relaxed, welcoming environment in which sales development can take place naturally. It has also been suggested by some trade union sources that high levels of physical security may stimulate violence against staff and customers in the sense that the raiders will need to use much more aggressive tactics in such circumstances. However, in these matters, as in so many other areas of branch security, there is a lack of quality data on which to make judgements.

5.2.2 The role of the security industry

Marketing analysts refer to the industry which provides for the security of retail financial services branches as the 'annunciation' business. In other words, the industry produces devices and systems which announce their presence to staff, customers and criminals and say, in effect, this area or premise is protected. The market is further divided into 'active annunciation' (alarms, sirens, lights, vacuum systems, rising screens, autolocking tills, guards etc.) which come into play when an incident occurs but are otherwise quiescent. They may be visible or not, according to the policy of the institution. The other category is 'passive annunciation' (static glazed screens, time delay safes and tills, reinforced counters, strengthened doors, windows and entry systems, continual video recording etc.) All retail financial services branches are fitted with some annunciation devices to protect staff and these may be active or passive, or, more typically, a combination of both types.

The security industry is made up of manufacturers, finishers and installers. Large primary producers are companies such as Pilkington, who make glass, and Chubb, who make a range of systems such as vacuum tubes, safes, rising screens. In the particular case of glass security screens, the original glass sheets have to be laminated with other materials, much in the way of a car windscreen, to resist the impact of a hammer, bullet or shotgun load. This work is done by finishers such as Security Laminators and Impactex who are constantly researching and developing new materials with greater attack resistance. Glass, however thick, when hit with a sharp, heavy object or a bullet will tend to splinter on the side that is being attacked. On the obverse of the glass there may be an effect known as 'spalling' in which chips of glass break out of the surface of the sheet. Both of these phenomena are highly dangerous to staff and customers and it is these that lamination prevents.

The manufacture and finishing of glass is tightly controlled by a number of British Standards (5544, 5051, 6206, 6262) although in many areas, the manufacturers and laminators apply their own commercial standards which exceed the performance requirements of the British Standards (Glass and Glazing Federation). All financial services businesses will specify the precise standards to which they want the glazed elements of the branch to conform and these will apply to all the glazed areas.

As far as the other devices and equipment are concerned, the security industry provides a huge range of items. The main additional installation which is visible to staff and customers is the continually recording camera. As its name implies, this is a video camera which takes a record of the branch public space. Its effectiveness has been well demonstrated by the television programme *Crimewatch*, which frequently shows extracts from the video films and these are equally frequently followed by arrests and convictions. A device which is common in Australia and North America is the 'rising shutter' and this is now being installed in the UK. The metal shutter is sunk into the counter, either on its own or in combination with a glazed screen and can be activated to rise in a fraction of a second to ceiling height. This seals off the staff from the raiders with an impregnable barrier and leaves the raiders with no staff targets and nobody to negotiate with. It has been suggested that the main effect of the rising shutter is psychological—the criminals are deprived of their main weapon, fear. However, any customers who are unfortunate enough to be in the branch public space at the time are left in the middle of a situation which is in some respects more dangerous. It has been argued that the rising shutter simply removes the staff from the confrontation and leaves the customers with the problem. There are also doubts about who carries the responsibility for activating the shutter in a confrontation where the staff may be threatened at gunpoint. Nevertheless, rising shutters are known to be effective where the staff are properly trained in their use and more tests are being carried out in the UK. There are also a number of other active devices being tested in the UK and overseas but it is not prudent to give details for public use.

Still other methods of protection rely upon the non-availability of cash in the event of a raid. All tills and safes can be locked automatically, time delay can be built into safe and till opening procedures and vacuum tube systems installed to move cash quickly from the counter area into a remote safe. Clearly, if little or no money is available to a raider at a particular branch then the prospect is that the branch will not be selected for attack.

One area of security protection which does give cause for concern is in the installation of glazed and other security devices. Although there are specialist installation companies such as Pearce Security Systems, Killby-Tann and Chubb (who also carry out some manufacturing), the majority of security devices are positioned as part of a general shopfitting contract, either for a new outlet or within a refurbishment. As with all shopfitting, this type of work tends to be carried out by small local companies—there are nearly 1,400 'shopfitters' in *Yellow Pages* nationally. Clearly, a security device is only as good as the strength and appropriateness of its attachments or mountings. Sources within the security industry have called for new British Standards and a Code of Practice to regulate the shopfitting of security equipment. Such an increase in regulation would benefit all professional installers, large and small, by making life more difficult for the few 'cowboys' who damage the standing of the majority of reputable installers in the industry.

5.2.3 The role of the employers

One of the main driving forces for change in the provision of security systems at branch level must be the attitudes of the employers since, at the end of the day, they have to pay for security devices and fit security policy into their overall trading practices. All employers in the financial services industry will wish to take the fullest steps possible to protect staff and customers in the event of an incident. On the other hand, there are a number of conflicts which appear in the formation of branch security policy and these make it an area of great difficulty.

It is theoretically possible to construct and shopfit a building society or bank branch which is impregnable to any form of attack, where any attack would fail and any raid would guarantee the capture of the criminals. The only problem is that it could not function as a retail outlet because the moment that the general public is admitted to any premises, the conditions for a raid exist. The 'bunker' concept of security has been replaced with more flexible security methods which act as a massive deterrent to crime but also allow the staff and customers to interact and to transact business. All the research carried out into staff and customer attitudes to security reveal ambivalent attitudes. All know of the necessity for protection but all resent the fact that it makes the branch environment less attractive and welcoming. Just as the concept of armed police is anathema in Britain, it is regretfully accepted as needed in certain circumstances.

So, branch security is, of necessity a compromise between level of protection and the need to function as a retailer, just as car design is a compromise between safety, cost and appearance. The question of the level and type of security appropriate to each branch is a matter for judgement, consultation with the local police advisers, use of the body of research knowledge of the manufacturers and consultants in the security industry and discussions with trades unions and staff unions.

The branches of retail financial services businesses tend to be in two quite distinct types of premises. Banks traditionally have occupied elderly and undistinguished Gothic temples in the high street and there has been a long tradition of bank premises design that the building should reflect solidarity and stern prudentiality. This traditional approach continues even today where banks utilize new premises in shopping malls and town centre redevelopments. It has been said that if you were suddenly transported into the middle of a modern multi-range retailer such as W. H. Smith, Boots, Menzies, Woolworth, Homebase etc., it would be difficult to work out from the design and shopfittings alone, which outlet you were in, and the same is certainly true of the banks. With the exceptions of a handful of 'concept' branches, the bank's internal style remains deeply conservative, almost reactionary. Although the proportion of the main banking floor devoted to the customer has increased from the 20 per cent estimated in 1970, in many branches the customer is still palisaded into a congested area, while through the glass screens, staff can be seen working, or, worse, chatting and wandering about. In the research into attitudes to banks, this aspect of waiting in a queue to be served at the one operating window, while other staff can be seen not serving the customer, is at the top of the dislike agenda. Why bank branches are designed so that the customer can see through into the 'office' remains a mystery. From a security point of view, a long counter with glass screens and plenty of staff in view must be the most difficult option to deal with effectively.

The changes anticipated in branch-based financial services are certain to be slowed and truncated by the current recessionary pressures on balance sheets and the need for financial services businesses to undergo a period of consolidation before investment in any aspect of branch operation can be contemplated. This is a critical problem since the activities of the criminal elements in society, whether they are pre-planned or spontaneous do not flow with the business cycle and all employers have a clear duty to both customers and staff to provide a safe and secure environment in which to carry out transactions and selling protocols. It is very difficult to form a consensus view of the future branch design intentions of retail financial services. Broadly, however, the common element is the need to provide more space for the customer to circulate. This means increasing the public space proportion to present an attractive and welcoming context, moving sales teams into the public area and arranging routine transactions in open sight. The implications of these new 'open plan' branches are far-reaching. The serious amounts of cash will be isolated behind a 'hi-cash' area, heavily screened and protected. The cashier points in the open area will be based on a sealed safe, time-delayed and video-surveyed. Office staff will be typically on the first floor and the branch will employ vacuum and other systems to remove cash quickly and securely into remote safes. The evidence from branches in the UK, Australasia and North America which have this combination of customer service and high security layout is that they have a better record of raids than conventional branches. The taking of hostages, either spontaneously or pre-meditated, still takes place, but there is no security system available, nor one that can be designed to cope with the hostage situation and this is true of all businesses, not just financial services. Indeed, financial services are probably better equipped than most to cope with such distressing and horrifying tactics.

Building societies did not inherit large property empires and during the rapid expansion of branches in the 1970s utilized smaller premises than the banks, in many cases little more than 'lock-up' shops. This was partly because the building societies at that time offered only the most basic services, which did not include money transmission, and the administration of accounts required few staff and less space. It was also due to the fact that it was easier to obtain 'change of use' from the planning authority for a small unit. Paradoxically, this provides the societies with a significantly greater problem in one direction and an easier solution in another. Because of restricted space, the societies have been compelled to reduce the amount of branch administration handled at branch level to an absolute minimum. This includes the 'truncation' of cheque clearing on the society's cheque accounts so that cheques do not need returning to the account holding branch but may be cleared centrally. This reduces the amount of paperwork involved in clearing by around one-third, albeit at an increased risk of undetected fraud. It is partly for this reason that most societies insist on ten working days before withdrawals may be made on cheque deposits. Most societies have established administration centres to handle paperwork remote from the branches, thus, releasing staff time for customer service and making maximum use of the space available.

So this is to the advantage of the societies who can devote more effective energy to the selling of loans and insurances for example. On the other hand, however, the restricted space in many building society branches means that selling space is at a premium and in particular, that members of staff may be placed outside the security area at sales desks or in cubicles. This not only reduces the amount of circulation space available to the customers but provides for vulnerable staff in the event of an incident. As the societies move increasingly into a wider role in the provision of financial services, they will need to balance the conflicting demands of security and effective selling, just as the banks have been doing for decades. It is important to recognize that no commercial gain can be worth increased risk to staff and customers.

5.2.4 The role of the government and government agencies

The government has no specialized interest in the security of financial services premises except through the operation of the general criminal law and the health and safety legislation. Obviously, the health and safety executive and the police authorities take a more direct and informed interest in these matters. This area is characterized by a proliferation of study groups and working parties; indeed, a financial services working group, sponsored by the health and safety executive, which had been working for some two years, recently produced the consultative version of its report. After the appropriate period for discussion and consideration by the many interested parties, a final version will be produced which may then form the basis for new codes of practice, new regulations and possibly new British Standards. Sources within the industries involved have suggested that the main recommendations will be surprise-free, more coherent policy; better training; improved liaison between authorities; enhanced data capture and research.

One of the more contentious suggestions is likely to be that local authorities should inspect financial services branch security installations under the Health and Safety at Work Act. This would put employee safety in financial services branches on the same level as operatives in hazardous circumstances in factory production where dangerous machines and equipment have to be properly isolated and fitted with guarding devices. It is deceptively easy to accept the analogy between potentially injurious circumstances in an industrial production unit and a branch likely to be subject to an armed raid. However, the analogy assumes that there is a 'right' way to protect an employee from the consequences of an armed raid just as there is a right way to guard an operative from the careless use of a lathe and, of course, this is not the case. There are as many opinions as to the optimization of retail security as there are companies in the field. If inspection of premises is introduced, then we will have to be more certain than we are at present of the efficacy of the active and passive devices available and their effect on the intentions of criminals of all types. We will also need to be confident that those chosen to carry out the inspections are fully trained and competent in the benchmarks of production, finishing and, importantly, the standards of good installation practice. All sides of the industry would agree that we are a long way from these conditions.

SUMMARY

Raids on financial services branches are growing in frequency and in the use of violence and weapons. All sides involved are making continual efforts to improve the degree of protection afforded to staff and customers but these efforts are hampered by lack of cooperation at local level, growing competitiveness and lack of investment in premises. There is a shortage of good industry-wide research data on raids, the effectiveness of various active and passive devices and into the trauma effects on staff.

While the production and finishing of devices is largely governed by British Standards, the installation of equipment is frequently carried out by local shopfitters to unknown specifications as part of an overall furbishment and not by one of the specialist security installers.

The modern open plan branch layout can place more staff in the public space where they are vulnerable to raid events, although the evidence is that such branches are less likely to be raided.

A new generation of active security devices such as rising shutters are currently being evaluated and should do much to increase staff safety although more data are needed. There is much greater consciousness on the part of employers as to the 'hidden' effects on staff of branch attacks; training and counselling are increasingly available to those affected.

REVIEW EXERCISES

1. You are the marketing manager of a medium size building society and you are planning to gauge staff and customer reaction to a radical new 'open plan' office which incorporates high level but unobtrusive security devices. Set out how you would approach such a research exercise focusing particularly on the likely objectives of the study and the need to take soundings over a significant period of time.
2. The senior negotiator of the staff union of your bank seeks a meeting with you to discuss the setting up of a training programme for staff to prepare them for the possibility of being involved in a branch raid and to help them recover afterwards. List the issues that you would put on the agenda for such a meeting and the particular areas of discussion you would prepare information for.
3. It has been said that the higher the level of protection present in a branch, the greater the possibility of a raid, and that the raid is more likely to involve violence to staff. Set out your views for and against this point of view.
4. It is clear that the greater the levels of competition which exist in an industry, so the more difficult it is to obtain cooperation even on matters of mutual and collective interest. Frame a set of recommendations for the setting up of a joint body to harmonize the policy approach to branch security issues in financial services. What major blockages do you anticipate to the effective function of such a body and how would you manage them?

5. Following a raid on one of your branches in which a quantity of money was taken but no one was physically injured, the local radio station asks you to take part in a 'phone-in' discussion of the event and the Board has agreed to provide a spokesman. In this role, what are the main points that you will wish to communicate?

REFERENCES

Banking Insurance and Finance Union (1992) 'The Hidden Cost—a review of policy and research on behalf of the Health and Safety Executive Financial Services Working Group', Piper-Hastings Management Consultants, London.

Ennew, C., T. Watkins and M. Wright. (1990), *Marketing Financial Services*, Heinemann, Oxford.

Glass and Glazing Federation (1987) General Information Sections 14.1; 6.3; 6.4. London.

Civil and Public Services Association (April 1990) 'Violence at Work—Guidance', London.

Civil and Public Services Association (August 1990) 'Violence at Work—Open Plan Offices', London.

National Union of Civil and Public Servants (1992) 'Violence at Work – Guidance for Union Representatives', London.

Note: Although the facts and opinions expressed in this chapter are entirely the responsibility of the writer, it is right that my grateful thanks are recorded to those many managers and staff in all sectors of the security industry, trades unions and employers who took the time out of their busy schedules to answer my questions helpfully and thoughtfully.

CHAPTER SIX

THE BRANCH ENVIRONMENT

Steven Greenland   Manchester School of Management

INTRODUCTION

Financial service branch environments are among the most sophisticated and complex facing the designer. They are multifunctional facilities aiming to provide an acceptable working atmosphere for staff, efficient service/product delivery for consumers and also an effective environment for communicating the required corporate messages/image. Due to the intangibility of financial service products, the design of a branch has an even more significant role to play, when compared to the importance of design in other settings. At the branch, the only tangible points of reference a customer has with which to associate an institution's products are the outlet's appearance, its functioning and layout, and the quality of service. Even service quality will be, to an extent, a function of the environment, as staff satisfaction and performance levels will be directly influenced by their work surroundings.

The appropriate designing of environments where products and services are offered is now recognized as being a powerful medium for improving efficiency and user satisfaction and for gaining a competitive advantage over adversaries. The relationship between a designed environment and the effects it has upon its users is, however, extremely complex. Nevertheless, a clear understanding of this relationship and how various design styles exert their influences is essential so that branches with the maximum likelihood of inducing the desired effects can be produced. In today's highly competitive financial service markets, where there has been an increasing drive towards competitiveness and branch accountability, this area has become a major focus of attention for many institutions. Recent industry activity and expenditure on researching and creating the most effective and user friendly branch environments has been enormous.

Over the past five years, the realization of the importance of the branch has caused its role and its form and layout to be re-evaluated. Specific branch design concepts and strategies have been developed by the UK institutions and are currently being applied across their networks. As a result, the appearance and functioning of the UK's financial service outlets is being revolutionized. This chapter describes these changes, provides details of branch design and reconfiguration programmes, discusses the key factors for consideration in retail branch design and evaluation, and goes on to consider various techniques for measuring design performance and evaluating the branch environment.

6.1   THE CHANGING ROLE AND FACE OF UK BRANCH DESIGN

The branch is a key element in the financial institution's marketing mix. Recently its importance has been more fully recognized and a great deal of resources have been channelled into

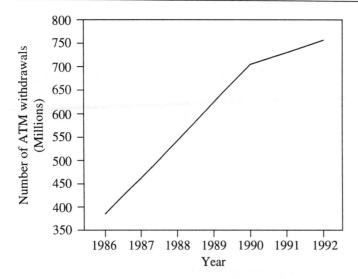

Figure 6.1 Number of ATM withdrawals of the leading five UK banks
Source: Calculated from figures in Table 6.04, Annual Abstract of Banking Statistics, Volume 10, Statistical Unit, British Bankers' Association 1993

improving the effectiveness of branch design. This section describes the important role of the branch in UK distribution strategies and discusses the main design changes that have occurred.

6.1.1 The role of the branch

As discussed in Chapter 4, the branch is and will continue to be the main vehicle for distributing personal financial services. While telephone banking, home banking and remote ATM networks will be playing increasingly important roles in the European financial markets of the future, both the current activities of institutions, as well as customer opinion, dictate that the decline in the importance of the branch will not be as 'radical' as predicted by some. Customers do experience certain advantages, especially in terms of convenience when using ATMs, telephone and home banking services. Accordingly, most larger institutions are experimenting with telephone banking, reducing their domestic networks in terms of branch numbers and intensifying the use of ATMs (see Figure 6.1). This increased ATM usage is, however, with a view to enhancing efficiencies, rather than the elimination of the branch as the main customer/institution interface.

In certain circumstances the lack of 'human' contact associated with automated and non-branch services can be a distinct disadvantage. The following responses selected from a series of group discussions conducted inside a working branch help to describe some of these and demonstrate the continuing need for the branch and its personal service.

For business you still need a bank branch, you still need advice and you still need to see somebody about some things.

If your statement's wrong you want to go in rather than just discuss it on the phone.

I prefer for the bank cashier to check that the money that I've given him is correct. For depositing the money I like the bank to stamp it, they tell me if any cheques haven't been signed.

My only criticism I have of UK bank is that everything is actually done over the telephone. Of course if you have a bank you can actually get a relationship going with the bank manager or the assistant manager, I think that it's a bit impersonal.

I find it easier if someone has been trained to talk about insurance and I can ask questions whereas you can't ask the machine questions, it's either yes/no, yes/no which is off putting.

(Greenland and McGoldrick, 1991b)

Undoubtedly there is a market segment to be catered for with non-branch services, especially among full-time employees. However, as weekday and weekend opening hours increase, the convenience attraction of telephone banking may be lessened. The promise of a personal service and the opportunity to develop friendly/personal financial relationships with institutions may be seen as being more valuable and thus the market for non-branch banking may actually decline. Another point to be emphasized is the fact that it is in the institution's own interest for these personal relationships to exist as they can be actively cultivated to promote image and stimulate cross-selling. This cementing of the business–customer association has been termed 'relationship marketing' (Martin *et al.*, 1989). In the impersonal atmosphere of a non-branch interchange, it is unlikely that the ATM or telephone personnel will be fully aware of a customer's financial needs and certainly will not have the experience, from an established face-to-face relationship, with which to back up such knowledge. The branch environment therefore has a valuable and continuing role to play in the retailing of financial services.

6.1.2 The increasing significance of branch design and a branch identity

Having established the continuing importance of the branch distribution channel, attention will now be given to its design. Traditionally, bank facilities were errand driven, transactional processing, service outlets. In terms of appearances, they projected images of reliability, security and stability through premises with impressive, timeless architecture and a rather stern ambience. Building societies generally had a friendlier image and less austere environments (McGoldrick and Greenland, 1992; Riley and Knott, 1992). During recent years, however, the role and design of the branch, especially for banks, have changed; its significance as an element in the marketing mix has increased dramatically and the outlet style and layout have been revolutionized. These changes were brought about by a complex series of developments, driven predominantly by the ever-increasing need to generate greater revenue through sales of services and to be more cost-effective with operations.

Intensified competition in times of economic hardship has encouraged marketing principles, found effective in product retailing, to be adopted by the personal banking sector. As a result, financial institutions are viewing their services from the point of view of customer needs more than ever before. This has proven essential in a market where bank promiscuity—consumers using more than one institution—is high, and increasingly sophisticated financial customers are becoming far more aware and discerning of competitors' offerings. It is difficult for financial service providers to differentiate themselves in terms of service range, price and interest rates etc. which, to a large extent, are determined by government economic policy; nor by product, as new product developments are easily and swiftly duplicated by competitors. Image and its media portrayal has therefore proven the key weapon in differentiation and positioning strategies. The major players are establishing specific market niches for themselves, aiming to outperform competitors in terms of sophistication and effective/appropriate service delivery to these segments. Within such positioning strategies, the branch, the frontline physical presence on the high street, has been playing an increasingly important role. Continued merger and acquisition activity has created added problems for some institutions' efforts to project a uniform image across their networks.

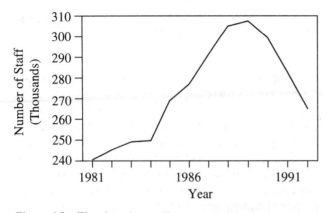

Figure 6.2   The changing staff numbers of the leading five UK banks
Source: Calculated from figures in Table 6.04, Annual Abstract of Banking Statistics, Volume 10, Statistical Unit, British Bankers' Association 1993

6.1.3   Enhancing design efficiency

New technologies, their continued miniaturization, along with the removal of 'back office' functions (processing and telephone enquiries) to central locations and the downgrading of certain outlets to produce more of a hierarchical delivery system, have released a considerable proportion of the branch area for alternative activities (for more details see Chapter 4). Such developments have enabled large savings in employee costs to be made: for example, 1992 seeing a further 15,000 people laid off in the financial services sector (Smith *et al.*, 1992). Figure 6.2 displays the current decline in the number of UK staff for the top five UK banks.

As a result of these trends, the traditional branch layouts and designs are no longer appropriate for the modern bank's marketing objectives. In order to remain competitive branches have been reorganized and retail merchandising techniques incorporated in efforts to more fully satisfy user requirements, maximize the selling opportunity and minimize operational and maintenance costs. This has proven even more essential with the massive rise in the actual number of products and services offered by financial service institutions. For example, a spokesman for a large UK building society indicated that premises functions within his organization had been altered most dramatically, post deregulation due to the fact that over the past ten years the number of products on offer had risen more than fivefold and would stand at between forty to fifty by the year end. Many institutions have been developing specialist services, such as 'mortgage shops', estate agencies, business centres etc. in efforts to cope with this change, segmenting the market with focused product ranges.

Figure 6.3 summarizes the principle motivating forces behind the revolution in the design of financial service outlets.

6.2   THE EVOLUTION IN BRANCH DESIGN

Since the late 1980s the realization of the valuable role that branch design can play in helping to fulfil marketing objectives has resulted in the dramatic change of the modern outlet's appearance. Indeed, this has become a major element of change in the physical charactersitics of retail areas in many towns and cities up and down the country (Greenland, 1993). Traditional working branches with their impressive stone architecture frontages are beginning to be deleted from the institutions' high street networks (see Figure 6.4). Internally, these branch designs are

1. Greater industry competition and economic hardship mean marketing must be more effective, as a result retail merchandising techniques have been adopted.
2. Merger/acquisition activity has produced a confused corporate identity across some networks.
3. Banks have to compete more directly with building societies and their friendlier image.
4. More sophisticated financial consumers, exhibit promiscuity amongst institutions and have more discerning needs that must be catered for.
5. Branch designs are now produced with the customers needs in mind.
6. The number of financial products and services on offer has grown substantially.
7. Outlets providing specialist services have been developed.
8. Technological developments and miniaturization have increased efficiencies and reduced space required for duties such as administration.
9. Processing and enquiry functions have been centralized.
10. Rationalization programmes and more hierarchical branch networks have evolved.
11. Many outlets dating from the 1960s/70s are out of fashion and need renovations to bring their interiors up to present day tastes.
12. The realization of the role the branch can play in achieving numerous marketing objectives.

Figure 6.3: Why branch designs and design strategies are changing, a summary of the principle factors

characterized by a low customer area to staff area ratio, extensive use of bandit screens, small windows and a low adoption rate of retail merchandising techniques in the banking hall area. Any personal interviewing tends to be conducted at counter windows or in the branch manager's private offices. The modern branches, however, have been designed more along the lines of stores, the services offered are considered the products and the staff, no longer bankers, but retailers who require an environment in which they can apply their selling skills. These differences are illustrated in Figure 3.12, Chapter 3 which displays a typical traditional and modern branch layout.

6.2.1   Fifteen key aspects of branch design evolution

There are 15 key areas in which modern branch design has developed. The following section summarizes the more common themes, trends and considerations of these modern design policies/strategies and the resulting evolution of the branch environment.

1.   Centrally coordinated design and refurbishment function   In the past, the branch design function tended to be operationally focused and regionally controlled. Institutions are now centrally developing and coordinating customer-oriented design strategies, creating retail outlets that are more effective in both the marketing and provision of services. Refurbishments and new branch developments are based around specific design concepts dictated and administered by a national rather than regional policy which is a far more efficient way for this function to operate.

2.   Cost restrictions   The size of networks, over 2,000 branches for the larger UK banks, and the cost of refurbishment, upwards of around £750,000 for larger customer service outlets has meant that a piecemeal approach had to be taken to the adoption of the new designs. The network is viewed in its entirety, in a nationally budgeted, coordinated and implemented 'roll out' refurbishment programme in which priority branches are identified and refitted first.

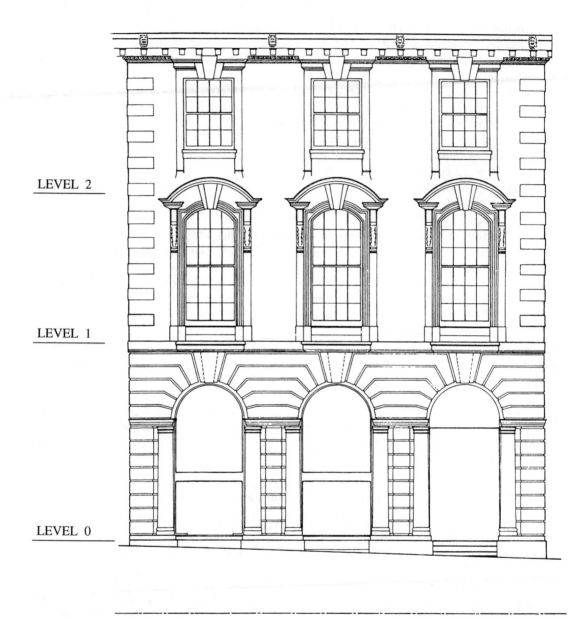

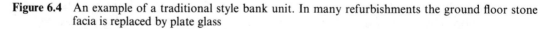

Figure 6.4 An example of a traditional style bank unit. In many refurbishments the ground floor stone facia is replaced by plate glass

3. Standardized designs and the corporate image The centralizing of network refurbishment programmes and the standardization of design have enabled institutions to portray a consistent corporate image through their branch network. Fixtures, fittings and finishings, ATMs, main and supporting colour schemes, symbols, crests, signage and even stationary are being standardized to ensure that the desired messages are visually transmitted. Some institutions have even introduced corporate dress and uniforms for their staff to help reinforce the bank/building society's identity. Lists of approved suppliers are circulated and as well as ensuring a consistent image, these allow very considerable costs savings from bulk orders to be made.

The new design will be standard nationwide, this allows economies of scale to be appreciated. For instance 60,000m^2 of carpet and 2000 designer cash counters have been ordered. (TSB premises manager, 1991)

4. Cost considerations Costs and long-term return on investment considerations have become of key importance and a much greater degree of accountability is emphasized in the modern design strategies. Suppliers are carefully selected and interiors are designed to be durable and adaptable, allowing partial refits and alterations to be made, without having to completely gut a premises. If a particular outlet feature is found to be more effective or an additional new service offering has been developed these new branches have the capacity and capability to adapt their environments to accommodate such changes with the minimum disruption and incursion of expense.

5. Use of design agencies Virtually all institutions use outside design agencies, mainly in the construction of design blueprints or concepts that can be successfully employed in the variety of premises size and shape found in the network. The agencies offer a more objective approach to branch design, and with their knowledge and experience from retail environments aim to create effective and aesthetically pleasing financial selling atmospheres. Agencies such as Fitch, McColl and Michael Peters all have major financial institutions on their customer lists.

6. High profile frontages Large glass, shop window type frontages with automatic doors have been incorporated into modern branch designs to enhance the approachability of outlets, enabling the interior to be seen as well as providing sites for promotional material. Eye catching signage and the effective use of lighting have also been added to exteriors to enhance the branches high street presence. The larger windows may also enhance the staffs' opinion of the branch setting as; 'window views have been found to influence life satisfaction as well as environmental satisfaction', Heerwagen (1990).

7. Increased customer space allocation The continued rationalization of the branch's operational effectiveness as a distribution system has allowed the maximum possible proportion of space to be devoted to the customer and to selling. Traditional style branch units have up to 90 per cent of their areas devoted to staff and operational functions. In the modern designs it is the retail service area that occupies the majority of space. A spokeswoman for Barclays gave the following details of typical customer to staff area ratios before and after refurbishment (see Figure 6.5). (For further examples see Figure 3.12.)

Other institutions quoted figures of up to 80 per cent of the premises area being commonly allocated to the customer/sales area. This change in space allocation has enabled customers to be drawn further inside branches, that have a maximum sales area and much more of a retail feel to them. The increased spaciousness of the banking hall area is also likely to have a positive influence on customer-to-customer relationships. 'Within countless service environments, customers potentially influence the satisfaction and dissatisfaction levels of other customers' (Martin et al., 1989). With this greater space, branch users do not experience such close physical proximity with each other and are thus given more freedom, control and choice over their interaction behaviour with other customers.

Processing and the other so called 'back office' functions are not considered complimentary to the selling environment. During busy, long periods, queuing customers express dissatisfaction at seeing branch staff performing any tasks other than serving. Accordingly, such functions have

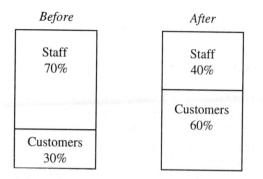

Figure 6.5   Revolution in the share of space for customers – The Barclays refurbishment example

either been removed and centralized in the network or placed out of the view of the main banking hall area.

8.   Open planning and bandit screen removal   Bandit screens have been selectively removed from certain functions in the new style branches. Reception, information and personal banking service desks have been placed out in the banking hall area in an open plan style without bullet proof glass barriers. Interviews are generally performed at these desks or in semi-enclosed or alcoved interview 'pods'. Some of the modern designs also have open, low cash withdrawal desks, which are, in fact, staff operated, automatic cash dispensers which increase the speed and quality of service. Withdrawals from these tend to be limited, frequently not more than £350. Cash is supplied to the tills via pneumatic tubes. Higher value cash withdrawals can be obtained from the screen protected 'high cash fortress area'. In some branches, even the screens from these have been removed, replaced instead with vertical lengths of wire to prevent over-the-counter entry/access. The reasons for removing or reducing the use of barriers in the branch are self-explanatory: the new designs are trying to create a place where people will feel free to interact in a lively and uninhibited fashion, allowing customer/staff relationships to be stimulated. Producing these open plan environments without physical barriers to communication has literally enabled staff to become closer to the customer. Initial security worries over these barrier free, open plan designs, were expressed by management, as well as health and safety departments. However, high profile cameras and video equipment have been installed in replacement of the screens. This, and the fact that the high cash fortress is usually located well inside the branch, seems to deter would-be robbers. Security is, of course, an important factor that needs to be accounted for in the branch retail mix. It adds to the confidence of consumers and staff, raising staff morale and thereby possibly leading to their providing a better service to their customers. (For more details see Chapter 5.)

9.   Prominent merchandising   Merchandising displays, leaflet dispensers and personal banking services staff have been given prominent positions in the banking hall to attract the attention of customers. This is further encouraged through the use of illuminated graphic display stands, eye catching signage and colourful leaflet dispensing carousels. Some of the larger branches have been divided up into specific, well signed, product areas forming what has been termed 'the financial supermarket'. Obviously, customers can only purchase products and services if they are first aware of the fact that the branch provides them. The product and display areas are highlighted with clear signs and through the use of direct and indirect lighting techniques. These strategies have enabled the array of services on offer to be more effectively displayed in a high profile and visual manner.

TRAFFIC FLOW

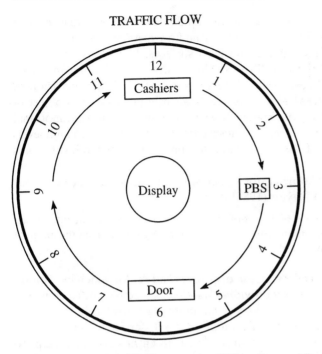

Figure 6.6   Branch traffic flow concept (PBS = Personal Banking Services)
Source: Barclays Bank plc

As the branch is also the work setting for staff, care must be taken to ensure the sales oriented lighting techniques do not interfere with the desired illumination levels for effective staff functioning. Spotlights may create glare problems which make seeing difficult and uncomfortable, and a lack of brightness can cause eye strain.

Poor lighting, due either to inadequate illumination or glare, gives rise to visual fatigue which can contribute to general fatigue. (Hayne, 1981)

Clearly ineffective lighting techniques might reduce staff performance and service quality levels, and must therefore be guarded against.

10. Controlling the direction of customer movement around the branch   Traffic flow concepts from environmental psychology and retail theory have been adopted in new branch designs. Entrances are located on the left hand side of premises and a clockwise direction of movement around the outlet, past displays and product areas is encouraged. The direction of customer movement is controlled and influenced by the branch layout, receptionist instructions, walkways, directional signage, the shape of counter fronts, lighting, as well as floor covering patterns, in efforts to maximize the promotional and selling opportunity. Figure 6.6 illustrates the basic traffic flow principle as communicated to branch managers in Barclays design training programmes.

11. Controlling the speed of customer movement around the branch   The division of the retail/service space into specific functional areas has facilitated the introduction of 'hard' and 'soft' zones to the branch. These zones are determined by the level of service provided and the length of time it is desirable, from the institution's point of view, for the customer to spend at particular points in the branch. Hard zones encourage rapid movement in areas of fast transaction services and are characterized by directional traffic flow methods, tile floor coverings, durable fixtures and finishings, stark lighting and hard surfaces. In contrast, soft zones encourage a slower movement of in-branch traffic through wider aisles, softer lighting and plush carpets and furnishings. In larger branches, comfortable seating areas with the provision of coffee, newspapers and sometimes childrens play areas are frequently included. The object of controlling the speed of movement around the branch is again to help maximize promotional and selling opportunities by keeping the customer for longer periods in the areas with high levels of merchandising activity. The features of the soft zones also aim to enhance the institution's friendly and more accommodating image.

Any attempts at influencing or manipulating customer behaviour must, however, be cautious not to overstep the mark. As McIver and Naylor (1986) state:

The rock on which a financial services business is built is confidence; and too obvious an effort to attract customers, particularly by what look like huckstering methods, may in the long run cheapen the image of the organization and detract from that essential confidence.

12.   Increased use of automated banking services   Cash dispensers and ATMs which in addition to the standard cash withdrawal facility, are now providing statements together with a considerable range of other automated service offerings, play a far more significant role in modern branches and receive high usage levels. The increasing adoption of self-service facilities adds to the high tech feel of new designs. They are generally located near to entrances, which helps to identify and bring those customers requiring higher levels of service further into the branch. These ATM facilities are frequently in lobby areas which can be card accessed and provide service outside normal banking hours. Such lobbies also offer additional display sites for supporting promotional campaigns.

13.   Improved ergonomics   The functioning of the new branch environments for both staff and customers has been improved. By examining operational efficiencies productivity rates can be increased and unnecessary activities eliminated:

Assume that some process requires 10 steps and a clerk completes it 20 times each day. If the process can be completed in five steps, the same clerk theoretically could complete it 40 times each day without increasing his or her effort.' (Barron, 1991)

A new accounts representative may only be required to open a few new accounts per day. This employee's productivity level will be extremely low unless additional duties are given. It is commonplace for modern teller and personal banking service positions to incorporate a 'work station' with VDU and database access allowing the staff to perform other tasks and keep busy when customer activity in the branch is low. Other efficiencies can also be gained in the removal/incorporation of machine cords, wiring and components into fully integrated design interiors, which reduces clutter and frees space for other use.

By providing staff with a comfortable work environment, performance output can be improved: 'Facility managers who have been implementing ergonomic principles in design say that the combined effect of supportive chairs, enhanced lighting, wall systems, abundant work surfaces and temperature and noise control reduces workers' stress and fatigue.

As a result companies save money through:

- Increased individual and collective productivity
- Reduced job turnover, training and recruitment costs
- Reduced sick leave and health care costs (Durante, 1989)

Increased efficiencies in customer actions are achieved in the hard zone areas. The institutions aim to keep a swift flow of traffic through these. A common feature developed for the modern branch is the 'queue line merchandiser' (Hawk, 1989). These are narrow, desk top surfaces with the necessary deposit slips, pens etc. that allow the customer to immediately join a queue line and fill in any required details while they wait. The fixture also includes leaflet dispensers and promotional displays to help merchandise services. This system increases the rate of customer flow through teller queue lines, as well as providing another focal point for communicating the institutions offerings.

14. Staff training/reorientation The styles in which branches are refurbished represent a great change to traditional designs, indeed their very function has been altered with the greatly enhanced retail orientation. As a TSB premises manager indicated:

One problem with trying to enhance the retail image has been staff attitudes, the staff have to alter their ideas and turn from bankers into retailers .... The staff are now being encouraged to cross-sell products and services.

Many institutions run training programmes in conjunction with the implemented refurbishments to help ease staff through this transition and reorientation.

15. Design evaluation/monitoring Once new designs and alterations have been incorporated into the branch networks, information concerning the functional desires and criticisms of staff and consumers are monitored so that any problems can be solved and designs 'tweaked' on an incremental basis, to be incorporated into future refurbishments. This helps ensure increased efficiencies for branch designs in the future.

6.3 BRANCH DESIGN AND RECONFIGURATION PROGRAMMES

This section describes the design teams and the reconfiguration and refurbishment programmes of some of the UK's leading financial service providers. Details concerning the design research methods employed by the industry are given and suggestions regarding the effective structuring and organization of the design function and refurbishment programme provided.

In the past, branch design and refurbishment was an operationally-driven task, dictated by local staff/branch management and heavily influenced by concerns for their own convenience. Evidence of this non-customer orientation can still be observed today in the language of many bankers, an example being the retail sales area which is still frequently referred to as the 'front office' and the 'public space'. More recently, banks, as well as building societies, have been rationalizing their distribution networks and restructuring the premises function within their organizations, adopting a far more structured and customer-oriented approach to design and refurbishment. For the majority of institutions this has lead to the establishment of specialist branch design teams and entirely new branch reconfiguration programmes being developed and applied to the networks. An example of stages involved in one institution's reconfiguration programme is presented in Figure 6.7.

6.3.1 Design teams and their effective organization

With the increasing emphasis on the branch as a marketing medium and the demand for a more cost-effective distribution strategy, many institutions have formed new premises design and refurbishment teams in attempts to better coordinate their branch activities. The size and

1. Establish a mission statement (where we want to be).
2. Establish consumer and staff views on branch environments.
3. Produce a design brief.
4. Construct a warehouse prototype branch mock up.
5. Research and evaluate the functioning of the prototype branch.
6. Amend specific design problems.
7. Perform a high street pilot study on selected branches incorporating the new design.
8. Monitor performance of newly reconfigured branches in terms of sales and user attitudes to their environments.
9. Incrementally improve the design.
10. Pilot the new design to other branches.
11. Refurbish all branches in the fashion of the continuously monitored/updated design concept.

Figure 6.7   The stages of the reconfiguration programme of a large UK financial service provider

composition of these teams varies considerably between organizations. Generally, however, they consist of representatives from premises, marketing, operations and market research functions, as well as individuals from external design and architectural consultancies.

An interdisciplinary design team is the most effective. 'A serious commitment to making branches more functional as selling environments will require communication and cooperation across departmental lines. It does not matter where the initiative begins—in marketing or branch management or strategic planning—the process will ultimately involve virtually everyone associated with the branch' (Hawk, 1990a). The level of resource input required and the long-term ramifications of any decisions made, concerning branch format also necessitates the inclusion of a high ranking team leader. Hawk (1990a) summarizing work by Retail Planning Associates, Columbus US, suggests the following team structure as being the most effective:

- Marketing and/or retail banking executive officer: to provide strategy information and adjudicate/control decision making.
- Market research manager: to provide customer and product specific information relating to branch needs. Attention to the needs of specific user groups such as people with disabilities should also be given.
- Branch administrator and/or branch employee: to provide input on employee branch user needs.
- Merchandising manager: to coordinate in-branch merchandising/promotional strategies.
- A facilities/operations manager: to assist in the re-orientation of both branch premises and staff from an operations to a retail service driven function as well as ensuring design regulations are adhered to.
- 'Out-house' external organizations; to provide expert opinions on certain branch design issues.

The extent to which external organizations are used will depend on the organization's existing functional infrastructure, as well as its resource base. The design briefs for these interdisciplinary teams also vary between institutions, but common factors for consideration and improvement include corporate identity, communicating and reinforcing corporate messages, selling and promoting products, keeping customers, attracting new customers, queue management, open plan areas, product areas, encouraging browsing, security, customer confidence and satisfaction, costs and the longevity of branch design. A more detailed discussion of the possible objectives for design strategies can be found in Figure 6.9.

6.3.2   Branch design research phases

The preliminary research, conducted by UK institutions to generate design concepts for the ideal branch, has typically employed surveys, focus groups and studies using stimulus material such as branch models or photographs of different types of environments and branch layout options, known as 'mood boards'. These qualitative studies aim at furthering the understanding of consumer and staff attitudes to, and behaviour within, branches as well as providing guidance 'on specific issues such as the implications of varying inter-relationships between counter space and personal interview facilities, the degree of privacy required for interview on various subjects, the degree of conservatism deemed appropriate to (building society) branch environments' (Peters, 1986). Branch designs are drawn up on the basis of information gained from these preliminary research studies. The majority, but not all of the larger institutions used outside design consultancies to produce the new branch formats. In some cases up to three consultancies had been contacted with the brief of the preliminary research findings and instructed to produce appropriate branch designs. Where no external agencies had been used, institutions had recently 'poached', or employed individuals with retail design experience.

Several different approaches were adopted by institutions for the piloting and testing of proposed new designs. The most resource intensive technique used was the construction of prototype branches in warehouses. Staff and customers were transported to these mock ups and given different tasks and transactions to perform. Questionnaire surveys and group discussions were then used to evaluate the branch format and layout, and subsequent design improvements made accordingly. This technique has, however, received considerable criticism, stemming mainly from the warehouses' imitation environment and the substantial costs involved. These prototypes are very expensive to produce, costing considerably more than the refurbishment of an existing branch and the accuracy reliability of data produced by them is dubious. The role playing exercises, for instance, are not real life and are performed by individuals acting out parts. No indication of environment effects, on factors such as length of branch visit, attraction of new customers and sales, can be gained in this setting. In addition, the warehouse environment itself is false and does not allow an accurate evaluation of lighting and heating levels and the impact of windowed frontages.

A more favoured approach to branch piloting has been the refurbishing of selected high street branches with the new designs. An assessment of their effects on customer/staff attitudes and behaviour, and their impact on branch performance indicators is then conducted to reveal how successfully the branch design objectives have been achieved. It has, however, proven difficult to accurately assess the impact of different environments on branch performance as many institutions do not have the necessary databases to provide this information. Furthermore any changes recorded could be the result of many variables not necessarily related to the design alterations, staff retraining being such an example.

Results and findings from the branch design research phases are then assimilated and a more effective design solution produced. The details of the branch design solution make up the institution's design manual. These document and illustrate the new styles to be introduced throughout networks, providing lists of approved suppliers and detailing comprehensive and specific guidelines to be adhered to, as far as possible, within the constraints imposed by individual sites. Once an effective design solution has been decided upon, most institutions still maintain some level of monitoring and continued evaluation of their new branch's performance, as well as customer and staff complaints/suggestions. Some institutions maintained pilot branches to experiment with new ideas or technological/product developments. In this way designs are incrementally improved, alterations being centrally coordinated and communicated with minimal effort to branches nationwide.

6.3.3   Roll out of reconfiguration programmes

Once institutions had formulated an effective design strategy, plans for the systematic refurbishment of the whole network were developed. Networks of the UK's larger institutions are enormous and so most adopt a piecemeal approach that allows the core profit making branches to be the first to be refurbished, usually over a period of one to three years. The majority will have completed the implementation of their reconfiguration programmes by the early to mid 1990s. Members of the networks branch design team coordinate the programme, liaising with regional head offices and disseminating the design guidelines down the organizational hierarchy. A strategy for implementing network changes, adopted by several of the larger institutions has been to train and brief regional head office managers on the required branch design concepts, detailed in a branch design manual, who then run their own regional network reconfiguration programmes.

6.3.4   The refurbishment process from branch selection to refit completion

Once a site has been targeted to accommodate the new design, the refurbishment process begins. This will usually be the responsibility of an established premises refurbishment team. An example of a well-known institution's nine stage refurbishment process is presented below:

1. Produce site/premises plans 1:50 scale and obtain shopping centre plans that indicate the immediate premises functions and directions of pedestrian flow.
2. Visit and survey the site with parties involved in the design of the outlet. Typically this will include individuals from a variety of functions, at both national and regional levels and from different hierarchies of the organization, who will provide specific inputs to the refurbishment process.
   National level
   (a) 'Premises controller'; oversees the process and ensures the solution fits into the design concept.
   (b) 'In-house designer/architect'; produces plans to be discussed and altered accordingly.
   (c) 'Structural engineer'; assesses the feasibility and costs of any proposed structural alteration.
   Regional level
   (a) 'Regional controller'; assists in selecting the most effective design, providing marketing and operational input.
   (b) 'Area bank manager'; provides site knowledge, as well as personal design requests.
   'Out-house'
   (a) 'Fitters' tender formal offers/bids for the cost of the refit and estimate time of completion.
   (b) 'Design/architectural agencies' may be brought in for a site with peculiarities such as special structural or security considerations.
   It is desirable to involve, as far as possible, only 'in-house' personnel in the 'roll-out' refurbishment programme. This makes the process far simpler and more effective as less

briefing is required and greater expertise and knowledge is gained along the institution's learning curve. However, some situations inevitably demand outside assistance. For instance, the Alliance and Leicester Building Society hired a York-based architect because of his expertise in dealing with listed buildings and the 'York style'. In this particular case, the refurbishment of a branch occupying a fifteenth century listed building was the problem facing the branch design team. Another common circumstance when outside involvement may be sought is where planning restrictions are anticipated and contacts to aid the 'politicking' process are desirable.

3. Hold branch design meetings to consider and discuss potential formats for the outlet. These must adhere to the branch design manual guidelines. During these meetings, the interested parties discuss any site specific problems posed by the unit, such as structural columns, frontage orientation etc. and opinions for the characteristics of the new layout are voiced. Opinions frequently reflect individuals' functional background and the premises controller has to act as adjudicator. Operations personnel, for instance are typically sales-oriented and therefore inevitably tout for more counters etc. The branch manager may be more concerned with 'back office' facilities etc. The 'in-house' designer sketches out the suggested layouts, upon tracing paper overlays on the existing unit plans. In the light of these, the merits of each branch format are discussed further.

4. Once a format has been decided upon formal plans for the proposed branch layout are drawn up and any further ideas/suggestions are incorporated.

5. Planning permission for any proposed structural alterations or change of building use are applied for.

6. Implementation is instigated with fire and building inspectorate reports. Tenders are invited from five to six fitters/suppliers from the design manuals approved list. Any required agreements, with tenants of associated premises are arranged.

7. If required, a temporary branch will be established while refurbishment takes place. A nearby vacant premises or a portable building are commonly used.

8. Prior to/during refurbishment, marketing and personnel functions will have the responsibility of training staff in the operation and retail orientation of the new outlet, as well as communicating the refurbishment and its benefits to customers.

9. Refits generally take approximately twelve weeks. When complete, opening functions/events are organized to advertise the new style branch in efforts to enhance the customer base.

6.3.5   Flexibility in the design concept

The most successful branch design concepts are those which are readily adaptable to the different sizes and shapes of outlets in the network. Clearly, smaller branches will not contain all the components of larger sites, but the general principles and design messages can still be incorporated. Some institutions are very rigid over the control of their branch environments. Others are less authoritarian, allowing branch managers to apply their own ideas to their outlet's environment. In some branches, for instance, piped music, branch facilities such as children's play areas, teletext share prices, plants, novel merchandise displays etc. have been included at the manager's request. At other sites, concessions on items such as the number of interview rooms/booths have been made. These requests have tended to come from smaller town branches where managers perceive the consumers of such communities to be more familiar with each other and therefore more secretive about their money, demanding greater privacy from the branch environment. Other branches demand the adjustment of the design concept due to their distinct/peculiar character:

- Branches among high quality shops or in central business districts tend to be more opulent in appearance compared to branches in less prestigious sites. An outlet with a large volume of business dealings may have quality finishings installed into first floor offices.
- Sites in 'historical' areas have to have their frontages designed to fit in with their surroundings. Older buildings with preservation orders need special attention and external alterations such as the installation of glass frontages and ATMs will usually be prohibited.
- Frequency of 'hold ups' will also influence the format of a refurbishment. Branches raided once tend to be prone to attack. Such outlets may not position staff in the banking hall area as these pose a hostage taking risk and bullet proof screens may be maintained or a 'pop up' screen can be installed, these spring up at the touch of a button sealing off staff from the banking hall area.
- Branches dealing with the armed forces, especially those in Northern Ireland are also unlikely to accommodate all the refurbishment guidelines.

6.3.6   Organizing the design function and refurbishment programme

The earlier description of the strategies adopted by various UK institution's design functions, in the development of their refurbishment programmes, has revealed the complexity of this task. US financial service design consultants (McDonnell and Albers, 1988) consider a logical structuring of these activities to be a prerequisite for production of the most cost-effective design solutions and roll out programmes. Their suggested approach has been assimilated, along with the successful key elements from the strategies of UK institutions to produce a framework which summarizes how effective retail designs can be developed and successfully implemented into branch networks. This framework is presented in Figure 6.8.

6.3.7   Future trends in UK reconfiguration programmes

Implementation of new design concepts will continue across the branch networks of the UK institutions. In the future, it is unlikely that many more prototype warehouse experiments will be conducted. The real 'acid test' is on the high street and it is here that any branch piloting will take place. Many institutions have formed design teams and now employ their own in-house designers and architects, this trend is likely to continue and the future use of external design consultancies might then be expected to decline. The incremental improvement of branch designs will also continue and any research into new developments will probably take place as environmental experiments in pilot test branches. As yet, very little environment specific research has taken place; this aims at assessing the effects that different environment components have upon the attitudes and behaviour of branch users. For instance, it is not fully appreciated how branch spaciousness, large glass frontages, removal of bandit screens etc. interact with behaviour and effect user attitudes. A small amount of work has been carried out assessing the impact of music on branch users, but on the whole, the sectors' research into this area has been lacking. As branch performance assessment techniques and databases are improved and more systematic approaches to design development are investigated, the specific effects of the various environment elements may become the focus of attention for the design departments. A systematic approach to design evaluation is discussed in the last section of this chapter.

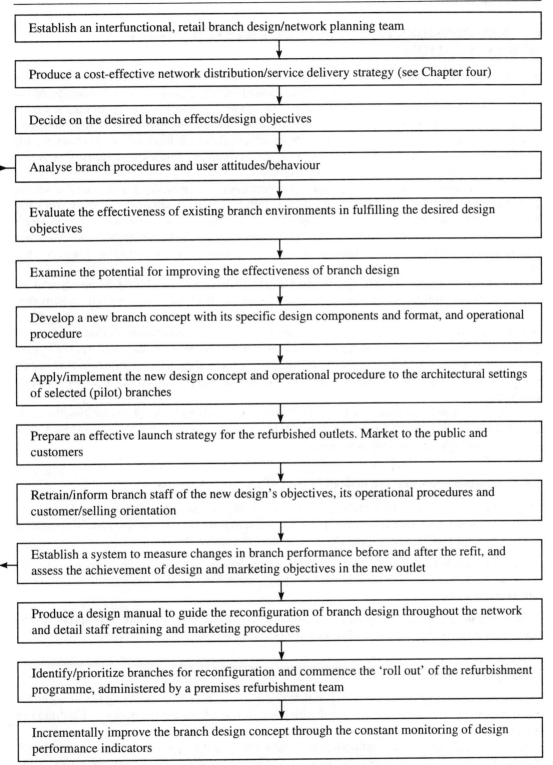

Figure 6.8 Framework for organizing the branch design/refurbishment programme

6.4 KEY CONSIDERATIONS IN RETAIL BRANCH DESIGN AND EVALUATION

Before the creation of an effective branch design can even be considered, appropriate knowledge concerning the environment must first be established. There has to be an appreciation of the multitudinous components and dimensions that make up the branch environment and a comprehension of how they interact with the behaviour and attitude of its users. Only then can a justified and well-reasoned branch format be constructed, which has desired and scientifically proven impacts upon staff and customers. With this knowledge, designs based upon fact, rather than designer whims and fantasy, can be produced.

There is a research and literature base that examines the retail design of financial service branches and other 'servicescapes' (e.g., Bitner, 1992). However, substantially more work has been performed on product retailing outlets (i.e., Grossbart et al., 1990) and an even larger volume exists in the area of design and environmental psychology. Despite the distinctive characteristics and differences of financial service settings much of this indirectly related work is very relevant.

Branch environments are among the most sophisticated and complex of designed environments. They are multifunction facilities, accommodating both working and selling activities, and provide an important medium for marketing messages to be communicated to consumers. 'Because the products are intangible, the environment of the institution is that much more important' (Price, 1988). The intangibility of financial service products dictates that the branch environment and the quality of branch service are key factors by which consumers evaluate an institutions offerings. Even service quality is, to an extent, a product of the branch environment.

The following section details the possible desired effects of retail branch design, elucidates the components of this environment, suggesting key design considerations and discusses how individuals actually perceive atmospheres.

6.4.1 Atmospherics and the desired impact of the branch design

The branch is the financial institution's most prominent physical manifestation and its design has a significant role to play assisting in the achievement of the organization's marketing objectives. Kotler (1973) developed the term 'atmospherics' to describe:

the conscious designing of space to create certain effects in buyers. More specifically, atmospherics is the effort to design buying environments to produce specific emotional effects in the buyer that enhance his purchase probability.

This description is specific to product retailing, a broader definition, more appropriate to the vast array of different product and service providers, is as follows:

Atmospherics is the tailoring of the designed environment to enhance the likelihood of influencing users, and potential users in a desired manner.

In the case of financial service retailing outlets there are some 13 key marketing functions of the 'environment mix' that can be enhanced with the effective use of atmospherics as illustrated in Figure 6.9.

The potential atmospheric influences represent the possible desired impacts of the branch design, which are likely to vary between institutions. Deciding the design objectives is the initial, essential key consideration in the design process.

The design and layout of an outlet can be tailored to influence how cost-effectively successful it is for:
1. Initially, visually attracting customers to the institution.
2. Communicating the desired corporate branch and product images, differentiating them from those of other institutions.
3. Creating the most effective balance between products and functions.
4. Selling, promoting and advertising products and services, as well as the institution.
5. Encouraging the customer to browse around the branch and maximize the time spent in it.
6. Supporting and giving 'environmental substance' to media campaigns.
7. Providing an ergonomically sound environment freeing more bank employees time for sales-oriented activities.
8. Facilitating efficient and quality service delivery.
9. Developing customer/staff relationships.
10. Giving user satisfaction, for both staff and customers, aesthetically, emotionally and in terms of functionality.
11. Enabling the rapid implementation of any future environment alterations or refurbishments.
12. Providing an acceptable design life cycle.
13. Preventing robbery/fraud and imparting staff and customers with confidence in their safety and security.

Figure 6.9   Potential atmospheric influences/design objectives for consideration in the branch design brief

The first obvious step in doing environment–behaviour research is to identify the problem, or in the case of consumer behaviour research to identify the behaviour that one wants to understand or control. (Bitner, 1986)

Once the desirable design–behaviour responses have been selected a detailed design brief can be produced, only then should an examination of the influence of specific environment elements be considered. After all, without an effective design brief there is little or no hope of producing an effective design.

6.4.2   Components of the branch environment

Before an understanding of the effects of specific branch environment features can be gained a listing or classification of its salient elements is essential. Financial service institutions' premises design manuals provide detailed lists and descriptions of items composing the branch environment. The number of individual components and suggested measurement details for a branch are enormous. They usually come under general headings such as:

Frontage	Interview desks	Terminals
Entrances	Interview pods	Ceiling
Fascia	Interview rooms	Lighting
ATM external	Branch managers office	Electrical
ATM internal	Staff offices	Heating and ventilation
Banking/retail hall	Strong room	Furniture
Counters	General office	Floor coverings

Queue lines	Computers	Wall finishes
Merchandise stands	Security TV	Intruder alarms
Enquiries	Office machines	Corporate dress
Reception	Filing	

Under each of the headings are sub-sections with numerous more elements and details. Lists such as these are useful starting points for generating a list of components making up the branch environment. They do not, however, reveal which components and factors are the most instrumental in effecting the attitude and behaviour of branch users.

6.4.3   Environment factors and the branch user effects

Baker *et al.* (1988), researching the design of US branch facilities, proposed five main categories of branch environment variables that affect users:

1. *Ambient conditions*—background stressors tending to impact the subconscious (e.g., air quality, temperature, sound, scent and lighting).
2. *Aesthetics*—more obvious/visual elements, relating to design features (e.g., colour, style, architecture).
3. *Privacy*—both auditory and visual, relating to design features (e.g., enclosed/open plan offices, spaciousness).
4. *Efficiency/convenience*—design factors affecting efficiency, productivity and convenience (e.g., directional signs, queuing systems, hard and soft zones etc.).
5. *Social factors*—these influence attitude and behaviour of the environment users, both staff and consumers.

Such a framework allows an environment to be simplified, enabling further study of its atmosphere to be performed in a more meaningful and manageable way.

Greenland and McGoldrick (1991b), researching customer opinions on UK branch environments, enlisted over 100 observers to spend time in bank and building society outlets and catalogue features that had a positive or negative effect on the perceived quality of those retail environments. From this, a detailed typology of the major components of the branch environment was generated. Branch characteristics, perceived as favourably influencing the retail environment, are presented below in the form of a checklist. They have been categorized under general headings, which are based upon the key underlying dimensions of the branch environment, as suggested by a factor analysis performed on data from a subsequent exploratory questionnaire survey utilizing the typology.

Information and security in the customer banking hall area
Promotional leaflets/posters within easy reach/view of queuing area
Information on current interest rates
TV/video screen information on bank services offered
Visible TV security cameras
Bandit screens

Decor, fixtures and finishings
Plush carpets and furniture
Plants/flower displays/paintings etc.

Figure 6.10   A checklist of the main environment factors/considerations influencing customer perceptions of the financial service outlet

Tasteful decor and colour schemes
Attractively designed stationery
Separate consulting/information desks
Adequate customer facilities; comfortable chairs, kids play areas etc.

Automated services
At least one exterior cashpoint machine
Easily accessible interior ATM
All ATMs working
Express deposit letterbox

Factors affecting outlet convenience/efficiency
Staff numbers
Few other customers in the branch
Organized queuing
Fast moving queues
All cashier counters open when busy
Pleasant staff
Layout of branch designed for simple and efficient use
Proximity to car parks, place of work, homes, shops

Factors effecting privacy and the amount of customer interaction
Privacy at information counters/desks
Spacious area on customer side of counters
Ample desk top surfaces to write on
All the pens working
All the withdrawal/deposit slip trays full
Clock and date easily visible
Private interview rooms available

Architecture and structural features
Impressive building
Large glass frontage
Wide entrance
Automatic doors
Clear eye catching exterior signage
Visibility of back office area behind counters
Branch locality

Physical conditions
Adequate level of lighting
Comfortable air temperature
Clean and tidy
Soft background noise/music
Little noise from outside traffic and ATMs
Pleasant/freshly smelling
Fresh air/comfortable air conditioning

Counter accessories/details
Lighted arrows/instruction indicating when cashier/teller free
Different counters/positions for different services
Function of counter clearly labelled
Clock and date prominently positioned

Staff accessories/details
Name of cashier on desk/badge
Employee tree with staffs' name, photo and position
Attractive staff uniform

Figure 6.10   Continued

Branch design dimensions:

Utility	Privacy	Air quality	Perceived cost
Organization	Security	Temperature	Activity
Space	Lighting	Comfort	Colour
	Acoustics	Tidiness	Potency

Figure 6.11   Design dimensions of financial service outlets

The checklist shown in Figure 6.10 helps to identify the branch attributes that can favourably influence customer attitude and behaviour and intimates which general branch qualities or dimensions are affected.

The concept of design dimensions or themes has been developed by environmental psychologists such as Canter (1969), Kasmar (1970) and Cass and Herschberger (1973). These dimensions represent distinct design concepts or themes, as seen from the users' point of view and help in the standardized descriptions of environments. Gifford (1987), using the work of Cass and Herschberger (1973) identified certain dimensions of designed environments that frequently emerged in studies employing many diverse descriptors. Based on his conclusions, the 15 dimensions shown in Figure 6.11 are proposed for describing financial service facilities.

By obtaining user ratings of branch environments along these dimensions, a quantitative description of their design performance can be obtained.

6.4.4   How the branch environment is appreciated

Kotler (1973) maintained that a place's atmosphere or environment is experienced through four of the five main sensory channels:

1. Visual   (sight)   e.g., colour, brightness, size, shapes
2. Aural   (sound)   e.g., volume, pitch, background noise, music
3. Olfactory   (smell)   e.g., scent, freshness
4. Tactile   (touch)   e.g., softness, smoothness, temperature

The cognitive interpretation of these experiences will determine an individual's response to a particular environment.

If an accurate understanding could be ascertained, of the relative importance users attach to each branch attribute/design dimension, then it would be relatively straightforward to design branches with a corresponding representation of those features. Unfortunately, the process is not that simplistic. Many of the visual, aural, olfactory and tactile environmental elements exert their effects at, or below, the level of consciousness. This factor creates difficulties in the investigation of environment–behaviour relationships and can lead to inaccuracies and misinterpretations of findings. The following example illustrates this point. As part of a pilot study appraising the design of bank branches, customers were asked to indicate the perceived importance of 53 branch environment attributes (Greenland and McGoldrick, 1991a). This approach was considered applicable, as importance ratings had been utilized in a study by Baker *et al.* (1988), for assessing branch environments, with some reported success. A large glass frontage was rated as the least important element examined by the pilot study. However, other more qualitative work (Greenland and McGoldrick, 1991b) involving interviews with branch design managers and group discussions performed in branch during banking hours, revealed that windows were a significant contributor to the overall ambience and utility of the design;

they affected lighting levels as well as allowing users to see in and out of the branch. The contradiction in the research findings suggests that environmental appraisal cannot be conducted accurately using an instrument as simplistic and direct as importance ratings, posing a particular challenge for researchers and practitioners alike.

As Holahan (1978) stated:

Our commonsense notions of the relationship between architecture and activity are often erroneous ... Thus, an adequate appreciation of the human impact of architectural settings needs to be founded on a systematic empirical evaluation.

Unless a technique, that accurately appraises the environment, is evolved and utilized, it will be difficult to make well-founded and effective design solutions. Any approach adopted must therefore take account of the more subtle or subconscious impacts of design.

6.4.5   The emotional impact of the designed environment

Subconscious branch environment effects can be investigated by exploring their users' emotional response to the design. Research from environmental psychology has revealed the importance of examining emotional states when considering the impact of designed environments as these serve as mediators between environmental stimuli and corresponding user reactions. The focus of such work has been the ability of an environment to induce specific emotional responses which in turn influence an individual's behaviour, such as the desire to remain in and further explore that environment.

Mehrabian and Russell (1974), in their original work, revealed two key dimensions of emotion, relating orthogonally to one another, that describe how a person feels when in an environment. They discovered that in a more pleasant environment, the greater the degree of arousal, the more likely it would be for individuals to display approach behaviour both towards that setting and to individuals in it, whereas in an unpleasant environment the greater the arousal, the more likely it would be for individuals to display avoidance behaviour. They also suggested the emotional response of dominance, describing the extent to which the individual feels in control of a situation when in an environment, as influencing approach and avoidance behaviour. Later, however, research by Russell and Pratt (1980) and Donovan and Rossiter (1982) questioned the significance of this dominance factor. An environment's information rate; its novelty, complexity and spaciousness, has been shown to affect its arousing quality and thus the resulting approach/avoidance behaviour. A summary of the main components influencing an individual's approach/avoidance behaviour is displayed in Figure 6.12. By measuring each of these a greater appreciation of some of the more subtle or subconscious impacts of different designs can be gained.

Having considered and discussed key aspects of retail branch design and associated problems with assessing design performance, the actual measurement of the effectiveness of different branch styles is now examined.

6.5   MEASURING DESIGN PERFORMANCE AND EVALUATING THE BRANCH ENVIRONMENT

Accurate assessment and evaluation of the branch environment is essential in order for design shortcomings and improvement areas to be identified. The design effectiveness of an outlet can be measured in post-occupation studies by assessing various design performance indicators. These performance indicators will involve measurement of:

- The fulfilment of design objectives
- Performance along design dimensions
- The emotional impact of the design

6.5.1 Techniques for assessing the fulfilment of design objectives

Figure 6.9 listed 13 possible design objectives. Some of these, such as; a design's life cycle, the style's ability to deter/prevent robbery and whether the format enables rapid implementation of future alterations are performance elements, that can only be assessed by monitoring branches over a considerable time period. However, branch performance in the other objectives can be assessed more immediately through a variety of assessment techniques. Some factors are relatively straightforward to assess while others are difficult to gain an accurate performance appraisal of.

6.5.2 Branch productivity measure

The ultimate branch design objective will be to drive up sales and profit per square metre in the long term. It would be relatively straightforward to compare a branch's productivity before and after refurbishment. However, few institutions have developed sufficiently complex databases that enable this. As Lee (1991) states:

Measuring productivity in a service environment is a perplexing task for managers. The types of work involved are nowhere near as clear-cut as in manufacturing environments. Units of output and input, not to mention the quality of them, cannot be easily defined and calculated. Many service processes are not repetitive, nor are services clearly visible in most industries. Once services have been created and rendered to customers they cannot be seen or measured. These characteristics make services very difficult to quantify and measure objectively.

Even if accurate productivity measures are established, any changes recorded after a refurbishment will be the result of many variables not necessarily related to the design alterations. For instance, many refurbishments go hand in hand with staff retraining programmes and occur in town centre areas where much of the current network rationalization activity is focused. Any increase in the number of new accounts being opened could therefore be due to numerous

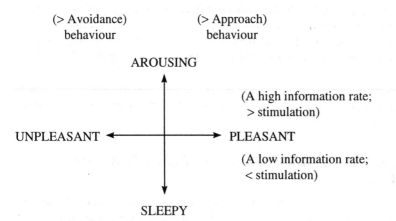

Figure 6.12 Two dimensions of emotion, the information rate and their influence on approach and avoidance behaviour

factors, such as closure of other branches in the vicinity, promotional activity, demographic changes, local housing/employment developments etc., and not be the result of a more visually attractive/eye catching exterior. The reliability of branch productivity measures, in accurately indicating design effectiveness is therefore questionable. In any case, productivity measures would only allow a very few of the design objectives to be investigated.

6.5.3   Monitoring/observing branch activity

Monitoring and observing the behaviour of both staff and customers in the branch is a useful activity. It can reveal deficiencies in the ergonomic functioning of a branch and help to examine the effectiveness of specific design attributes such as window and in-branch displays/promotions. Recording the number of leaflets taken from dispensers at different points in the branch, for instance, can help to indicate the locations and the display techniques that are most effective in attracting customer attention. Recent research into shopping habits has also examined how shoppers are lured to window displays (Highfield, 1991). Similar approaches could be adapted to financial service outlets to investigate which displays and window frontages are the most effective in attracting the attention of passers by. Observation of in-branch behaviour can provide greater knowledge and insight into customer and staff habits. It is especially useful for assessing the effects of experimental design/branch features such as comfortable seating areas, provision of coffee and newspapers, and piped music. Some bank branches do have piped music, research from retail observation studies suggest that:

The tempo of instrumental background music can significantly influence both the pace of in-store traffic flow and the daily gross sales volume. (Milliman, 1982).

Music can also affect branch staff performance, limited research examining the influence of music in offices suggests that for certain types of office work.

Employee satisfaction seemed to improve somewhat with the introduction of music. Output did not appreciably improve although it did not decline either. (Sundstrom, 1986)

Monitoring and observing user activity in branches with music might help to reveal its effects in a financial service retail environment.

6.5.4   Survey research

Surveys encompass personal interview, focus group discussion and questionnaire techniques and are particularly useful for assessing performance in many of the design objectives. They are able to provide both quantitative and qualitative information on perceptions, attitudes and opinions about different environments, as well as providing insights to their users behaviour (Zeisel, 1985). However, for these techniques to be fully effective they must be used actually inside the branch setting. This is due to the transient nature of effects induced by environment (Lutz and Kakkar, 1975). Individuals are really only aware of, and able to describe, how an environment affects them when they are actually inside it. Also, because emotional responses will need to be measured when investigating opinions and emotional responses, it is essential to question individuals while the feelings and thoughts are fresh in their minds.

Even if people are willing to answer as faithfully as possible, are they really able to remember the required information? Indeed the bigger the time lag between the event and the report of it, the more likely it is that the outcome is a rationalization and an interpretation. ... (Scherer et al., 1986)

6.5.5   In branch focus group discussions

Separate group discussions, lasting approximately 90 minutes, for customers and staff of refurbished branches, can also prove useful for providing a qualitative branch appraisal. As Greenland and McGoldrick (1991b) found, this exercise is most productive if performed in groups of six to eight individuals, inside the branch, during working hours and in two phases. As previously mentioned, effects and opinions concerning environments are a difficult subject for people to talk about in the abstract surroundings of an office or living room. In the first phase, 20–25 minutes should be spent in the banking hall area and on the street outside its frontage. The group should be split between two researchers who lead the discussions and ask for impressions on the branch and its features. Hand-held audio equipment should be used, to record the conversations, allowing mobility inside the branch. The remaining time should be spent in a comfortable 'back office' room, following the format of a more standard group discussion. Here, the two smaller groups merge, provide further details and comments about the branch and enable some of the vaguer/subtler aspects of emotional response to be pursued. Criticism and approval of different branch attributes can be uncovered and, once established, respondents can be probed further to discover why and what they like and dislike about them. When the transcriptions of the recorded conversations are broken up under headings of the various branch dimensions, very useful and revealing qualitative descriptions can be gained. These indicate areas where the design is performing well or poorly and can suggest possible improvements. Such information can clearly be useful in helping to provide more detailed design briefs and more user friendly and facilitative branch designs.

It is beneficial to hold one discussion group with bank customers who are unfamiliar with both the branch and the institution in question. These individuals are more able to give an objective opinion on the image presented by the outlet. They also tend to comment about other features of the environment and offer different opinions compared to the branch's own customers. This group is important as it might represent potential customer attitudes, who visit the branch for the first time, maybe with a view to opening a new account. Their opinions on how easily they spotted 'new accounts' desks, the reception area etc. will be very relevant in assessing the branch designs performance.

6.5.6   Questionnaires and structured interviews

Questionnaires and structured interviews can incorporate self-reported ratings of branch attributes and provide valid numeric data by which the design performance of different outlets can be quantitatively compared. They are an especially useful technique as they can be structured around the many specific features of the designed environment, some of which may escape attention in the less rigid group discussion. The respondents are focused onto specific factors, which is essential in environment–behaviour research, as frequently individuals;

when questioned about places, have great difficulty in putting their thoughts and reactions into words. (Canter, 1977)

Many of the design objectives can be measured using a questionnaire/structured interview with the following components:

- Behaviour/attitude indicators
- Assessment of perceived quality of service and institution
- Assessment of design dimensions
- Emotional response and perceived branch approachability indicators

The following section proposes suitable performance measures and possible questions for assessing each of the above components. They could be used in a questionnaire aiming to elicit branch design appraisal from the point of view of the customer.

6.5.7   Design performance measures

Behaviour and attitude indicators might involve rating the following factors:

- How important is it for you to get in and out of the branch as quickly as possible?
- In the branch to what degree do you feel friendly and talkative towards the other customers?
- In the branch how regularly do you spend time browsing at the information leaflets and posters?
- To what extent do you try to avoid visits to the branch?
- To what degree are you a satisfied customer of this bank/building society?
- To what extent do you like the inside of this branch?
- To what extent do you enjoy being a customer of this branch?
- If you knew somebody who wanted to change financial institutions, to what extent would you recommend this branch?

The key dimensions of service provided by financial service outlets were investigated by McGoldrick and Greenland (1992). Seven main factors emerged, and these can serve as the dimensions of service for customers to rate the branch and institution:

1. The branch provides helpful/efficient service
2. The branch is understanding, providing a flexible/cooperative service
3. The branch provides clear impartial advice
4. The branch is trustworthy and reliable
5. The branch staff pressurize customers into making decisions
6. The branch is convenient in location and service range offered
7. The branch manager is approachable

Possible design dimensions along which a branch's performance could be measured have already been presented in Figure 6.1. Possible emotional response and approachability indicators are presented in the Figure 6.13. These provide quantifiable measures of the framework described in Figure 6.12

By comparing the various design performance measures of refurbished and non-refurbished branches, an indication of the degree of improvement obtained by the new retail environment can be gained.

6.5.8   A comparison of customer perceptions from modern and traditional style branches

Ongoing research performed by Greenland and McGoldrick (1994) investigating the design effectiveness of specific branch environments utilized some of the techniques discussed above. The following section provides a summary of results from this work, in which data from over 2000 questionnaires were produced as part of a major survey involving 16 branch environments of five leading UK banks. The branches varied according to specific style and location characteristics and the questionnaires were distributed inside by the bank staff. The results discussed here are based on the responses from the four most traditional and the four most modern branch designs included in the survey sample, which have sufficiently similar customer bases to allow

Emotion	Emotional descriptions	
Pleasure	Pleasant	Unpleasant
	Nice	Dislikeable
	Appealing	Unappealing
	Attractive	Distasteful
Arousal	Active	Inactive
	Lively	Sleepy
	Alert	Slow
	Bustling	Unused
Dominance	Approachable	Intimidating
	Understanding	Authoritative
	Humble	Impressive
	Obliging	Daunting

Proposed information rate dimension	Bipolar measure	
Novelty	A novel branch	A standard branch
	Unusual	Common
Complexity	Varied	Repetitious
	High technology	Low technology
	Complex	Simple
Spaciousness	Too big	Too small
	Crowded	Uncrowded

Figure 6.13   Measures to illicit emotional responses to and the information rates of the branch environments
Source: Mehrabian and Russell 1974; Russell and Pratt 1980; Donovan and Rossiter 1982

comparisons to be made. As mentioned previously, traditional branches are characterized by a lower customer area to staff area ratio, extensive use of bandit screens, small windows and a low adoption rate of retail merchandising techniques. Modern branches are characterized by a higher customer area to staff area ratio, reduced use of bandit screens, large windows and a high adoption rate of retail merchandising techniques.

The research results indicated that customers of modern branches were more likely to be satisfied with their branch, and recommend it to others than customers of traditional style branches. Comparatively, it was also not important for them to get in and out of the branch as quickly as possible, suggesting a greater selling opportunity in the modern branch.

Service quality comparisons and the levels of usage for the majority of service types, between the traditional and modern branches in the survey, revealed little difference. This is perhaps a surprising result given the emphasis of the new designs on breaking down staff and customer barriers, enhancing service efficiency and maximizing the selling opportunity. Qualitative research with staff and customers suggests the concept of territoriality as a possible explanation of these rather unexpected results. 'By virtue of having a physical territory in which the individual's influence is recognised, the occupant can use the control to regulate contacts with others' (Sundstrom, 1986). The staff-customer boundaries have been altered in the new style branch with staff positioned in what was traditionally the customers' territory. This territory has been intruded upon by staff members who were previously content in their 'back' office areas. This may have had a negative effect upon the staff morale and/or the customers' perceived psychological boundaries, and thus upon the interpersonal relationships in the branch. This is clearly an avenue demanding further exploration.

Institution image perceptions of customers from modern branches proved to be significantly better than traditional ones. Customers of the refurbished, new style branches perceived that institution/bank as being more fashionable, impressive, high-tech, approachable and less authoritative, when compared to the views of customers of the older style outlets.

For the design dimensions of the factors below the modern branches rated significantly more favourably statistically than the traditional designs:

Aesthetics	Space	Privacy	Light
Temperature	Comfort	Tidiness	Perceived cost
Potency	Colour	Activity	Air quality

Some of these findings might be expected, as they reflect some of the key physical modifications to the traditional styles, such as the increase in the size of the banking hall area, the inclusion of air conditioning systems, the creation of brighter and more attractive designs etc. The fact that modern designs had higher privacy ratings than the traditional outlets is an interesting result in that the new layouts are more open plan with information desks and interview points actually in the banking hall area. Perhaps the greater space associated with modern branch interiors helps to explain this result.

In terms of emotional response and information rate measures, the modern style branches were the more satisfactory performers. The modern branch environments were considered as being more pleasant and arousing, generally less domineering and had higher information rates indicating that greater approach behaviour would be expected in such branches. Using techniques/calculations developed by Mehrabian and Russell (1974), this data can be used to assign an empirical value for the affective quality of each branch environment examined. These values can then be used to help determine the impact upon emotional response caused by the variations between each branch's environment elements and components.

The results and associated discussion indicate that modern branch designs rate more highly on many design dimensions and have a more favourable impact upon customers' emotional states and upon direct and indirect evaluations. From these findings, and an assessment of qualitative staff interview data, intimations can be made concerning the effects of design features upon customer attitude and behaviour. The importance of satisfying staff, as well as the customers' environment needs has been highlighted. For more quantifiable and proven relationships, between environment and user behaviour, to be identified an in-depth examination of the characteristics of each branch needs to be performed and analysed against their users' responses.

6.5.9 The environmental audit

Each branch environment needs to be audited and where possible described quantitatively to enable an accurate statistical assessment of the effects of specific branch features on the behaviour of their users. Branch features which can be described quantitatively in such an environmental audit include:

- The actual number of branch facilities such as, counters, desks, ATMs, banking hall staff, promotional displays, leaflet dispensers, chairs, windows, queue lines, surfaces to write on, plants etc.

- Whether or not functions are signed, information and exchange rates are displayed, staff have uniforms and name badges/plaques, any back office functions are visible, there is a hard and soft zone, lighting is uniform or selective, there is a traffic flow system, piped music is played, interview desks are alcoved or open, etc.
- Physical measurements concerning the age of building and fittings, the area of bandit screens, windows, banking hall, visible back office, counter surfaces, hard/soft zones, promotional displays, the length of frontage, counters, exterior signage, ceiling height etc.

Correlation and regression relationships between these quantitative details and user attitude and behaviour variables can then be investigated. In this manner it should be possible to reveal which design features have a positive or a negative effect upon branch users. At the very least, an examination of the interrelationships between variables measured will provide a greater understanding of the branch environment–behaviour relationship. The indirect effects model in Figure 6.14 depicts the theorized branch environment–customer behaviour relationship. The model provides a framework for investigating the effects that a designed environment has upon its users and attempts to summarize the links between environment variables and outcome variables. The outcome variables selected represent some of the desired atmospheric influences or design objectives presented earlier in Figure 6.8. Using the same components, but with a slightly different focus the model could easily be adapted to examine the staff–environment behaviour relationship. An understanding of the specific effects of different branch attributes upon users' attitudes and behaviour will enable systematic design improvements to be made. Once general principles are revealed and more fully understood concerning the emotional and behaviourial impact of different design features, then a designer will know that certain environmental stimuli will evoke predictable responses in the branch user, and more effective designs can accordingly be produced.

SUMMARY

The branch environment has an extremely important role to play in financial institutions' distribution strategies. A branch design has considerable influence upon both staff and customer satisfaction levels and can be tailored to help achieve numerous specific marketing objectives. The need for greater efficiency and the recent realization of the potential benefits to be gained from an effectively designed service environment has created a revolution in branch appearance, its functional emphasis, as well as in the structuring and organization of the design and refurbishment function within banks and building societies.

Modern branch formats have been created by newly centralized, specialist refurbishment teams who dictate design policy across the network as a whole. Their aim has been to develop highly cost effective branch strategies which increase operating efficiencies while both enhancing customer satisfaction and maximizing the in-branch selling opportunity. Staff of these new retail-oriented facilities, however, have found their work environments and roles radically altered. This, in some ways, may have adversely affected their job satisfaction levels. Refurbishment teams, when considering the retail branch design concept must strike a balance between both customer and staff satisfaction levels, as there is bound to be at least some conflict between the needs and wants of each user group. After all, any aspects that lessen the employees' levels of satisfaction with their work environment will reduce job performance and service quality, which will ultimately affect the consumer. The most effective branch formats will be produced by a well-structured and organized, interfunctional design team, which appropriately interprets the specific environment needs of the particular user groups.

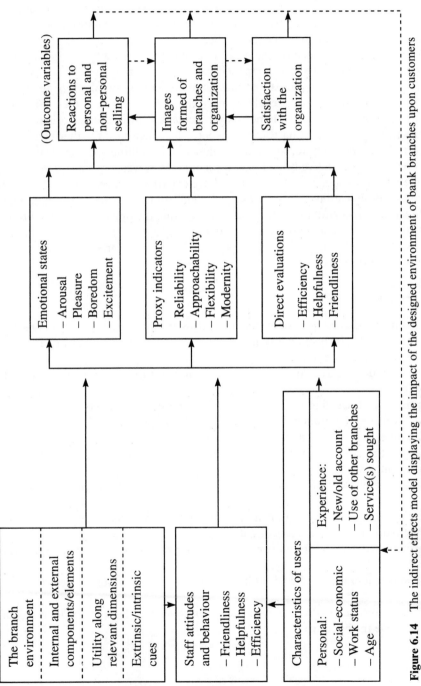

Figure 6.14 The indirect effects model displaying the impact of the designed environment of bank branches upon customers
Source: Greenland and McGoldrick, 1994

Once branch objectives and user requirements have been established, a design brief can be produced, which will determine the desired format. The design team will aim to construct a service facility that effectively fulfils the instructions in the brief. To do this requires a detailed understanding of the branch environment–behaviour relationship. The greater the comprehension of how specific outlet features interact with and affect the attitudes and actions of staff and customers, the more effective the design concepts will be.

The modern branch designs do outperform the traditional styles in many ways, especially from the point of view of customers and in the achievement of several marketing objectives. However, there is still room for improvement and most institutions incrementally tweak their designs on the basis of results from post-occupation evaluation studies of refurbished sites. Financial institutions have only recently adopted retail concepts and become more consumer-oriented, and as such are relatively new at incorporating these ideas into their facilities. Further changes in outlet appearance are therefore likely to continue as banks and building societies learn from their mistakes and create more effective branch environments. However, any subsequent alterations are very unlikely to be as radical as those which have occurred in recent years. The more effective new designs and design adjustments are likely to stem from an enhanced understanding of the interaction between branch and user. Research investigating the impact of specific branch environment attributes upon user attitudes and behaviour, utilizing the design performance measures described in this chapter, might therefore prove to be the most productive avenue for further exploration in the future.

REVIEW QUESTIONS

1. 'The branch environment is a key element in the financial institutions' marketing mix'. Discuss.
2. You are given the task of refurbishing a typical traditional style branch. What alterations/adjustments would you propose to make and why?
3. What should be the main tasks and objectives of an institution's branch design and reconfiguration team?
4. The level of importance attached to the branch has increased substantially over recent years. How has this fact affected the branch design strategies of UK institutions?
5. Why is designing an effective branch environment such a difficult task to undertake?
6. Compare and assess the different techniques for evaluating the performance of a branch's designed environment.
7. 'A branch design can only ever be as good as its design brief'. Discuss the implications of this statement.
8. Why is the emotional impact of the branch environment an important factor to be considered when evaluating the effectiveness of a design?
9. Account for the increased demand for more effective branch designs which has emerged over recent years.
10. What are the main considerations when establishing and organizing a branch design/reconfiguration team?
11. Have modern branch designs really achieved their objectives and how might incremental improvements be made in the future?

REFERENCES

Andrus, D. (1986) 'Office atmospherics and dental service satisfaction', *Journal of Professional Services Marketing*, **1**(4) (Summer), 77–85.
Anon, (1986) 'Music while you shop', *Retail*, **3**(4), 36.

Anon (1991) 'Victorian branch given a face-lift for the future', *Bankground*, July, 3.

Baker, J. (1986) 'The role of the environment in marketing services' in *The Services Challenge*, Czepeil J. *et al.*, eds., American Marketing Organization Chicago, 79–84.

Baker, J. (1990) 'A framework for examining the informational value of store environments', *Working Paper, Department of Marketing*, Texas A and M University, College Station.

Baker, J., L.L. Berry and A. Parasuraman (1988) 'The marketing impact of branch facility design', *Journal of Retail Banking* X, **2**, 33–42.

Barron, P.I. (1991) 'Cost/benefit analysis helps streamline procedures', *Profitable Banker*, 3(3),1.

Bitner, M.J. (1986) 'Consumer responses to the physical environment in service settings', in M. Venkatesan *et al.*, eds., *Creativity in Services Marketing*, American Marketing Association, Chicago.

Bitner, M.J. (1992) 'Servicescapes: the impact of physical surroundings on customers and employees', *Journal of Marketing*, **56**, April, 57–71.

Brantley, R. L. (1989) 'Customer contact is a key to better service quality', *Savings Institutions*, **110**(8), 101.

British Bankers Association (1993) *Annual Abstract of Banking Statistics*, Vol. 10, Statistical Unit, British Bankers Association.

Buchan, J. (1992) 'Called to account' *The Independent on Sunday*, 7 June, 3–4.

Butler, D. and P.M. Biner (1987) 'Preferred Lighting levels: variability among settings, behaviours, and individuals', *Environment and Behaviour*, **19**(6), 695–721.

Campbell, J.M. (1983) 'Ambient stressors', *Environment and Behaviour*, **15**(3), 423–433.

Canter, D. (1969) An intergroup comparison of connotative dimensions, *Environment and Behaviour*, **1**, 37–48.

Canter, D. (1977) *The Psychology of Place*, The Architectural Press, London.

Cass, R.C. and R.G. Herschberger (1973) 'Further toward a set of semantic scales to measure the meaning of designed environments', *Environmental Design Research Association*, Conference EDRA, Vol. 2.

Carr, C.D. (1987) 'Architecture in today's banking environment', *Bank Administration*, **63**(11), 66–70.

Council on Financial Competition (1988) *Excellence in branch banking: volume 1 transforming the branch system with speciality branches*, Council on Financial Competition, June, Washington.

Dohr, J.H., M. Sarmaida and M.B. Portillo (1990) 'Volume color: environment and behaviour systems approach', *Environmental Design and Research Association Conference*, EDRA **21**, 80–81.

Donovan, R.J. and J.R. Rossiter (1982) 'Store atmosphere: an environmental psychology approach', *Journal of Retailing*, **58**(1), 34–57.

Duffy, H. (1991) 'Seeking competitive advantage in retail delivery', *Bank Management*, February, 20–26.

Durante, J. (1989) 'Companies find comfort can be cost-effective', *Retail Control*, **57**(6), 18–21.

Evans, G.W., S. Cohen and P. Brennan (1986) 'Stress and properties of the physical environment', *Environmental Design and Research Association Conference*, EDRA **17**, 91–98.

Farbstein, J. and R. Wener (1980) *Evaluation of correctional environments*, National Institute of Corrections, Boulder, Colorado.

French, D. (1986) 'A different kind of branch office', *Bankers Monthly*, **103**(6), 33–34.

Friedman, A., C. Zimring and E. Zube (1978) *Environmental Design Evaluation*, Plenum Press, New York and London.

Gifford, R. (1987) *Environmental Psychology: Principles and Practice*, Allyn and Bacon, Boston.

Greenland, S.J. and P.J. McGoldrick (1991a) *Consumer Attitudes to the Retailing of Bank and Building Society Branches: Results of the Pilot Survey*, FSRC, School of Management, UMIST Working Paper.

Greenland, S.J. and P.J. McGoldrick (1991b) *Group Attitudes Towards the Retail Environment of a Refurbished Bank Branch: Assessment and Implications*, FSRC, Manchester School of Management, UMIST, Working Paper.

Greenland, S.J. and P.J. McGoldrick (1992a) 'Researching the effects of retailing environments upon customer behaviour in the financial services sector', *European Marketing Academy Conference*, May, Aarhus.

Greenland, S.J. and P.J. McGoldrick (1992b) 'Towards developing a standardized environmental evaluation instrument for bank branch retail service outlets', *Marketing Education Group Conference*, July, Salford.

Greenland, S.J. and P.J. McGoldrick (1992c) 'Modelling the impact of designed space upon users' attitudes and behaviour, *British Academy of Management Conference Paper*, September, Bradford.

Greenland, S.J. (1993) 'Change in the high street: Banks that want planners to say yes', *Town and Country Planning*, June, **62**(6), 152–153.

Greenland, S.J. and P.J. McGoldrick (1994) 'Atmospherics, attitudes and behaviour: Modelling the impact of designed space', *The International Review of Retail Distribution and Consumer Research*, January, 4, 1.

Grossbart, S., R. Hampton, B. Rammohan and R.S. Lapidus (1990) 'Environmental dispositions and customer response to store atmospherics', *Journal of Business Research*, **21**(3), 225–241.

Hawk, K. (1989) 'The terrific transformation of the bank store', *Bankers Monthly*, **106**(10), 88–90.

Hawk, K. (1990a) 'Branch retailing—a team effort' *Bank Marketing*, **22**(4), 26–33.

Hawk, K. (1990b) 'The new branch', *Bank Marketing*, **22**(5), 26–30.

Hayne, C. (1981) 'Ergonomics light and colour', *Occupational Health*, **33**(4), 198–205.

Heerwagen, J.H. (1990) The psychological aspects of windows and window design, *Environmental Research Design Association*, Conference, EDRA, Vol. 21, 269–281.

Highfield, R. (1991) 'Why the stores are watching your step', *The Daily Telegraph*, 27 December, 7.

Holahan, C.J. (1978) *Environment and Behaviour*, Plenum Press, New York.

Kasmar, J.V. (1970) The development of a usable lexicon of environmental descriptors, *Environment and Behaviour*, **2**, 153–169.

Kotler, P. (1973) 'Atmospherics as a marketing tool', *Journal of Retailing*, **49**(4), Winter, 48–64.

Lanphear, S. (1990) 'How well do you sell', *Credit Union Magazine*, **56**(6), 70–75.

Lee, J.Y. (1991) 'Measuring productivity for service firms: it is tricky, but it can be done', *Business Forum*, **16**(2), 11–13.

Lutz, R.J. and P. Kakkar (1975) 'The psychological situation as a determinant of consumer behaviour', in *Advances in Consumer Research*, Vol. 2, Schlinger, M.J. ed., Association for Consumer Research, Chicago, 439–453.

Marams, R.W. (1982) 'Evaluating open and conventional office design', *Environment and Behaviour*, **14**,3 (May), 33–35.

Marsh, J.R. (1988) *Managing Financial Services Marketing*, Pitman Publishing, London.

Martin, C.L. and C.A. Pranter (1989) 'Comparability management: customer to customer relationships in service environments' *The Journal of Services Marketing*, **3**(3), 5–15.

McDonnell, D. and J.E. Albers (1988) 'Making the bank a store', *Bank Administration*, **63**(8), 26–28.

McGoldrick, P.J. and S.J. Greenland (1992) 'Competition between banks and building societies in the retailing of financial services' *British Journal of Management*, Vol. 3, 169–179.

McIver, C. and G. Naylor (1986) *Marketing Financial Services*, Second edition, The Institute of Bankers.

Mehrabian, A. and J.A. Russell (1974) *An Approach to Environmental Psychology*, MIT Press, Cambridge, Mass.

Milliman, R.E. (1982) 'Using background music to affect the behaviour of supermarket shoppers', *Journal of Marketing*, **46**, 86–91.

Mintel, (1988) 'Retailing financial services—an impossible dream', *Personal Finance Intelligence*, Vol. 2, 5.1–5.30.

Moos, R. and S. Lemke (1977) Multiphasic environmental assessment procedures (MAEP) preliminary manual social ecology laboratory, Stanford University, Palo Alto.

Ornstein, S. (1990) 'Linking environmental and industrial/organizational psychology', in Cooper, C.L. and I.T. Robertson (eds), *International Review of Industrial and Organizational Psychology*, **5**, 195–228.

Peters, M. (1986) *Alliance and Leicester Building Society/Michael Peters Branch Design Research, Research Report*, A and L and BMP The Planning Partnership, Unpublished Company Report.

Price, J. (1988) 'Dynamic branch designs guarantee visual publicity', *Savings Institutions*, December, 62–65.

Riley, D. and P.A. Knott (1992) 'Through the eyes of the customer: research into the new look and functioning of bank and building society branches', Paper presented to the *155th ESOMAR Seminar* on Banking and Insurance, January.

Rose, P.S. (1989) 'Banking's next key objective', *Canadian Banker*, **96**(1), 54–63.

Rosenberg, R. (1980) 'Branch banking in the year 2000' *Long Range Planning*, Vol. 13, October, 65–69.

Rossotti, H. (1983) *Colour*, Princeton University Press, NJ.

Russell, A. and G. Pratt (1980) 'A description of the affective quality attributed to environments'. *Journal of Personality and Social Psychology*, **38**, August, 311–322.

Russell, J.A. and L.M. Ward (1982) 'Environmental psychology', *Annual Review of Psychology*, **33**, 651–688.

Scherer, K.R., H.G. Wallbot and A.B. Summerfield (1986) *Experiencing Emotion*, Cambridge University Press, London.

Schneider, B. and D.E. Bowen (1985) 'Employee and customer perceptions of service in banks; replication and extension', *Journal of Applied Psychology*, **70**(3), 423–433.

Schroeder, H.W. (1984) 'Environmental perception rating scales', *Environment and Behaviour*, **16**(5) September, 573–598.

Scuri, P. and D. Skene (1990) 'Spaces without Windows', *Environmental Research Design Association* Conference, EDRA Vol. 21, 291–294.

Sharples, S. (1987) 'Lighting up time: illumination and the retail environment', *Retail and Distribution Management*, May/June, 43–45.

Smith, D., A. Lorenz and M. Lynn (1992) 'Anatomy of a recession', *The Sunday Times Business*, 4 October, 11.

Smith, W. (1989) 'Trends in retail lighting', *Retail and Distribution Management*, September/October, 30–32.

Stokols, D. and I. Altman (1987) *Handbook of Environmental Psychology*, John Wiley and Sons, New York.

Sundstrom, E. (1986) *Work Places: The Psychology of the Physical Environment in Offices and Factories*, Cambridge University Press, London.

Weber, A. (1988) 'Financial centers push two Ohio banks to the lending edge', *Bank Marketing*, **20**(6), 16–17.

Wener, R.E. (1982) 'Standardization of testing in environmental evaluation', *Environmental Design Research Association* Conference, EDRA, Vol. 13, 77–84.

Wineman, J.D. (1982) 'Office design and evaluation: an overview', *Environment and Behaviour*, **14**, 271–298.

Wineman, J.D. (1987) 'Natural lighting in the office, the worker's perspective' *Environmental Design and Research Association Conference*, EDRA **18**, 7–13.

Zeisel, J. (1985) *Inquiry by Design*, Cambridge University Press, London.

THREE

OTHER ELEMENTS OF THE MIX

SEVEN

PRODUCT RANGE DEVELOPMENT

Peter J. McGoldrick

Manchester School of Management and Manchester Business School

INTRODUCTION

There are some problems in defining the scope and form of 'the product' in the retailing of financial services. For butchers and bakers, the product is more clearly defined. For brokers and bankers, 'the product' is an amalgam of prices, practices and promises. For them, the product is more deeply entwined with other elements of the marketing mix. In the context of financial services retailing, the product could be defined as each individual service offered by the retailer. Conversely, the entire service offered by the financial institution could be perceived as the product. The former definition is applied within the context of this chapter.

The similarities and differences between financial services and consumer goods retailing were discussed in the introduction to this book. A number of lessons can be learnt from the concepts and strategies used in the development of physical products. The differences must not, however, be overlooked:

Financial products are a means to an ends, not an end in themselves.

They are not, in themselves, interesting or tasty or focal. They are abstract. It takes quite a lot to get people to change their financial behaviour. (Russell-Walling, 1990)

Neither should the differences be overstated. Many physical products provide a means to an end, and many are far from interesting, tasty or focal! The above quote does, however, draw attention to an important aspect of financial products, namely, the problems of achieving effective differentiation and of effecting behavioural change. Loyalty and/or inertia in the use of financial services tends to be high; it is a great challenge to design a product with benefits sufficiently powerful, which can be communicated sufficiently persuasively, to cause consumers to switch their patronage.

Differentiation can be achieved only rarely by the invention of an entirely new product. More frequently, it is the particular features or the additional 'extras' which differentiate product A from product B. The product is sometimes depicted as comprising three levels:

1. *The core product*—a current account provides money transmission services, which represent the core benefit.
2. *The actual product*—a particular type of current account will provide a brand name and specific features, such as cheque book, cards, access to ATMs, etc.
3. *The augmented product*—these are the additional features, such as interest free overdrafts up to a specified level. These may be optional extras, with or without additional cost.

This concept can be a useful model to assist product development but should not be applied too rigidly in the financial services context. What may be classified as part of the augmented product for one set of consumers may be the core product benefit for others. It should also be appreciated that financial services may be the 'augmented' part of another, more tangible product. For example, warranties and credit arrangements are frequently offered as the augmented benefits associated with the purchase of consumer durable products.

This chapter examines two main elements in the development of the product range. The first section looks at the development of new or adapted products, the courses of new ideas and the factors associated with success. Strategies and processes of new product development are then considered. The second section of the chapter turns to the concept of the product range sold under a given brand name or set of names. Strategies of range development are examined, as are the alternative directions for growth and diversification. Finally, approaches to evaluating the growth potential and profitability of the range are considered, including portfolio analysis and the concept of the product life cycle.

7.1 PRODUCT DEVELOPMENT

The dynamic nature of the financial services environment, discussed in Chapter 1, makes it essential that retailers maintain a strong focus upon innovation and product development. The high level of inter-type competition between retailers, since deregulation, has brought strong pressure to innovate and to respond. Possibly because the new retailers of a given service have approached the task from a different background, and with a different set of resources, the rate of development has certainly increased.

In this section the term 'new product' has been generally avoided, as this in itself raises many problems of definition. Innovations do not necessarily require new products, and may be classified into three main categories:

1. *Continuous innovations*—These have the least disruptive influence upon consumers' established behaviour patterns, e.g., automatic ordering of new cheque books.
2. *Dynamically continuous innovations*—These have some disrupting influence upon patterns, e.g., the use of debit cards instead of credit cards at the checkout.
3. *Discontinuous innovations*—These do require new patterns of behaviour, e.g., the use of ATMs or home banking.

Note that the above classification relates to the level of newness from the customer's viewpoint, an essential perspective to take when trying to predict reactions and rates of diffusion. From the technology perspective, or the viewpoint of financial services retailers, the debit card is actually the most radical innovation among the above examples.

7.1.1 Sources of ideas

Rarely is it possible to identify one overriding source or impetus for a product innovation. Most often we see an evolutionary process, driven by competitive forces, technological change and, hopefully, retailers' perceptions of customer needs. At some stage in this process, however, new ideas are required to produce the product innovation, however slight, that will help to differentiate the product from existing competition. At the simplest level, ideas may be classified as being of internal or external origin. Internal sources of ideas may include specialist research and development, individual executives or any other company employee. While the specialist

Table 7.1 Product development orientations

| Orientation | Size of institution | | | |
	Large	Medium	Small	All
Technology driven	2.3	2.1	1.3	2.1
Market driven	4.4	4.1	4.2	4.3
Competitively driven	3.9	4.2	4.4	4.1

Note: Means based on 1–5 scale, in which 1 indicates 'not at all', 5 indicates 'to a great extent'.
Source: Edgett, S. (1993), Developing new financial services within UK building societies, *International Journal of Bank Marketing,* **11**(3), 36 and 37

research departments may provide the formal process of market appraisal and product development, new solutions to customer needs can sometimes be spotted by those relatively junior employees who work most closely with the customer. External sources of ideas are somewhat more diverse, including research and technological developments within various outside agencies. In truth, the majority of ideas are derived from other companies, be they competitors, distributors or associated companies. In the financial services sector, a very major impetus for development is government legislation and, increasingly within Europe, EC directives (Department of Trade and Industry, 1992). Another, very powerful source of ideas can be the customers or potential customers themselves. Some companies are very weak at harnessing customers' ideas, seeing comments and complaints as something to be dealt with, rather than as free but valuable product/market information.

In a survey of UK building societies, Edgett (1993) sought to obtain ratings of the extent to which product development was driven by technology, the market or competition. The means in Table 7.1 are derived from a 1–5 scale, in which 5 indicated 'a large extent' and 1 indicated 'not at all'. Overall, the societies claimed to be driven primarily by the market, followed by competitive considerations and technology. Edgett does, however, question these claims, finding little substantive evidence that the market-driven approach is the most common. Table 7.1 suggests that the largest of the societies were the most reluctant to admit to being competition-driven in their product developments. These three orientations to product development will now be considered.

The extent of competitively driven innovation increased considerably, following deregulation, diversification and the entry of new players to the retailing of financial services. Lawrence (1990) observed that the high cost of wholesale borrowing forced the specialist lenders towards greater product innovation. According to Larner (1991) 'Almost any bell or whistle that building societies now boast as part of their repertoire was conceived by a new player trying to gain a marketing edge'. Building societies responded to their new challengers with numerous adaptations to their mortgage products. In particular, they have been active in developing schemes to attract first time buyers, usually taking the form of discounts off base rate for the first 6 to 12 months of the mortgage (Planned Savings, 1990).

Financial institutions can, and frequently do, claim many instances of market-driven innovation. For example, the Home Purchaser Plan introduced by Scottish Amicable was based upon the institution's own consumer research (Swift, 1991). This showed that customers were interested primarily in the core attributes of cost, protection, security and prospect of early repayment.

Specialist agencies may also play a role in market-driven product innovation, For example, the product development consultancy Groton, Lodge and Knight assisted NatWest in the launch of its Gold Plus service and its Small Business Advisory service (Russell-Walling, 1990). Just as financial service providers are relative newcomers to the techniques of retail marketing, the techniques of researching market needs are also at the development phase. Hill (1990) identified a number of problems, including:

1. Researching new financial products is a relatively recent development and therefore little or no history is available to build upon.
2. This in turn means less likelihood of technique validation.
3. The wide range of products and product types makes it difficult to build upon a consistent database.
4. Product categories are often less well defined than in the area of fast moving consumer goods, so brand shares are not necessarily meaningful or measurable.

A great deal of evidence is available of consumers' usage of existing specific financial services, via the NOP/FRS database, discussed in Chapter 2. Research into product opportunities has not reached this level of sophistication.

The impact of technology has been manifold in the retailing of financial services. From a consumer viewpoint, the spread of ATM facilities has been one of the most clear manifestations. For example, the National Westminster Bank increased its network of ATMs from 514 to 2,775 between the end of 1981 and the start of 1992, their rate of ATM cash withdrawals increasing from 396 million to 6,500 million over the same period of time (British Bankers' Association, 1992). EFTPoS has represented an even greater development in technology terms, although some doubts are being expressed as to whether UK institutions have adopted the appropriate technology by using the relatively unsophisticated magnetic strip cards (Meall, 1992). The more sophisticated smart cards, although costing nearly ten times more per card, have contributed significantly to lower levels of card fraud in France.

In assessing the sources of ideas and the stimuli for change, it should be remembered that market, competitive and technological factors are closely interrelated. Based upon a Delphi study of expert opinions within the financial services sector, Marr and Prendergast (1992) identified a number of factors that would continue to promote technological change, including:

- Consumer demand for enhanced services
- Cooperation between financial institutions
- Increasing security problems
- Legislation supporting technology
- Increasing competition for retail customers
- Top management support
- Effective marketing
- Increasing availability of software and front end technology
- Rising costs of processing paper
- Rising costs of labour
- Changes in financial institutions in other countries
- Customers acclimatized to computers from school onwards.

7.1.2. Success factors

Although products are developed with the clear intention of achieving success, this outcome can arrive in many different forms. Hart (1993) provided a comprehensive review of the dimensions

Table 7.2 Dimensions used to measure service project success

---

1. *Sales/market share performance*
   - exceeded market share objectives
   - exceeded sales/customer use objectives
   - exceeded sales/customer use growth objectives
   - high relative sales/customer use level
   - high relative market share
   - high overall profitability
   - strong positive impact on company image/reputation
2. *Competitive performance*
   - superior service outcome and experience relative to competitors (perceived)
   - superior unique benefits relative to competitors (perceived)
   - gave important competitive advantage
3. *'Other booster'*
   - enhanced sales/customer use of other products
   - enhanced profitability of other products
4. *Cost performance*
   - substantially lowered costs for firm
   - performed below expected costs
   - achieved important cost efficiencies for the company

Source: De Brentani (1988, 1989), quoted in Johne and Pavlidis (1991), p. 17

and criteria of success in several fields of product development. While some would argue that financial criteria are the only true measure of success, others would point to the other important spin-offs that may occur from product development:

Success is defined as the achievement of something desired, planned or attempted. While financial return is one of the easily quantifiable industrial performance yardsticks, it is far form the only one. New product 'failure' can result in other important by-products, organizational, technical and market developments. (Maidique and Zirger, 1985)

Johne and Pavlidis (1991) reviewed studies that had addressed the issue of product development success in banking. It was observed that success can be measured at two levels: the programme level and the project level. A specific project may therefore fail to meet the financial or market share targets set, whereas it may contribute to the success of an overall programme. Such a contribution may arise through spin-offs in technology, expertise, publicity, etc.

Drawing upon studies by De Brentani (1988, 1989), Table 7.2 illustrates some of the criteria that are used to assess product success.

In a subsequent study of product development within banks, building societies and insurance companies, Johne and Vermaak (1993) utilized six measure of success:

1. Level of profits achieved
2. Rate of increase in profits achieved
3. Level of market share achieved
4. Rate of increase in market share achieved
5. Level of sales achieved
6. Rate of increase in sales achieved

In each case, the level or rate was compared with that of the most successful competitor on that criterion.

Whatever criteria are adopted for measuring success, there are no simple formulae for achieving it. The reader may encounter case histories depicting product development success and the factors that appeared to contribute to that success. For example, Icole (1990) provided a detailed account of the development and launch of new savings products in France. It was concluded that the following factors had contributed to their success:

1. Preliminary market analysis, prior to launch
2. Targeting of offers and client incentives
3. Effective marketing organization
4. Preliminary introduction campaigns
5. Positioning compatible with the institutional background
6. Effective motivation of the network
7. Good timing

As the above illustrate, it is especially difficult in the case of financial services to isolate the inherent success of the product from the success or otherwise of its delivery. While useful in themselves, such case histories can provide only lessons, not panaceas. Product success is often achieved by breaking the rules or conventions, rather than by following them. Some guidelines for the product development process are, however, provided in the sections following.

In that many 'product development' projects fail to achieve the targets set, a number of generalizations have been derived of the factors associated with failure. Although the study is now somewhat dated, the four factors identified by Berry and Hensel (1974) are still entirely topical:

1. Failure to look at new products through the eyes of the consumer
2. Failure to creatively research the needs of market segments
3. Failure to consider the degree of behavioural change required of the consumer
4. Failure to communicate clearly a new product's benefits

From the wider field of product and service development, a number of other generalizations can usefully be added. For example, from Mason and Ezell (1993):

1. Lack of superior benefits over existing products
2. Problems in market research
3. Poor corporate strategic match
4. Target market too small to serve profitably
5. Technical problems with the product
6. Poor positioning strategy
7. Managerial problems.

7.1.3 Product development strategies

Earlier, it was noted that the inspiration or impetus for product development tends to come from competition, technology and/or the identification of customer needs that are not currently being satisfied within the marketplace. One of the primary strategic decisions therefore, is whether to take a reactive or a proactive approach to product strategy (Urban and Hauser, 1980). Under different sets of circumstances and resource constraints, each type of approach may be the more appropriate.

Reactive strategies may be classified as:

- Defensive
- Imitative
- Second but better

Defensive strategies essentially seek damage limitation if a competitor launches an innovation which cannot be copied or improved upon quickly or profitably. For example, a response to the 'high tech' banking products of a competitor might be to stress personal service and traditional, solid values. The imitative or 'me too' strategy copies the competitor's new product as quickly as possibly, before the competitor has had time to establish a significant competitive advantage. Given the relative ease with which most product developments in financial services can be copied, this is a more common approach than many would prefer to admit! The strategy defined as 'second but better', while essentially reactive, is a more sophisticated approach. For example, the innovator may encounter many problems that were not fully anticipated during the initial screening processes. This gives competitors the opportunity to wait, research the market and learn from these problems, prior to introducing their products. The full scale launch of debit cards in the UK showed some evidence of this approach. The appeal of the 'second but better' strategy is that it may prove significantly less expensive and less risky than being the original innovator. Like most reactive strategies, however, it would be unlikely to contribute towards genuine innovation within the marketplace.

Proactive strategies suggest that the organization initiates the major change. Given the intangible character of financial services, they may in reality be less common approaches to product development than those outlined above. They are, however, important in enabling some organizations to achieve differentiation, albeit usually temporary, and in providing a stimulus for change within the market. In one of the classic treatments of new product strategy, Urban and Hauser (1980) identified four main types of proactive strategy:

- Research and development
- Marketing
- Entrepreneurial
- Acquisition

In any context, especially that of financial services, one could argue that the first two should operate in close harmony. However technically brilliant, a product will achieve widespread adoption only if it satisfies customer needs more successfully than existing products. The muted customer response to the early EFTPoS schemes in the UK reflected a technology and cost-driven innovation, the customer benefits of which were not sufficiently well communicated at that stage (Ironfield and McGoldrick, 1988). This point was given further support from the study by Johne and Vermaak (1993) of 21 banks, insurance companies and building societies. Table 7.3 shows a number of factors that may be important influences on product development. The importance of these was rated on a 1 to 5 scale; means scores are presented for the successful and the less successful product developers. The strength of the marketing function within the organization was the factor that differed most significantly between these two groups.

The importance of a strong customer orientation, whether or not this is manifest through a strong marketing function, is frequently reiterated. Without this orientation, there is little possibility of achieving genuine added value in product development. According to one insurance company:

We reflected on what each of our products was offering customers and decided that the best way to create sustainable competitive edge was through beefing-up the support we provide. Accordingly, we have decided that we are no longer going to be a low cost supplier. (Johne, 1993)

Table 7.3 Factors impacting on product development decision taking

| | Mean scores (1–5 scale) | |
	SPD	LSPD[1]
Exogenous factors		
Degree of market regulation	4.83	4.67
Competitiveness of market	4.83	4.33
Growth potential of market	2.17	2.67
Potential profitability of market	3.83	3.33
Endogenous factors		
Explicitness of business strategy	3.17	2.67
Supportiveness of leadership	2.17	2.00
Permanence of organizational structure	1.83	1.67
Formality of managerial systems	2.17	2.67
Relative number of marketing staff	4.83	2.67[2]
Experience of the skill base	1.83	1.67
Pervasiveness of shared values	3.83	2.67[3]

Notes: (1) SPD = successful product developers
LSPD = less successful product developers
(2) Difference highly significant (t-test, p = 0.00)
(3) Difference of modest significance (t-test, p = 0.11)

Source: Johne, A. and L. Vermaak (1993), 'Head office involvement in financial product development', *International Journal of Bank Marketing*, **11**(3), 31

Among the other proactive strategies for product development, the 'entrepreneurial' approach may describe the activities of some of the smaller, new lenders. Within such organizations, the impetus comes typically from a small group or maybe from just one individual entrepreneur. This approach need not be denied to large, established organizations, some of which have set up special project teams to develop and initially to manage new ventures. Under such circumstances, it is clearly essential that the members of these teams are given sufficient freedom from their normal duties. Such teams are able to capture most of the benefits of rapid decision making and single-mindedness, while enjoying the infrastructure support of the large organization. Table 7.4 summarizes the approaches to product development from a sample of 67 building societies. Project teams, committees or *ad hoc* groups have the advantage of drawing together relevant expertise from within the organization. De Brentani (1993) identified the importance of widespread involvement in product development:

Personnel at all levels need to think in innovative terms, and firms must establish and support systems that stimulate communication and involvement by employees who represent specialised functions and who have different skills and points of view.

A proactive development strategy which avoids the lead times and, to an extent, the product failure risks is that of acquisition. As discussed in Chapter 1, the 1980s saw many mergers and acquisitions within the financial services industry, some oriented to buying market share, others to buying new product ranges. Such diversification does involve other potentially greater

Table 7.4   Approaches to managing product development

	Frequency of using the approach		
	Never %	Sometimes %	Always %
New venture teams	56.1	40.9	3.0
New product committee	22.7	53.1	24.2
Temporary new product committee	32.8	59.7	7.5
New product department	73.1	16.5	10.4
New product manager	73.1	15.0	11.9
New product group	61.2	34.3	4.5
Product (brand) manager	51.5	30.3	18.2
Ad hoc group	24.6	61.6	13.8

Source: Edgett, S. (1993) p. 39

financial risks, which will be discussed in the second section of this chapter. An alternative is the formation of alliances or partnerships, for example, the partnerships between finance houses and some smaller building societies.

7.1.4   Product development process

A logical approach to reducing the risk of product failure is to evaluate carefully the concept and product at each stage in the development process. Figure 7.1 depicts the orthodox stages of this process, from the influences upon idea generation through to the full launch and evaluation. Because of the number of stages involved, and the time needed to undertake some of them thoroughly, the timespan can be large. For example, it took National Westminster Home Loans (NWHL) 18 months to design and to establish their Flexible Mortgage (Mortgage Finance, 1991). There is some incentive to try to reduce this timescale because of the dangers of imitation as developments move towards the launch stage. For example, NWHL developed their Flexi Two mortgage product within six months, a drastic reduction upon the typical 12–18 month schedule. Unfortunately, the rush to the market can sometimes lead to insufficient screening or testing. Schedules can, however, be shortened without necessarily sacrificing rigour of analysis, by a number of means:

1. A tight-knit project team, with sufficient autonomy, can react and decide more quickly than a more ponderous committee, meeting less frequently.
2. New techniques and technologies in concept testing and market research can speed the evaluation stages.
3. The use of critical path analysis can help to identify tasks that can run concurrently, for example, the various design, testing and training components depicted in Figure 7.1. For a full discussion of critical path analysis applied to product development, the reader may consult Urban and Hauser (1980, p. 469).

The process of idea screening is the first 'filter' within the product development process. At this stage the investment in the project is usually still modest and the screening can occur with little

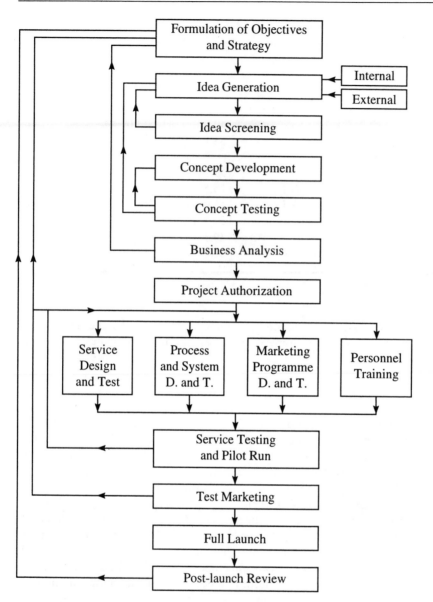

Figure 7.1 The financial product development process
Source: Developed from Sheuing and Johnson (1989)

danger of competitor reaction. In his study of building society product development, Edgett (1993) found the following approaches to screening:

Individual using formal system	:	17.9 per cent
Individual using informal system	:	14.9 per cent
Group using informal discussion	:	62.7 per cent
No screening process used	:	4.5 per cent

These results suggest that informal systems predominate, although these are likely to be based, at least implicitly, upon some form of checklist. A more formal checklist or rating system is likely to include the following criteria:

1. *Market opportunity*—demand, market share and growth potential.
2. *Competitive edge*—differentiation and unique selling points *vis à vis* competition.
3. *Capabilities and resources*—does the organization have the required skills, personnel, distribution channels, etc.?
4. *Congruence*—is the development in accord with overall image and objectives?
5. *Financial*—timescale for breakeven and profit projections.
6. *Legal and government*—is the product consistent with current and anticipated regulations?

The next evaluation stage is that of concept testing, which introduces a slight risk of the project becoming exposed to the competitors. Whereas screening can be conducted within the organization, concept testing typically requires some elements of customer research. A range of qualitative techniques which can assist at this stage was described by Hill (1990). These include the discussion of 'fact sheets', evaluation of advertisement drafts, various projective techniques and role reversal, whereby customers take on the role of the product management team. Unfortunately, it is difficult to forecast accurately the future demand for products, on the basis of expressed intentions:

High loyalty to banks and building societies, plus enormous inertia, make estimating very difficult; i.e., people say that they will acquire/buy/invest but they never quite get round to doing it. (Hill, 1990)

Apart from the testing of the individual components of the product, the final evaluation stage before the launch, is test marketing. Test marketing may be conducted in a limited geographical area to test market reaction and acceptance. In practice, test marketing is used in the minority of product launches by UK banks, insurance companies and building societies. Mohammed-Salleh and Easingwood (1993) identified five main factors that inhibit the use of test marketing:

1. Test marketing can be as expensive as a full launch.
2. No need, as the product is a copy of a competitor's product.
3. Research has already established the value of product benefits.
4. Difficult to produce test market conditions.
5. The time taken to test market thoroughly could allow competitors to imitate and launch at the same time or earlier.

In the financial services setting, factors 1, 2 and 5 are valid justifications in some cases. Given the difficulties of forecasting real demand from attitude research, factor 3 is more questionable, as too is factor 4. There is no doubt a very real tension between the desire to get from idea to launch as quickly as possible, and the desire to minimize risk of product failure by careful evaluation at each stage. Organizations that short-circuit evaluation at each critical stage do so at their peril. Urban and Hauser (1980) depicted an alternative 'model' of product development processes:

1. Exultation
2. Disenchantment
3. Confusion
4. Search for the guilty
5. Punishment of the innocent
6. Distinction for the uninvolved

Although offering a humorous contrast with conventional models, such as Figure 7.1, it does unfortunately reflect the patterns observed in all too many cases. The enthusiasm and career

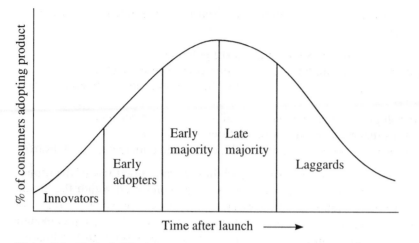

Figure 7.2 Typical diffusion curve

ambition of key individuals can destroy even the best designed of processes; it can certainly distort the flow of information and the conduct of the evaluation stages.

7.1.5 Adoption and diffusion

Understanding the process of product adoption, and diffusion within the market, is valuable for the projection of turnover and profit growth. The speed with which individuals are likely to adopt a product is dependent upon need and risk. A product that fulfils a major need with little apparent risk will probably achieve rapid adoption. The level of need fulfilment is, of course, highly dependent upon individual circumstances and requirements. The level of risk is a highly subjective concept, some individuals perceiving far higher levels of risk than others. Various types of perceived risk can inhibit product adoption:

1. *Performance risk*, e.g., the direct debit systems fails to advise of changes in the payment level.
2. *Financial risk*, e.g., the investment fails to yield the expected returns.
3. *Physical risk*, e.g., being robbed as you leave the ATM.
4. *Social risk*, e.g., relatives may not approve of you taking out an equity release scheme!
5. *Psychological risk*, e.g., taking a store card for a down-market company may be incompatible with your self-image.
6. *Time-loss risk*, e.g., switching current accounts involves time taken to change salary instructions, direct debits, etc.

There is a tendency among product developers to concentrate more upon the needs than the perceived risks, as a result of viewing the product from their own standpoint. This can lead to an adoption rate that is far slower than was forecast. It is also quite difficult to research accurately levels of perceived risk as customers are often reluctant to 'admit' to some of their fears, especially of the social and psychological risks.

Diffusion theory suggests that different types of customers tend to adopt products at different times after their launch. Figure 7.2 depicts a typical diffusion curve, which has been found to resemble a normal distribution. The 'innovators' typically comprise the first 2–3 per cent to adopt, tending to be younger, well-educated and/or high income consumers, willing and able to take risks. For example, foreign currency mortgages were adopted by some of the more sophisticated innovators, especially when UK rates were very high (Fee, 1991).

Table 7.5 Awareness of investment schemes

Scheme	Socio-economic group: % aware			
	AB	*C1*	*C2*	*DE*
TESSAs	38	32	16	10
Personal equity plans	21	16	7	4
Shares	38	26	16	11
Unit trusts	24	19	11	7
Investment trusts	16	9	6	4

Source: Key Note (1992) *Personal Finance in the UK*, Key Note Publications, London, p. 11

Table 7.6 Adoption of debit card payment

	Percentage of debit cardholders	
	Ever used for payment	*Used in the last 4 weeks*
All adults	64	45
Social class		
AB	67	51
C1	66	48
C2	60	41
DE	56	33
Age bands		
21–24	72	54
35–44	66	48
55–64	56	36

Source: NOP (1992), *The Financial Consumer 1992/93*, NTC Publications, Henley on Thames

The 'early adopters' are a somewhat larger group, comprising typically 12–15 per cent of consumers. These are key targets for product marketers, being the opinion leaders who can influence the patronage patterns of the later majorities. Table 7.5 illustrates that awareness of the more sophisticated products is skewed towards the higher socio-economic groups. In the case of financial services, early adopters are not necessarily younger, given the very specific age targeting of some products.

The first three adoption categories in Figure 7.2 comprise the first 50 per cent of consumers in terms of adoption rates. Some socio-economic bias still tends to be apparent among the early majority. Debit card payments could be seen as approaching that stage of diffusion. Table 7.6 illustrates that considerably more of the AB and C1 consumers who held such a card had used it for payments within the last four weeks.

The last two categories tend to be more down-market and risk aversive. Given the nature of many financial products, some of these typically late adopters may never adopt the specific financial product. It is important to appreciate, therefore, that the diffusion curve is a very generalized concept which cannot be applied as a precise forecasting tool. It is, however, of value in helping to anticipate the characteristics of adopters at each stage, and in helping to direct marketing communications more effectively.

7.2 MANAGING THE RANGE

The emphasis so far has been upon the development of products, be they innovations, modifications or downright copies. The task of managing the product range requires the constant re-evaluation of every product within the organization's portfolio, most likely leading to some product repositioning and some deletions. As the products offered by most financial services retailers have proliferated, the concepts of range management have become increasingly relevant. This section considers firstly the concept of the brand, which provides the perceptual link between the products within the range. The objectives of range developments are examined, with regard to the overall strategic aims of diversification and growth. Various strategies for developing the range are then compared, using examples of closely targeted products. Frameworks for evaluating the suitability of the product mix are then discussed, including forms of portfolio analysis and product life cycles.

7.2.1 Developing the brand

A detailed treatment of the techniques of brand advertising is provided in Chapter 9. At this stage, it is appropriate to note briefly the twofold role of branding in the management of the product range:

1. A strong brand name, which has acquired the trust and confidence of consumers, can help the process of diversifying into product areas new to the company. The great strength of the Marks and Spencer and St Michael brand names enabled that company to diversify from its core areas into credit cards, loans and unit trusts (Levene, 1991).
2. Branding can help to differentiate products or ranges, especially important given the similarity of many financial products. With regard to life insurance companies, Watkins (1988) noted 'the most common approach to new product development is to copy competitors' products and to attempt to differentiate them from those of competitors by the use of branding, particularly the name of the brand'.

A successful brand therefore offers customers added values, communicated through advertising. The advertising expenditures in 1991 of some of the best known financial brands were:

National Westminster   £24.4m
Halifax   £24.1m
Abbey National   £20.1m
Nationwide Anglia   £18.7m
Barclays   £17.5m
Prudential   £10.1m
(NOP, 1992)

The added values conveyed through advertising may be rational, functional issues, such as longer opening hours, or emotional elements, such as brand personality. Given the rather intangible nature of some financial services, the distinction between the functional and the emotional may be somewhat blurred.

The components of financial services brands were illustrated in a study of savings account brands by De Chernatony (1993). Table 7.7 shows the main brand components, derived through factor analysis of 15 attitude statements. The first component includes most of the personality elements, whereas components 2 and 3 are more functional in nature. Analysis of this type can help to understand how brands are perceived and how consumers differentiate between them.

Table 7.7   Savings account brand components

Factor	Attitude statement
Component 1	For organized people who plan ahead
	Offers high interest rate
	Used by sophisticated people
	Not for young people
	Not for social people
	For people with high aspirations
	For wealthy people
Component 2	Not for people with a family
	Not an easy to use account
	Needs large cash amount to open account
Component 3	More like a current account
	Offers more means of withdrawing money

Source: De Chernatony, L. (1993), 'Categorising brands: evolutionary processes underpinned by two key dimensions', *Journal of Marketing Management*, **9**(2), 173–188

Product managers must therefore take into account both the functional and the personality attributes of their brand(s). If a product or range is being 'branded' for the first time, the choice of a name is clearly of immense importance to the personality of that brand. A number of general guidelines may be applied in the choice of a name:

1. It should be easy to pronounce, easy to remember and easy to recognize.
2. It should link to the special benefits of the product/range.
3. It should avoid negative connotations, including those in other languages if the brand is to be international.
4. It should convey clearly the product category.

Qualitative research should be used to assist in the development and testing of a brand name. Hill (1990) describes the research leading to the launch of 'Private Reserve', a 90 day notice account from the National and Provincial Building Society. Other such research led to the development of a 'goal related savings product' in the form of a Holiday Saver account.

   In spite of the similarity of many rival products, brands may also be judged on their functional attributes. In a comparative evaluation of mortgage lenders, *Which Mortgage* (1991) based its awards upon a number of functional criteria, including:

1. Competitive rates
2. Timing of rate reductions
3. Range of discounted products
4. Levels of service
5. Clarity of propositions
6. Geographical coverage

The value added by the brand can therefore be a blend of functional and personality attributes. Value added may also be achieved by the integration of a number of financial services. For example, Serrano Alda (1992) describes the successful development of 'Salary Service Packages' in Spain, which incorporate a range of basic and leisure related facilities. The basic package includes a bill payment service, debit and credit cards, low interest loans, advances against salary and accident insurance. Special facilities and discounts apply to car insurance, travel and theatre tickets; these services may be utilized by telephone or at the bank branches. In this way, the financial services retailer may further develop its brand while extending the relationship with the customer into other related services areas.

7.2.2 Developing the range

Diversification and segmentation have been the cornerstones of product range strategies in recent years. Acutely conscious of the competitive threats to their traditional areas of business, most retailers of financial services have looked for new areas of growth. Generalized product-market strategy options were discussed in Chapter 3. Most organizations have followed the route of diversification and have greatly increased the range of products offered to their existing customers. At the same time, they have become increasingly adept at tailoring their ranges to the needs of identifiable segments of the market.

Some of the most conspicuous range extension has been seen in building societies, some of which expanded from mortgage and deposit account business into current accounts, credit cards, stockbroking, insurance products, estate agencies and housing development (Hopton, 1991). Not all have followed the diversification route quite so vigorously. For example, the Woolwich took a more measured view of its product range developments. According to their head of financial services:

We decided against share dealing. We were right. Only one or two societies are still in that market. We decided against underwriting our own mortgage indemnity business, even though it was seen as a licence to print money. Now we know otherwise. And we decided against personal pensions. Deposit-based pensions have hardly set the world alight. (Levene, 1992)

Banks have also been active in extending product ranges beyond their traditional boundaries. In France, the financial services market has become largely dominated by the big banks, which have learned to leverage their customer relationships to sell a wide range of products (Schwartz, 1992). In the United States, the concept of the financial supermarket gained some appeal. A detailed account of several such operations was provided by the Council on Financial Competition (1987). These cases illustrated the problems of developing or acquiring the expertise required to provide a wide range of services, from brokerage to travel to retirement planning. The 'supermarkets' had also encountered the need to vary the range of services offered, according to the characteristics of the catchment areas. Valuable lessons could be learnt from the diversification activities of major product retailers. In the late 1970s and early 1980s, some superstores and hypermarkets, with room to spare, started to sell clothes, washing machines and even cars. Most retreated from these areas, except for the more basic clothing ranges. The reasons for these withdrawals related to problems both of supply and of demand:

1. Although powerful in its core product areas, a retailer may have little bargaining power in other areas.
2. Product expertise is required for product selection and selling; this expertise may be expensive to acquire.
3. New ranges were not always congruent with the core image; a highly reputable retailer of low risk, frequent purchase products may none the less have low credibility for the sale of big ticket items.

Table 7.8   Key segments for market managers

Segment	Product range needs
Youth market	Money transmissions services. Overdraft or loans. Simple savings account. Travel facilities.
Independent market	Budget facilities. Mortgages, savings accounts. Consumer loans and credit cards. Insurance. Travel facilities.
Family market	Mortgages and home improvement loans. Longer-term savings for education funding. Insurance and wills. Pensions. Consumer loans. Savings accounts for children.
Empty Nesters market	Savings and investments. Occasional borrowing. Replacement mortgage or home improvement loans. Financial advisory services. Travel facilities.
Retired market	Management of capital/income. Trust services and financial advice.

Source: Wilson, A. (1992), 'The changing nature of the marketing function within retail banks and building societies'. Paper presented at the *British Academy of Management Conference*, Bradford, p. 6

4. Purchase patterns for routine, lower cost times are entirely different from those for major purchases. The latter normally includes more extensive information search and decision-making processes. The two activities do not always fit well together on the same visit.

Effective development of product ranges must focus upon the needs of customer groups which can be satisfied, profitably. The astute cross-seller offers solutions to the customer's various needs, not simply a list of disparate products (Sonnenberg, 1988). In response to this challenge, some banks and building societies have introduced market managers to focus upon key market segments, such as students or individuals of high net worth (Wilson, 1992). Table 7.8 illustrates how such a management structure can focus upon the needs of clearly defined segments.

This approach can also highlight the segments that may not be especially well served by the existing range. In recent years, the youth market has become a particular focus of attention, in the hope of building loyalty from early stages. For example, the Halifax Building Society offers the following for its younger age segments:

The Little Extra Club: for children aged 11 or under, offering junior account holders a number of extras, including a membership card, money box, sew-on badge, bike sticker and a club magazine.

Quest: the club for 12–16s, which also offers a club magazine, a careers guide for school leavers and Cardcash for 14 year olds and over.

Extra Help for under 21s: a range of benefits including added interest on certain accounts, preferential overdraft facilities and full card facilities.

Bienstman (1991) explained the approach of one Belgium bank to its youth market. Research had shown the younger age customers to be strongly in need of the sense of independence that could be provided by the appropriate range of products. Although the youth market was not especially profitable to the bank, much emphasis was given to the strategy of early recruitment. At the other end of the age spectrum, many retailers have identified the benefits of better serving the pre-retirement and retired segments. Their needs clearly differ from those of the young segments and the product manger can develop and promote a sub-set of the range for these groups.

Age is, of course, just one of many possible segmentation variables, including income, house ownership status, lifestyle, values and attitudes. For effective target marketing, the segments must be measurable, accessible and economically viable. If the segmentation system meets these criteria, it is likely to provide a strong basis for range development that is customer, rather than product, oriented.

7.2.3   Analysis of unit profitability

The emphasis to this point has been upon the development of products, brands and the range. Product range management involves not only the creation of products, it also involves the continual reappraisal of existing products. In each case, a decision must be made between retailing, modifying or killing off the product. Such an evaluation can also suggest the level of marketing support that should be devoted to each element of the range.

In the wild scramble for diversification in the late 1980s, financial services retailers were often less than precise in their predictions of profit contributions from new products. This led to a realization that popular areas of diversification may not always be profitable ones (Mabberley, 1989). Systems of measuring unit profitability, which are commonplace in product retailing, came to be adopted by some financial services retailers (*Economist*, 1989). These included profits per square metre, as a way of comparing the productivity of branch space, and DPP (direct product profitability).

DPP is an attempt to allocate all the costs involved in obtaining, marketing and retailing each product, to provide a clearer picture of the product's real contribution. High margin products with high retailing costs may therefore produce a low, or even negative DPP, whereas lower margin items with low retailing costs may actually produce a better DPP contribution. Such measures alone are not a substitute for product management decisions; it may well be entirely sensible to retain some low DPP items as 'loss leaders'.

The evaluation of item profitability has been assisted by developments in retail technology and associated software. As Trout (1992) points out, the analysis of unit profitability should focus upon the product, the customer and the branch:

The account manager will need to know who are the 50 least profitable customers, why are some customers unprofitable, and which products should be sold to which types of customer?

The product manager should know which products make the greatest profit contribution, which product and customer combinations are most profitable and to what extent is product Y a loss leader?

The unit manager should have statistics on which office is the most profitable and why, which account officers contribute most to organisation profits, and what are the relative contributions of offices servicing the same customers?

One example of such a system is the software package 'On-Q', developed by Corporate Solutions International and capable of being run on a powerful personal computer. Using this system, Coutts and Co. are able to analyse the profitability of each of its 50,000 customers, or of specified segments. Similarly, the profitability of each of 150 products can be analysed. According to their project manager:

Coutts is now in the enviable position of being able to deal with the external problem of balancing quality of service against adequate profit generation, as the system matches effort (and hence costs) with related income at both the product and customer level.

7.2.4   Portfolio analysis

The more precise analysis of cost and profitability is a major step towards more effective management of the product range. The organization must also take a broader view of its 'product portfolio', *vis à vis* competition, market size, market growth and internal strengths. A number of frameworks are available to assist in this process, including the BCG (Boston Consulting Group) market growth/market share matrix. An adapted version of this is shown in Figure 7.3.

This matrix suggests that products, or business units, can be classified according to the growth of the market overall, and the share of that market held by the organization. Four broad classifications are defined as follows:

1. *Problem children*—the industry growth is strong, but share is low, indicating that competitors are in a strong position. At this stage, the organization must decide between building share with a vigorous and probably expensive marketing support programme, or withdrawing if the prospects for success seem poor. Because of the fundamental decisions required at this stage, such products are also known as 'question marks'.
2. *Stars*—with high share in a high growth industry, the prospects for this product are good. It will, however, also offer an attractive area of potential for rivals, so strong marketing support is still essential.
3. *Cash cows*—well-established products in a low growth, probably mature market. A 'holding' strategy may be appropriate if the market is strong and stable. If the market and/or share is weakening, a 'harvesting' strategy may be appropriate, i.e., cutting back on expenditure and marketing support to maintain product profitability as long as possible.
4. *Dogs*—with low growth and low share, these products appear to offer low potential and should be considered for harvesting or immediate deletion.

A product that is new to the organization may well pass through the four categories in the above sequence. Strong marketing support may transform some problem children into stars. As

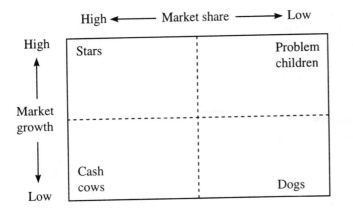

Figure 7.3   The market growth/market share matrix
Source: adapted from Boston Consulting Group

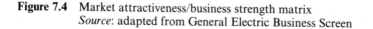

	High ◄——— Market attractiveness ———► Low		
High	Invest for growth	Invest selectively for growth	Develop for income
Business strength	Invest selectively and build	Develop selectively for income	Harvest or divest
Low	Develop selectively Build on strengths	Harvest	Divest

Figure 7.4 Market attractiveness/business strength matrix
Source: adapted from General Electric Business Screen

markets mature, some become cash cows and, if competition proliferates or support is removed, move to the 'dogs' category.

Frameworks of this type cannot provide accurate forecasting tools or definitive prescriptions for product marketing decisions. In the financial services sector, there are many mature but very large product markets, the shares of which are divided between many competing retailers. Using the market growth/market share matrix literally, such would be classified as 'dogs', but may none the less be entirely profitable products. Furthermore, an organization may achieve a high share within its target market segment yet hold a low share of the market overall; there are clearly some difficulties in defining 'markets' and 'shares' under such circumstances. In spite of these limitations, the matrix does serve to draw attention to some of the external forces of relevance to product range decisions.

As discussed earlier in Section 7.2.2, the internal strengths and capabilities of the organization are also highly relevant to product portfolio decisions. This is recognized by the 'General Electric Business Screen', an adapted version of which is shown in Figure 7.4. Within this matrix, the horizontal axis represents 'market attractiveness', comprising an amalgam of size, growth, stability, ease of entry, types of regulatory constraints, industry capacity and profitability; the vertical axis, 'business strength', incorporates relative share, company capacity to supply, company/brand image, product quality, financial strength and management expertise.

The recommendations associated with each of the nine 'cells' of the matrix are summarized within Figure 7.4. The concept suggests that organizations should attempt to match strengths within the company with opportunities and conditions within the marketplace. As in the case of the BCG matrix, there are enormous problems involved in summarizing complex sets of variables into simple 'attractiveness' and 'strength' scales. Again, the value of this matrix derives less from its ability to provide precise answers than from its ability to provoke decision makers to take a broader view. As many retailers of financial services discovered, diversification into markets of moderate attractiveness, armed with inadequate business strength in the field, can be a very expensive mistake.

7.2.5 Product life cycles

In an industry for which permanence was regarded as a major virtue, the concept of life cycles may not have gained early acceptance. Yet as products proliferate, competition abounds and technology advances, it is increasingly relevant to apply this concept in the context of financial services. Figure 7.5 illustrates the generalized form of the life cycle, within which products are seen to pass through the stages of development, introduction, growth, maturity and eventually decline. This concept may be applied at the level of the product class, such as savings accounts; the product form, such as high interest accounts; or the branded product, for example, the Royal Bank of Scotland's Gold Ninety Account. The life cycles of branded products tend to be shorter than those of the more general product category, although the continuity of a brand can be maintained by changing and evolving the specific products that carry the brand name. Product innovation is leading to shorter life cycles; mortgages have had a very long history but some specific types of mortgage have proved less durable. Technology is also speeding the process:

EFTPoS will complete the life cycle and its place in the industry will see widespread acceptance of the Smartcard. Home banking will reach most customers, as part of the overall trend towards an increasing number of homes having personal computers. (Marr and Prendergast, 1992)

The stages of the life cycle will be considered briefly, with an indication of the marketing activities appropriate to each phase:

1. *Development and introduction*—This phase is characterized by expenditure, rather than profit, as the product is prepared and launched. Competition is typically low or non-existent, unless of course the product is simply a 'me-too' version of competitors' products. Marketing emphasis should be upon raising awareness, stimulating trial and encouraging adoption. A great deal of effort was expended to encourage trial of the early EFTPoS schemes, with publicity and leaflets designed to emphasize the benefits and allay the fears.
2. *Growth*—Assuming that the product is successful at launch, the growth phase represents the most rapid development of sales revenue and profits. It is likely to see competitors entering the market, given the relative ease with which most financial products can be copied. It is important for the initiator to continue with strong marketing support to press home its first mover advantages. To accelerate growth, the company may also improve product features, explore new market segments and consider other ways of delivering the product/service.
3. *Maturity*—Sales revenues peak but profits start to fall as competitors consolidate their positions. Overcapacity often leads to price cutting, further depressing profit levels. Companies at this stage typically look for cost cutting opportunities and may decide to focus their attention upon the most profitable market segments. To delay the onset of decline, loyalty incentives may prove cost-effective in retaining valued customers.
4. *Decline*—At this stage the product becomes a possible candidate for replacement, although deletion is not the only viable strategy. As the number of competitors also tends to decline, it may be marginally profitable to maintain the product on a low expenditure basis. Organizations must also assess the extent to which key customers may be alienated by the deletion of the product.

Not unlike the portfolio matrices discussed previously, the life cycle concept cannot be applied as a precise forecasting tool. Rarely do life cycles follow the smooth lines of Figure 7.5. Durations are especially difficult to predict; growth can often be rekindled by product modifications; sometimes life cycles are truncated while seemingly at the growth stage by a major legislative or technological change. In spite of these many limitations, the concept does highlight

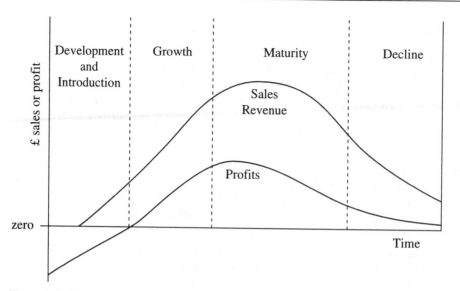

Figure 7.5   The product life cycle

the dangers of becoming too reliant upon products in late maturity or decline. It can also assist in the effective allocation of marketing resources between the products within the range.

SUMMARY

The product is fundamental to the offer of financial service retailers; without products that are well tuned to the needs of customers, expenditure on price discounts, advertising, personal selling and branch environments will be largely wasted. The tasks of developing products and of managing the product portfolio are therefore of crucial importance to management.

Product ideas can be derived from many sources but development tends to be driven by competition, the market and/or technology. Given the relative ease with which most financial products can be copied, there are many instances of 'me too', competition-driven developments. Organizations that listen to their customers, either directly, through their front-line staff or through research programmes, are clearly more likely to emerge as the innovators of successful products. Product failures can be costly and tend to arise because of a lack of customer orientation, a failure to segment the market, a failure to understand the adoption process and/or a failure to communicate product benefits effectively.

A number of different product development strategies may be identified, that are reactive or proactive in nature. The latter may be pursued through research and development, market analysis, entrepreneurial flair and/or acquisition. The process of product development typically occupies a timescale of 6–18 months, depending upon the extent of behavioural and technological change required. In their desire to get to the market quickly, and to avoid the attentions of potential imitators, organizations often tend to avoid full scale test marketing of financial products.

The rate of product adoption and subsequent diffusion is highly dependent upon levels of need and perceived risk. These risks may relate to concerns about performance, financial loss, physical danger, social approval, psychological risks or the loss of valuable time. Early adopters of products tend to differ in many respects from later adopters, suggesting some changes in marketing strategies during the product diffusion process.

Following the vigorous diversification strategies of many retailers of financial services, it is increasingly important to manage the product range effectively and profitably. The brand name(s) provide the link between items within the range and a successful brand can convey many functional and emotional attributes. A powerful brand can also provide the vehicle to assist with diversification into related product areas. Many retailers have suffered the consequences of a 'diversification too far'. A successful product range development strategy tends to look for common threads, both in terms of management expertise and customers' perceptions of the organization's competence. A strategy which focuses upon clearly defined, viable and accessible market segments can prove highly successful. Some retailers have appointed market mangers to ensure that the product range, communications and service mix is appropriate to their targeted market segments.

As information technology develops, so too does the ability to evaluate the true profitability of products within the range. It may be entirely sensible to allow the continuation of 'loss leaders', which help to retain customers and to sell more profitable products. An accurate analysis of profit contribution is, however, essential to effective range management. Similar information systems can also highlight the profitability of specific customers, segments, staff or branches.

The management of the product portfolio should also consider the relative positions of products with regards to market share and growth within the market. The particular strength of the organization within the product area may also be a factor in the decision to develop, harvest or divest of a product. There is also evidence that products tend to follow a form of life cycle, from introduction, through growth, maturity and decline. Although the duration and stages of the cycle are difficult to predict with any degree of accuracy, the concept can help to avoid overdependence upon products that are entering late maturity or decline. Very different marketing strategies may be appropriate at different stages in the life cycle.

REVIEW QUESTIONS

1. Taking one financial product of your choice, explain the elements that comprise:

    (a) the core product
    (b) the actual product
    (c) the augmented product

2. What are the main sources of ideas for product innovation in financial services? Why are some sources more likely than others to result in effective product differentiation?
3. Define the concept of 'success' in the development of financial products. How can a product that does not reach profit targets still contribute to the success of the overall product development programme?
4. What characteristics of a product or the development process tend to be associated with product failures?
5. Distinguish between reactive and proactive strategies of product development. Describe circumstances under which each type of strategy is likely to lead to the most profitable outcome.
6. With reference to a specific financial product, construct a flow chart to show the sequence of the product development process.
7. What are the dangers of:

    (a) test marketing financial products?
    (b) failing to test market them?

8. Define and explain the forms of perceived risk that may inhibit the adoption of:

   (a) ATMs
   (b) store cards
   (c) shares

9. Why have major retailers of financial services been prepared to incur very high expenditures in the development of their brands? Based upon one example of a strong financial brand, what are the brand values that differentiate it from rival products?

10. Discuss the benefits and possible problems of moving from a product management orientation to a structure within which market managers play a more prominent role.

11. You have been asked to develop a methodology for producing more precise analyses of unit profitability. What factors should be included in the calculation of:

    (a) individual product profitability?
    (b) individual customer profitability?
    (c) individual branch profitability?

12. Taking the product range of a financial services retailer with which you are familiar, show how you could appraise the product portfolio using:

    (a) the BCG market growth/market share matrix
    (b) the General Electric market attractiveness/business strength matrix

    What conclusions emerge for management of the product range? What are the limitations of these forms of portfolio analysis?

13. Provide one example of a financial product at each of the four main stages of the product life cycle. What techniques would you recommend to extend the span of the growth phase, based upon the example chosen to illustrate that phase.

REFERENCES

Berry, L.L. and J.S. Hensel (1974) 'Why do some new bank products fail?' In L.L. Berry and L.A. Capaldini (Eds.) *Marketing for the Bank Executive*, Leviathan House, London.

Bienstman, M. (1991) 'A comprehensive approach to the youth market', *Savings banks International*, **3**(91), 11–16.

British Bankers' Association (1992) *Annual Abstract of Banking Statistics*, Vol. 9, Statistical Unit, BBA, London.

Council on Financial Competition (1987) *Organization of Financial Supermarkets*, Council on Financial Competition, Washington DC.

De Brentani, U. (1988) *New Product Performance in Industrial Service Firms*, Working Paper 88–11–38, Concordia University, Quebec.

De Brentani, U. (1989) 'Success and failure in new industrial services', *Journal of Product Innovation Management*, **6**, 239–258.

De Brentani, U. (1993) 'The new product process in financial services: strategy for success', *International Journal of Bank Marketing*, **11**(3), 15–22.

De Chernatony, L. (1993) 'Categorizing brands: evolutionary processes underpinned by two key dimensions', *Journal of Marketing Management*, **9**(2), 173–188.

Department of Trade and Industry (1992) *The Single Market: Financial Services*, DTI, London.

Economist (1989) 'Why saying yes isn't enough', *Economist*, 3 June, 117–118.

Edgett, S. (1993) 'Developing new financial services within UK building societies', *International Journal of Bank Marketing*, **11**(3), 35–43.

Fee, G. (1991) 'Translate foreign loans into sterling gains', *Financial Adviser*, 20 June, 38.

Hart, S. (1993) 'Dimensions of success in new product development: an exploratory investigation', *Journal of Marketing Management*, **9**(1), 23–41.

Hill, P. (1990) 'From dairy desserts to debit cards—new product research in consumer and financial markets'. In ESOMAR *How to Market Financial Services in an Increasingly Competitive Environment*, ESOMAR, Amsterdam, 71–85.

Hopton, C. (1991) 'Keeping customers sweet', *Mortgage Finance*, January, 56–58.

Icole, E. (1990) 'Le lancement de nouveaux produits d'epargne en France'. In ESOMAR *How to Market Financial Services in an Increasingly Competitive Market*, ESOMAR, Amsterdam, 107–118.

Ironfield, C.E. and P.J. McGoldrick (1988) 'EFTPoS systems—determinants of shoppers' awareness and usage', *International Journal of Retailing*, **3**(4), 24–42.

Johne, A. (1993) 'Insurance product development: managing the changes', *International Journal of Bank Marketing*, **11**(3), 5–14.

Johne, A. and P.M. Pavlidis (1991) *Product Development Success in Banking: a Review of the Literature*, Working Paper 118, City University Business School, London.

Johne, A. and L. Vermaak (1993) 'Head office involvement in financial product development', *International Journal of Bank Marketing*, **11**(3), 28–34.

Key Note (1992) *Personal Finance in the UK*, Key Note Publications, London.

Larner, D. (1991) 'Days of experimentation are now over', *Financial Adviser*, 7 November, 37.

Lawrence, S. (1990) 'Innovative schemes for remortgages', *Financial Adviser*, 8 November, 23.

Levene, T. (1991) 'It's all in the name', *Planned Savings*, April, 13–16.

Levene, T. (1992) 'Profile', *Planned Savings*, October, 17–18.

Mabberley, J. (1989) 'It may be popular, but is it profitable?', *Building Societies Gazette*, December, 59.

Maidique, M.A. and B.J. Zirger (1985) 'The new product learning cycle', *Research Report Series, Innovation and Entrepreneurship Institute*, University of Miami, Florida.

Marr, N.E. and G.P. Prendergast (1992) 'Home banking versus personal banking in the retail market—the experts' view of the future'. In ESOMAR *Banking and Insurance: Pressure on Profits: Pressure on Research*, ESOMAR, Amsterdam, 71–96.

Mason, J.B. and H.F. Ezell (1993) *Marketing Management*, Macmillan, New York.

Meall, L. (1992) 'Smart cards: whose flexible friend?', *Accountancy*, June, 100.

Mohammed-Salleh, A. and C. Easingwood (1993) 'Why European financial institutions do not test market new consumer products', *International Journal of Bank Marketing*, **11**(3), 23–27.

Mortgage Finance (1991) 'Loan flexibility', *Mortgage Finance*, February, 58–59.

NOP (1992) *The Financial Consumer 1992/93*, NTC Publications, Henley on Thames.

Planned Savings (1990) 'Building society mortgages', *Planned Savings*, September, 45–46.

Russell-Walling, E. (1990) 'Financial services come to the rescue of NPD', *Financial Weekly*, 22 June, 20–21.

Serrano Alda, F. (1992) 'Added value products: Servei Familiar'. In ESOMAR *Banking and Insurance: Pressure on Profits: Pressure on Research*, ESOMAR, Amsterdam, 237–248.

Scheuing, E.E. and E.M. Johnson (1989) 'A proposed model for new service development', *Journal of Services Marketing*, **3**(2), 25–34.

Schwartz, S. (1992) 'Service providers chip away at French banks' supremacy', *International Money Marketing*, 21 February, 12–13.

Sonnenberg, F. (1988) 'The power of cross-selling', *Journal of Business Strategy*, **9**(1), 10–16.

Swift, S. (1991) 'Uniquely well endowed', *Money Week*, 19 June, 17.

Trout, N. (1992) 'Product and customer profitability reporting: turning a profit', *Banking Technology*, April, 22–24.

Urban, G.L. and J.R. Hauser (1980) *Design and Marketing of New Products*, Prentice-Hall, Englewood Cliffs, NJ.

Watkins, T. (1988) 'Developing trends in the marketing of life insurance', *Journal of Marketing Management*, **4**(1), 71–87.

Which Mortgage (1991) 'Best lender 1991 awards', *Which Mortgage*, December, 13–16.

Wilson, A. (1992) 'The changing nature of the marketing function within retail banks and building societies', paper presented at the *British Academy of Management Conference*, September, Bradford.

EIGHT

PRICING OF FINANCIAL SERVICES

Malcolm Hughes   Watermill Consultants

INTRODUCTION

The price of a product or service is the symbol of acceptance of the existence of a contract of exchange. In simpler terms, if I buy an item from you, at an agreed price, then I am saying, in effect, that a bargain has been made. Price is therefore that point in the economy where the interests of supplier and consumer coincide; a point of agreement; an expression of mutual satisfaction with the transaction. It is possibly an exaggeration, but not much of one, to say that customer satisfaction can only be said to exist in the framework of price; if there is no price, then the concept of customer satisfaction is without substance. Price thus determines the armature on which the fundamental relationship between the supplier and the consumer is based.

Price also has a meaning in accounting terms, since casting the 'correct' price for a product or service is a determinant of cash flow, earnings and, ultimately, the presentation of shareholder value. If the purpose of all business activity can be described as 'the over-recovery of fixed and variable overheads' (a somewhat unromantic definition!) then price and pricing tactics are firmly in this equation as key success factors and major strategic influencers. This is one of the surprising things about price—it is not the element in the marketing blend which is simply calculated by cost accountants. It is, without doubt, the pre-eminent, fundamental marketing variable and price setting should be undertaken at the most senior counsels in the organization in the context of the overall corporate mission (Lancaster and Massingham, 1988; Kotler, 1988).

This chapter examines the context of pricing in the framework of service pricing overall, providing a brief survey of the key theoretical issues which arise in the pricing of financial services and then looking in detail at the strategic and tactical pricing of investment, lending and payment instruments by sector. The conclusion of the chapter consists of a summary of main elements, together with selected practical exercises prepared by the author. It is recommended that you attempt these exercises—they will assist the reader to become more familiar with the ideas expressed and to relate the chapter material to business activity.

8.1. THE PRICING OF SERVICES IN CONTEXT

8.1.1 Pricing and the market mix

Having defined the landscape, we can address the point which has often been addressed by others. Is there any primary difference between the pricing of goods and the pricing of services? The immediate observations rest upon the clear evidence that while the marketing of services and the marketing of goods possess both similarities and differences, then so the elements of the marketing blend must reflect such similarities and differences. This will include all the 'Ps' of the traditional marketing mix and the other members of the acronym menagerie such as STEP, PEST, MECCO and PLC. So, in what ways are the elements of the pricing of services different from those of products?

In the use of STEP (segmentation, targeting, evaluation, positioning), pricing occupies a key role in each element and there are businesses such as the travel trade which survive on the use of price segmentation as a primary marketing tool. Because of the intangibility of services relative to products, pricing levels must be more closely based on customer expectations (Cowell, 1984). PEST (political, environmental, social, technological) is a valuable acronym in the wider analysis of the role of price relative to external factors. For example, it is known from conjoint or 'trade-off' analysis that customers are prepared to invest in 'green' unit funds and to pay more for products and services that do less damage to the environment. In this widely used computer-driven technique, which has been used effectively in both product and service marketing research, modelling is used to assist in the design of a realistic compromise between price and features, thus avoiding the 'free Rolls-Royce' effect of conventional research into what customers see as their 'ideal' service or product. (Vandercammen, 1992).

In order to overcome the lack of tangibility in financial products, the 'virtual reality' technique can be used in conjoint research. In VR research, the full packaging of the account is mocked up, including newspaper 'articles' and radio 'features' dealing with the new product. It is possible to make this VR package so realistic that respondents claim to have read and heard of the (imaginary) new product! MECCO (markets, environment, customers, company) summarizes the nature of the inputs to the pricing decision. Again, the problems encountered in pricing a service are different by both nature and degree. For example, in product marketing it is accepted that the area of 'pricing discretion' rests between the lower limit of costs and the upper limit of consumer demand. But in service marketing decisions, these limits are not to be found exactly, and in some financial services (e.g., small-value credit) these limits do not exist—the minimum loan rate is several multiples of the basic wholesale cost of funds—and the customers in this market appear to be completely insensitive to rates (McGoldrick, 1990).

PLC (product life cycle) is geared closely to the pricing strategies of products and services (Wilmshurst, 1984). A fundamental use of the PLC, often missed in the arguments about whether it 'applies', is that all the marketing mix strategies, including pricing, need to be reconsidered as a product or service ages in the marketplace. With financial services products, this ageing process is often deliberately engineered on the empirical grounds that with new products, both investment and lending will achieve most of the business that they are likely to capture in the initial stages of their life cycle and then need to be placed quickly under the counter so that the next cycle of innovation can have a clear run. The first immediately apparent difference is, self-evidently, that services have less tangibility than goods (Schlissel and Chasin, 1991). This is a polite way of saying that the consumer is thought to be less able to detect whether a price is valid for a service than for a physical product. Or, even more crudely, that the supplier can 'get away' with more in the service markets and that the customer is less sensitive to the relationships between prices and values. This idea which, if true, would be regrettable, begs many questions about consumer's grasp of values, both mechanistic and added. The introduction of conjoint or trade-off research techniques has allowed more precision to judgements in this field (Ennew, Watkins and Wright, 1990). In any case, like all generalizations about the marketing profession, generalizations about customer sensitivity to service pricing will be true only in part and there will be as many exceptions as there are conforming examples.

8.1.2 Price awareness and sensitivity

It cannot be sensible to suggest that long-term success in the marketing of a service can rest on the assumption that pricing can be pitched at a higher level on the grounds that the customer is less likely to notice. Nor that the devices which operate in the competitive markets for products to regulate and moderate prices are somehow faulty in service marketing. At the far end of this idea is the conclusion that services are deliberately made confusing and ambiguous, hard to compare, framed in small print for the goal of greater profit. Certainly the temptation is present, but consumerism, the proliferation of regulatory authorities such as OFTEL and OFWAT, and the vigilance of the media must mean that transgressions of competitive price responses must either be rare or undetected monopolies!

The second point is also self-evident. The operation of price mechanisms for products is determined by the uncoordinated behaviour of the mass market (Lipsey, 1987). For example, the collapse of the UK motorcycle industry in the 1970s was caused by large numbers of prospective purchasers opting to buy cheaper (and high quality) imported Japanese machines and by all the domestic producers failing to respond to this challenge. These two conditions (mass consumer behaviour; mass lack of producer response) created circumstances in which the market switched like a ratchet from one state to another. If only a few potential customers had responded and/or several UK producers had responded with better, cheaper machines, then the outcome would have been different. So, if market responsiveness is a condition of the effect of price on behaviour, then is this different between goods and services?

Without doubt, it is less easy to compare price and value of services than of products. Even less easy are the comparisons of price and value of financial services products because of the hidden, or at least more obscure, elements of both price and value which we discuss in later sections of this chapter. We might thus suggest that the price elasticity of demand of a service is less than, in general, the price elasticity of demand of a product. That we all feel this to be intuitively true is without argument; and it is also supported as an idea by academic economists (Beardshaw, 1986).

Part of the difference between products and services is that services are infrequently purchased compared to goods. We have ample opportunities to compare the prices of different brands of fabric detergents, petrol, canned soups, carrots as against sprouts, cabbage versus cauliflower—these are routine buys, every week or so. The person buying provisions for a household, quickly becomes wise to both absolute ('carrots are expensive this week') and relative ('lamb is better value than beef this week') concepts of price and apparent value. Services yield less easily to this kind of analysis. They are either of such small order of magnitude (e.g., a bus fare; a telephone call) or of such limited alternative choice (e.g., a gas bill; an electricity bill) or next to impossible to compare (e.g., a bank account; an insurance policy) or so infrequently bought (e.g., a funeral; legal advice; conveyancing) that informed and sensible decisions based on experience are less available. The purchaser thinks 'what's the point in shopping around?—I can't understand the nature of the service and anyway I only buy it once or twice in my life.'

Of course, there are non-financial services where comparisons are more available and these tend to have a greater content of uniformity (e.g., dry cleaning; car servicing) or a significant element of deliverables or tangibility (e.g., holidays; restaurants; education).

8.2 Theoretical considerations in the pricing of financial services

The role of tangibility is critical to the setting of price not only in terms of service perishability— that is, the consumer cannot buy and store services—but also from the point of view of the price setter. With an intangible service, the limits of production capacity are less defined; the service content can be easily and quickly changed; new products can be launched in a few days (and just as easily copied). Thus, for the marketer, efforts must be made to invoke substance in the service product. This can be seen in financial services in the proliferation of 'product packs' for new accounts—often glossy and heavily 'designed' outer containers for simple print items such as cheque books, pay-in slips and statement wallets. The actual price for many financial services is unseen.

8.2.1 Elements of cost

In a common example, the price paid for an endowment assurance policy in support of a mortgage, will contain significant elements of payment of commission to the salesman or distributor. In other words, not all the premium paid by the customer will be invested in the selected fund; a proportion will be diverted to selling costs. This is clearly a price, but it is not shown or seen as such. This is described as a 'covert' price, as distinct from the 'overt' price, paid as a premium for a household contents insurance policy direct to the insurer, for example. It continues to be urged that the insurance industry 'disclose' their commission payments; but there are real difficulties in devising a system which is fair to direct sales offices, broker offices and company representatives. For simple investment products, there appears to be no price involved in the purchase of the service. However, these services are supported by marketing programmes, distributed through costly branch networks and managed by teams of specialists in offices. These have to be paid for and they are paid for by the customer. The price is therefore the theoretical difference between the interest rate paid on the investment instrument (say, a building society deposit bond) and the rate that could be paid if no costs were apportioned to the instrument.

Typically for a medium-sized building society with costs in the median range, around two per cent of the interest paid (say ten per cent gross) is absorbed in this way. The amount of cost absorbed by expenses varies with the amount of activity on the account and many of the accounts maintained by building societies and banks are unprofitable because the transaction levels are high. Put another way, the pricing mechanisms of banks and building societies are not sufficiently sensitive to allocate costs to the customers who cause them—they have to be carried by all. The recent initiative by the Halifax Building Society, although criticized, to introduce charges on smaller, more active accounts is a courageous strategic move and suggests that the industry is finally coming to grips with the fact that it is subsidizing many millions of customers at the expense of its shareholders and more significant or less active investors. This concept of trading off one group of customers against another, or trading out of an unprofitable area of the market by dropping the rate paid is unusual to financial services, but is not unique. Many seasonal businesses, for example, hotels, will knowingly sell services at a loss in the low season simply to keep the hotel staff busy and provide some cash flow. This is trading off one group of customers against another and is risky in the sense that it is based on the assumption that profitable customers will appear in the high season. Similarly, the whole mechanism of the market maker in common equity stock is based on the principle that buyers can trade out of the market when they do not want to buy stock and this is done by dropping the offer price to an unattractive level at which none will sell.

Price considerations in the buying of financial service can be blurred by adding value to the service and thus providing points of difference from the commodity nature of many of its provisions. In some cases, this can be a simple reversion to the 'heap and label' philosophy of service marketing—at its most unimaginative this consists of taking a batch of existing services, bundling them together and branding them as if they were a coherent entity. Midland Bank created a range of 'new' accounts by bolting together existing money transmission and savings vehicles and branding the results with baffling titles such as 'Orchard', 'Vector' (now defunct) and 'Meridian'. This attempt to escape from the commodity behaviour of the chequeing market into a selective, segmented, targeted and positioned world of added value has to be applauded for courage and there are some who would argue (myself included) that the experiment, in the case of Vector, was not given long enough to mature.

In North America, banks are marketing 'universal' or 'unified' accounts in which a wide range of transmission, credit and investment services are operated as one account, providing great flexibility and, importantly, value for money to the customer.

We have already discussed the task of price as the recruiter of fixed and variable costs, but this begs the very large question that such costs are identifiable in the marketing of financial services. One of the perennial problems in all kinds of financial services—wholesale and retail, simple and enigmatic, core and peripheral—is that the allocation of the costs of the service to the operating characteristics of that service is largely a matter of opinion rather than fact (Ward, 1989). Clearly, the basic input and output interest rates are easy arithmetic. If you acquire money on the global medium-term markets for, say ten per cent, make it into domestic mortgages and sell them through life brokers to people buying houses at 14 per cent then the basic margin is self evident. But what proportion of your costs of operating your wholesale mortgage business do you attribute to this mortgage product? If you have many different product lines, what rules apply for the allocation of the variable costs of items such as communications costs, clerical labour, IT and data processing time, sales time, training, personnel, telephones? If, as is typical, you advertise your trading name in the umbrella sense, what proportion of your overall advertising and promotional spend do you allocate to each service line?

Most companies—even the very largest—have grappled with this issue, decided that it cannot be solved and take product line profitability down to the 'contribution' level, i.e., to the point where we start to become uncertain of the rational sense of the cost allocation tools that we have. This produces a situation where, for example a typical mutual life office, product line costs allocated only absorb 30 per cent of costs, leaving 70 per cent of operating costs generally recovered but not specifically captured to product line profitability. This is one of the major reasons why the pricing of financial services is at times so difficult to understand and so erratic—the producers do not, in the main, have any real idea of accurate product costs!

8.2.2   Price–cost relationships

Figure 8.1. shows the classic relationships between costs and output and gives the break even point (A) at which the recovery of total fixed and variable costs is complete and profit begins to emerge. Figure 8.2. demonstrates the changes in break even points that arise from variations in prices (BEA, BEB, BEC). The important issue arising from these analyses is the significant sensitivity of profit beyond break even point to changes in the assumptions that are made about the allocation of costs, particularly fixed costs. Quite small increases in the levels of fixed costs can mean unprofitability for the product line under consideration and, importantly, exaggerated profitability for the other products in the range. Since the allocation of fixed costs by product line is very much a matter of guesswork, then many pricing decisions must be defective and many companies must be carrying range members that are unprofitable at the current prices charged.

While in theory, therefore, the prices of financial services are based on the same principles as the pricing of other services and goods (company earnings objectives; customer demand; product life cycle; customer expectations; external forces), these apply differently in the pricing of financial services and have different weights and importance in the mix. It follows, therefore,

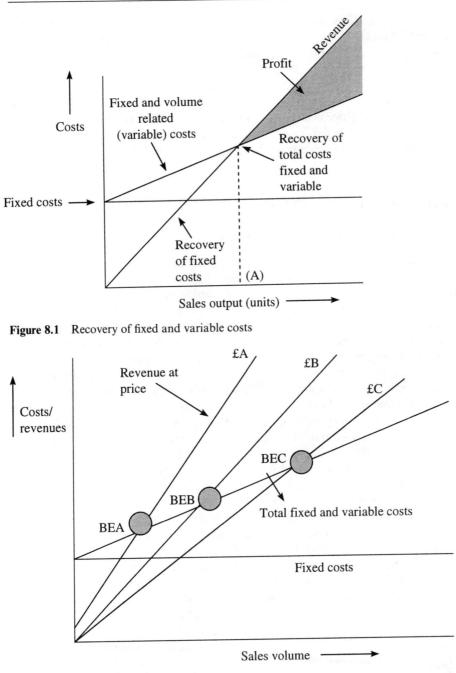

Figure 8.1 Recovery of fixed and variable costs

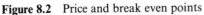

Figure 8.2 Price and break even points

that the research tools used to determine the relationships between pricing, non-price features and demand in financial service have to be much more sophisticated and precise than those that can be tolerated in the marketing of ordinary products and services. One example of this difference already mentioned is in the use of conjoint or trade-off research to aid the design of financial products.

A further issue that distinguishes financial services pricing theory from other fields is the concept of 'bought risk' (Stanlake, 1987). When some kinds of financial services are purchased by the customer, paying either an overt or covert price, then the risk of loss of capital is present. With commodities and futures there are high risks, with bank and building society deposits, the risk can be considered negligible. Where there are high risks, the customer may make significant gains in the market and recover the costs of the deal many times over. Conversely, all the capital may be lost—the ultimate price! Price is also related to liquidity—money deposited or invested over a long term tends to attract higher rates of interest (a lower price to the investor) than money which is entirely liquid. In, for example, a bank current account, little or no interest may be paid for full liquidity.

8.3 FINANCIAL SERVICES PRICING IN PRACTICE

8.3.1 The pricing of deposit and savings instruments

We have already touched on the concept of price for investment services as being the difference between the interest rate that could be paid in the absence of non-interest costs and the rate paid in practice. Bearing in mind that the consumer appeals of a deposit product are various, and that interest rate is only one of such appeals, then we can begin to understand the wide variance in rates paid. It is, for example, possible to obtain as much as three to four times the level of interest for a similar invested amount at similar terms from one institution compared to another. Since money is essentially an homogeneous commodity, then the fact that many billions of pounds is invested at much less than the rate it could command elsewhere, and thus at a higher price, can only be explained by inertia in the broadest sense. This is not to imply that consumers are lazy and ignorant, although some undoubtedly are, but that the customer who happily accepts a return of two per cent on a bank deposit will have other motives for continuing with such a disadvantageous arrangement. This can be as simple as the fact that the branch is convenient and the staff professional and friendly.

There is considerable debate from time to time over whether the practice of 'cascade marketing' is or is not ethical. Cascade marketing can be applied to both deposit and savings instruments and has been applied to my certain knowledge from the early 1970s. In this marketing device, deposits or debts are attracted at low prices (high or low interest rates respectively). Having attracted a tranche of new customers in this way, the prices are slowly increased, usually under the cover of general changes in rates and greater and greater profits are taken from the portfolio. Some losses of customers are inevitable and planned for—typically the 'money aware'—but the bulk of the customers will stay put as their investment or loan becomes progressively less value to them and more profitable to the institution (see Figure 8.3).

Much debate has centred on the relevance or otherwise of the product life cycle in financial services. In the view of many marketing practitioners, financial services is the only area of marketing activity where the PLC exists and that is because it is engineered as a matter of strategic planning. It is clear that the product range within a financial services institution is capable of almost endless extension and iron discipline is required if the distribution channels are not to be clogged with a proliferation of barely distinguishable offerings. Some would argue that this unhappy state has already been reached. Nevertheless, novelty and the cascade principle of marketing for new money lay the foundation for an active programme of innovation. Independent distributors such as brokers and company representatives also like to see fresh ideas from time to time, even if vaguely familiar or 'me-too's'. This can only lead to the managed life cycle wherein the new product is speedily progressed to obsolescence, its tactical usefulness exhausted.

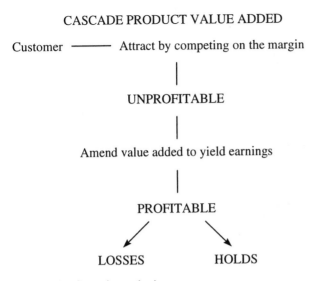

Figure 8.3 Cascade marketing

Technically, very few financial services products can be withdrawn; witness the advertisements in the press giving the terms and interest rates of 'accounts no longer available to the public'. These graveyards are the ultimate last sector of the PLC—not decline but morbidity.

Price is an important component of the marketing mix but only insofar as it serves the overall objective of controlling the cost of onboard funds. Usually, the cost of fresh incoming funds are higher than the cost of those already in house. This can produce distortions in the balance of assets and liabilities, particularly in a situation where the output side (the lending markets) are tougher and margins that can be retrieved are smaller. There is thus a natural tendency to emphasize the other aspects of the mix, away from price. This can be seen in heavy advertising, sales promotion, product features such as withdrawal terms and minimum investment levels. Where transactions are permitted on deposit and investment accounts, it is critical that these are controlled, since significant utilization of these facilities can swiftly run entire segments of accounts into losses. Penalties and charges for such excessive use of facilities will become more common as the financial pressures on sources and uses of funds become more acute.

Figure 8.4 shows the familiar 'U' shaped profitability curve for a bank chequeing account. Those with low balances and high numbers of transactions are profitable because they are paying bank charges and overdraft interest; those with high balances and low transactions are profitable because they are, in effect, lending the bank money interest free and hardly using the services. The average customer with a modest balance and reasonable number of transactions is usually unprofitable—it is in this key area that effective pricing strategy is needed and where it so often fails.

The great unknown in the marketing of investment and deposit instruments is, of course, the new product development ambitions of the Chancellor of the Exchequer from time to time. When John Major adorned the Treasury as its first Minister, he was clearly exercised by the need to design and launch new financial products with attractive tax breaks—TESSA and improved PEPS were his architecture. Suffice to say that the financial community responds with enthusiasm to any assistance from the Treasury in the form of tax breaks and National Savings has been sharpening up its marketing as its ability to pay interest gross and without declaration is now a monopoly condition.

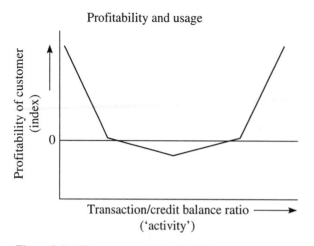

Profitability and usage

Figure 8.4   Cheque account profitability

8.3.2   The pricing of equity shares and mutual funds

When an investor buys or sells shares in a quoted company or in government debt (called 'gilt edged'), the market maker with whom the deal is made will charge commission on the value of the deal, usually subject to a minimum fee for any deal. For example, if a customer sells shares through a broker, a commission will be charged of (typically) 1.75 per cent on the sales value. In real terms, this would work out at £50 for the sale of 1,200 Marks and Spencer shares at the price of 242p. Of course, this is not the only charge inherent in buying or selling shares. For certain trades, VAT, transfer costs, contract levy and stamp duty may be charged. Clearly, if a share is bought, then the price of the share has to rise by at least two to three per cent in order to recover these costs. As with mutual funds (or unit trusts), there is also a spread between the buying price (offer price) and selling price (bid price). The bid price is the price at which the fund management company will repurchase units from customers who want to sell and the offer price is the price at which the company will sell units to customers who wish to buy. Why they are not simply called the sell and buy price is a mystery. One way to remember it is that as 'B' is before 'O' in the alphabet, so the bid price is less than the offer price. Most of the newspapers that have a city page show unit trust prices and there may also be additional information such as price changes over the year and yields.

Dealers manipulate their positions in the market essentially by varying their prices up and down so that they attract, or do not attract, the buying or selling of a particular share. For example if a market maker has an order for 10,000 shares of Marks and Spencer, then the shares must first be located and then bought from another market maker who is seeking to make such a sale on behalf of one of the clients. In this way, supply and demand for shares is matched. If the demand for a share exceeds the available supply then the price will rise until sellers appear and the demand is satisfied. Similarly, if there is selling pressure behind a share, then the price will fall until buyers feel that it is a bargain. Ironically, when there is great activity on the stock market, as at times of national crisis, and share prices are falling sharply, the popular newspapers talk of 'panic selling'. Given that all deals have to be matched, it would be just as true, although less dramatic, to talk of 'panic buying'! In October 1987, when stock markets round the world underwent one of the worst falls in the history of all markets, not only were tens of millions of shares sold as prices fell vertically, but somebody bought them.

This double cost of buying and selling shares (commissions plus the buy/sell spread) makes the carrying out of small deals expensive. This has caused concern for some time in that it discourages the 'small' investor and the admirable concept of 'wider share ownership'. Unit trusts or mutual funds were introduced partly to offset this high cost of direct ownership and also to allow the smaller investor to spread the risk of loss over many holdings. The investor in unit funds still has to bear the cost of the bid/offer spread, but can buy direct from the marketing company and may pay only a small front-end commission. During marketing programmes, it is possible to buy new units at a discount price. Other actively marketed investments such as PEPs and investment trusts are based on the principle of reducing the entry cost and dealing costs to a minimum to attract the more modest purchaser.

It is not appropriate in a book of this nature, and it is also illegal under the financial services legislation, to give advice on the selection of investments. However, the holding of good quality shares in well known companies has, over the long run, protected the value of capital against inflation. Since most institutional investment is based on share investment, at least in part, then the ordinary citizen has an important stake in the business community through his or her pension or life policy. Most of us would not think of ourselves as 'stock market investors', but we are, even if indirectly.

8.3.3   The pricing of mortgage and credit products

This area of pricing seems, on the face of it, to be more straightforward. A mortgage is simply a long term secured loan using a domestic property as security. It can be repaid at termination from the proceeds of matured life assurance policies or other similar investments, such as unit funds and pension plans; it can be repaid at termination from funds from any source; or it can be repaid (as is usually the case) in monthly instalments over its life. The price, in all these cases, is mainly the interest rate charged by the lender, although some lenders will also charge setting up fees and there are many other costs in buying a house, such as solicitors' fees, conveyancing charges, stamp duty. One of the difficulties encountered in obtaining a true charge for credit (known as the annual percentage rate or APR) is the extent to which these essential charges should be reflected in the rate.

The APR is a classic example of the operation of regulation in a way almost guaranteed to confuse the customer. The intentions of those who introduced the concept of APR were entirely honourable, to provide a common base upon which the various types of credit available could be price compared. In practice, APR is not at all understood by the less certain customer—in other words those who are not used to borrowing money. APR is calculated according to a set and complex formula which takes into account the fact that lenders make fixed charges for setting up loans and that loans are repaid during their life and that the interest rate will thus rise progressively as the capital is repatriated to the lender. It is widely accepted that the APR method has not helped customers to pay more realistic prices for credit; indeed in all my years experience of retail branch work, I have never once been asked for the interest rate of a loan, just 'Can I have the money', and 'What are the monthly repayments?'

The way in which mortgage rates are set by lenders has changed a great deal since the days in the 1970s when the Council of the Building Societies Association would meet in solemn secrecy and decide on the rate to be charged. The changes to building societies brought about by the legislative innovations of the 1980s (Building Societies Act, 1986), plus the emergence of other lenders into the market, such as the banks and wholesale lenders, have meant that the supply of funds into the market is 'clearing' the market—supply is matching demand; rationing is not in operation. This has had major implications for the price of mortgages; not as some would hope to reduce the price, but rather to ensure that the price of all credit has been and remains high. This seems to argue against the economic truth that competition will lower prices in a perfect market and so it does. We need to recall that the supply of funds for credit is piped directly from the savings and investment markets. Competition for the investors' money in these supply markets increases prices (interest rates), as institutions jostle with each other to attract money with more attractive terms. This feeds straight through into the lending markets.

I once enjoyed an argument with a quite senior politician who regarded it as a sacred truth that competition always reduced prices and found it impossible to accept that in the investment markets, increased competition means increased rates; and while competition for lending will have a downward pressure on interest rates charged, the price of incoming funds will place a floor under these rates and hence the prices of credit from time to time.

8.3.4 The pricing of life, pensions and general insurances

The premium which the customer pays to a life assurance company for the provision of a life policy or a pension policy covers a number of liabilities. Note that the fundamental provisions of a life policy and a pension policy are the same; we need to make a distinction between 'endowment' policies, where there is an element of investment, and policies which simply pay out on death but provide no lump sum at maturity. Both are invested in the funds of the life company and both pay benefits on death or at a fixed point in time. At maturity, the proceeds of a life policy are paid to the holder, typically as a lump sum without further tax deducted. With a pension plan, the lump sum is, normally, used to buy an annuity (this is also a form of life assurance) which will release an income for the rest of the life of the holder. This income is taxable through the PAYE system. The premiums paid by pension plan holders are, within certain limitations, deductible from income before tax is assessed and the relative price of pensions as an investment vehicle is reduced; life assurance premiums do not attract tax relief. There is no doubt that successive chancellors have regarded the tax advantages of pension funds as far from a level playing field and have repeatedly sought to palisade these concessions. It may not be too distant that pension fund contributions will no longer be relieved of tax and the subsequent rise in the price of a personal pension may provide one of the most significant readjustments in the investment markets since the end of tax relief on life assurance premiums in the 1970s.

The premiums (or price) paid, often monthly, cover the costs to the life company of insuring the life of the customer in the event of death before the end of the policy term. This can be considered as the underwriting or actuarial element of the policy. The amount of the premium which is taken by this element will depend on the age of the policyholder since the probability of death rises with age—eventually becoming 100 per cent! The calculations carried out by actuaries ensure that these premiums are fair and also that the fund has adequate assets to cover its liabilities at any point. This will depend to a great extent on the age profile of the pool of lives which comprise the fund. Very young children cannot be insured in this way—the actuarial calculations are too complex. Another part of the premium, and it can be as much as 60 per cent, is absorbed by the operating costs of the insurance company and the remainder is invested for the benefit of the policyholder in the life fund or funds.

Within the operating cost element, an amount will be paid at the start of the policy to the salesman or other distributor such as a building society, bank or broker who arranged the sale of the policy. Again, the amount of commission paid varies considerably, but can be as much as the entire first year of premiums for a long-term life policy or pension plan—a notable example of a covert price. These commissions are very lucrative for the sales organizations involved. In its

1991 accounts, Nationwide Building Society shows commission earnings in excess of £100 million, a sum which approaches half its operating profit for the year. For some smaller building societies, such earnings account for all their profits. There have been and continue to be attempts made to obtain full disclosure of these commissions paid from the policyholders' premiums but the life assurance industry is less than enthusiastic about this prospect.

It is true to say that the market for endowment assurance (i.e., where there is an investment element) is entirely supported by the mortgage related market and that commission payments to lenders are a powerful hidden price that the housebuyer has to pay. Such mortgage related policies, particularly the 'low start' variant which allows higher borrowing at a lower price, are one reason for the high expectations which characterize the UK housing market and may also serve to support house prices at a higher level than otherwise. However, government interference in the housing market has always been timid, probably for sound political reasons!

The markets for general insurance are widespread and complex—all the way from film stars insuring parts of their anatomies to permanent health insurance; from liability for entire aircraft to a theft policy on a child's bicycle. The prices here are straightforward; you pay a premium which is assessed depending on the degree of risk and the underwriting experience of the type of risk that the insurer has in the category. For this price you obtain cover against stated events occurring. This statement of the process explains a number of things about general insurance: first that the price of general insurance can only be calculated on past events, so that a company that has had a bad run of house contents claims must raise its prices after the event and may find itself charging higher prices as the general level of, say, theft from homes is falling—a difficult public affairs position; secondly, that general insurers are classic users of price as a segmentation tool. If an insurance company has a good experience in a particular area, for example, older drivers, then it will offer attractive prices for motor policies to this group so as to attract more business. Other companies will respond and the customers in this segment will benefit from better value. Obversely, younger drivers can be actively discouraged by companies who set their rates so high that little or no business will be attracted.

Furthermore, the risks covered have to be precisely defined so that the pricing of the policy is fair to the insured and the risk taker. This can, and does, lead to feelings of disaffection from policyholders who can experience situations where the event that happened to them is the very one that is excluded by the policy. The old insurance joke about the policy which covered against being attacked by a hippopotamus while riding a bicycle along the river bed as being the only policy on which the claims could not be fraudulent, has elements of truth. It is believed within the insurance industry that the majority of household contents claims are fraudulent either in part or in whole—this clearly increases the prices for those who claim honestly or do not claim at all.

Of course, using price as an active marketing variable in this way can become self defeating, since even good risk groups will become unprofitable at very low price levels and other marketing devices from the mix should be invoked. There is the famous example of the special cheap house contents insurance for dog owners which has proved a popular piece of targeting. It is based on the assumption that dog owners have better claims experience than non-owners and thus command a lower price. Plausible but untrue: the claims experiences are identical; it is just a clever piece of packaging!

8.3.5   The pricing of payments systems

There are few topics guaranteed to cause more heat than light than a discussion of bank charges. One can have every sympathy with the hapless customer who has been taught from childhood that financial services are 'free' at point of use and to suspect any attempt by institutions to charge for the use of 'my' money. This is not an appropriate place to offer a defence of the UK banking industry, often much and unjustly maligned. But it is worth asking why 'free banking' should ever have been used as a marketing tool, as it has many times in the past and will be again. It is self-evident that stopping 'free banking', when conditions are opposed to it, will cause guaranteed public disaffection and easy media targets. So the long-term losses of 'free banking' in terms of public relations are incalculable and must far outweigh the shorter term gains.

But how sensitive are typical current account holders to the price of current account banking? The answer seems to be that some are and some are not. The introduction by all the clearers, over the last five years, of interest bearing or lower priced current accounts has left a significant proportion of accounts (30 per cent) and, by implication, vast funds in non-interest bearing accounts. These accounts tend to carry smaller balances than average and, of course, the banks have skilfully positioned their services to maximize their on-board non-interest bearing funds. But the take-home conclusion is that the majority of these account holders, simply do not care. It cannot be lack of awareness on the part of account holders—anyone who claims not to know of the existence of interest bearing current accounts must have been living in a cave for the last few years. So inertia, as with the cascade marketing of the building societies, emerges as a powerful marketing tool allowing, ethics aside, the more flexible use of pricing policy.

One other burden that the banks carry in the current thankless environment is that of supporting the business community. It is seldom said, and less realized, that the bulk of ordinary industrial and commercial activity in any trading nation depends on the banks' provision of credit into the payment system at reasonable prices. Without the provision of flexible trade credit, no business could trade which has to buy goods and services, add value and resell them. The remarkable thing to notice about the perennial uproar around the banks' behaviour towards small businesses is not how bad the situation is, but how good. For every individual case where the price of credit and other services is shown to be heavy-handed or unreasonable, there are thousands of cases where business people are loyal and committed to the bank that gave them a start and are prepared to pay the fees and charges appropriate to the risks involved.

Bank managers are a much disliked race, in some cases rightly so, but during a recession the most fine and balanced judgements are needed about the trading performances of many hundreds of businesses, large and small, unless the recession is to be tipped into a slump. The use of segmented pricing of credit and transmission services is the only alternative to withdrawal of facilities in many cases. In any event, the cost of banking services for businesses with annual turnovers of less than £5 million is below 0.5 per cent and we need to remember that of all businesses, over 30 per cent are net investors in the banking system and thus benefit from higher interest rates.

Another area where the blessed inertia of the UK financial services customer has come to the rescue both of the marketing managers and the bottom line is in the introduction of fees for credit cards. Up to 1990, the UK was one of the few countries in the world where a credit card could be obtained without price and, if used simply as a payment instrument and not for borrowing, operated without any cost at all. The financial affairs of the credit payment systems operators are shrouded within the annual reports of their parents—usually banks. Therefore the actual profits of, say, Barclaycard, Access and Trustcard are opaque to the casual enquirer. Insider opinion, however, suggests that no credit card operator in the UK has ever made a profit as a stand alone business and those that have do so because of the conventions of the parent as to the allocation of overheads. This state of affairs is caused by the bizarre combination that nearly half of all card holders never borrow on credit and of the half that do borrow, the defalcation levels are alarming. The use of pricing in the form of direct fees has always been inevitable, given this marketing dilemma that profits cannot be created by advancing credit more aggressively because the customers who tend to borrow also tend to be poor at repayment. Theft and fraud also contribute to the need to increase the prices of card services.

Since the introduction of card fees, which are now almost universal, the number of card holders has fallen overall but is showing signs of rebuilding. Customers are deduplicating—for example, not holding both Visa and Access (Mastercharge), and marginal users are dropping out of the market altogether. Since the trick when introducing pricing is to lose only the customers that have little value, then the tactic can be said to be working. In this case, the charging of fees has encouraged the use of direct debit cards such as Connect and Switch as an alternative method of payment. These are free at point of use and help to relieve the flood of paper payments in the clearing system.

SUMMARY

This examination shows that pricing has a very different and distinctive role in services; in general and financial services in particular. It calls into question the predication that service pricing is simply a minor development of product pricing and is based on the same principles.

In financial services, pricing can be of two kinds: 'covert', that is lost interest, commissions, offer/bid spreads etc., and 'overt', that is fees, premiums and interest payments.

The degree of elasticity of demand in financial services varies from virtually nil in some markets (e.g., mortgages) to very high levels (e.g., new lump sum deposits).

In the mass markets for money transmission, short term credit and demand deposit savings, customer behaviour is segmented into 'sensitives' and 'insensitives' and appropriately targeted pricing strategy can be aimed at each segment, as in the banks' current account charging tactics and the building society's 'cascade' investment pricing strategies.

Little use is made in the UK of offering a package of related financial services at a discount price in order to encourage cross-selling, as with the so-called 'universal' accounts in North America which provide a range of credit and payment services within one account at competitive prices. It is known that such accounts have been extensively researched, but the conclusions have been that the relative lack of sophistication of the UK financial services consumer renders them less appealing. Furthermore, the institutions themselves lack the database management systems to introduce such combined accounts.

Insurance products are priced using a combination of actuarial, underwriting, segmentation and selling costs inputs. Disclosure of the true costs of sales commissions to customers might well cause a major reappraisal of the value of some of the products in these markets.

Research methods into the pricing of financial services have to use advanced techniques such as conjoint (trade-off) or virtual reality (VR) analysis if the results are to be decision reliable. This is another important difference from products where less radical research methods can be tolerated.

The role of government monetary policy, the activities of the Treasury in the liquidity markets, the ability of the authorities to create tax advantage can, at times, overwhelm the market-based pricing policies of conventional producers.

The housing market is the key to much of the insurance market and also governs the pricing of mortgage credit and thus indirectly rates paid in the deposit markets.

REVIEW EXERCISES

1. You are planning the launch of a new investment product for the Cleckheckmondthwaite Temperance Permanent Building Society, which is a local society operating 7 branches, all

within 22 miles of the eponymous Yorkshire town. Draw up a launch checklist of factors that you will need to take into account when setting the interest rate, or rates for your new product.

2. Select a clearing bank and describe ways in which product pricing might be used in the commercial banking market for small businesses (up to £5 million annual sales turnover) to provide sustainable competitive advantage.

3. Do you think that the product life cycle exists in financial services marketing insofar as it has an influence on product and service pricing? Support your views with examples for and against the PLC, paying particular attention to the role of price in the various discrete stages of the life cycle of a financial product.

4. What are the influences of distribution systems on the pricing of financial services? Give examples of situations where selected distribution systems might increase and decrease the price of the delivered service.

5. In the advertising of investment and mortgage products, interest rates are frequently featured in large type, dominating the message of the product features. Yet research shows that many customers are unsure of the meaning of interest rates and that a tiny minority grasp the meaning of terms such as APR, fixed rate and withdrawal penalty. Comment constructively on an advertisement of your choice and indicate what steps you would take, either regulatory or code of practice based, to improve the communications values of price advertising in financial services.

6. It has been said that the cost of dealing in shares and government debt is not the factor preventing wider share ownership—the main reason is that ordinary people should concentrate on ordinary methods of saving and investing and leave the securities markets to the experts. To what extent do you agree with this view? Do you think that if the price of equity investment were made cheaper and more easily available, significant numbers of savers and investors would choose direct involvement? Give full reasons for your answers in the context of events such as recent privatizations.

7. If the allocation of fixed and variable costs to members of a product line is an inexact science, then what mechanisms can you suggest might be investigated to improve this allocation? To what extent do you think that the accurate costing of financial services products is an important component in the setting of prices or do you feel that the other influences on price are of greater importance? Illustrate your answer with examples.

8. There are around 2,000 authorized unit trusts actively marketed in the UK. Theory would suggest that such intensive competition in a relatively small market would reduce the cost of purchasing units for the individual and hence the price of dealing in company securities using this route. With limited exceptions, however, all unit fund management companies charge the same or similar prices in terms of spread and commission. Why is this the case?

REFERENCES

Beardshaw, J. (1986) *Economics—A Student's Guide*, Pitman Publishing Company, London, 138–154
Building Societies Act (1986) HMSO, London.
Cowell, D. (1984) *The Marketing of Services*, Heinemann, Oxford, Ch. 8.
Ennew, C., T. Watkins and M. Wright (1990) *Marketing Financial Services*, Heinemann, Oxford, p. 113.
Kotler, P. (1988) *Marketing Management*, Prentice-Hall, NJ, Ch. 17.
Lancaster, G. and L. Massingham (1988) *Essentials of Marketing*, McGraw-Hill, Maidenhead, England, Ch. 9.
Lipsey, R. G. (1987) *An Introduction to Positive Economics*, Weidenfeld and Nicholson, London, Ch. 6.
McGoldrick, P. J. (1990) *Retail Marketing*, McGraw-Hill, Maidenhead, England, 211–236.
Schlissel, M. R. and Chasin, J. (1991) 'Pricing of services, an interdisciplinary review', *The Service Industries Journal*, **11**(3).
Stanlake, G. F. (1987) *Introductory Economics*, Longman, Harlow, Essex. Ch. 4.

Vandercammen, M. (1992) 'The use of conjoint analysis in determining financial services pricing', ESOMAR, Amsterdam.

Ward, K. (1989) *Financial Aspects of Marketing*, Heineman, Oxford, pp. 141, 258.

Wilmshurst, J. (1984) *Fundamentals and Practice of Marketing*, Heinemann, Oxford, 42.

NINE

PROMOTION AND ADVERTISING

Yvette Kirk   Milward Brown Market Research Ltd

INTRODUCTION

The financial market is particularly complex and competitive, becoming increasingly so over recent years. The Financial Services Act, passed in legislation in 1986 to improve standards within the industry, came into force in 1988, and totally changed the structure of financial distribution in the UK. The act precipitated a financial revolution, with organizations eager to diversify into the other 'traditional' areas of activity. The FSA exacerbated the already fiercely competitive environment in which financial organizations operated. One response to this new environment has been an increasing interest in marketing and in advertising in particular. Advertising, communication with a view to increasing sales, is one of the most important, and one of the most expensive, marketing activities to understand.

It is important to recognize that in such a complex market, advertising may have many roles. The following are examples of these roles.

Acquisition of new customers   A primary objective of advertising is often to attract new customers to the organization. New customers may come from those entering the relevant life stage category for a financial service or by attracting customers from other financial organizations.

Retention of existing customers   While it has to be acknowledged that there is still a degree of customer inertia, which varies quite markedly across financial product fields, customers are becoming increasingly demanding in terms of provision of financial services and increasingly likely to change supplier if they become dissatisfied with the service. One advertising objective may therefore be to maintain loyalty among existing customers.

Cross selling   The cross-selling of additional services to existing customers in order to maintain profitability has been a key objective behind the diversification of many financial organizations.

Staff morale   The effect of advertising on the organization's own employees may be particularly important given their role in portraying the image of the organization and in converting sales in branches.

Corporate stability   The advertising investment itself serves as a statement of confidence and stability to a wider audience such as intermediaries, shareholders and so forth.

Advertising within this market does not only have to contend with the dynamic and competitive nature of the environment; the following hurdles also have to be crossed:

Consumer apathy   A specific feature of financial products is that, although they are recognized as being important, very few consumers regard them as interesting.

High risk purchase   The purchase of a financial service is generally a relatively high risk, serious purchase, which occurs without the ability for trial. It is high risk, not only in the sense that it may involve the investment of large sums of money, but also in the sense that it is an intangible benefit. Additionally, some financial products are open to public display after purchase, and are, therefore, susceptible to social pressures of, for instance, acceptability among peer groups.

Plethora of sources of information   Advertising is only one of a number of channels of information available to the consumer; the target market is also influenced by other things it sees and hears. The consumer can actively seek information from a variety of other sources—friends, relatives, newspaper advice, independent financial advisers etc., and the extent to which these sources are used will vary between consumers. Given the dynamic nature of the marketplace, a consumer re-entering the financial market will typically have to re-evaluate the alternatives. Advertising also interacts with channels of information that are not actively sought. The consumer is continually bombarded with information about the financial market place, about specific organizations and their services. On the one hand, this information can be positive and serve to reinforce the advertising message of, for instance, a caring attitude towards customers; on the other hand, the information may be dissonant with the advertising message. Unfavourable media coverage concerning the retail banks' credit policy during the economic downturn of the early 1990s would appear to have directly contradicted the intended message of their small business advertising.

Minority of consumers in the market   At any one time, only a minority of the population will actually be in the market for the advertised service. Consequently, with broadcast media, the advertiser will also have to aim to achieve something with the majority who are not about to buy, if they are to avoid 'wasting' a lot of the advertising expenditure.

Commodity purchase   Much of what is on offer to the consumer is a commodity-based product which could be supplied by anyone. The consumer needs to be given a reason for choosing one supplier over another. The combination of the essentially commodity-based purchase and the increasing competition for consumer finance necessitates a distinctive corporate positioning. However, the majority of financial institutions, and especially those with no direct relationship with their customers, lack a clear identity and positioning in consumers' eyes. For instance, insurance companies, whose dealings are often through a broker, are particularly prone to a weak identity; conceptually, consumers tend to think of them as a homogeneous category.

The magnitude of the task becomes apparent!

The purpose of this chapter is to examine the role of advertising within the market. The first section reviews the trends in expenditure over recent years; and goes on to discuss the various decisions that need to be made in terms of budget setting, media usage, choice of advertising agency and strategy.

Attention then turns to the crucial issue of how advertising is thought to generate sales of financial services, since without an understanding of how advertising works it is difficult to maximize its potential. The contrasting ways in which the various media are consumed and the implications of this on producing effective advertising for financial services are explored. The chapter concludes with a review of the main research approaches to evaluating advertising performance.

9.1 ADVERTISING EXPENDITURE

Reviewing the amount of expenditure on financial advertising gives no indication about its effectiveness, but illustrates the commitment of financial organizations to media advertising. Mintel (1991) examines the levels of advertising of financial products both above and below the line, and notes that above the line activity was almost unheard of until the last 20 years. Increased competition resulting from legislative changes that enabled institutions to diversify out of their traditional areas of expertise and increased consumer spending in the 1980s, fuelled the growth of advertising expenditure. Table 9.1 shows the main media financial advertising expenditure as a proportion of total advertising expenditure. Financial services expenditure has grown steadily throughout the 1980s and at a greater rate than all advertising expenditure; financial advertising accounted for an increasing proportion of the total advertising expenditure to 1988.

Table 9.2 shows the level of expenditure broken down into major financial service sectors. In 1986, the Building Society Act allowed building societies to increase their range of products and services and to change their status to that of a joint stock bank. At this point in time, the building societies overtook the banks as the biggest media spenders. Mintel (1991) examines the main media advertising spend on financial services in the major product areas, enabling an examination of the growth of spend by individual financial sectors between 1980 and 1990.

Mintel points out that advertising expenditure is concentrated among a small number of financial organizations. In 1990, £110.8 million was spent in the banks sector, five banks (NatWest, Barclays, Lloyds, Girobank and TSB) accounted for nearly three-quarters of this; and while there are in excess of 100 building societies, five account for nearly 64 per cent of the spend for the building society sector.

9.2 DECISIONS IN ADVERTISING

9.2.1 Budget determination

A fundamental decision facing the advertiser is how much should be allocated for the advertising budget. There is no simple and straightforward formula that answers this question, and it is common for advertisers to regularly use more than one method to help set advertising budgets. Large scale surveys suggest that there is increasing emphasis on a more considered approach and the use of more sophisticated databased budgeting techniques, although, perhaps surprisingly, a number still rely upon the more judgemental or arbitrary approaches to budget determination (Hooley and Lynch, 1985; Lynch, Hooley and Shepherd, 1988).

Broadbent (1989) provides a comprehensive guide to setting advertising budgets and discusses the various advantages and disadvantages of different approaches. The following outline the main methods of budget determination:

Affordable or residual   Advertising allocation is decided upon the basis of what can be afforded. Once the revenue has been reduced by other costs, the remainder is divided between the advertising budget and other items.

Inertia   The inertia approach, where the budget is retained at the same level as the previous year, is more likely to be used when advertising is a small part of the marketing mix.

Media inflation multiplier   The budget used in the previous year is increased by a factor reflecting the estimated increase in media costs.

Table 9.1 Main media advertising expenditure, at rate card cost discounted using Advertising Association discount factors, 1983–90

	Total expenditure £m	Index	Financial expenditure £m	Index	% of total
1983	1,743	100	152	100	8.7
1984	1,961	113	177	116	9.0
1985	2,154	124	217	143	10.1
1986	2,532	145	258	170	10.2
1987	2,873	165	317	209	11.0
1988	3,224	185	368	242	11.4
1989	3,484	200	380	250	10.9
1990	3,653	210	397	261	10.9

Source: Mintel (1991)

Table 9.2 Main media advertising spend by major financial service sectors rate card cost, 1980–90

	1980 £m	1982 £m	1984 £m	1986 £m	1988 £m	1990 £m
Banks	23.1	38.8	61.4	68.6	99.5	110.8
Building societies	21.0	44.3	60.2	75.9	101.0	121.7
Other financial	13.8	20.9	31.7	54.5	66.6	58.1
Financial services	12.6	19.3	27.0	42.2	53.2	47.6
Insurance companies	12.5	24.4	38.0	62.9	96.3	90.6
Credit cards	4.6	9.3	11.6	16.7	22.8	12.0
Unit trusts	2.9	6.2	10.6	25.6	23.9	24.3
Investment bonds	1.1	0.6	0.8	2.8	1.1	1.9
Total	91.6	163.8	241.3	349.2	464.4	467.0

Source: Mintel (1991)

Advertising to sales ratio Allocation is determined either as a proportion of the estimated sales revenue for the next year or as a proportion of sales from the current or previous years. Such an approach is relatively easy to use once the definition of 'sales' and this 'proportion' itself has been agreed. A particular difficulty of the financial market is the definition of 'sales' in the first place. Unlike the FMCG market, the definition is not necessarily straightforward, for instance in the savings product field, should the measure be applications, account openings or deposits?

In some cases, the proportion may be based upon an industry norm. Ideally, the proportion should be updated annually, although the fact that the one used is often that of habit means that the method is essentially one of inertia. An implicit disadvantage of the advertising to sales approach is that the effects of advertising on sales is not taken into account. Little direct account is taken of competitor activity, of advertising effectiveness or of the advertising targets and objectives. So, as Broadbent (1989) points out, the result of adherence to an advertising to sales method in a situation of falling sales would be a reduction in expenditure, whereas increased expenditure may be the appropriate action.

Competitive parity A relatively easy approach to budget setting is to examine the spend of major competition and set the budget at a level in line with it. The advantage of this approach is that it is less inwardly looking given that attention is focused upon the competitors' advertising activities. The assumption, that may be incorrectly made, is that the competition is spending the 'correct' amount, and as with other ratio methods, advertising efficiency and the effect of advertising on sales are ignored.

Objective and task Using this approach, the method of setting advertising budgets is based upon an understanding of the marketing and advertising objectives, and a calculation of the budget that is required to meet the stated objectives. An attraction of this approach is that the emphasis is placed upon the outside world, and upon what needs to be achieved.

Broadbent notes that this method is often linked with the zero-based approach which states that 'nothing should be taken for granted in budget-setting: the inertia, same as last year method is specifically rejected, instead a bottom up approach is used, with each part of the budget being explicitly justified, the justification often being the task to be achieved by advertising'.

It is generally agreed that objective and task is the best approach to determining expenditure levels. Practically, it is the most difficult, since accurate costings of the media required to achieve the objectives is complex. Reviewing the data available about the market and the competition, and about one's own advertising history is often a first step. Experimentation, essentially area tests where heavy weight is applied to one or more TV region may help to set the budget directly, although experimentation is often expensive and there is no guarantee of clear conclusions. It is worth noting that thus far the assumption has been that all advertising is equally effective; in reality campaigns vary markedly in their ability to address the advertising objectives and as such advertising 'efficiency' is an important variable to be considered. A combination of the various approaches outlined enables the advertiser to determine a budget level.

9.2.2 Media usage

Depending on budget size, communication objectives and the nature of the target audience (all of which are interdependent), there is a wide range of media available for the financial advertiser to choose from, including television, print, outdoor and radio. Below the line activity such as direct mail and in branch activity can also be used.

Table 9.3 shows the percentage of media split for the financial services industry between 1986 and 1990. Unlike other markets, the press medium attracts the greatest share of advertising revenue with both tactical and longer term strategic executions in both black and white press and colour magazines. Around a fifth of advertising expenditure is on television advertising; with one per cent spend on advertising using radio as a medium.

Mintel (1991) points out that different institutions within each sector show different emphasis on the type of media favoured. As an illustration, NatWest in 1990 concentrated 75 per cent of its advertising on TV, while TSB had only 38 per cent of its advertising spend directed at television, 53 per cent directed at press and the remaining 9 per cent at independent radio advertising.

The advantages and disadvantages of the main advertising media are briefly discussed below.

Table 9.3 Advertising media split for financial services, 1986–90

	1986 %	1987 %	1988 %	1989 %	1990 %
Press	80	78	75	75	77
Television	20	21	24	24	22
Radio	*	1	1	1	1

* less than 0.5 per cent

Source: Mintel (1991)

Print Print is used extensively and is a large and important sector of the advertising market. The relatively cheap advertisement production costs and short copy dates give creative and marketing flexibility.

Various forms of the press media offer virtually total coverage of the advert population. Increased colour facilities in the primarily black and white medium may carry greater impact than colour in magazines.

There is the ability to choose widely contrasting vehicles for the advertising message, therefore targeting the advertising to the relevant audience in terms of demographics. Financially aware ABC1s may be reached by a print schedule of the quality dailies and Sundays rather than 'popular' press. Magazines have a longer life than newspapers, and can have an audience far wider than sales since copies can pass along many readers beyond the buyer.

Regional and local press give the opportunity for geographical targeting.

Television Television is often chosen as a method to create high awareness, its advantage of broad reach is, however, counterbalanced by high expense. TV is sold in 'spots' or intervals of time. The cost of any commercial varies primarily according to the time and day of week it is scheduled to be transmitted. Rate segments are classified broadly into peak and off-peak.

Television is a mass medium, although selectivity of different target groups within the total television audience is possible to an extent. There is a dichotomy of opinion as to whether programmes should be targeted. Many within the advertising industry intuitively believe in quality airtime, a system by which added value is claimed to be achieved by buying slots in specific breaks. On a practical note, some believe that slots in the middle of a TV programme are better than those at the end of a programme—a belief that more of the audience are likely to leave the room (and therefore miss the advertisement) in an end of a programme break than a middle of programme break. There is also a 'halo' effect theory, the hypothesis being that if advertisements are bought around programmes the target audience particularly likes then they are enhanced, achieving borrowed image values for the advertiser. Furthermore because it is airtime bought at a time when the programme has the viewers' full attention, it thereby achieves higher impacts for the advertisement. However, even if quality airtime is accepted as providing added values, the value which is thought to exist may be swamped when the cost of buying specific slots is taken into account.

Radio While radio advertising is a relatively inexpensive method of delivering high frequency, and is good at reaching the younger, lighter ITV viewer, this medium is yet to be used extensively by financial advertisers. As with advertisers in other markets, the use of radio has essentially been restricted to that of a secondary support medium. An advantage of the media is that it is not hampered by production delays and deadlines experienced in other media. Its flexibility means that the advertiser can quickly take advantage of special situations or unexpected conditions.

Cinema The cinema audience offer the advertiser the opportunity to reach a young audience at an age where they are just acquiring spending power and are in the market for financial services for the first time. It is also a medium which is key to those who believe in quality airtime. Cinema is a flexible medium that can be used in its own right or in conjunction with other media. It can be used selectively both in terms of audience demographics and geography.

Direct mail Direct mail, the sending of promotional advertising material through the post to specified individuals, can enable precise targeting and the dissemination of information directly to selected segments of the market. However, the success of this approach is dependent upon the quality of the customer database. Databases are often out of date or contain duplicate information, and for a variety of reasons it may be difficult to access the relevant information in the desired format. Additionally, financial organizations have a responsibility to their customers which is recognized within the Data Protection Act. If direct mail is used, caution needs to be taken to ensure that the information is appropriate to the recipient, and that individuals are not repeatedly receiving material and thereby causing a negative reaction to the institution.

9.2.3 Agency selection

Practically all major campaigns of leading advertisers are placed through an advertising agency. Financial advertisers vary in their approach to dealings with advertising agencies; some decide to use different agencies to satisfy their various advertising needs, although the majority use a single agency.

While it is unusual for an advertising agency to handle competitor accounts, it is not unheard of; Bartle, Bogle and Hegarty (BBH), for instance, handled both NatWest and Girobank over 1991. Very often, agencies handle one company from different sectors of the market; BMP DDB Needham was the appointed agency for Barclaycard, Alliance and Leicester and Scottish Amicable in the first quarter of 1992, and Ogilvy and Mather were working for both the Woolwich Building Society and Eagle Star Insurance. It may be that as the boundaries between financial institutions blur, the perceived conflict of interest of an agency being appointed to more than one financial organization results in advertisers insisting an agency restricts its services to a single financial organization.

One of the debates over the years has been whether clients are in a better position if they use a full service agency to do the media planning and buying, rather than using a media independent which does no creative work but concentrates on media. Although in most cases, media buying is probably not as important as creative work in terms of agency selection, the main benefit of using an independent media buying company is often seen to be one of cost, and such companies are taking a greater share of the market. The benefit of using a full service agency is not only one of convenience, but also enables the application of the agency's knowledge of the market to the planning and buying of the media.

Marketing Week commission an annual survey from 150 of the top 300 UK advertisers. In the survey, advertisers are asked to rank the importance of seven business criteria for agencies using a ten point scale. As in previous years, 'creativity' and 'value for money' were ranked as the first two most important criteria, with 'media buying and placement' achieving the third highest ranking.

Table 9.4   Importance of criteria

89	90	91		% rating 9 or 10 v. impt'	Average rating
	Rank				
1	1	1	Creativity	61	9.01
2	2	2	Value for money in results achieved	60	8.98
3	3	3	Media buying and placement	35	7.7
4	5	4	Quality of account managers	31	8.32
5	4	4	Attentiveness and adoptability to client companies	31	8.08
6	6	6	Marketing strategy and analysis	25	7.56
7	7	7	Coverage of markets outside the UK	7	3.77

Source: Marketing Week (1991)

The advertisers were also asked to assess the performance of 50 prominent agencies on the seven criteria, naming the three best agencies in each category. An overall league table was then compiled by adding up the nominations for each agency. In this way, the survey attempts to measure agencies' reputation; the results suggest that different agencies have very marked areas of perceived strengths and weaknesses (see Table 9.4).

9.2.4   Content and message

The selection of the appropriate content and message format is clearly a major decision to be taken. Such decisions are ideally based upon extensive research into consumer motivation and images. Strategically, advertising content should be compatible with the overall brand strategy and, while being capable of carrying the brand towards its desired positioning, should not be so dissonant with the current positioning to lack credibility with the brand heritage. In formulating the approach, a major consideration is that advertising does not work in isolation from everyday reality. For instance, hostile press over the recent recessionary period has left the banks with an image badly in need of repair. Many of the high street banks have consequently changed strategy adopting a very different tone in the recessionary mood of the 1990s than was present in their activity over the buoyant economic climate of the 1980s. The imagery is softer, reflecting the mood of the environment in which they are operating, presenting the organizations as friendly, and emphasizing approachability, stability and customer service.

In the late 1980s, there was marked product proliferation. Midland was an extreme case of this, and unlike the majority of financial organizations, Midland adopted a FMCG style approach to branding its core accounts, 'Vector', 'Orchard' and Meridian'. Interestingly this situation has appeared to have reversed itself. Such a strategy has the accompanying difficulties of product differentiation to overcome, and the dilemma of supporting the sub-brand at the possible expense of the corporate brand. The state of development of the brand, that is, the position of the organization on the brand development cycle is of primary importance in deciding upon the advertising message. Essentially there may be thought to be two main advertising tasks: advertising is usually required to either create awareness and build a personality for the organization or to continue the dialogue of well-known brands (occasionally, it may be required to change the strategy or message about a well-known brand). So advertising works to build financial organizations in several possible ways.

- Financial institution is already well known—advertising reinforces perceptions which already exist and builds further interest around them (for example, Lloyds' TV advertising in the late 1980s featuring Leo McKern, Nigel Havers and Jan Francis).
- Financial institution has a pale identity and needs to establish itself not only in awareness but also in imagery (for example, Alliance and Leicester's TV advertising in the mid 1980s featuring Fry and Laurie). Advertising strategy for the smaller regional building societies may be to increase awareness of the organization rather than trying to build an identity. Prior awareness of the financial institution is probably a pre-requisite for use and therefore particularly key in the health of the organization.
- Advertising puts the financial institution on the consideration list for account openings, when previously it was not well-known. Arguably, Girobank advertising works in this way; or even advertising in product fields for which the organization does not automatically come to mind—Halifax may not spring as readily to mind for current accounts as for mortgages or savings.
- Although successful strategic re-thinks are rare because, to start with, they fight against existing brand perceptions, a financial institution may have the wrong identity and need to be relaunched.

9.3 MECHANISMS VIA WHICH ADVERTISING MAY GENERATE SALES

Fundamental to this entire chapter is a discussion of the various ways in which advertising is thought to influence sales of financial services. The material discussed is based upon a private seminar 'Effective advertising of financial services,' held by Millward Brown Market Research Ltd in October 1991, and widely attended by advertising decision makers in this market. The seminar was a development of ideas which have been publically expounded via a number of papers (Brown, 1991; Hollis, 1990). The hypotheses forwarded are empirically derived and based upon extensive advertising research conducted over the last ten years. It is generally accepted that the effects of advertising on sales are of at least two kinds: immediate effects and those operating in the longer term. A campaign may operate on more than one level, having both short-term and longer term effects; indeed, the ideal is often to execute the short-term tactics in a way which helps build the long-term personality of the brand.

  This section first discusses the mechanism via which advertising may influence sales immediately by communicating a new and relevant message which activates or motivates the minority of consumers who may be ready to buy a particular product or service and who are predisposed to attend the message with more than casual interest. Advertising mechanisms which may also influence sales in the longer term, by creating or reinforcing the organization's reputation or credibility, and stimulating interest and curiosity are then examined.

9.3.1   Short-term sales

Advertising within the financial services market is very often offering new services and disseminating specific new information. For this reason it is perhaps more common than in other markets for the advertising to work via what may be described as the 'traditional' theory of advertising. The theory being that if an individual noticed an advertisement and heard new information about a financial service or organization, there would be a resulting better opinion,

IMMEDIATE CHALLENGE

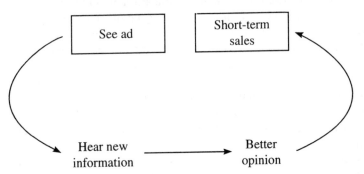

Figure 9.1   Advertising which generates immediate sales

an immediate decision to investigate the service, and an increase in sales. Advertising for the first interest bearing current accounts, which offered a new, relevant and interesting claim, probably worked via this mechanism.

Brown (1991) refers to this mechanism, via which advertising generates immediate sales, as 'immediate challenge' and notes that any immediate decisions are likely when the advertising is telling the consumer something new which is of perceived value or relevance so that they believe or accept it, 'a combination of novelty, relevance and credibility determine the power of a commercial to challenge consumers immediately'. There is, in fact, mounting evidence to support this view. Sylvester (1992) in summarizing the key findings from the IRI (Information Resources Inc.) 'how advertising works' study, which represents an extensive case analysis of advertising's effect on short-term sales, states that 'In general, the status quo is not enough to drive incremental volume', and that, 'TV advertising is more likely to work when there are changes in brand/copy strategy, media strategy or category dynamics. An increased sales effect is more likely when copy strategy is new, introductory or intended to change rather than reinforce attitudes.'

For the majority of consumers, financial services are not intrinsically interesting the majority of the time. Financial services command interest when the consumer requires the particular service, at which time the service may be of very high interest not only because it is now relevant to their current needs, but also because purchase within the market is relatively high risk. Any immediate sales effects are likely to come most readily from motivated consumers who currently require the advertised service. These consumers are in the state of heightened interest that immediately precedes the purchase decision—they are in what may be termed the 'decision window'—from the advertiser's point of view, a window of opportunity. If the advertised message is communicated clearly, it may be relevant enough to justify the consumers' thinking about the advertisement and making up their mind there and then to find out more about the service. Forming a better opinion of the advertised service or organization is a decision which requires mental processing and immediate reappraisal, the mental processing is probably less likely to take place among those who are not currently in the decision window.

The duration of time for which consumers are in the decision window, and the motivation of respondents once in the window, will vary between services. The length of time a consumer is in the mortgage decision window, *actively seeking* a mortgage, is relatively short compared to the duration typically spent in the pensions decision window. Once a property has been found, the decision of who to approach for a mortgage will normally have to happen relatively quickly, whereas much longer is normally taken in deciding which organization to approach for a pension. Consumers within the decision windows are not one homogeneous mass. The motivation of the individuals within each window will vary enormously. At the one extreme, individuals may trawl all of the organizations offering a service and at least attempt an assessment of the advantages and disadvantages of each option. These 'earnest' individuals appear to be mainly driven by rational decisions, although the ability to make a purely rational decision will be constrained by the amount of information an individual can actually assimilate. At the other extreme, some individuals are more 'casual', feeling that it is impossible to resolve all the issues properly. Psychologically, this group may be more influenced than the earnest group by the emotional values that advertising can impart. Thus, if consumers are in the decision window, or if the advertising says something new, there may be an immediate decision in favour of the organization or service or a consciously better opinion of it. With broad coverage media, however, advertising expenditure cannot usually be justified if it is only thought to have an immediate effect on the minority of consumers who are currently in the decision window. In optimizing the advertising, it seems that the key criterion is to try to achieve longer term strategic effects while generating short-term tactical gains.

The extension of the 'immediate challenge' mechanism to account for longer term sales has intuitive appeal. That is, having given consumers a better opinion of your organization, they would retain this opinion and the advertising would, therefore, have influenced sales in the longer term when the consumers are next in the decision window for the advertised service. However, empirical data does not substantiate this hypothesis.

Figure 9.2 shows the level of endorsement a high street bank achieved on the image measure 'a bank I'd be happy to join if I closed my current account', and illustrates a general finding that perceptions, though quickly gained, tend to die away quite rapidly. The new campaign (advertising burst B) increased the number of people who felt they would go to this bank if they closed their current account, but most of the improvement was temporary. The immediate challenge mechanism cannot be extended to account for longer term sales effects because the 'better opinion' is not retained in the longer term.

Not only is the improvement temporary but repeated exposure to the same advertisement does not generate a correspondingly cumulative improvement in opinion. This follows from the finding that opinions may move in response to advertising that is new, but that subsequent exposure to the same message does not tend to produce further improvement in opinion because the message is no longer new. It seems that the consumer does not process the advertisement to the same extent when they are repeatedly exposed to the same creative treatment. The following section discusses the mechanisms via which advertising *is* thought to influence sales in the longer term.

9.3.2 Long-term effects

Advertising may work in a variety of ways to generate sales in the longer term. There is a wide range of processes whereby advertising images generate interest and curiosity in the organization and where lively advertising memories will convey status on the organization, such that it is taken seriously in the decision process. This is referred to as the 'interest-status' mechanism. On the other hand, advertising memories may enhance the way organizations and services are perceived even when they are being assessed apparently rationally; the 'enhancement' mechanism. These mechanisms are summarized in Figure 9.3 and discussed in detail over this next section.

'A BANK I'D BE HAPPY TO JOIN
IF I CLOSED MY CURRENT ACCOUNT'

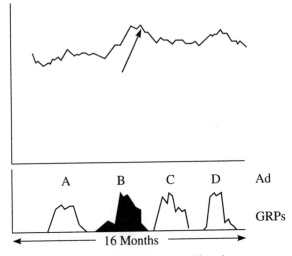

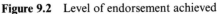

Figure 9.2   Level of endorsement achieved

'Interest-status' and 'enhancement'

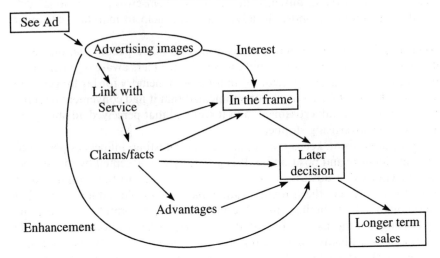

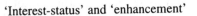

Figure 9.3   Advertising effects

Mechanisms of 'interest-status'   Repeated showing of the same advertisement builds associations between the organization and the particular service, so that, when a service is required,
that organization is in the frame for consideration. Organizations that have recently diversified
into non-traditional areas of expertise will probably lose out in some markets if they do not come
to mind easily in that context.

Awareness of claims made in the advertising also places the organization in the frame
for consideration, and actually affects the decision process itself since any other source of

Have convenient opening hours

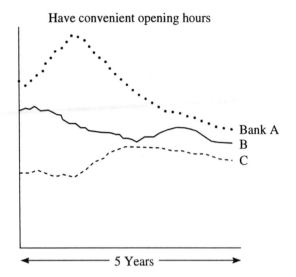

Figure 9.4 Perceived advantage: long term effect

information validating an advertising claim represents confirmation of prior information and therefore powerful reinforcement. Indeed, purchase decisions are themselves post-rationalized, and the presence of rational product supports in advertising can help to maintain customer loyalty.

While an advertisement will wear out in terms of its ability to make people reappraise an organization, it will not wear out in terms of its ability to keep consumers aware of a perceived advantage and such perceptions are generally retained in long-term memory for far longer than overall opinions. Bank A in Figure 9.4 effectively communicated that it had convenient opening hours by repeated bursts of the same advertisement, and it still had that perceived advantage in people's minds, years after the advertising stopped.

Simply remembering the advertising keeps the organization interesting, influences perceived size and builds a corporate identity and positioning. It is generally well accepted by marketeers of fast moving consumer goods that advertising is a major contributor to the 'brand'. Jones (1986) states that 'a brand is a product that provides functional benefits plus added values that some consumers value enough to buy'. In the financial services market, the brand is, in effect, the organization and advertising is a means of differentiating between organizations that provide essentially the same services. A distinctive image helps build and maintain loyalty via emotional commitment. Ditchburn (1990) argues that 'the corporation is the brand, or central adjective' and that financial service marketing activity is therefore a corporate issue, and 'all its communication modes from advertising to sponsorship must march to the same drum.' He notes that unlike goods which can be touched, tasted, and their performance and reliability judged over time, the service it provides is even more dependent on the intangible, emotional values evoked by the brand. Lively advertising memories convey status on the organization, and provide an emotional reassurance to the consumer making major financial decisions.

Mechanism of 'enhancement' Advertising images may generate interest, or they may enhance the way financial organizations and services are perceived, even when they are being assessed apparently rationally.

Enhancement of strengths   Advertising may enhance the consumer's awareness of strengths of the organization. For instance, TSB probably helped people think of them as a bank, playing down negative image differentiation between them and the big four high street banks and playing up the positive friendly side of the bank's historic origins with their slogan 'The Bank that likes to say Yes'.

Enhancement via simplifying summary   Enhancement may operate through a simplifying summary; the phrase the 'Listening Bank' has perhaps served as a way of hanging together all of the new services Midland provided so that the whole was emotionally more than the sum of the parts.

Enhancement via positive social feedback   A well-known method in which advertising images can enhance brands is via positive social feedback. For those financial services which are open to public display, brand choice is open to the powerful influence of approval or otherwise by the customer's peer group. Advertising, which is simply admired will itself give positive feedback to the consumer.

Enhancement via conditioning   Advertising memories condition encounters with organizations so that advertising claims and images are converted during experience into beliefs about the organization through enhancement.

9.4   INFLUENCES INTERACTING WITH ADVERTISING

Advertising activity does not occur in isolation; rather the consumer is bombarded with a plethora of influences some of which are working in conjunction with the advertising, others not. Alternative sources of information may result in an organization being considered for its financial services. Information may come from other marketing activity such as direct mail, branch posters, leaflets. It may come from word of mouth, from friends or relatives. *Yellow Pages*, financial programmes on television, news items and simply high street presence may all contribute to putting the financial organization in the consideration frame for a service.

Advertising is also competing against negative media information. For instance, small businesses advertising in 1991 occurred against a background of negative PR concerning the bank's unsympathetic attitude to small business customers during the recession. Savings advertising at the beginning of 1992 occurred in the context of the UK's largest building society, Halifax, announcing the introduction of charges on savings accounts where the balance fell below £50 for more than 30 days in any one quarter.

9.4.1   Relationship with the organization

One of the key influences interacting with the advertising is the nature of the relationship with the organization. In the first place, customers of an organization are more likely to notice a TV advertisement than those who do not have a relationship with the organization. In fact, analysis of advertising's ability to generate branded advertising associations suggests that customers are 50 to 60 per cent more likely to remember an advertisement for their bank or building society than non-customers (Brown, 1991). It seems likely that customers are more interested in their own financial organization when its name comes up—the advertising has a greater relevance to those that have dealings with the organization. In fact, this seems to be particularly marked among very small organizations, or those with little advertising history, where it may be that

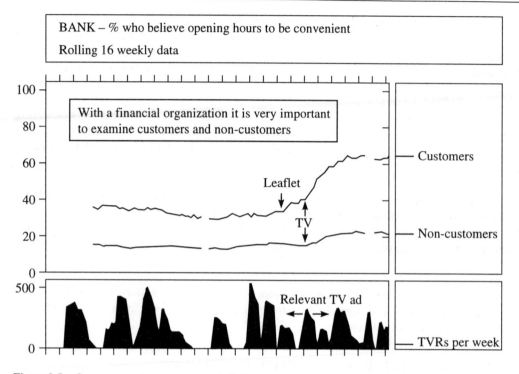

Figure 9.5   Customer and non-customer beliefs

being on TV at all was interesting for customers. In terms of communication from TV advertising, it seems that while the psychology of communicating to customers and non-customers may be the same, the response is not always the same, depending upon the mental set and experience which each brings to the advertising. In some cases, customers are more likely to register advertising claims than non-customers, in other cases non-customers are more receptive. The primary difference between the two groups is the influence each is exposed to. Customers are very often exposed to marketing activity that does not reach non-customers (direct mail, statement inserts, in-branch activity) and so forth. Indeed, synergy between media has been shown to be a cost-effective approach to maintaining imagery initiated via more 'expensive' media.

Figure 9.5 shows that from the advertising for a high street bank, the customers of the organization started to believe that it had convenient opening hours sooner than non-customers did. The non-customers were responding to the TV advertising, but the customers were responding to a leaflet that went out earlier.

Customers are also exposed to the organization's staff and services—advertising claims may be rejected among customers on the basis of personal experience. Figure 9.6 is an illustration of this, non-customers appear to accept the advertising claim that the organization is particularly friendly, and show an improvement on a relevant image measure, whereas the customers do not show a similar improvement in response to the advertising. On the other hand, where personal experience is consonant with the advertising, it can be a very powerful reinforcement of the message.

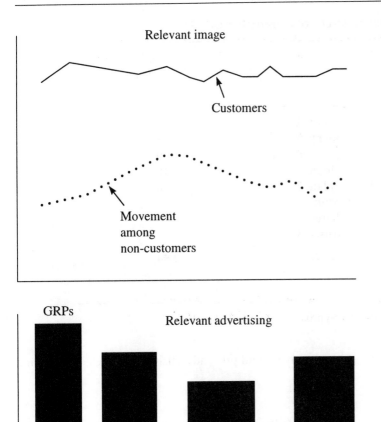

Relevant image

Customers

Movement
among
non-customers

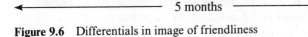

GRPs   Relevant advertising

5 months

Figure 9.6   Differentials in image of friendliness

9.4.2   Relevance of advertised service

In the same way that customers are more likely to notice a TV advertisement for their organization than non-customers, those that are in the decision window for a financial service are sometimes more likely to notice a TV advertisement for that service, than those for whom the service is not immediately relevant.

Table 9.5 shows the proportion of the adult population who are considering taking out various financial services. Only 5 per cent, for instance, are seriously considering opening a savings account, thus with broadcast media, the advertising is usually attempting to influence a far wider audience than the minority currently in the market for a service.

Relevance of the message for those in the decision window means that this group is more likely to consider going to the financial organization, that is, short-term sales are more likely to come from this group.

9.5   EFFECTIVE ADVERTISING IN THE MARKET

Having reviewed the mechanisms via which advertising is believed to influence sales of financial services, this next section discusses how different media are consumed and the implications of

Table 9.5 Penetration levels for considering services

	Seriously consider next few months %	Might do next 12 months %
Current account	2	4
Life insurance policy	5	8
Mortgage	6	9
Personal loan	5	10
Private pension plan	5	8
Savings/deposit account	5	8
Stocks and shares	5	8
Unit trusts	3	5
None of these	71	59

Base: (c. 6000)

Source: Millward Brown Syndicated Tracking Study

this for creativity. It concentrates primarily on TV and press advertising, although outdoor and direct mail are also mentioned.

9.5.1 Television

Television viewing is essentially passive. If viewers decide to stay in the room during the commercial break, they are subjected to a series of advertisements, each following immediately on from the previous one, the result being that there is no time for the viewer to think about and process any one advertisement. Attention is essentially limited to spot length. Involvement in this medium is about entertainment. The passive nature of the viewing experience, where viewers are not paying individual attention to each and every element of each advertisement, results in a phenomenon whereby it is the involving elements or themes within the advertisement that are remembered. Brown (1991) terms this phenomenon the 'creative magnifier' effect—the marked tendency for advertising memories to concentrate selectively on the parts of the advertisement that are found entertaining, involving and creative. Figure 9.7 illustrates the creative magnifier effect. When people were asked to describe a financial advertisement for one of the banks, one particular scene that lasted for only 7 per cent of time of the advertisement, accounted for 38 per cent of all the comments referring to it. That one short scene was disproportionately remembered because the creative elements were interesting and involving.

Finding which advertising memories are retained by consumers and which are interesting and involving to the viewer should have a major effect on the advertisement. The objective of the creative person is to develop a message that will stand out; but consumers do not anxiously await each advertising message, rather they pay attention only to that which interests them. If the advertisement is going to communicate the desired message about the financial organization, then the organization, the service and the benefit must all be integrated into the relevant part of the advertisement. The message that will be communicated when the advertisement is seen in real

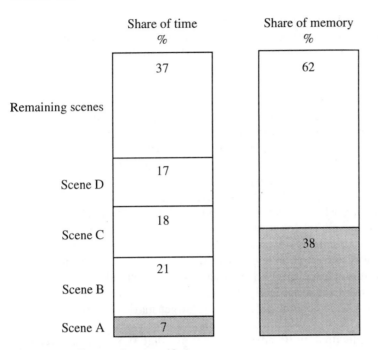

Figure 9.7 The creative magnifier

life, in the unmotivated viewing situation, will be whatever associations derive from the memorable themes and elements.

So, if the message is voiced over in a boring way, it is unlikely to be retained in long-term memory and will probably not achieve its communication objectives. Similarly, the advertisement is likely to be remembered in association with the financial institution if what is involving and memorable relates to the organization. If the creative idea links with the brand, the service and the imagery and binds them together in an uncontrived way, then the likelihood is that consumers will notice and remember them irrespective of whether they are interested in financial services or not.

The link that has proven to be the most difficult to establish is that between the organization and the creativity of the advertisement. This partly results from financial institutions tending to have weak individual identities, and therefore there is not much in the concept of the 'brand' that the creative people can attach the advertising ideas to. Consequently, there are a number of financial advertisements that offer an end benefit without attributing that to a particular organization. The advertisement could be for any financial institution which offers that service. There is increasing evidence from the sales validation of tracking study data to support the view that advertising which is not remembered in association with the brand will not benefit the 'brand'. For advertising memories to keep the financial organization interesting, to associate advantages with it, and to enhance perceptions, the advertising must come to mind when you think about the organization or when you think about the product field, the organizations and the advertising memories must come to mind.

9.5.2 Print

Print, on the other hand, is consumed more actively, the reader is actively turning the pages of the publication and is consciously deciding what to stop at and what and how much to read. The print advertisement must therefore have the ability to catch the reader's attention and involve the reader so that the advertisement is processed. Unlike TV, print advertisements for interesting product fields are noticed much more than advertisements for the more 'boring' product fields such as financial services.

The issue of how print advertisements actually work and their consumption is explained by three tiers: first an instant level of absorption of the product category, message and brand; the next stage, if the advertisement has succeeded in holding the reader's attention, is one of absorbing additional rational or emotional information; the third and final stage is where the details of the supporting copy might be read completely or almost completely.

The implication of the way in which print is consumed on the role of creativity in print advertisements is that it is most likely to be effective if it arouses curiosity and does not create confusion. Very often, the reader of the financial pages of newspapers will be actively seeking information; the minority of readers who are particularly interested in specific financial services, especially those in the 'decision window' for a service, will pay a lot of attention to press advertising, so attention to pages and items is selective. Those readers looking for information will read the advertisement if it is perceived as relevant to them, and this perception must be gained almost immediately. In this respect, print advertisements are potentially 'self targeting'. With financial tactical advertisements, it seems likely that the main hook should be the product field so that the focus of interest will then coincide with the target market's desire for information.

The other implication for individual print advertisements is, that if people are reading newspapers and magazines in a sort of editing mode, deciding what they will attend to and what they will not, individual print advertisements will 'wear out'. People keep seeing the individual press advertisement repeatedly and stop noticing it.

9.5.3. Direct mail and outdoor

Direct mail seems to have elements of both television and print. As with television, all individual items may be scanned, albeit passively and rapidly; but to be read, or retained, before being placed in the rubbish bin, the direct mail leaflet or brochure must, in the same way as press, very rapidly announce its origin and purpose. Posters, in the same way, must work very rapidly.

9.6 ALTERNATIVE PROMOTIONAL VEHICLES

As the financial market place becomes more competitive, companies seek increasingly innovative ways of communicating with their target markets. For instance, TSB was one of the first banks to produce a magazine, *TS Beat*, which was aimed at the young and sent out to schools. Alliance and Leicester have run a participatory game in conjunction with *Radio Times*, enabling the society to reach millions of people.

Financial institutions have historically used promotional gifts to encourage younger consumers to join an organization. However, the use of these promotional techniques has declined over recent years (Mintel 1991). Sponsorship, a form of promotion distinct from advertising, in which the sponsor and sponsored gain mutual benefit, has seen remarkable growth in recent years—in expenditure and in type and number of activities sponsored. The growth in sponsorship as a method of communicating message and image to the target market, has been fuelled by the high cost and clutter of the more 'conventional' media advertising and by the opportunity to target key segments. The purpose of this section is to briefly discuss the growth in sponsorship as a marketing tool and the use of this communication vehicle by the finance sector.

9.6.1 Sponsorship

Abratt, Clayton and Pitt (1987) note that 'all companies exist within the business environment and there must be interaction between the company and the environment', they define sponsorship as:

an agreement in terms of which a sponsor provides some aid to a beneficiary, which may be an association, a team or an individual, to enable the latter to pursue some activity and thereby derives the benefits contemplated in terms of its promotion strategy.

They note that one of the benefits contemplated may be to gain exposure on TV and other media, to create name awareness of the product or company, to promote public relations of the firm, or in general terms to generate publicity. A number of broad corporate objectives in becoming involved in sponsorship are identified:

- Community involvement
- To increase public awareness of the company
- To alter public perception of the company
- To build goodwill among opinion-formers and decision makers
- To reassure policyholders and stockholders
- To counter adverse publicity
- As an aid to staff relations
- To assist staff recruitment
- To identify with a particular market segment
- To facilitate prospecting for the sales force

Financial institutions have become involved in diverse areas of sponsorship including opera (e.g., Barclays, NatWest) and concerts (e.g., Midland Bank). Sports sponsorship is the largest area of sponsorship overall, attracting approximately 70 per cent of sponsorship funds (Mintel, 1987); with the finance sector being the most active in sports sponsorship, accounting for 20 per cent of the total (Parker, 1989). Table 9.6 serves to demonstrate dominance of the finance sector in this area, with half of the top ten sponsors coming from this market. While exposure on TV is one benefit that may result from sponsorship, Parker (1989) examined the scheduled hours of television coverage within the top ten TV sponsors of sport and found that the scheduled hours of television coverage varied dramatically. He suggests that the other issues which should be considered include the synergy of the company/brand with the event and its image, the likely appeal of the event to the company/brand's target market, its suitability for corporate hospitality and the track record of others who have been involved in similar sponsorships'.

Synergy between the sponsor and sponsored event seems to be a particularly important issue; inherent compatibility can act as an important aid to the association being remembered by consumers. It seems that ideally there should be a logical association between the company, the event and the audience. This may be a particularly key issue if the event has been historically supported by other sponsors, since it has been found that these sponsors which enter at an early stage can make a long-term impact. Wright (1988) quotes English cricket as an example, where the awareness of the current sponsor's name was at half the level as that of Gillette who had withdrawn from sponsorship of cup competition more than ten years earlier.

More recently, there has been a move in the UK towards the sponsorship of television programmes. A number of financial organizations have negotiated such sponsorship deals. The sponsorship of television weather forecasts by Legal and General in 1991 may be particularly relevant given its umbrella branding device; incidentally, this sponsorship coincided with a large

Table 9.6 Hours of scheduled TV among the top 10 TV sponsors

	Company	Sport	1988
1.	Cornhill	Cricket	185
2.	Embassy	Snooker	97
3.	NatWest	Cricket	38
4.	Barclays	Soccer	36
5.	Refuge Assurance	Cricket	34
6.	Merchantile Credit	Snooker	33
7.	Rothmans	Snooker	31
8.	Benson and Hedges	Cricket	31
9.	MIM Britannia	Snooker	30
10.	Fidelity	Snooker	29

Source: Admap

reduction in that organization's expenditure on television and newspaper advertising. Barclay-card's sponsorship of the travel programme, *Wish you were here*, is another example of a financial organization using such vehicles. Again, there is the logical association between a credit card and that type of television programme which presumably assists in building awareness of the association.

Synergy in promotional activity, by combining sponsorship with other modes of marketing communication is typical, and indeed it seems accepted that those companies that do best support the sponsorship with additional promotional expenditure in at least a 1:1 ratio. For instance, Miles (1987) suggests that related expenditure should equal or exceed the actual cost of sponsorship.

9.7 EVALUATION OF ADVERTISING

Given the high costs associated with advertising, it is obviously essential to understand how the investment by the company impacts on and involves the consumer in the marketplace. This next section briefly reviews the various techniques that are available and in common use to evaluate and understand the advertising performance. No single research tool is capable of providing a complete evaluation of advertising performance; rather, an understanding of how the marketing activity is working for an organization is only attained when the advertiser utilizes a number of approaches.

Papers from the IPA advertising effectiveness awards clearly demonstrate that advertising can be proved to work against measurable criteria. For example, advertising was demonstrated to have achieved both its short-term tactics and long-term strategy by affecting the short-term promotion of loans, while contributing to more long-term image changes for Lloyds Bank (*Advertising Works 3*, 1985).

Twyman (1986) reviewed the general approaches to the monitoring of advertising perform-ance, and summarized the appropriateness of each for assessing specific aspects of the advertis-ing. While this summary provides a useful framework for discussing the different approaches, increasing sophistication and the development of research techniques, particularly in the area of pre-testing, would currently result in a more positive appraisal of the ability of the approaches to assess different aspects of advertising performance.

9.7.1 Measurement in terms of sales

It is generally agreed that the ultimate objective of advertising is to influence sales—to sell more than could have been sold in the absence of advertising. It is not surprising, therefore, that some believe a demonstration of a relationship between advertising activity and sales to be the most appropriate measure of advertising effectiveness. While such an analysis is a valuable tool in conjunction with other measures, there are two main drawbacks to the technique when used in isolation. First, measurement of a sales return from advertising does not in itself explain how a campaign produced a specific result. Secondly, the analysis works best in assessing short-term rather than longer term sales effects, although sales effects are often too small in the short-term to justify the expenditure. Essentially, econometric analysis aims to represent sales in a market by means of a mathematical equation. Typically this equation represents the movements of sales (the dependent variable in the equation) in terms of a number of other factors (the independent variables). The outcome of the analysis is an identification and quantification of the factors influencing sales.

A practical consideration before embarking upon sales analysis is the problem of identifying the relevant measure of sales in the first place. For instance, consider the measure of sales for a savings account advertisement; should one take the number of accounts opened or gross receipts attributable to the new accounts opened? If the latter is chosen it may be appropriate to exclude the percentage of receipts through reinvestments of maturing schemes and transfers of money from other types of accounts.

Having identified the relevant measure, it is often the case that the analysis is constrained by the format in which the data are actually available. Both the sales data and data about all the factors in the market that are thought likely to contribute to the movement in sales, are needed for regular intervals covering at least two or three years, so that any seasonal variation can be accounted for. The difficulty that any sales modelling exercise has in terms of disentangling advertising influences from the many other factors that influence sales, is exacerbated by the extended purchase cycles that characterize the market.

9.7.2 Tracking studies

There are essentially three components of tracking studies:

1. Quantitative surveys
2. Interviews conducted at different points in time
3. Essentially consistent questionnaire

There are essentially two approaches to tracking; interviewing can either take place on a continuous basis throughout the year, or intermittent measures can be taken. The technique of continuous interviewing is widely used by major advertisers in the UK, its advantage being that changes in key consumer measures can be related to the precise timings of advertising activity. The alternative methodological approach of intermittent measures which are usually taken at some point in time after the end of the burst of advertising activity has an advantage in terms of cost, but has a number of inherent disadvantages. These two approaches are discussed below:

Intermittent measures The approach of conducting a survey prior to the campaign and again after the campaign, aims to detect movements on measures such as 'attitudes towards the organization', 'awareness of the organization', 'advertising awareness', etc., the difference being attributed to the advertising. While this represents a relatively inexpensive research methodology, the limitations of the pre-post technique frequently results in inconclusive measures. There are three notable drawbacks:

- The level obtained at the post stage depends upon the timing of the measure in relation to the pattern of spend, consequently the peak effect of the advertising may be missed.
- The timing of the measures will not usually be appropriate to assess the performance of other brands in the market. Hence there is a lack of competitive context against which to judge advertising performance.
- Factors other than the advertising will have an influence between the measures (for example, competitive activity, PR, general market trends) and it is difficult to disentangle these from advertising effects.

Continuous tracking   A continuous methodology overcomes the limitations of the intermittent approach. Interviewing is carried out throughout the year and typically rolling data are used to create an ongoing measure. Such market monitors enable an understanding of competitor activity and accounts for planned and unplanned activity.

9.7.3   Area experimentation

Area tests are used to explore reactions to changes in copy or advertising weight by exposing different advertising in different parts of the country. However, other factors (such as the proportion of the population who deal with a financial organization) also vary by region; and the evidence of the effect of the increased advertising may not emerge for months.

9.7.4   Pre-testing techniques

Pre-exposure research evaluates the advertising before media exposure takes place. An advantage of conducting research at this stage is that it can avoid the advertiser allocating large amounts of media money on advertising that does not deliver on the objectives. However, pre-exposure research conducted on finished executions rarely results in the decision for the creative treatment to be withdrawn—it is too painful a decision to make after the investment that has already occurred. In reality, therefore, the value of conducting research at this finished stage is essentially in providing a detailed understanding of how the creative treatment is working, and a prediction of its likely performance when media exposure takes place. If research is conducted at an earlier stage in the development process, on animatic film or drafts of a print execution, there is the opportunity of developing the execution in accordance with the research findings.

Traditionally, there has been a debate between the relative value of qualitative and quantitative pre-exposure research. Qualitative research tends to be used during the developmental stages of advertising although qualitative pre-testing can add to the understanding of advertising, particularly the 'softer' values:

- The mood, the tone and the 'feel' of the commercial as a whole can be explored.
- The brand personality measures which need to be tapped into can be investigated. This is particularly important in the financial market where there are relatively few actual product differences—where the competitive points of difference are perceived to be emotional rather than rational.
- The user imagery measures which require sensitive probing.
- The 'what if' issues, i.e., how the creative execution can be developed and improved.
- The overall campaign 'feel' rather than focus on individual executions.

There are a wide range of pre-exposure quantitative tests which Feldwick (1992) divides into the two main groups; those that are based upon the principle of attitude shift, and those that measure impact, recall and/or communication. 'Attitude shift' techniques start from the assumption that the main problem with advertising is not to get itself noticed, but to persuade people to have a different attitude toward the brand. There have been various techniques including the use of matched samples (a test group being exposed to the advertising, with a control group having no exposure), and theatre tests (respondents recruited to watch a programme in a theatre, commercial break includes test advertisement, and responses are compared pre- and post-exposure). More recently, the theatre tests are being superseded by placing video cassettes with respondents.

'Impact and communication' techniques essentially consist of some sort of exposure to the test advertisement followed by a battery of commonsense questions covering, for example:

- Comprehension of the advertisement
- What the respondent saw as the message
- Attitudes to the advertisement
- Persuasiveness, credibility, relevance

Not surprisingly, there is increasing demand across the industry for validation of pre-testing techniques against on-air performance and ultimately against sales. It seems likely that those techniques which validate their performance in this way will thrive.

SUMMARY

The financial market is complex and dynamic, with recent legislation accelerating the pace of change and fuelling an increasingly aggressive competitive environment. The role of advertising and promotional activity within this sector is particularly important and equally as complex as the market in which it operates. There are a number of roles which advertising may serve and a wide range of mechanisms via which advertising may influence sales of financial services. The same campaign may operate via more than one mechanism; and indeed should ideally be capable of generating short-term tactical gains while achieving the longer term strategic aims of the organization.

A good persuasive advertisement can lead to a better opinion of a financial product or organization and an immediate decision to investigate, thereby resulting in rapid sales effects. However, the extent to which these short-term effects can be produced seems to depend upon the financial product field and the extent to which the communication is perceived to be relevant, credible and new. For most financial products, there are very few people actively 'in the market' at any particular point in time; and for some products, such as mortgages, there is little or no chance of bringing consumers into the 'decision window' through advertising. Thus it often appears difficult for financial advertising to have a major effect on sales in the short term. In other areas (such as savings and current accounts), it may be possible to propel consumers into the 'decision window', but this tends to happen only when advertising a product which warrants attention by being a particularly good offer.

If there is 'news' to transmit, it will probably open accounts if it is relevant and credible to consumers; for example, Barclays' announcement of 'Saturday opening' and Midland's 'free banking'. It seems reasonable to suggest that it is worth delivering such 'big news' of general relevance on TV, thereby reaching as many people as quickly as possible. Interestingly, if the message contains relevant news, the advertising skills brought to bear on it are arguably not as critical to the advertisement's success as in those situations where there is nothing new to say—the nature of the information may almost 'guarantee' sales.

However, advertising on TV cannot usually be justified unless it is likely to achieve longer term strategic effects among a general sample, as well as immediate tactical effects among the minority of consumers 'in the decision window'. Consumers tend to view financial brands as parity—they are often seen to offer the same services. The role of advertising in the longer term, therefore, is very often to build and sustain a unique positioning which offers the consumer an emotional advantage over the competition. The generation and maintenance of saliency and appropriate advertising memories influence sales in the longer term.

Advertising does not occur in a vacuum, it is only one of many channels of communication an organization has with the consumer. Intended advertising messages interact with other variables and with other sources of information; some of these will support the advertising claim and provide powerful reinforcement, others will not. Neither does advertising impact on a homogeneous mass of consumers; rather, there is a continuum from those who have no committed view of a financial organization, who may not even have heard of it before, through to those who hold either very positive or very negative committed views. Advertising impacts on all these consumers, and in reaching conclusions about its likely effects, it is necessary to understand the attitude of the consumer. As McDonald (1986) states 'the advertising task is very different for consumers with different kinds of involvement, and the criteria for success and failure must differ'. The current recessionary climate has meant that more than ever budgets are under close scrutiny. Increasingly, financial organizations use a range of media and communication vehicles to achieve their tactical and strategic aims. Sponsorship, particularly sports sponsorship, is used extensively within the market and will presumably continue to grow in the future.

It is not uncommon for advertising agency renumeration to be linked to advertising performance with a bonus for what is perceived to be exceptional performance and a penalty for underachievement. This factor has played a part in fuelling the quest to understand the role of advertising and to validate its effect on sales. A combination of research techniques and expertise has been capable of unravelling the various strands and provide an evaluation of advertising performance but as McDonald (1986) states, there is no simple relationship, 'the way advertising interacts with attitudes and behaviour is not simple, not homogeneous, not generalizable'.

REVIEW QUESTIONS

1. Discuss the role of advertising for financial organizations in different sectors.
2. How does promotion and advertising within one financial sector differ from that in other markets? Discuss the implications of this on the main types of advertising.
3. Contrast the various approaches financial institutions may take in budget determination.
4. How does a financial organization decide what to communicate and which media to use?
5. Discuss the different mechanisms via which advertising is thought to influence sales in the financial market.
6. Discuss the role 'creativity' has to play in producing effective advertising in the print and TV media.
7. Discuss the role of sponsorship as a method of communicating with the consumer. What are the disadvantages compared with main advertising media?
8. Compare the various approaches to the assessment of advertising effectiveness.

REFERENCES

Abratt, R., B.C. Clayton and L.F. Pitt (1987) 'Corporate objectives in sports sponsorship', *International Journal of Advertising*, **6**, 299–311.
Broadbent, S. (1989) *The Advertising Budget*, Institute of Practitioners in Advertising.

Brown, G. (1991) *How advertising effects the sales of packaged goods brands: a working hypothesis for the 1990s*, Millward Brown International plc, available on application.

Brown, G. (1992) 'How advertising works—some new thinking in the light of modern evidence', *Journal of the Market Research Society*, **35**(26), 239–256.

Ditchburn, B. (1990) 'Financial service marketing: the corporation as adjective', *Admap*, **26**, 18–21.

Feldwick, P. (1992) 'Headaches and flat feet—a review of current quantitative pre-testing practice', *Journal of the Market Research Society*, **35**(24), 221–230.

Hall, M. (1992) 'Using advertising frameworks—different research models for different campaigns', *Admap*, **316**, 17–21.

Hollis, N. (1990) 'Separating advertising from promotional effects with econometric analysis', *Journal of Advertising Research*, June/July.

Hooley, G.J. and J.E. Lynch (1985) 'How UK advertisers set budgets', *International Journal of Advertising*, **3**(3), 223–231.

Institute of Practioners in Advertising (1984) *Advertising Works 3 Papers from the IPA Advertising Effectiveness Awards*, Holt, Rinehart and Winston.

Jones, J.P. (1986) *What's in a Name? Advertising and the Concept of Brands*, Lexington Books.

Lynch, J.E., G.J. Hooley and J. Shepherd (1988) *The effectiveness of British marketing*, Interim Report on Economic and Social Research Council Project F20250017, University of Bradford Management Centre, England.

Macdonald, A. (1992) 'Modelling TV effectiveness—predicting ad awareness through reach and frequency', *Admap*, **315** 32–36.

McDonald, C. (1986) 'Advertising effectiveness revised', *Admap*, 191–195.

Marketing Week (1991) 22 November, 40.

Miles, L. (1987) 'Sporting Life', *Marketing*, 28 May, 26–28.

Mintel (1987) *Opportunities in Sponsorships*, Mintel, London.

Mintel (1991) 'Advertising financial services into the 1990s', *Personal Finance Intelligence*, Vol. 2, Mintel, London.

Parker, K. (1989) 'Measuring the impact of sponsorship', *Admap*, 44–48.

Sylvester, A. (1992) 'What works, what doesn't. Practical applications of the Adworks material', *Admap*, **316**.

Twyman, A. (1986) 'Monitoring advertising performance: a canter round the field', *Admap*, **250**, 131–135.

Wright, R. (1988) 'Measuring awareness of British football sponsorship', *European Research*, **16**(2), 104–109.

TEN

CUSTOMER SERVICE AND QUALITY

Barbara R. Lewis   Manchester School of Management

INTRODUCTION

Financial services organizations have adopted, over the last 20 years, a professional marketing orientation. This is evidenced by their focus on customer needs and on market segmentation, product development, pricing policies, personal selling and advertising and promotional programmes, discussed in the preceding chapters. The major financial services providers have increasingly sophisticated strategic and marketing planning, and respond not only to customer needs, attitudes and behaviour but also to business and economic conditions, government and legislative impact, and technological developments. Additionally, in recent years, a major concern for all organizations and in particular those in service sector industries, is consideration of customer needs in relation to *service levels*. Customer service and service quality is now a critical focus of any corporate or marketing strategy, and high levels of customer service are typically seen as a means for an organization to achieve a competitive advantage. For financial services retailers, customers' needs are influenced by the characteristics of financial services which present quality problems and challenges and also by trends particular to their environment—which are summarized in this introduction, together with the benefits that might result from achievement of high levels of service.

The major thrust of the chapter is then to focus on definitions of service and quality, dimensions of service, measurement of service quality, the role of personnel (internal customers) in service delivery, and the monitoring of service quality. In addition to the theoretical concepts and academic reference sources cited for further reading, findings from empirical work among customers and employees of financial services providers are presented in some detail.

10.1 CUSTOMER SERVICE IN CONTEXT

10.1.1 Characteristics of services

The particular characteristics of services were discussed in the introduction to this book, but it is useful at this stage to recap briefly on those aspects of particular relevance to services and quality. Financial services are characterized by *intangibility*: there is usually little or no tangible evidence to show once a service (e.g., investment or mortgage advice) has been performed. As a result of this, organizations will provide peripheral tangible clues which become elements of the service, e.g., relating to the physical environment as evidenced in the re-design of bank branches with a focus on atmosphere and decor (see Chapter 6).

The production and consumption of many financial services are *simultaneous*, and the service may not be separable from the person, and the customer may be involved in the service performance (again, financial advice services). Thus, the service process, including staff at the customer interface, becomes integral to service quality. Related to this is the notion of *heterogeneity*. Because of the elements of intangibility and inseparability, variability often exists in financial services as a function primarily of labour inputs and non-standardization of delivery, and so the use of quality standards in the conventional sense is not possible. This increases consumer risks and also the possibilities for inconsistent reliability, but also provides a company with the opportunity to give staff the responsibility to address individual customer needs more effectively.

Furthermore, many financial services cannot be stored to meet fluctuations in demand (e.g., people's time, purchase of shares in a privatization issue, mortgage payments) and so companies need to develop systems to manage supply and demand. For example, speed of service in a branch is very important to customers, but peak demand and queuing is largely predictable and can often be accommodated by part-time staff and/or use of automated facilities. Finally, financial services usually have complex delivery systems, e.g., the 'front-counter' person represents the organization to the customer but is often dependent on an efficient 'back-room' team.

10.1.2 The service environment

Turning to the environmental trends which impact on customer service and quality issues, one needs to consider consumers' awareness and expectations, technological developments, and competitive elements. Consumers are increasingly aware of the alternatives on offer (both financial services products and provider organizations) and rising standards of service, and so their expectations of service are elevated and they are increasingly critical of the quality of service they experience (see Leonard and Sasser, 1982; Takeuchi and Quelch, 1983; Albrecht and Zemke, 1985). Expectations are what people feel a service should offer and relate to the company and its marketing mix, to include the traditional elements (product, price, place and promotion), which are extended in the service sector to include physical evidence, process and people (see Booms and Bitner, 1981).

The physical environment of a bank or building society branch will include various tangible clues which might be essential (information leaflets, computers) or peripheral to the service being bought (seats, decor, uniforms). The service process or systems is also critical. If systems are poor (e.g., breakdown of computer access to customer accounts), employees get blamed and consumers perceive poor quality service. The banks' personnel are also integral to the production of the service as already referred to and, although their degree of contact with the customer varies, all have a contribution to make.

Advances in technology have obviously made a major contribution in financial services to facilitate the customer-company exchange and increase levels of service, e.g., management information systems, marketing information systems to include customer databases, the bankers' automated clearing system, direct debit facilities. Increased mechanization and computerization can depersonalize services (e.g., ATMs, home banking), but also result in increases in speed, efficiency, accuracy and improved services. The other side of the coin is, however, that electronic banking in depersonalizing service could lead to less customer loyalty. But, generally, high 'tech' and high 'touch' go hand in hand; better personal service with enhanced technological efficiency. Technology can free employees' time and allow them to concentrate on the customer and enhance customer–staff interaction. Technology will not replace people in the provision of financial services.

Major developments are also apparent in the business and economic environment. In particular, recent legislation (e.g., deregulatory activities) has contributed to a more complex and competitive marketplace with widened customer choice and sophistication. The reaction of financial services providers has been, on the one hand, to emphasize operations and financial efficiency, and/or more focused product and market strategies. In addition, they may also have an appreciation of the importance of customer service and quality, and the possible opportunities for attaining differentiation and achieving a competitive edge by providing superior service, i.e., service quality is seen as a mechanism to achieve pre-eminence in the marketplace and the battle for market shares and so becomes a factor in strategic planning (see Leonard and Sasser, 1982; Berry *et al.*, 1989). Service quality is such a pre-eminent issue that no major financial services provider can now stand still while others are enhancing service levels.

10.1.3   Benefits of good service

Without a focus on levels of service, financial services retailers face problems and complaints with both employees and customers, and associated financial and other costs. Furthermore, a (small) proportion of dissatisfied customers will complain and tell a number of others, generating adverse word-of-mouth publicity and possibly accusations of blame between personnel in the organization, and a proportion may switch to competitors. With a service quality programme, an organization can expect a number of benefits:

- The most often mentioned is enhancing customer loyalty through satisfaction. Looking after present customers can generate repeat *and* increased business and may lead to the attraction of new customers from positive word-of-mouth communication. This is significantly more cost-effective than trying to attract new customers. Cost savings also accrue from 'getting things right the first time.'
- Major financial services providers also highlight the additional benefits of increased opportunities for cross-selling (see Smith and Lewis, 1988). Comprehensive and up-to-date product knowledge and sales techniques among employees, combined with developing relationships and rapport with customers, enables staff to identify customer needs and suggest relevant products.
- In relation to employees, benefits are seen in terms of increased job satisfaction and morale and commitment to the company, good employer–employee relationships, and increased staff loyalty; which contribute to reducing the rate of staff turnover and the associated costs of recruitment, selection and training activities.
- In addition, good service quality enhances corporate image and may provide insulation from price competition; some customers will pay a premium for reliable service quality. Overall, successful service quality leads to reduced costs (of mistakes, operating, advertising and promotion) and increased productivity and sales, market shares, profitability and business performance.

10.2   DEFINING SERVICE

10.2.1   Service encounters

At this point it is useful to introduce the concept of service encounters, also referred to as 'moments of truth' or 'critical incidents' (see Albrecht and Zemke, 1985). A service encounter is

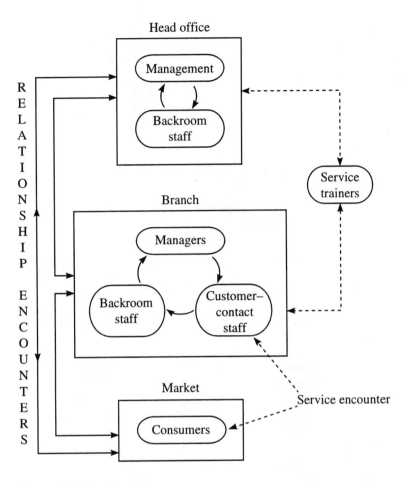

Figure 10.1   Service encounters
Source: Lewis and Entwistle, 1990, p. 49

the direct interaction between a service organization and its customers and may take varying forms. For example, a bank customer wishing to make an account enquiry may choose between an interaction with an ATM, or with a bank employee, by telephone, letter or face-to-face in a branch. Every time the customer comes into contact with any aspect of the bank and its employees there is an opportunity to form an impression of the bank and its service. Service encounters, in particular those involving bank employees, have a high 'impact' on consumers and the quality of the encounter is an essential element in the overall quality of service experienced by the customer.

   Service encounters also have an impact on employees in relation to their motivation, perform-ance and job satisfaction, and their rewards. Consequently, financial services providers need to manage their service encounters effectively for the benefit of customers and employees and for the achievement of corporate goals. This concept is developed further by Lewis and Entwistle (1990), see Figure 10.1 which illustrates the variety of encounters which prevail for a financial services retailer and which together impact on customer service and quality. This will be returned to in Section 10.4.

CONSUMER

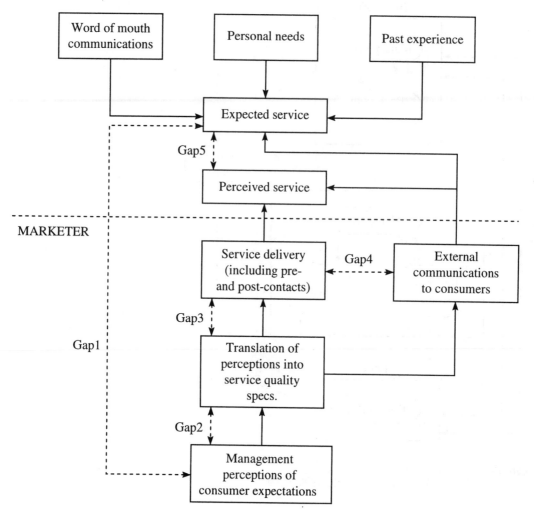

Figure 10.2 A conceptual model of service quality
Source: Zeithaml *et al.* 1988, p. 36.

10.2.2 Definitions of service quality

Service quality is variously defined but essentially is to do with meeting customers' needs and requirements and how well the service level delivered matches customers' expectations (see, for example, Lewis and Booms, 1983). The term 'expectations', as used in the service quality context, differs from the way it is used in the consumer satisfaction literature, where expectations are seen as 'predictors' (probabilities) made by a consumer about what is likely to happen during an impending transaction (Oliver, 1981). In relation to service quality, expectations are seen as desires/wants, i.e., what we feel a service provider *should* offer (rather than *would* offer), and are formed on the basis of previous experience of a company and its marketing mix, competitors and word-of-mouth communication. Consequently, quality becomes a consumer judgement and results from comparisons by consumers of expectations of service with their perceptions of actual service delivered (see Gronroos, 1984; Berry *et al.*, 1985, 1988). If there is a shortfall then a service quality gap exists which providers would wish to close. However, one needs to bear in mind that:

- Higher levels of performance lead to higher expectations.
- To find expectations greater than performance implies that perceived quality is less than satisfactory, but that is not to say that service is of low quality; quality is relative to initial expectations—one of the issues to take into account when measuring service quality.

The concept of service quality gaps was developed from the extensive research (including manager interviews and customer focus groups in a bank), in the late 1980s by Berry and his colleagues (Parasuraman *et al.*, 1985; Zeithaml *et al.*, 1988) (see Figure 10.2). They defined service quality to be a function of the gap between consumers' expectations of the service and their perceptions of the actual service delivery by an organization; and suggested that this gap is influenced by several other gaps which may occur in an organization:

Gap 1: Consumer expectations—management perceptions of consumer expectations Managers do not necessarily know what customers (both internal and external) want and expect from a company. This may be remedied by market research activities (e.g., interviews, surveys, focus groups, complaint monitoring), and better communication between management and personnel throughout the organization.

Gap 2: Management perception of consumer expectations—service quality specifications actually set Even if customer needs are known, they may not be translated into appropriate service specifications, due to a lack of resources, organizational constraints or absence of management commitment to a service culture and service quality. The need for management commitment and resources for service quality cannot be overstated.

Gap 3: Service quality specifications—actual service delivery This is referred to as the service performance gap and occurs when the service that is delivered is different from management's specifications for service due to variations in the performance of personnel—employees not being able or willing to perform at a desired level. Solutions are central to human resource management and will be returned to in Section 10.4.

Gap 4: Actual service delivery—external communications about the service What is said about the service in external communications is different from the service that is delivered, i.e., advertising and promotion can influence consumers' expectations and perceptions of service. Therefore, it is important not to promise more than can be delivered (or expectations increase and perceptions decrease), or fail to present relevant information. Success in this area requires appropriate and timely information/communication, both internally and to external customers.

Gaps 1 to 4 together contribute to consumers' expectations and perceptions of actual service (Gap 5). Financial services providers need to identify the gaps prevalent in their organization, determine the factors responsible for them, and develop appropriate solutions.

10.2.3 Dimensions of service

A major thrust of this chapter is to focus on Gap 5, and in particular to provide an indication of the dimensions which lead to quality evaluation in financial services retailing and their assessment. Dimensions of service quality are multifarious and relate to both a *basic service package* and an *augmented service offering* (Gronroos, 1987). A basic or core financial service product, that the consumer receives, might be a current account with associated services which are *required* to facilitate consumption of the core service (e.g., a cheque book) and supporting services which are not required but may enhance the service and differentiate it from competition (e.g., a cashpoint card).

The augmented service offering includes how the service is delivered (process) and the interactions between the bank and its customers which can include: the accessibility of the service (e.g., number of bank clerks and their skills, branch layout); customer participation in the process (e.g., use of ATMs, the need to fill in forms) and the interactions between employees and customers, systems and customers, and the physical environment and customers.

Dimensions of service (quality) have been discussed for a number of years. Gronroos (1984) referred to the *technical* (outcome) quality of the service encounter, i.e., what is received by the customer, and the *functional* quality of the process, i.e., the way in which the service is delivered—in relation to bank staff this would include their attitudes and behaviour, appearance and personality, service mindedness, accessibility and approachability. In addition, there exists the 'corporate image' dimension of quality which is the result of how customers perceive a bank, and is built up by the technical and functional quality of its services. This model was later synthesized with one from manufacturing which incorporated design, production, delivery and relational dimensions of quality (Gummesson and Gronroos, 1987).

Other key contributors have been Lehtinen and Lehtinen (1982) who refer to process quality (as judged by consumers during a service) and output quality (judged after a service is performed) and suggest that corporate image is a key dimension, as do LeBlanc and Nguyen (1988). Both researchers also focus on staff–customer interactions. Edvardsson *et al.* (1989) present four aspects of quality which affect customers' perceptions:

- Technical quality—to include skills of service personnel and the design of the service system.
- Integrative quality—the ease with which different portions of the service delivery system work together.
- Functional quality—to include all aspects of the manner in which the service is delivered to the customer to include style, environment and availability.
- Outcome quality—whether or not the actual service product meets both service standards or specifications and customer needs/expectations.

However, the most widely reported set of service quality determinants is that proposed by Parasuraman *et al.* (1985 and 1988). They suggested that the criteria used by consumers that are important in moulding their expectations and perceptions of service fit ten dimensions:

- Tangibles: physical evidence
- Reliability: getting it right first time, honouring promises
- Responsiveness: willingness, readiness to provide service
- Communication: keeping customers informed in a language they can understand
- Credibility: honesty, trustworthiness
- Security: physical, financial and confidentiality, e.g., ATMs
- Competence: possession of required skills and knowledge of *all* employees, e.g., to carry out instructions
- Courtesy: politeness, respect, friendliness
- Understanding/knowing the customer, e.g., needs and requirements.
- Access: ease of approach and contact, e.g., opening hours, queues, phones

These ten dimensions vary with respect to how easy or difficult it is to evaluate them. Some, such as tangibles or credibility are known in advance, but most are *experience* criteria and can only be evaluated during or after consumption. Some, such as competence and security, may be difficult or impossible to evaluate, even after purchase. In general, consumers rely on experience properties when evaluating services.

Subsequent factor analysis and testing by Parasuraman *et al.* (1988) condensed these determinants into five categories (tangibles, reliability, responsiveness, assurance and empathy), to which Gronroos (1988) added a sixth dimension—*recovery*. Parasuraman's dimensions of service provided the basis of the SERVQUAL questionnaire (Parasuraman *et al.*, 1988). This is a 22-item scale with good reliability and validity which can be used to better understand service expectations and perceptions of consumers:

Service Expectations: e.g., 'Customers should be able to trust bank employees'

'Customers should not have to queue'

'Banks should tailor loans to customer requirements'

strongly agree..................strongly disagree
1   2   3   4   5   6   7

Perceptions: e.g., 'I can trust the employees of my bank'

'I do not have to queue at my bank'

'My bank tailored my loan to meet my needs'

strongly agree..................strongly disagree
1   2   3   4   5   6   7

SERVQUAL may be used to: track service quality trends and improve service; categorize customers; compare branches of a bank or building society; and compare an organization with its competitors. However, it is limited to current and past customers as respondents need knowledge and experience of the company.

10.3   MEASURING SERVICE QUALITY

The dimensions of service quality, together with associated measurement tools, have been investigated in the last decade by both theorists and practitioners. An early example in financial services was the experience of a British bank (Buswell, 1983) which considered the quality of service received by its customers, service being defined as the offerings to customers of benefits and satisfactions beyond the product which are controllable and which may or may not incur costs. Customers used attitude statements to assess the quality of service they received in relation to knowledge of staff, communications, expertise of staff, willingness to lend and branch design. The bank was able to develop benchmarks and a system which had the ability to reveal changes in service at a particular branch over time and to distinguish between branches at the same point in time. Furthermore, Richardson and Robinson (1986) assessed the functional qualities of service provided by bank staff, Tansuhaj *et al.* (1987) measured both the technical and functional items of quality in banks, and Loizides (1991) assessed customers' images and perceptions of 28 service related features in a central European bank.

A study by Lewis (1989) collected data from *employees* of a UK bank rather than customers. They were asked what they understood by service quality and customer care and a number of elements emerged which had either a *customer* focus (customer satisfaction, putting the customer first, anticipating and commitment to customer needs, tailoring products to customer needs and establishing customer relationships) or a *product* focus (quality of service, personal service, polite/caring service, advice/problem solving, efficient/quick/accurate service, getting it right the first time, and maintaining standards).

Several projects completed by researchers in the Financial Services Research Centre in the Manchester School of Management have focused on service quality. Major objectives have been to investigate the service quality gaps, to identify key dimensions of service (from previous research, in-depth interviews and survey questionnaires), and to assess service performance with respect to these dimensions for a number of major financial service providers—primarily banks and building societies in relation to both personal and small business customers.

10.3.1 Customer perspectives on service

One major project (Lewis and Smith, 1989) culminated in a survey questionnaire whose respondents included 227 bank and 247 building society personal customers. Their expectations of service were assessed using an importance scale and their perceptions of service delivered via a satisfaction scale, in respect of 39 service quality criteria. The overall rankings for these criteria are shown in Table 10.1 and relate to four dimensions.

Table 10.1   Ranking of service elements

	Banks		Building societies	
	Expectations	Perceptions	Expectations	Perceptions
Physical features and facilities				
Location	2	3	2	3
Appearance of building	10	2	10	2
Parking facilities	7	11	7	11
Interior decor and atmosphere	8	5	8	4
Interior layout	5	7	6	7
Appearance of credit cards, cheque books, etc.	11	9	11	8
Equipment used	3	8	4	5
The number and behaviour of other customers	9	4	9	6
Privacy	1	6	1	10
Physical safety	4	10	3	9
Appearance of staff	6	1	5	1

continued

Table 10.1   Ranking of service elements—*continued*

	Banks		Building societies	
	Expectations	Perceptions	Expectations	Perceptions
Reliability				
Accuracy of transactions	1	1	1	1
The ability to do things right the first time	2	3	3	4
The ability to keep promises	3	2	2	3
The competence of staff you do not have face-to-face contact with	4	4	4	2
The staff with whom you come into contact				
Honesty and trustworthiness of staff	1	1	1	2
Reliability of staff	3	4	3	3
Knowledge and skill of staff	5	6	4	5
Politeness and friendliness of staff	7	2	7	1
Helpfulness of staff	4	3	6	4
The respect and consideration staff show me	9	7	9	6
Staff knowing my personal needs	10	10	10	10
Staff giving me individualized attention	11	11	11	11
Staff giving adequate explanations of service	8	9	8	9
The way in which staff handle complaints	6	8	5	8
Confidentiality of dealings and discretion of staff	2	5	2	7
Responsiveness to your needs				
Speed of service in the branch	2	5	2	8
Speed of service at the cash point	5	4	7	5
Time taken to answer the telephone	11	8	11	9
Time taken to post information	9	7	9	6
Opening hours	6	10	8	7
Prompt service	4	3	4	4
The availability of information in the branch/cash point	8	6	6	3
The availability of information by telephone	10	11	10	10
Being informed of new services, etc., by post	13	9	13	12
The willingness of staff to help with problems/queries	3	1	3	1
The willingness of the manager to help with problems/queries	1	2	1	2
The use of customer suggestions to improve service	12	13	12	13
The number of staff available to serve	7	12	5	11

Source: Adapted from Lewis and Smith (1989)

Physical features and facilities   Most of these were felt to be important, in particular location, privacy, physical safety and equipment; and respondents were generally very satisfied with all but one (parking facilities), the highest ratings being given to convenient location, appearance of buildings and appearance of staff.

Reliability   All four elements of reliability (accuracy of transactions, ability to do things right, ability to keep promises and competence of back-room staff) were felt to be very important *and* seen to be very satisfactory.

The staff you come into contact with   All but one of the characteristics of contact staff were felt to be important or very important, the most important being honesty and trustworthiness—followed by staff knowing personal needs, confidentiality and discretion—a function of the nature of the service encounter in these organizations. The characteristics of staff with which respondents were most satisfied were honesty and trustworthiness: thus, their expectations were met. Only two characteristics received poor evaluations: staff not knowing personal needs and not giving individualized attention.

Responsiveness to needs   Again, all but one of the determinants of responsiveness were believed to be important or very important, the most important being willingness of staff *and* management to help with problems or queries; and speed of service. High ratings were also given to speed of service at the cash point. Evaluations of responsiveness were generally very positive, in particular with respect to willingness of management and staff to help with problems and queries. However, a number of respondents were not informed about new services, a large minority felt that customer suggestions were not used to improve service, and a number felt that there were not enough staff available to serve.

A variety of open-ended questions added to the value of the data. For example, particularly good aspects of service were highlighted relating to staff personal qualities, but also some particularly poor aspects of service, such as not enough staff at peak times, slow service, staff not attentive enough, poor knowledge, mistakes and poor complaint handling—which could lead to account closure.

In addition, it was discovered that automated facilities are used mainly for cash withdrawal and balance of accounts, customers appreciating the 24-hour facilities provided and the time-saving element with perceptions that service has improved as a result of such facilities being available. Nevertheless, the questioning also brought to light the adverse characteristics of automation: breakdowns, lack of facilities, concern for personal safety, privacy and machines running out of cash.

Findings indicated that half the respondents had come to expect a better service from their bank or building society in recent years and that more than half believed that service had improved. Almost all were satisfied or very satisfied with the overall service received, but the range of questions and the assessment of service quality gaps indicated dimensions of service which could be improved upon.

A further project, using the same measurement tool enabled an international comparison to be made between retail customers of banks in the USA and the UK (Lewis, 1991) which brought to light some behavioural as well as attitudinal differences. The US customers visited their banks more frequently, largely explained by the practice, still prevalent, of a majority of working people receiving payment by cheque rather than by cash or direct credit transfer to an account. This necessitates a visit to a bank branch or an ATM to pay in the cheque.

Expectations and perceptions were assessed for 39 service related variables covering the physical features and facilities, reliability, customer contact personnel and responsiveness. UK customers attached more importance to privacy, appearance elements and using customer suggestions to improve service. US customers were more concerned about location and parking facilities (possibly as a function of driving to banks rather than having convenient high street sites as in the UK), opening hours, the number of staff available to serve (with associated perceptions of slow-moving queues), and several of the personal characteristics of bank staff they came into contact with.

With regard to perceptions, US customers were more satisfied with location and parking, and UK customers with appearance elements, all the personal characteristics of staff and the elements of banks' responsiveness to their needs. This is reflected in their responses to questions about the overall quality of service they receive from their bank: only 79 per cent of US customers were satisfied with overall service quality, as compared with 94 per cent of UK bank customers. These findings illustrate one of the problems of customer surveys: population groups may differ and, in particular for the coming years, cultural differences in attitudes and behaviour within the European community may well impact on expectations and perceptions of service.

10.3.2 Small businesses—expectations of banks

The UK banks are presently striving to attract small businesses as demonstrated by their advertising campaigns, increasing range of products and other information aimed at this sector. This interest by the banks is partly a result of government policy to help small businesses: they become attractive customers both now and as they grow, hopefully, into large companies. The banks need to know the service quality criteria which are important to a small business owner/manager in a banking relationship and how they are performing with respect to these criteria, in order to attract and retain such customers. Smith (1990) identified four key areas of service from in-depth interviews in 50 companies.

- *Bank personnel* A major criticism levelled by small businesses is the inability of bank staff to understand the business and make informed judgements relating to the potential needs of a client company.
- *Organization and structure of banks* The oligopolistic market structure of the UK banks, characterized by non-price competition and their size, is reflected (for small businesses) in apparent bureaucracy and remoteness of policy-makers from managers in the field.
- *Pricing policy* The lack of price competition and high price risk creates problems for small companies, e.g., high interest payments, charges, collateral requirements and problems in raising initial/additional finance.
- *Product offerings* Product requirements may be 'relatively simple' to the bank but not so to the small business manager. This has implications for information needs, etc.

In addition, 55 service factors were incorporated into structured rating questions for respondents to indicate their expectations (on an importance scale) and their perceptions/satisfactions (on an agree-disagree scale). The most important factors were seen to be:

- Accuracy or competence aspects
- Confidentiality and trustworthiness of the manager
- Promises kept
- Reliability in the branch and at head office
- Speed with respect to decision making, transactions and dealing with customers in the branch and on the phone, resolving problems and queries—all of which reflect a need for responsiveness and competence in a banking relationship

In relation to bank managers, in addition to trustworthiness and speed of decision making, important factors are: an understanding of the business and having authority to make decisions which affect the business; having an interest in the customer's business; and availability and personal qualities. For other bank staff, efficiency and reliability are key factors, as are product knowledge and personal qualities.

The small business customers are very satisfied with a number of these factors such as: trustworthiness and approachable bank manager; accuracy of account information and statements; information about accounts readily available; confidentiality and reliable staff—promises kept. In contrast, major dissatisfactions relate to: queuing with personal customers; charges and interest rates, plus lack of explanation; collateral requirements; lack of facilities for the business person in the branch and errors.

10.3.3 Service levels—additional dimensions

Further to identifying dimensions of services, a financial service retailer should also consider the recent contribution of Johnston et al. (1990) and Silvestro and Johnston (1990) who investigated service quality in a large number of UK organizations and identified 15 determinants which they categorized as hygiene, enhancing, or dual threshold factors.

- Hygiene factors are those which are expected by the customer and failure to deliver will cause dissatisfaction, e.g., carrying out instructions with respect to standing orders, confidentiality of financial affairs, lack of queues and return of phone calls.
- Enhancing factors lead to customer satisfaction, but failure to deliver will *not* necessarily cause dissatisfaction, e.g., bank clerk addressing you by name.
- Dual threshold factors which are those expected by the customers, failure to deliver will cause dissatisfaction and delivery above a certain level will enhance customers' perceptions of service and lead to satisfaction, e.g., explanation of a mortgage service—repayment level, interest charges, payback period and other relevant conditions.

Zones of tolerance   Consumers' expectations with respect to dimensions of service are generally reasonable, e.g., they expect ATMs to have sufficient cash, and not to have to wait most of the time when they visit a bank branch. They also expect basics from a bank in terms of security and cleanliness and to be treated with respect. However, expectations vary depending on a host of circumstances and experiences and they rise over time. Furthermore, experience with one service provider (e.g., hotel, doctor) can influence expectations of others (bank, lawyer).

In addition, consumers have what Parasuraman et al. (1991) refer to as 'zones of tolerance', i.e., the difference between *desired* and *adequate* expectations. The desired level of service expectation is what customers hope to receive, a blend of what *can* and *should* be, which is a function of past experience. The adequate level is what they find acceptable, based in part on their assessment of what the service will be—the 'predicted' service—and depends on the alternatives that are available. Tolerance zones vary between individuals, service aspects and with experience, and tend to be smaller for outcome features than for process dimensions. In addition, if options are limited (e.g., general practitioner services), desires may not decrease, but tolerance levels may be higher; conversely if many alternatives are available (e.g., financial services), it is easy to switch and tolerance zones are more limited. Furthermore, expectations are higher in emergency situations (e.g., theft of a cheque book, loss of credit card) and when something is not right the first time.

Parasuraman et al. also highlight a number of managerial implications of their model, that service providers need to:

- Demonstrate fair play.
- Be reliable as expectations increase when service is not performed as promised—manage promises.
- Leverage the process dimensions, i.e., enhance the willingness and ability of personnel to deliver—and recover if necessary. This has implications for human resource management, e.g., recruitment, training, empowerment, evaluation and rewards.
- Build relationships.

10.3.4   Measurement issues

It has been shown that investigation of the determinants of service is of prime concern to financial services providers. Not only are consumer needs and expectations changing and dimensions wide ranging, but also measurement schemes and tools are varied and are continually being developed, each with its advantages and drawbacks. The issues relating to the statements and scales used in measurement are highlighted by several researchers, e.g., Lewis and Mitchell (1990) and Orledge (1991). These include:

- Evidence that not all service dimensions are equally important and so, ideally, a weighting of factors is needed.
- Change of attributes and weights over time.
- The use of double negatives is confusing to respondents
  (e.g., the bank manager does not take time to discuss my business
  agree.................disagree).
- Use of two lists of statements for the same items, as in SERVQUAL; rating companies in general—'banks should have convenient opening hours'—and specific companies 'my bank has convenient opening hours'.
- Seven point Likert scales have a potential to restrict answers.
- Interpretation of adjectives used influences responses.
- Timing of measurement: before, during or after a particular service delivery.
- Customers' responses are generally with respect to routine service situations: an organization also needs to consider non-routine encounters.

Orledge (1991) took account of some of these difficulties and experimented with a graphic scale as compared with SERVQUAL in assessing the attitudes of university students with respect to their banks' and building societies' provision of service in general, and loan/overdraft facilities in particular. The graphic scale turned out to be a slightly better predictor of overall satisfaction, although neither accounted for much of the variation in overall satisfaction with the bank or building society. Further discussion of measurement issues is offered by Lewis (1993) and Parasuraman *et al.* (1991a, 1993).

10.4   THE ROLE OF PERSONNEL IN SERVICE DELIVERY

Having assessed customer needs, financial service providers must set standards and systems for service delivery to include the relevant dimensions of customer service, i.e., to avoid Gap 2. This implies a requirement for management commitment to a service culture and service quality, and the allocation of appropriate resources—in relation to products, systems, environment and people.

The subsequent challenge is to ensure that the service delivered meets the specifications set. This depends on the performance of *all* employees who must be *able* and *willing* to deliver the desired levels of service. Employees' contributions in meeting customer needs and thus influencing customer perceptions of service cannot be overstated, and success depends on the development of enlightened personnel policies for recruitment and selection, training, motivation and rewards for *all* employees. Both customer contact and back-room staff, in the branch, at region and at head office.

10.4.1 Internal marketing

An understanding of the concept of internal marketing is central to personnel policies. It views employees as internal customers and jobs as internal products (see Berry, 1980), and a company needs to sell the jobs to employees before selling its service to customers, i.e., satisfying the wants of internal customers upgrades the capability to satisfy the needs of external customers. Gronroos (1981) refers to three objectives of internal marketing:

- *Overall*   To achieve motivated, customer conscious and care oriented personnel.
- *Strategic*   To create an internal environment which supports customer-consciousness and sales-mindedness among personnel.
- *Tactical*   To sell service campaigns and marketing efforts to employees—the first market-place of the company—via staff training programmes and seminars.

Berry (1981) developed the concept in terms of the possibilities for market research and segmentation. He rightly suggests that organizations should carry out research among employees to identify their needs, wants and attitudes with respect to working conditions, benefits and company policies. Furthermore, he indicates that people are different as employees and as consumers and might be segmented in a number of ways. For example, with respect to flexible working hours, which lead to increased job satisfaction, increased productivity and decreased absenteeism. In addition, 'cafeteria benefits' could be appropriate with respect to health insurance, pensions, holidays etc., the notion being that employees use 'credits' (a function of salary, service, age etc.) to choose their benefits. Berry is suggesting staff benefits to embrace and satisfy the needs of the heterogeneity of the labour force, and thus upgrade an organization's capacity to satisfy the needs of its external customers.

10.4.2 Recruitment, training and rewards

Personnel issues are addressed by Lewis and Entwistle (1990) who develop the concept of service encounters to include encounters or relationships within the organization—at all levels and between levels—which contribute to the quality of service delivered to the final customers. This includes relationships between:

- Customer contact and back-room employees
- Branch, head office and regional employees
- Operations and non-operations staff
- Staff and management at all levels and locations

For example, customer contact personnel may want information and responsiveness from either back-office or operations employees in the branch or head office or from a management team, to facilitate serving the customer. If these internal encounters are poor, the customer may be dissatisfied, complain and blame the customer contact personnel. Thus, a financial services provider needs to be aware of these relationships and manage them effectively. Lewis and Entwistle (1990) highlight the need for service providers to consider systems, environment and personnel to successfully manage their service encounters, and go on to focus on personnel/

staffing considerations with comments on selection, training and implications for customer care/service quality programmes. Recruitment and selection of the 'right' people is obvious. Key characteristics for employees to perform effectively may relate to:

- Process and technical skills
- Interpersonal and communication skills
- Flexibility and adaptability
- Empathy with the customer

Next it is vital to identify the training needs of new and present employees with respect to technical and interpersonal dimensions, and also to consider employment conditions, i.e., employees' wants and attitudes, with regard to working conditions, benefits and welfare, which can then be packaged to suit individual needs. Subsequent training programmes may be developed to provide product, company and systems knowledge and also interpersonal and communication skills. Zeithaml *et al.* (1988), in relation to Gap 3, indicate that success will depend on:

- *Teamwork*   Demonstrated by a caring management and involved and committed employees.
- *Employee-job fit*   The ability of employees to perform a job.
- *Technology-job fit*   Are the 'tools' appropriate for the employee and the job?
- *Perceived control*   E.g., do employees have flexibility in dealing with customers? If not stress levels may rise and performance decrease.
- *Supervisory control systems*   Based on behaviours rather than 'output quality'.
- *Avoidance of role conflict*   For employees in satisfying employees expectations of the company *and* expectations of customers.
- *Avoidance of role ambiguity*   I.e., employees should know what is expected of them and how performance will be evaluated and rewarded.

Such training programmes are today encouraging a customer service orientation. Customer care programmes are typically designed to move a company to a service oriented culture by breaking down barriers and improving internal communications. Advantages are seen to be creating an atmosphere of all working towards a common goal, understanding the work of others and encouraging all staff to have responsibility and authority for achieving corporate objectives—which includes empowering employees to exercise judgement and creativity in responding to customers' needs.

Employees also need to be supervised and systems set to monitor and evaluate their performance (e.g., product knowledge tests, mystery shoppers) and satisfaction. In addition, financial services providers have a variety of recognition and reward schemes for excellent employees, e.g., American Express have a Great Performers programme for employees who have gone to extraordinary lengths to assist customers. Customer service awards may be financial or not, and may involve career development.

10.4.3   Personnel—the research experience

Although the need for internal marketing, enlightened personnel policies and successful internal service encounters is accepted, their implementation requires further emphasis and refinement. This is demonstrated in the findings from a survey of bank and building society employees (Lewis, 1989). Four hundred and nineteen personnel, mainly customer-contact, provided opinions with respect to internal service encounters and relationships, perceptions of customer service in their organizations, training for customer service and areas for service quality improvement.

Perceptions of service A variety of elements in the provision of customer service/quality relating to both the organizations' operations and to the characteristics of staff were seen to be important and all respondents agreed that customer service is essential and that the public's expectations of service have risen. But only one-quarter believed that their company was able to meet the public expectations *all* of the time, and only two-thirds agreed that staff are able to offer a good service to all customers, and deal effectively with customer queries/problems.

Relationships within the company Respondents were critical of interpersonal relationships within their organizations, with respect to the attitude of back-room staff to customer contact staff and towards customers. There was also some evidence of poor relationships between branch staff and head office staff and between staff and management. Furthermore, only half agreed that their company looks after its staff and one-quarter believed that not all staff are trained to give a good service.

Service that the company provides Personnel were generally positive about the service their organization provided and believed that the public received a high standard of service. They saw the pros and cons of modern technology in the provision of customer service, but felt that the role of personal service will remain high. There was some criticism of organizations' staffing and training policies, for example, one half had negative perceptions about organizational policies and two-thirds felt that there were insufficient staff to deal with customer demands. Three-quarters felt that staff needed more product knowledge and more sales-related training and 90 per cent felt a need for more customer care training. There was an overwhelming view that more staff, more training and more knowledge would lead to better customer service.

Organizational environment Most employees have been on customer care/customer service training activities. However, few tend to be involved in activities concerned with relationships between staff and management, branch and head office staff, and between front-line and back-room personnel.

Overall, these findings emphasize the need for financial services providers to further develop their personnel initiatives and customer service training activities and in so doing to change the corporate cultures towards a commitment and responsiveness to external customers and their needs by all staff and management. There is also a need to include training and related activities concerned with relationships—within the organization, and between the organization and its customers.

Subsequent research by Koula (1992), in a European bank, was focused on Gap 3 and involved surveys among senior managers and other personnel throughout the bank. Comparisons were made in a number of areas including:

- Customer and service orientation of the bank
- Role of personnel in service delivery
- Corporate objectives with respect to personnel
- Internal communications
- Recruitment procedures
- Personnel training
- Interpersonal attitudes and behaviour (e.g., relationships, teamwork, cooperation)
- Employee commitment
- Appraisal and rewards
- Staff benefits
- Areas for improvement

The findings enabled a number of shortfalls to be determined, which might be remedied in the continuing development of recruitment, selection, training and rewards programmes.

10.5 SERVICE DELIVERY

In relation to service delivery, financial services companies need to avoid Gap 4, i.e., a failure to deliver the service as promised. Once a company has assessed customer needs, translated them into service systems and standards, and recruited and trained employees, it must then manage its 'promises'. A company needs appropriate advertising and promotion so that the service that is offered in external communications matches the service that the organization is able to deliver. Advertising and promotion affects consumers' expectations and perceptions of the delivered service and so it is important not to promise more than can be delivered, i.e., realistic communications are needed so as not to increase expectations unnecessarily and decrease perceptions of quality. Recent research by Nevitt (1992) has focused on the relationships between banks and their small business customers in relation to Gap 4, which is seen to exist, in particular, in relation to loan availability, financial advice, charges, and interpersonal attitudes and behaviour.

10.6 MONITORING SERVICE QUALITY

A critical element in any customer service strategy is for a company to have in place systems to monitor success. These include research and evaluation among employees and customers, using focus groups, discussions, surveys and interviews, and sometimes mystery shoppers and 'control' branches. Collection and analysis of customer complaints and complementary letters is often also valuable and, for some organizations, key indicators are provided by unconditional service guarantees and recovery activities.

A number of service providers now offer unconditional service guarantees; e.g., a hotel chain which offers cash compensation if difficulties are not resolved in 30 minutes; a pizza delivery which becomes free after a certain time delay; British Telecom promises with respect to waiting periods for telephone installations and repair of faults and the Royal Mail's compensation for late/lost delivery and damaged items. The use of such guarantees in the retailing of financial services may not yet prevail, but might do so in the future. Nevertheless, the UK banks now each have a code of practice in which they outline their commitment to customers, advise them of their consumer rights, and provide 0800 telephone numbers for customer service/advice/queries/ complaints etc.; e.g., 'We want our relationship to be a partnership based on confidence and trust' (National Westminster Bank) and 'Our commitment is to deliver to you a sound banking relationship, without compromising on traditional standards of honesty and fair dealing' (Bank of Scotland).

Hart (1988) summarizes key considerations relating to service guarantees. A good service guarantee is unconditional, easy to understand, communicate, invoke and collect on. It should also be meaningful, in particular, with respect to payout which should be a function of the cost of the service, seriousness of failure and perception of what is fair, e.g., 15-minute lunch service in a restaurant or a free meal. Ideally, a service guarantee should get everyone in the company to focus on good service, and to examine service delivery systems for possible failure points.

To turn to customer complaints, service providers now realize that only a small proportion of dissatisfied customers complain. The reasons why dissatisfied people keep quiet are discussed by Goodman et al. (1986) and Horovitz (1990) and include the following:

- Fear of hassle or finding it too much trouble to complain
- No one is available to complain to, or there is no easy channel by which to communicate disquiet
- No one cares and it will not do any good
- Do not know where to complain
- Customers attributing themselves as a source of service problems by their failure to perform in the creation of the service

Hart *et al.* (1990) refer to the additional costs of replacing customers over those of trying to retain customers who may be dissatisfied. They also refer to evidence of customers who have complained and who have received a satisfactory response subsequently being more loyal to an organization, more likely to buy other services, and more likely to engage in positive word-of-mouth communication.

Financial services retailers should strive for zero defects in their service delivery—to get things right the first time. Consequently, banks and building societies develop service quality systems which tend to be rigid with sophisticated techniques and structured personnel policies—to try to provide consistent high quality service. However, problems do occur (e.g., employees may be sick and absent) and mistakes will happen (e.g., a lost cheque book or an incorrect statement). The challenge for the banks/building societies is to recover the problem or mistake and get it right the second time.

Service recovery represents a planned process of returning an aggrieved/dissatisfied customer to a state of satisfaction with the company/service and making a special effort to get things right for the customer when something is wrong. Recovery is important to service providers as it has economic value, can increase customer loyalty, as well as assisting in identifying organizational problems, and improving overall service quality awareness. When something does go wrong, customers have recovery expectations. They expect an apology, to have a problem fixed, a promise kept, to be treated well and to be recompensed if necessary. Service recovery is 'emotional and physical repair': organizations need to fix the customer first and then fix the customer's problem. Consequently, in order to expedite service recovery, organizations can do a number of things:

- Acknowledge the problem: accept responsibility, believe the customer and avoid defensiveness
- Apologize
- 'Fix' the problem: respond to the customer, personalize the response, try to keep the customer
- Recompense explicit and hidden costs if appropriate

Critical to the service recovery process is the empowerment of front-line employees. It is essential to give personnel the authority, responsibility and incentives to identify, care about and solve customer problems and complaints; to allow them to use their judgement and to act with respect to the best solutions to satisfy customers. The personnel implications of empowerment are highlighted by Schelesinger and Heskett (1991). In particular, empowerment is seen to lead to better job performance and improved morale; it is seen as a form of job enrichment, which is demonstrated by increased commitment to jobs and reflected in attitudes towards customers. Knowing that management has confidence in employees helps create positive attitudes in the workplace and good relationships between employees and between employees and customers.

Overall, service recovery may be seen as not just solving problems *after* they have occurred, but to focus on critical service encounters and anticipate possible failure points. Ideally, an organization could identify potential problems and develop strategies for response to and solution of such difficulties.

SUMMARY

This chapter, has highlighted the need for excellent customer service (service quality), with respect to both external customers and employees, together with discussion of dimensions of service and measurement issues, illustrated with various empirical evidence.

Customers of the major financial services retailers are today generally satisfied with service levels, which are a reflection of the activities to date of these organizations. But evidence of dissatisfactions, complaints and switching behaviours provide an indication of aspects of service which might yet be enhanced, i.e., there are service quality gaps which need to be addressed, particularly as expectations of service may be rising and zones of tolerance, in some situations, may be narrow.

The key areas on which financial services retailers might focus may be summarized in terms of:

- *Systems and procedures* Must be customer and employee focused and reflect the need for responsiveness, flexibility and reliability
- *Technology* Must improve speed, accuracy and efficiency, and provide new products
- *Retail design* Physical design (including privacy, queuing) and emotional or atmospheric impact
- *Personnel* Require product knowledge and communication skills; abilities to understand and respond to customer needs, and personal qualities and commitment to the organization and to the customer

Consequently, financial service retailers need service strategies which embrace both internal and external customers. If an organization cares about its personnel and appreciates their role in service delivery, then success at managing internal service encounters will precede success in managing relationships with external customers.

Customer service strategies also need the commitment of top managers. There should be a corporate culture, which encourages a commitment to a consumer orientation throughout the organization, together with visible leaders. Berry *et al.* (1989) define true leaders as those who have a vision of the business; communicate their vision of the business/lead by example; are entrepreneurial and are obsessed by excellence.

Finally, together with a clearly defined strategy, management commitment and leadership, an integral element of a successful service quality programme will be to continually monitor the changing environment with respect to consumer needs and expectations; systems, technology and product development; legislative and political moves; business and economic conditions and competitor activities. Customer service/quality initiatives need to be monitored, reviewed and revised on a continuing basis.

REVIEW QUESTIONS

1. Discuss the environmental trends which impinge on customer service and which highlight quality concerns for financial service retailers.
2. In what ways do the characteristics of financial services present customer service problems and challenges?
3. What are the benefits which may be achieved from excellent levels of customer service? What are the costs of poor service?
4. How might a financial services retailer define good customer service?
5. Identify the major determinants of service quality. How might they be categorized for a financial services retailer?

6. What are major problems that an organization needs to be aware of in measuring service quality?

7. Technology plays an increasing role in the delivery of service. Discuss the pros and cons of 'high touch' versus 'high tech'.

8. If a financial services retailer is considering Europeanization or internationalization, to what extent will cultural differences need to be taken into account when developing customer service initiatives?

9. Outline the various service encounters which need to be considered by service organizations.

10. What is understood by internal marketing? Discuss the main implications for a financial services retailer.

11. Financial services organizations need enlightened personnel policies to achieve service excellence. What are the central concerns of such activities?

12. How do customer complaints impinge on service quality programmes? Discuss the importance of service recovery.

REFERENCES

Albrecht, K. and R. Zemke (1985) *Service America: Doing Business in the New Economy*, Dow Jones-Irwin, Homewood, Illinois.

Berry, L.L. (1980) 'Services marketing is different', *Business*, **30**(3), 24–29.

Berry, L.L. (1981) 'The employee as customer', *Journal of Retail Banking*, **3**(1), 33–40.

Berry, L.L., V.A. Zeithaml and A. Parasuraman (1985) 'Quality counts in services too', *Business Horizons*, **28**(3), 44–52.

Berry, L.L., A. Parasuraman and V.A. Zeithaml (1988) 'The service-quality puzzle', *Business Horizons*, July–August, 35–43.

Berry, L.L., D.R. Bennett and C.W. Brown (1989) *Service Quality: A Profit Strategy for Financial Institutions,* Dow Jones-Irwin, Homewood, Illinois.

Booms, B.H. and M.J. Bitner (1981) 'Marketing strategies and organization structures for service firms', in J.H. Donnelly and W.R. George (eds), *Marketing of Services*, American Marketing Association, Chicago, 47–51.

Buswell, D. (1983) 'Measuring the quality of in-branch customer service', *International Journal of Bank Marketing*, **1**(1), 26–41.

Edvardsson, B., B.O. Gustavsson and D.I. Riddle (1989) *An Expanded Model of the Service Encounter with Emphasis on Cultural Context*, Research Report 89:4, CTF Services Research Centre, University of Karlstad, Sweden.

Goodman, J.A., T. Marra and L. Brigham (1986) 'Customer service: costly nuisance or low cost profit strategy?', *Journal of Retail Banking*, **8**(3), 7–16.

Gronroos, C. (1981) 'Internal marketing—an integral part of marketing theory', in J.H. Donnelly and W.R. George (eds), *Marketing of Services*, American Marketing Association, Chicago, 236–238.

Gronroos, C. (1984) *Strategic Management and Marketing in the Service Sector*, Chartwell-Bratt, UK.

Gronroos, C. (1987) *Developing the Service Offering—A Source of Competitive Advantage*, September, Swedish School of Economics and Business Administration, Helsinki, Finland.

Gronroos, C. (1988) 'Service quality; the six criteria of good perceived service quality', *Review of Business*, **9**(3), 10–13.

Gummesson, E. and C. Gronroos (1987) *Quality of Products and Services: A Tentative Synthesis between Two Models*, Research Report 87:3, Services Research Centre, University of Karlstad, Sweden.

Hart, C.W.L. (1988) 'The power of unconditional service guarantees', *Harvard Business Review*, July–August, 54–62.

Hart, C.W.L., J.L. Heskett and W.E. Sasser (1990) 'The profitable art of service recovery', *Harvard Business Review*, **90**(4), 148–156.

Horovitz, J. (1990) *Winning Ways: Achieving Zero Defect Service*, Productivity Press, Cambridge, Mass.

Johnston, R., R. Silvestro., L. Fitzgerald and C. Voss (1990) 'Developing the determinants of service quality', in E. Langeard and P. Eiglier (eds), *Marketing, Operations and Human Resources Insights into Services*, First International Research Seminar on Services Management, IAE, Aix-en-Provence, 373–400.

Koula, S. (1992) *Expectations and Perceptions of Employees in a European Bank*, unpublished M.Sc. Dissertation, Manchester School of Management.

LeBlanc, G. and N. Nguyen (1988) 'Customers' perceptions of service quality in financial institutions', *International Journal of Bank Marketing*, **6**(4), 7–18.

Lehtinen, U. and J.R. Lehtinen (1982) *Service Quality: A Study of Quality Dimensions*, Working Paper, Service Management Institute, Helsinki, Finland.

Leonard, F.S. and W.E. Sasser (1982) 'The incline of quality', *Harvard Business Review*, **60**(5), 163–171.

Lewis, B.R. (1988) *Customer Service in a Major UK Bank*, Financial Services Research Centre, Manchester School of Management.

Lewis, B.R. (1989) *Customer Care in the Service Sector: The Employees' Perspective*, FSRC, Manchester School of Management.

Lewis, B.R. (1991) 'Service quality: an international comparison of bank customers' expectations and perceptions', *Journal of Marketing Management*, **7**(1), 47–62.

Lewis, B.R. (1993) 'Service quality measurement', *Market Intelligence and Planning*, **11**(4), 4–12.

Lewis, B.R. and T.W. Entwistle (1990) 'Managing the service encounter: a focus on the employee', *International Journal of Service Industry Management*, **1**(3), 41–52.

Lewis, B.R. and V.W. Mitchell (1990) 'Defining and measuring the quality of customer service', *Marketing Intelligence and Planning*, **8**(6), 11–17.

Lewis, B.R. and A.M. Smith (1989) *Customer Care in the Service Sector: The Customers' Perspective*, FSRC, Manchester School of Management.

Lewis, R.C. and B.H. Booms (1983) 'The marketing aspects of service quality', in L.L. Berry, G.S. Shostack and G. Upah (eds), *Emerging Perspectives on Service Marketing*, American Marketing Association, Chicago, 99–107.

Loidizes, A. (1991) *Consumer Images, Attitudes and Behaviour with Respect to Banks in Cyprus*, unpublished M.Sc. Dissertation, Manchester School of Management.

Nevitt, A. (1992) *Delivery of Service Quality: Relationships between Banks and Small Businesses*, unpublished M.Sc. Dissertation, Manchester School of Management.

Oliver, R. (1981) 'Measurement and evaluation of satisfaction process in retail settings', *Journal of Retailing*, **57** (Fall), 25–48.

Orledge, J. (1991) *Service Quality: An Empirical Investigation of Two Measurement Techniques*, unpublished M.Sc. Dissertation, Manchester School of Management.

Parasuraman, A., V.A. Zeithaml and L.L. Berry (1985) 'A conceptual model of service quality and its implications for future research', *Journal of Marketing*, **49**, 41–50.

Parasuraman, A., V.A. Zeithaml and L.L. Berry (1988) 'SERVQUAL: a multiple item scale for measuring consumer perceptions of service quality', *Journal of Retailing*, **64**(1), 14–40.

Parasuraman, A., L.L. Berry and V.A. Zeithaml (1991a) 'Refinement and reassessment of the SERVQUAL scale', *Journal of Retailing*, **67**(4), 420–450.

Parasuraman, A., L.L. Berry and V.A. Zeithaml (1991) 'Understanding customer expectations of service', *Sloan Management Review*, **32**(3), 39–48.

Parasuraman, A., L.L. Berry and V.A. Zeithaml (1993) 'Research note: more on improving service quality measurement', *Journal of Retailing*, **69**(1), 140–147.

Richardson, B.A. and C.G. Robinson (1986) 'The impact of internal marketing on consumer service in a retail bank', *International Journal of Bank Marketing*, **4**(5), 3–30.

Schelesinger, L.A. and J.L. Heskett (1991) 'Breaking the cycle of failures in service', *Sloan Management Review*, **32**(3), 17–28.

Silvestro, R. and R. Johnston (1990) *The Determinants of Service Quality—Hygiene and Enhancing Factors*, Warwick Business School, Warwick.

Smith, A.M. (1990) *Quality Service and The Small Business-Bank Relationship*, unpublished MSc. Thesis, Manchester School of Management.

Smith, A.M. and B.R. Lewis (1988) *Customer Care in the Service Sector: The Suppliers Perspective*, FSRC, Manchester School of Management.

Takeuchi, H. and J.A. Quelch (1983) 'Quality is more than making a good product', *Harvard Business Review*, **61** (July–August), 139–145.

Tansuhaj, P., J. Wong and J. McCullough (1987) 'Internal and external marketing; effects on consumer satisfaction in banks in Thailand', *International Journal of Bank Marketing*, **5**(3), 73–83.

Zeithaml, V.A., L.L. Berry and A. Parasuraman (1988) 'Communication and control processes in the delivery of service quality', *Journal of Marketing*, **52** (April), 35–48.

FURTHER READING

Berry, L.L. and A. Parasuraman (1991) *Marketing Services: Competing Through Quality*, The Free Press, New York.

Brown, S.W., E. Gummesson, B. Edvardsson and B.O. Gustavsson (1990) *Service Quality: Multi-Disciplinary and Multinational Perspectives*, Lexington Books, Lexington, Mass.

Czepiel, J.A., M.R. Solomon and C.F. Surprenant (1985) eds, *The Service Encounter: Managing Employee/Customer Interaction in Service Businesses*, Lexington Books, Lexington, Mass.

Gronroos, C. (1990) *Service Management and Marketing: Managing the Moments of Truth in Service Competition*, Lexington Books, Lexington, Mass.

Zeithaml, V.A., A. Parasuraman and L.L. Berry (1990) *Delivering Quality Service: Balancing Customer Perceptions and Expectations*, The Free Press, New York.

SUBJECT INDEX

NAME INDEX

AA, 87
Abbey Life, 113
Abbey National Building Society, 26, 31, 32, 95, 107, 127, 212
Abratt, R., 259
Access, 88, 236, 237
Admap, 260
Albers, J.E., 179
Albrecht, K., 267, 268
Alliance and Leicester Building Society, 114, 177, 246, 248, 258
Allied Dunbar, 4
American Express, 48–9, 90, 281
Ansoff, H.I., 86, 92, 93
Arnold, S., 116

Baker, M.J., 78
Baker, J., 182, 184
Ballachey, E.L., 59, 68, 71
Banc One, 97, 98
Banca Commerciala Italiana, 114
Banco Portugues do Atlantico, 115
Bank of America, 98
Bank of Credit and Commerce International (BCCI), 60, 115
Bank of England, 28
Bank of International Settlements, 29
Bank of Scotland, 283
Bankers Trust, 98
Banking Insurance and Finance Union (BIFU), 154, 155
Barclaycard, 88, 236, 246, 260
Barclays Bank, 32, 37, 55, 80, 108, 126, 127, 169, 171, 212, 242, 259, 260, 263
Barlow Clowes, 60
Barnett, M., 28
Barron, P.I., 172
Bartle, Bogle and Hegarty (BBH), 246
Bateson, J.E.G., 3, 42, 63
Bauer, R.A., 60, 63, 80
Bayton, J.A., 45, 57
Beardshaw, J., 226
Bennett, R.O., 144
Benson and Hedges, 260
Berry, L.L., 41, 42, 43, 64, 65, 79, 182, 184, 204, 268, 271, 280, 285
Betts, E., 41
Bienstman, M., 216

Bitner, M.J., 4, 43, 44, 180, 181, 267
Black Horse Financial Services, 113
Blackwell, R.D., 52, 74
Bliss, M., 126
BMP DDB Needham, 246
Board of Inland Revenue, 13
Boleat, M., 14
Bon, M., 85
Booms, B.H., 4, 41, 43, 267, 270
Boots, 159
Borden, N. H., 4
Boston Consulting Group, 217
Bradford and Bingley Building Society, 9, 20
Bristol and West Building Society, 95
British Bankers' Association, 128, 129, 164, 166, 202
British Gas, 72
British Telecom, 283
Broadbent, S., 242, 244
Brown, G., 248, 249, 256
Brown, S.W., 44
Buchan, J., 125, 126
Building Societies Commission, 26, 32
Buswell, D., 273

CACI Ltd., 104, 138
Campbell-Keegan, 101, 102
Canter, D., 184, 188
Carrick, R.J., 126
Cass, R.C., 184
CCN, 138
Channon, D.F., 3, 88, 111
Chase Manhattan Bank, 98
Chasin, J., 225
Cheltenham and Gloucester Building Society, 26, 33, 95, 107
Chisnall, P.M., 65
Christaller, W., 132
Chubb, 157, 158
Citibank, 89, 96
CitiCorp, 95, 96, 97
Civil and Public Services Association, 155
Cockrell, H.A.L., 76, 78
Cohen, J.B., 63
Coleman, R.P., 52
Coles, A., 14
Connect, 37, 237
Conran, T., 98

295